More Praise for *Blue on Blue*

"A compelling, educational, memorable account of Campisi's rise through the police department ranks until he was ordered to accept an assignment no cop ever wanted: to become part of the Internal Affairs Bureau. . . . **This superb memoir can be read for its sheer entertainment or as a primer on police work—or both.**"

—*Kirkus Reviews* (starred review)

"The thing about Chief Charles Campisi is that he's a truth teller. *Blue on Blue* takes the reader into a shadow world where police officers confront evil and often lose that confrontation. This is a serious look at American police work from a man who has seen it all. **You will learn an enormous amount by reading this book.**"

—Bill O'Reilly, former anchor at FOX News Channel

"A compelling, fascinating, and often harrowing read. In taut prose, Charles Campisi describes the evolution, formation, and institutionalization of a truly professional Internal Affairs Bureau, which he commanded from the mid-1990s until his recent retirement, and which stands as the most important and beneficial development in the modern history of the NYPD—indeed, it is arguably the single greatest achievement in the history of American police work generally. **This is a riveting history, wonderful for general readers and essential for all modern police forces to study and absorb.**"

—Caleb Carr, *New York Times* bestselling author of
The Alienist and *Surrender, New York*

"The ultimate insider's view on police brutality and corruption . . . There are myriad books by street cops and detectives, but a voice telling what it was like to work internal investigations is rare indeed. . . . **An unflinching exposé and a riveting read.**"

—*Booklist* (starred review)

BLUE ON BLUE

AN INSIDER'S STORY
OF GOOD COPS
CATCHING BAD COPS

CHARLES CAMPISI

Former Chief, NYPD Internal Affairs Bureau
with GORDON DILLOW

SCRIBNER
New York   London   Toronto   Sydney   New Delhi

Scribner
An Imprint of Simon & Schuster, Inc.
1230 Avenue of the Americas
New York, NY 10020

First Scribner trade paperback edition February 2018

SCRIBNER and design are registered trademarks of The Gale Group, Inc., used under license by Simon & Schuster, Inc., the publisher of this work.

For information about special discounts for bulk purchases, please contact Simon & Schuster Special Sales at 1-866-506-1949 or business@simonandschuster.com.

The Simon & Schuster Speakers Bureau can bring authors to your live event. For more information or to book an event, contact the Simon & Schuster Speakers Bureau at 1-866-248-3049 or visit our website at www.simonspeakers.com.

Interior design by Jill Putorti

Manufactured in the United States of America

10 9 8 7 6 5 4 3 2

Library of Congress Control Number: 2016054545

ISBN 978-1-5011-2719-9
ISBN 978-1-5011-2720-5 (pbk)
ISBN 978-1-5011-2721-2 (ebook)

To my grandchildren,
Charles, Lauren, Cocomi, and Sarah.
Of all the gifts God has given me, you are the most precious.

CONTENTS

AUTHOR'S NOTE

This is a work of nonfiction. Everything in it is true to the best of my memory and the memories of others, although any errors are mine alone. A few details have been altered to protect sources and methods, including the names and descriptions of undercover officers and informants. Some other names have been changed or omitted to protect the innocent and the family members of the guilty.

TIMELINE

October 1952—Future NYPD cop Charles Campisi born in Bushwick, Brooklyn.

March 1974—Police Officer Charles Campisi, Shield No. 791, graduates from NYPD Academy and is assigned to Manhattan Traffic Area and, later, Brooklyn's high-crime 73rd Precinct—also known as "Fort Z."

June 1975—More than five thousand NYPD cops laid off during the New York City financial crisis, Officer Campisi included. Campisi rehired twenty-two months later.

August 1989—Captain Charles Campisi appointed commanding officer of Manhattan's Sixth Precinct.

July 1992—Mayor David Dinkins appoints Mollen Commission to investigate corruption in NYPD. Corrupt cop Michael Dowd says he and numerous other cops routinely robbed drug dealers, sold drugs, and stole money from crime victims. Commission recommends permanent outside agency to monitor NYPD.

October 1992—Mayor Dinkins appoints former Marine and veteran NYPD cop Ray Kelly as police commissioner. Kelly launches new anticrime efforts, revamping old Internal Affairs Division (IAD) into Internal Affairs Bureau (IAB).

March 1993—Deputy Inspector Charles Campisi, currently head of the NYPD Cadet Corps, is "drafted" into IAB to head the new Corruption Prevention and Analysis Unit.

January 1994—Rudy Giuliani sworn in as mayor after running on anticrime platform. Police Commissioner Kelly is out, former Boston police chief Bill Bratton is in as new commissioner.

April 1996—After butting heads with Giuliani, Police Commissioner Bratton is out. Former US Marshals Service administrator and current New York City fire commissioner Howard Safir is in as commissioner. Murders in city drop below a thousand for first time in almost three decades.

July 1996—Safir promotes Deputy Chief Charles Campisi to a three-star position as chief of Internal Affairs Bureau.

August 1997—Haitian immigrant Abner Louima is sexually assaulted with a broken broom handle while in custody at the 70th Precinct station house in Brooklyn.

February 1999—Unarmed West African immigrant Amadou Diallo is shot nineteen times by four plainclothes NYPD officers in front of his apartment building in the Bronx.

August 2000—Commissioner Safir resigns to go into private sector. Mayor Giuliani appoints Department of Correction Commissioner Bernie Kerik as police commissioner.

September 2001—World Trade Center attacked. Internal Affairs Bureau assigned to compile final list of the dead.

January 2002—Michael Bloomberg sworn in as mayor, brings back Ray Kelly as police commissioner—the first commissioner in NYPD history to serve two nonconsecutive terms. New York City crime rates continue to dramatically decrease.

November 2006—Sean Bell shot and killed and two other men wounded outside a strip club in Queens by cops who fire a total of fifty shots. No weapon found on the men.

December 2008—Anonymous call about a single bad cop leads to a massive IAB investigation of ticket fixing by cops in the Bronx. Hundreds receive disciplinary charges in what will be dubbed the Tix-Fix scandal.

October 2012—So-called NYPD Cannibal Cop is arrested after joint IAB/federal investigation of allegations he plotted over the Internet to cook and eat women.

December 2013—Murders in New York City at lowest level in fifty years—only 335 killings.

January 2014—Bill de Blasio sworn in as mayor after running on platform widely perceived as antipolice and soft on crime. Ray Kelly is out as police commissioner; Bill Bratton is in—again.

March 2014—Chief Charles Campisi retires after forty-one years with the NYPD, including almost two decades as chief of Internal Affairs—the longest-serving Internal Affairs chief in NYPD history.

BLUE ON BLUE

Prologue

WE'RE WATCHING

The subject is moving now, coming out the front door of his two-story apartment building on a tree-lined street in the Bronx and walking to a red Mercury sedan that's parked up the street. It's his day off, so he's wearing jeans, running shoes, and a heavy North Face jacket against the February cold. Maybe out of wariness, maybe just force of habit, as he gets into the Mercury he throws a glance up and down the busy street, looking for anything unusual in the flow of pedestrians and vehicle traffic, but he doesn't see us—or if he does see us, all he sees is a young couple having a heated discussion in a drab Toyota parked at the corner, or a homeless man mumbling to himself as he picks through a garbage can halfway down the block. The subject doesn't make our undercovers for cops.

We've had him under surveillance for a couple weeks now, watching where he goes, who he meets, listening on a court-approved wiretap to his cell phone. We've run him through all the databases, put together a complete pedigree. We know all about his ex-wife and his girlfriend, all his known associates, where he grew up, what restaurants and bars he likes, the grades he got in school, how many times he's called in sick to work, where he goes on vacation; we know things about this guy that he's probably already forgotten about himself.

We also know that he's a criminal. Now all we have to do is catch him at it.

He's pulling the Mercury into the street now, and we're on him, but we're staying loose, not getting too close. The subject is experienced, he knows how to duck a tail, and if we jam him too hard we might lose him. We've got three cars on him, one ahead, two behind, keeping civilian blocking cars in between, so if he blows a light or squares a corner we can keep him in sight, maybe run a parallel on him until we bring the other units back on the tail. But except for occasional glances in his rearview mirror, there's no sign that the subject is concerned about being surveilled. Maybe he's feeling cocky, certain that there's no way we could be onto him. A lot of these guys are like that. Until the moment we put the handcuffs on them, they think they're smarter than we are.

He's crossing the Harlem River now, from the Bronx into Washington Heights, and still he doesn't seem to have a clue that we're watching him. He guides the Mercury onto a grimy side street off Amsterdam Avenue and parks near a five-story New Law tenement house, the kind with a combination courtyard and air shaft in the front; it's listed in our narcotics database as a known drug location. There's a lookout on the sidewalk in front, a young thug with a cell phone in his sweatshirt pocket, shivering in the cold, ready to signal if a customer's coming, or if he sees a bunch of narcotics cops in unmarked Crown Victorias come rolling up to serve a warrant. But the lookout can't make us; again, we don't look like cops, and we don't drive Crown Vics.

The subject gets out of the car and walks up to the front door. The lookout nods to him—the subject has been here before—and our guy disappears inside. From our informants, from our surveillances, from the wire we've got up on his phone, from everything we've put together on this guy, we know where he's going. He's going to a bare, cockroach-infested apartment on the fourth floor that some Dominican drug dealers are using as a stash house. Five minutes later he comes out the front door with a small black duffel bag in his hand—and we know that inside that duffel bag there are a couple kilos of crack cocaine.

Eventually, based on the information we give them, detectives from the Narcotics Division will put a case on those drug dealers on the fourth floor, sending in some of their own undercovers to make hand-to-hand buys and then banging the door with a battering ram and bursting in and arresting the dealers. But we don't care about the drug dealers right now. Yes, we're cops, but we aren't narcotics cops, and the only thing we care about right now, our only target, is the guy who's tossing that duffel bag full of crack into the trunk of his Mercury.

Because he's a cop, too.

He's a cop, but he's not a cop like us, or like most of the thirty-five thousand other cops in the New York City Police Department. Yes, he carries the same shield, the same badge, that we do. He carries a gun like we do, and he took the same oath. Maybe he even stood next to some of us on the day we graduated from the Police Academy, the day we all lined up in our shiny new blue uniforms and tossed our formal white gloves in the air in celebration and became part of the brotherhood that is the NYPD. Maybe back in the day he walked some of the same foot beats that we did, rode in the same patrol cars, arrested some of the same criminals, the same perps, maybe he took the same risks and suffered the same hardships to make this city a better and safer place. Maybe once he was a good cop.

But no longer. Now he's a crooked cop who's shotgunning drugs, transporting trafficker-weight cocaine shipments across the city and down the drug distribution ratline to points south in Maryland and Virginia and North Carolina. For the drug traffickers he's a perfect courier, because if he gets pulled over in a routine traffic stop or by some suspicious trooper on the Jersey Turnpike, all he has to do is flash that NYPD shield, maybe chat with the trooper for a few minutes about The Job, how long their respective Departments have been working without a union contract, how much their bosses suck, whatever, and then the trooper will wave him on, professional courtesy, cop to cop. That NYPD shield is his insurance policy, his guarantee that no cop will ever look inside that trunk.

And this is almost certainly not the first time that this cop has crossed the line, not the first time he has shotgunned a drug shipment or shaken down a drug dealer or beaten up a perp and taken his money or even pushed some citizen around just because he wears a badge and he's having a bad day. Bad cops are seldom bad cops just once.

But now all that is over. Because the moment that cop puts that duffel bag of coke into his trunk, we own him. He belongs to us. We're going to put this crooked cop in jail.

We could jump-collar him right now, pull him over as soon as he eases into traffic and turns the corner. But there's no hurry. We'll give him a little bit longer, we'll follow him a little further, let him cross the George Washington Bridge and go interstate with the drug shipment, which effectively doubles the years in prison he'll be looking at. If he was dead before, he's double dead now. He just doesn't know it yet.

So he heads south on the turnpike, still thinking he's safe. And now, finally, it's time. We have a couple of uniformed cops in a marked patrol car come up close behind the Mercury, then light him up and pull him over like it's a routine traffic stop. As expected, he comes out of the car holding up that NYPD shield, thinking he's going to badge his way out of it, but then we move in from behind the uniforms and grab him and take his gun and pat him down. All the while he's telling us he's a cop, he's a cop, there must be some mistake—but then he realizes who we are, what kind of cops we are, and he knows that it's over, that he's done.

Soon we'll sit him down at a table in a small, spare, windowless room somewhere, the same kind of debrief room where countless cops have confronted countless criminals with their countless crimes—and now he's just another one of them. Except that, like almost all the crooked cops we arrest, he's a virgin; no matter how many people he has arrested, he's never been arrested himself—and things look different from the perp's side of the table. He's a big guy, taller and heavier than most, but in a tiny room, surrounded by honest cops, he suddenly seems kind of small.

Maybe he'll be in a state of shock, stunned at how quickly he's been transformed from cop to perp—a lot of them are. Maybe he'll try to offer up some reason, some justification for crossing the line: My child support payments were killing me. I was just doing a favor for an old friend from the neighborhood. I got tired of seeing criminals and drug dealers making more money than I do. Everybody else is corrupt, so why shouldn't I get a piece? We've heard them all.

But whatever he says, we'll nod as if we believe him, and act as if we care. Then we'll take a run at him. Look, we'll say, you know you can't be a cop anymore, but if you cooperate, maybe we can help you help your-self. So tell us, who else is in this? Are there any other cops involved? Will you make a recorded phone call for us? Will you wear a wire against other crooked cops?

Maybe he'll go for it. Now that he's made the transition from cop to criminal, maybe to save his own skin he'll take that extra step and go from cop to criminal to rat, snitch, informer. Or maybe he'll tell us to go screw ourselves and ask for a lawyer.

Either way we've accomplished our primary objective. We've taken his shield away, and there's one less dirty cop in the NYPD.

It's a hard business we're in, a hard world in which we operate. It's a world full of lies and deception and betrayal, a world of snitches and informants, wires and wiretaps, surveillances and sting operations. It's a world of good cops gone bad and bad cops gone worse, of cops who rob and steal and deal drugs and abuse and rape and even kill people. There are never as many cops like that out there as some people choose to believe, but for us, and for all the honest cops, there are always too many. And they are the reason we exist.

By necessity we operate in the shadows, in secret, separate from the rest of the cop fraternity. Some cops hate us, many fear us; if we walk into a roomful of other cops, conversations trail off, looks are averted, people move warily away. Even the good cops who understand that the job we do is vital and necessary are glad that they don't have to do the job themselves. And so they hold us apart.

We understand all that, and we accept it. We have to. Because we are the Internal Affairs Bureau, the dreaded IAB. We are the cops who investigate other cops, the police who police the police.

And for us it's enough that every cop, good and bad alike, knows that every hour of every day, we are out there.

Watching.

Chapter 1

THE KIND OF COP I DIDN'T WANT TO BE

Three stories about the kind of cop I didn't want to be.

Story One. It's an early-summer evening in 1977, in Brooklyn's 73rd Precinct, the Seven-Three, and I'm chasing a kid down a cracked and cratered sidewalk lined with stripped cars and boarded-up and burned-out apartment buildings. There's another Seven-Three cop with me, and we're both yelling—Police! Stop! Police! Stop!—but of course the kid's not stopping. He keeps running—and the funny thing is, we're actually gaining on him.

Ordinarily we wouldn't have a chance with a kid like this. We're both wearing full NYPD gear—blue uniforms, hats, belts, guns, extra ammo, radios, nightsticks, handcuffs, flashlights, clunky Knapp shoes—while the kid, a teenager, is wearing a white T-shirt and dark pants and black Chuck Taylor Converse sneakers; he ought to be leaving us in the dust. But the kid's problem is that over his right shoulder he's carrying a big black plastic garbage bag filled with swag from a burglary, and it's holding him back.

Stop! Police! Police! Stop!

We're almost on him, and now the kid makes a decision. He lets go of the plastic bag and takes off like a shot. Without the bag slowing him down, it's like he's turned on the afterburners. No way we're going to be able to run him down.

And then something dangerous happens—something dangerous to the kid and, as it turns out, dangerous to my future as a cop.

Of course, dangerous occurrences aren't unusual in the Seven-Three; in this precinct, dangerous occurrences are just another day at the office. The Seven-Three, which covers the Brownsville and Ocean

Hill neighborhoods of Brooklyn, is what's known as an "A" Precinct or an "A" House, meaning it's a high-crime precinct—and for cops, it's a hard-luck precinct as well.

There are a lot of good and dedicated cops in the Seven-Three in 1977, but it's also fair to say that the vast majority of them wish they were somewhere else—almost anyplace else. A few Seven-Three cops like the action, but most wound up there either through bad luck of the draw, like me, or because they'd gotten jammed up with their bosses in another precinct and had been sent there as a kind of unofficial administrative punishment. A precinct like the Seven-Three has a certain end-of-the-line quality to it. The attitude is: So what if my shoes aren't shined at roll call? So what if I duck that radio run? What are they going to do, send me to the Seven-Three?

Still, even as they wish they were elsewhere, cops in an "A" House like the Seven-Three often take a perverse pride in working in a high-crime precinct. They look down on cops in lower-crime "B" and "C" precincts as something less than real cops, shirkers almost, and they give their own precincts nicknames that reflect the seemingly besieged and forgotten nature of their existence. The South Bronx has the 41st Precinct, the Four-One, which is called "Fort Apache"—later made famous in the Paul Newman movie *Fort Apache, The Bronx*—and to the west of us, in the Crown Heights section of Brooklyn, there's the 77th Precinct, the Seven-Seven, known as "The Alamo."

At the Seven-Three, we are "Fort Zinderneuf," or "Fort Z" for short, named after the far-flung and doomed French Foreign Legion outpost in *Beau Geste*. In the movie, the Legionnaires propped up the bodies of their dead comrades in the parapets to make the hostile tribesmen think the fort was more strongly defended than it really was. And that's what we are in the Seven-Three: bodies propped in the parapets, trying to hold crime at bay.

And crime—murder, rape, robbery, drug dealing—is the one thing Brownsville has no shortage of. Once a thriving immigrant community, with a commercial section of furniture stores and greengrocers and kosher butcher shops along Pitkin Avenue, over the preceding decades its population has dropped by half—and what's left is a mile-square portrait of urban catastrophe. Half of the apartment buildings are abandoned, and half of those are blackened hulks, victims of arson or squatters' cooking and trash fires; the rest are boarded up in a hopeless attempt to keep out the skells and the junkies. Garbage pickup is haphazard at best, stripped cars sit for months without being towed, most of the fire hydrants don't work; in 1977 the city is still in a financial crisis, and Brownsville, which is almost exclusively black and Hispanic, is the last place the city is going to spend any money it doesn't have to. The remaining shops along Pitkin Avenue—drugstores, shoe stores, pizzerias, small grocery stores, most of them white-owned—struggle to hang on, but they hide behind heavy steel grates and shutters, even in the daytime, and at the end of the day, ideally before darkness sets in, the owners close up and scurry away, fearing for their lives.

It's not that there aren't good people in Brownsville, and in Ocean Hill, too, another neighborhood in the precinct that's gone to rot. They're poor people—in 1977, except for the bigger drug dealers, every single person who lives in Brownsville is poor—and they're good people. But sometimes even the decent people look at us as if the disaster they're living in is our fault: You're the cops. Why can't you do something? As for the bad guys—the players, the dealers, the cornerboys, the gang members—they look at us with pure, undisguised hatred.

The hatred isn't always passive. Some years earlier a guy had lunged out of an alley near the corner of Saratoga and Blake and virtually decapitated a Seven-Three police officer with a butcher knife. Gunfire is a nightly occurrence, and you constantly have to watch out for "air mail"—bricks or bottles or chunks of concrete or other debris being thrown from a rooftop or a window onto your head. Seven-Three cops even have a little jingle they sing about it: Bricks and bottles rain down on me / Because I work in the Seven-Three!

Sometimes the missiles thrown at us are less dangerous but more disgusting. Once, earlier on, I'm in a sector car with a Seven-Three veteran when we get an Aided call at an occupied three-story apartment house—"Aided" means someone is having some kind of medical problem. When we roll up to the address I start to get out of the car, but my partner grabs my arm and tells me to hold on a second. He's looking through the car window at the building, up at the roof, and either experience or some sixth sense tells him something's wrong.

This is a piss-bag, kid, he tells me, and sure enough, a few seconds later—*splat!*—a waxed brown paper lunch bag full of piss hits the sidewalk next to the car and bursts apart. Someone had telephoned in a phony Aided call just for the sheer joy of throwing a bagful of human urine at us. And it wouldn't be the last time, either.

Piss-bags raining from the rooftops. Welcome to Fort Z.

Like I said, in 1977 there are a lot of good cops in the Seven-Three. But if you aren't careful, if you take the crime and the misery and the hatred and the piss-bags personally, there's a good chance you might start thinking about throwing the piss-bags back.

Which maybe explains what almost happens to the kid with the black plastic garbage bag.

I'm not a complete rookie, I've got a few years on the job, but I'm new in the Seven-Three, so I don't have a "seat," a permanent assignment; I show up at roll call and I go where they tell me. On this particular early-summer evening I'm assigned to a foot post on Pitkin Avenue between Rockaway and Stone, and the adjoining streets—about six blocks in all. It's been a quiet tour so far, and when I get to the boundary of my post I see another Seven-Three cop who's working the adjoining post.

I don't really know this guy—we'll call him Officer Romeo—but he's got a few more years on the job than I do, and he's been in the Seven-Three longer. I've heard some vague talk that he's got an attitude, and that some cops don't like to work with him. But it's just that, vague talk. So I walk across the street to his post to shoot the breeze for a minute.

Hey, what's goin' on?

Nothin' much. You?

Nothin' much.

Then, while we're talking, a citizen leans out of a second-story window in the building next to us and calls out: Officer! Officer! They're robbing the beauty parlor around the corner!

So Romeo and I take off running, and as we round the corner we see the kid clambering out of a first-story window with that big plastic bag. We see him, he sees us, and the chase is on.

There are a couple of things I notice at this point. One is that while the guy in the second-story window had said it was a robbery, which is the taking of property from a person by force or intimidation, it actually looks more like a burglary, which is criminal trespass with intent to commit a crime, in this case larceny. There's a "Closed" sign on the beauty parlor door, and the kid with the bag came out a window, so there's probably nobody inside the beauty parlor, which means it's not a robbery. Burglary and robbery are both felonies, but in practice burglary is a less serious crime.

And the other thing I notice is that after the kid drops the black plastic bag and starts to pull away from us, Officer Romeo draws his gun, stops running, and takes a combat stance with his .38 revolver pointed at the running kid's back. He's taking careful aim.

And I'm thinking: He's going to shoot this kid.

No way. I stop, too, and I reach out and push Romeo's gun toward the ground, yelling, Don't shoot! DON'T SHOOT! And Romeo gives me a look that's first surprise, and then pure rage.

What the fuck are you doing? he yells at me.

What are *you* doing? I yell back. We can't shoot! He's just a kid!

Fuck you! He's getting away!

In the old days it might have been different. Back then, under the law, a cop could in some circumstances legally shoot a suspect who was fleeing the scene of a dangerous or violent crime such as an armed robbery. But in the early 1970s both state law and NYPD policy began changing. Now the Department allows cops to shoot only if the suspect poses an imminent threat of death or serious injury to the cop or someone else. The short form is that in most cases you can't shoot a perp who's running away.

Still, there are gray areas—there always are. If Romeo shoots that kid, maybe he can claim that he thought the kid had reached for a weapon in his waistband. If he tells a good enough story, maybe the shooting will fly, especially if his partner, meaning me, backs him up.

Fortunately for the kid, and for Romeo, and for me, it doesn't happen that way. As Romeo and I are arguing, out of the corner of my eye I see the kid duck into an abandoned apartment building a half block down the street. Argument temporarily forgotten, Romeo and I run down the street and into the building.

Like the hundreds of other abandoned buildings in Brownsville, this one is a mess. The mongo men, the scrap metal scavengers, have already been through it, stripping out everything they can get a few cents on the pound for—plumbing, electrical wires, kitchen sinks, doorknobs and hinges, radiators. The skells and the junkies have camped out in it, throwing their garbage in the corners, sleeping or shooting up in one room and taking their dumps and pisses on the floor in another room—assuming they had the initiative to go to another room. The smell in the building is beyond belief—so bad, in fact, that even the junkies and bums have abandoned it.

With our flashlights out—guns out, too, just in case—Romeo and I start a room-to-room, looking for the kid. In a second-story apartment, in a trash pile with a hinge-less door dragged on top of it, I see a black Chuck Taylor Converse sneaker poking out—and the foot inside it is shaking.

All right, buddy, I call out, we got you. Come out of there, and let us see your hands.

So the kid crawls out, covered in trash, hands up and still shaking. Later I find out he's sixteen. He's probably expecting some street justice for having run from us—not a savage beating, but at least a few thumps. And maybe under other circumstances, with another cop, his expectations might be justified. Remember, this is 1977. And this is the Seven-Three.

Please don't hurt me, the kid says.

I don't feel sorry for this kid. He's old enough to know better, and chances are this isn't the first crime he's committed, and it won't be the last. But I don't take his running away from us personally.

We aren't going to hurt you, I tell him. But you're under arrest.

So we search the kid—no weapons—and then cuff him and start marching him back to the precinct. On the way we grab the black plastic bag, and inside it there's a bunch of old hair dryers and brushes and scissors and half-empty bottles of shampoo—junk. The whole score probably isn't worth ten bucks.

At the precinct, Romeo takes the arrest—it was his post, so it's his collar—and starts processing the kid into the juvenile justice system. I go back to walking my post.

And that should have been the end of it. Except that over the next couple days I notice that some of the other cops in Fort Z are looking at me sideways. Like I said, I'm pretty new in the precinct, and they're looking at me like they're wondering what kind of cop I am.

It turns out that after we brought the kid to the precinct, after I had gone back on post, Romeo started bad-mouthing me to other cops. I didn't back him up, he said. I was weak, he said. I was a pussy, he said, a coward.

Calling a cop a coward is the second-worst accusation you can make against him, especially in a precinct like Fort Z. If other cops think you don't have the guts to fight when fighting is necessary, or that you won't back up a partner, they won't want to work with you, or even talk to you. You'll be shunned, ostracized. The only way you could be more shunned and ostracized is if the other cops think you're a cheese-eating rat, an informer, a guy who squeals on other cops.

But what am I going to do? I can't go around saying: Hey, I'm no coward! That in itself would seem pathetic and weak. All I can do is keep my mouth shut and do my job.

The next day the Seven-Three delegate to the PBA—Patrolmen's Benevolent Association, the cop union—catches me in the locker room. He's a veteran, been there forever. He's heard the talk. So he asks me: Hey, kid, what really happened out there?

Talking to your PBA rep is a little like talking to a priest. He isn't going to tell the bosses what you say; you aren't ratting anybody out. So I tell him the whole story, and when I'm done he pats me on the knee and says: Well, kid, you probably saved yourself a trip to the grand jury—meaning that if Officer Romeo had shot that kid in the back, I probably would have been called before a criminal grand jury to testify.

I don't tell the PBA rep this, but if that had happened, I know what I would have done. I would have told the truth—that the kid was running away, that I hadn't seen a weapon, that in my opinion there was no reason to shoot. Even if it ruins my career as a working cop, even if in other cops' eyes it makes me a cheese-eating rat, I'll tell the truth.

After that I don't hear any more about it. The PBA rep doesn't really know me, but I guess he knows Officer Romeo, and he must have passed the word that I'm okay. I don't get any more sideways looks.

As it turns out, I don't stay in the Seven-Three that much longer— and neither does Romeo, although for different reasons. A few years later I hear that he'd gotten jammed up for shooting and wounding a family member during a domestic dispute and was kicked out of the Department.

Of course, in the context of the Seven-Three, this incident with the running kid was no big deal. Romeo hadn't actually done anything illegal, nobody got shot, we made the arrest.

But it made me realize something about myself. I knew that no matter how many piss-bags rained down from rooftops, no matter how much crime and violence and hatred I saw, I wasn't going to let the job turn me into the kind of cop who would shoot a running teenager in the back over a two-bit burglary. And if I saw another cop do something like that, no matter what the consequences, I wasn't going to cover it up.

That wasn't the kind of cop I wanted to be.

Story Two. It's the spring of 1974 and I'm fresh out of the Academy, assigned to Manhattan Traffic Area, which covers Manhattan south of Ninety-Sixth Street from the East River to the Hudson. I'm standing in a coffee shop on Second Avenue, arguing with the owner about whether I have to pay for a cup of coffee.

It's not what you think. I'm arguing that I *should* pay. And the coffee shop owner is arguing just as strongly that I shouldn't.

This little drama had started just a few minutes earlier. It's a rainy day, so my partner and I are in an RMP—Radio Mobile Patrol, a marked patrol car—in uniform, riding around and responding to radio calls. At one point, my partner, Ed, a classmate from the Academy, and I decide to get a cup of coffee.

Well, it's coffee for Ed. For me it's hot tea, milk no sugar. Yeah, I know. Cops are supposed to drink coffee, the blacker and more viscous the better; if your spoon won't stand up straight in it, it's not really coffee. But I like tea.

Anyway, we pull the car in front of a coffee shop on Second Avenue. It's my turn to buy, so Ed, who's driving, stays in the car while I go in.

It's a small place, half a dozen stools at the counter, a few booths along the wall; there are maybe ten customers in there. I walk up to the counter and give the counterman/owner my order—large coffee, black, extra sugar, large tea, milk no sugar, to go, please—and he turns around and walks over to the coffee machine. A minute later he comes back with two steaming Styrofoam cups.

This is 1974, remember, so a cup of coffee costs a dime, and the same for tea. I don't have any coins, so while the counterman is getting the coffee I fish a dollar bill out of my wallet. But when I try to hand him the dollar, he puts his hands in the air and steps back like the dollar bill is radioactive.

Oh, no, Officer, he says. For you, no charge. Free.

Thanks, I tell him, but I'll pay. Just give me the change.

No, no, no, he says. Free. No charge.

Thanks, but no, really, I want to pay.

Hey, like I said, no charge.

I know this coffee shop owner isn't trying to bribe me with the free coffee. He's not trying to give me free coffee because he's afraid if he doesn't I'll start hanging summonses on every car that's parked in front of his shop. He wants to give me the free coffee because he likes having uniformed cops in his shop. It's like an insurance policy against crime. Even the most brain-dead mope isn't going to try to rob a place that has cop cars parked out front and a steady stream of guys in blue going in and out. And for most cops, free coffee or a discount on a meal is just part of the job; they don't give it a second thought.

But I still want to pay. So we keep going back and forth like this, until the counterman, a short Greek guy, starts getting a little hot about it, like it's a point of honor or something. He's waving his arms and saying in a loud voice: Officer, for you, free! Finally he walks over to the far end of the counter and won't even look at me.

Now, as a cop, you're always watching people, but when you're in uniform you know that people are also watching you. As I'm standing there at the counter with that unwanted dollar bill in my hand, I can feel the eyes on my back, and I can imagine what the other customers are thinking.

Half of them are probably thinking: Whaddaya, nuts? Take the free coffee already. And the other half are probably thinking: A cop who won't take a free cup'a coffee? Gimme a break. What kind of scam is this cop running?

It's getting embarrassing. So finally I hold the dollar conspicuously up in the air and say, in what is probably a too-loud voice: I'm leaving the dollar on the counter! I slap the dollar on the counter, grab the coffee and the tea, and get out of there before the counterman can chase me down. I jump in the patrol car and we take off. And when I tell Ed what happened, about leaving the dollar on the counter, he starts laughing.

Of course, the story gets around. The veterans, the old-timers, start saying things like, Hey, kid! Are you the one who paid a dollar for a ten-cent cup'a coffee? And then they laugh like crazy. Naturally I don't tell them that it wasn't just a cup of coffee, that I got a cup of tea as well. That would have only made them laugh harder.

And they probably would have laughed harder still if they'd known that the incident at the coffee shop on Second Avenue—which I never went back to—wasn't the only time I'd had trouble paying for hot tea or a sandwich while I was in uniform. It happened all the time—although in most cases, when I insisted on paying, the owner or cashier would eventually shrug and say: Okay, if that's the way you want it.

The fact is that in my entire career as a cop, I never took a meal or a cup of coffee—or tea—on the arm. Never.

Maybe you're wondering why.

It's not just because the Patrol Guide, the NYPD cop's bible, prohibits accepting gratuities of any kind, free coffee and sandwiches included, and I'm afraid I'll get caught. The Patrol Guide prohibits a lot of things, from wearing white socks with your uniform to using a blue-ink pen instead of a black-ink pen to write a parking ticket. The Patrol Guide is about four inches thick, and even the most conscientious, by-the-book cop in the Department probably can't get through a shift without violating some obscure section of it. Besides, who's going to turn you in? The restaurant owner who, without being asked, gives you the free coffee or the discounted meal in the first place? Or your partner? C'mon.

And I don't refuse to accept free meals because I really believe all those cautionary tales they told us in the Academy, about how taking even a single cup of coffee on the arm would inevitably put you on a slippery slope that will end up with you stealing wallets from DOAs (dead people) or ripping off drug dealers. I never thought a good cop turned into a bad cop because of a ten-cent cup of coffee.

And it's not because I'm some kind of naturally saintly guy. I never lack for things to talk to the priest about when I go to confession.

No, the reason I turn down the free coffee is because I figured out early on that, except for the occasional argument with a cashier, it just makes the job easier. If I take a free sandwich, it makes it harder to say no if the coffee shop owner wants me to give him a break on double-parked delivery trucks, or if he wants me to drop what I'm doing and scatter some teenagers who are loitering in front of his shop. I might bounce the teenagers or give a break on the delivery truck anyway, but it won't be because I think I owe the guy something. I'll do it because it's good police work—nothing more, nothing less.

And when you do your job that way, the word gets around. Oh yeah, you're the one who paid a dollar for a cup'a coffee. You develop a reputation among other cops as a straight shooter, a guy who follows the rules and puts in an honest shift—a straight eight. As long as they don't suspect you of being a rat, other cops, even the less than honest ones, don't hold being an honest cop against you. They figure, hey, that's just the way he is.

The point is that despite what some people may believe, in the NYPD being an honest cop doesn't hurt you with other cops. In fact, a reputation for being a straight shooter protects you.

Which is why I can also say that during my entire time as an NYPD police officer, with the exception of a cop taking an occasional free cup of coffee or a discounted meal, I never once personally witnessed an NYPD cop engaging in an act of financial corruption.

That may not sound believable. After all, I came on the job just after the Commission to Investigate Alleged Police Corruption—better known as the Knapp Commission—had held hearings and released its final report. After hearing testimony from honest cops like Frank Serpico, later portrayed by Al Pacino in the popular film, and from dishonest cops who'd gotten caught, among others, the commission concluded that corruption was "an extensive, Department-wide phenomenon," ranging from cops shaking down tow-truck drivers and prostitutes to cops selling drugs. According to the commission, corruption in the NYPD was rampant and systemic.

So how can I not see it? Am I blind? Or just stupid?

I'm neither. What you have to understand is that especially after

Knapp, when the anticorruption heat was on, no bad cop with half a brain is going to rifle a cash register after a burglary call or roll a well-dressed drunk at a bus stop in front of you unless he's absolutely certain you're a corrupt cop, too. If you have a reputation as an honest cop, he would no more steal money in front of you than he would steal money in front of the police commissioner himself.

And your reputation will follow you. Even in a Department with thirty or forty thousand cops (the number varies) there's always somebody who knows somebody who knows somebody who knows you. Calls will be made and the word will get around—and if you're an honest cop, the bad cops will leave you alone.

So yeah, I was the cop who paid a dollar for a ten-cent cup of coffee—and a tea. If I hadn't paid, if I had accepted that free cup of coffee, it wouldn't have been any big earthshaking deal.

But that wasn't the kind of cop I wanted to be.

Story Three. It's 1978, a couple weeks before Christmas, and after a twenty-month layoff caused by the city's 1975 financial crisis—more on that later—and another stint at the Seven-Three, I'm back in Manhattan Traffic Area, assigned to the Scooter Task Force. On the Task Force we ride around in two-wheel Lambrettas or three-wheel Cushmans, mostly handling traffic and security and crowd control for special events—demonstrations, parades, VIP visits, and so on—but also taking other radio jobs as well. It's a good assignment for me. The hours are regular, and since I've just gotten married, and have been studying for the sergeant's test, that's important.

True, it's not as exciting as being in the Seven-Three. Positive side? In 1978 Manhattan South still has its share of crime, but you generally don't have piss-bags raining down on you from the rooftops.

On this particular day there's a demonstration scheduled at City Hall by tow-truck drivers, who are mad about something—in New York, somebody's always demonstrating about something—so I'm at the corner of Church and Dey Streets, on Scooter No. 3830, getting ready to divert traffic away from the demonstration area. Then at exactly 9:10 a.m.—the timing is important here—a cab pulls up next to me.

Hey, Officer, the cabbie says, a fare left her briefcase in the backseat. She was gone before I saw it. What should I do?

The Patrol Guide has the answer. It has the answer to almost every conceivable circumstance, including "found property" in the back of a yellow cab. I radio my patrol sergeant that I've got some found property and then I take the briefcase out of the backseat—it's nothing fancy, just a plain hard-leather briefcase—and put it on the trunk of the cab. I take out my memo book and start writing down the t/p/o—time, place, occurrence—and the cabbie's pedigree: name, address, phone number, medallion number, and so on. The briefcase isn't locked, so we open it together and look inside. There's not much, just a single credit card and some business papers that have a woman's name, address, and phone number on them. I inventory it all in my memo book, and I give the cabbie a receipt with my name and badge number. While I'm doing this the sergeant shows up, and I tell him what happened and he "scratches"— signs—my memo book with his name and the date and time: 12/13/78, 9:20 a.m.

The cabbie leaves, and I've still got the briefcase. I don't want to carry it around with me in the scooter, so I ask the sergeant if I can take it over to the First Precinct house and voucher it. He's says okay, but be back by ten a.m.

No problem. I drive over to the precinct, and the DO—the desk officer, a lieutenant—enters my name and the date and time in the Interrupted Patrol Log, which records why I'm off my post. The lieutenant checks the briefcase contents and hands me the voucher, which I put in my memo book. I go over to a typewriter and start pecking out the found property report, in carbon-paper quadruplicate. Then I call the phone number on the business papers and reach the woman who lost the briefcase. I tell her where she can pick up her briefcase, and what was in it when I opened it, and she agrees that there were just some papers and the one credit card. She's grateful—the papers aren't valuable, but they are important—and she keeps thanking me. No problem, ma'am, all part of the job. I hang up, log out at the desk, and I'm back on my post at 9:50.

And then I don't give the incident even a second thought until just after Christmas, when I'm at roll call and the sergeant hands me a letter ordering me to report to the Manhattan South Field Internal Affairs Unit the following week, and to bring my memo book for December 13.

Internal Affairs. The cops who go after other cops.

Before the Knapp Commission, most police corruption and misconduct allegations were handled—or, some would charge, not handled—by precinct or borough commanders. After Knapp, the Department created the Internal Affairs Division, with a central office on Poplar Street in Brooklyn, and Field Internal Affairs Units stationed in every borough command. In the late 1970s there are about a hundred cops assigned full-time to Internal Affairs and another two hundred to the borough FIAUs.

And with the possible exception of their mothers and their wives, everybody hates them.

Sure, most cops acknowledge the need for some kind of internal anticorruption effort. As Knapp made clear, the old system obviously hadn't worked. But that doesn't mean that you have to actually like the IAD guys—and even the most honest and by-the-book cops don't.

The IAD guys have a terrible reputation among the cop rank and file. As far as most cops are concerned, other cops go into IAD for only three reasons: one, they're cowards or shirkers who are too afraid or too lazy to work on the street; two, they're rats who got jammed up by their own corruption or misconduct and agreed to work for IAD and rat out other cops to save their own skins; or three, they're zealots who simply get a sick and twisted pleasure out of persecuting cops.

It might not have been so bad if IAD also had a reputation for rooting out serious corruption and misconduct. But it doesn't. In the rank-and-file view, IAD seems more interested in busting cops for administrative violations—not wearing their hats when they get out of a patrol car, calling in sick so they can go to their daughter's dance recital, that sort of thing—than in spending the time and effort to go after really bad cops.

Of course, the stereotype of IAD guys isn't accurate in every individual case. Some cops went into IAD so they could get the necessary investigative experience to qualify for a detective's gold shield, and IAD was one of the few avenues open to them. Some guys went into IAD because they honestly wanted to help rid the Department of bad cops.

Still, the stereotype is accurate often enough that it is the stereotype.

The regular cops are us, and IAD is them. They're the "rat squad," and nobody wants anything to do with them.

But even as cops despise the IAD guys, they also fear them. Cops figure that even if they're innocent, the IAD guys can always find something. So a summons from Internal Affairs isn't something to be taken lightly. For a good cop it's a source of concern; for a cop with problems, it's a source of mortal dread.

They never tell you what you're being called in for, what the allegation is. But the date of the memo book pages they order you to bring can give you a hint. So I go back and look at my memo book for December 13. There weren't any really unusual incidents, no arguments with a citizen that could have generated a complaint, no use of force, no complicated reports that I might have screwed up.

The only thing that stands out on that day is that briefcase in the back of the taxi.

I know I'd done everything by the book, and then some. But who knows? Maybe the woman changed her mind and decided that there had been some cash in the briefcase that was missing. Maybe the cabbie had used the credit card to make a quick purchase before he turned it in to me, and when the woman got the card statement she filed a complaint. It doesn't seem likely, but it's possible.

Still, I have everything documented, so I'm not worried—or at least not too worried. Per SOP (standard operating procedure), I call my PBA rep and tell him I've been summoned, and he says he'll meet me there.

So the next week at the appointed time I show up at the Manhattan South FIAU offices, which are on an upstairs floor at the 17th Precinct. I meet my PBA rep outside, and I ask him what's going on, why have I been called in? He shrugs and says, I dunno, something about a Christmas tree.

Huh? What? A Christmas tree?

Now I'm really confused.

Two Internal Affairs guys in suits and ties are waiting for us. One of them is a regular police officer, a young guy who's the case officer, the other an older IAD sergeant. They aren't smiling, and they don't shake our hands. They usher us into a small, windowless, bare-walled room with a plain wood table and some chairs. It's exactly the sort of room in which squad detectives interview suspects—except in this room the suspects are cops. In police jargon it's called a "GO" room—"gee-oh"—an outdated but still used reference to General Order 15, the old NYPD regulation concerning administrative disciplinary hearings.

On the table there's one of those old reel-to-reel tape recorders, and when the PBA rep and I sit down the IAD guys turn on the tape, identify themselves, state the date and time, and then tell me to state my name and shield number. Then they inform me that this is an official administrative hearing under PG Section 118-19, and they read me what's known as my Garrity rights.

"Garrity" was a 1960s Supreme Court case that grew out of a police ticket-fixing investigation in New Jersey. Basically it held that a public employee can be ordered to give a statement in an administrative disciplinary hearing and can be fired if he refuses to answer or lies. But it also held that since it's a compelled statement, made under threat of termination, under the Fifth Amendment anything the employee says cannot be used against him in a criminal proceeding.

Do you understand your rights, Officer Campisi? the IAD guy asks me. Are you satisfied with your representation? Are you ready to answer questions?

I tell them I am.

Officer Campisi, he says, were you on duty with the Manhattan Traffic Area Scooter Task Force on December 13 at approximately 9:30 a.m.?

Yes.

What was your scooter number?

Three-eight-three-oh.

Officer Campisi, the IAD guy says, were you aware of a Christmas tree lot situated at the corner of Greenwich and Seventh Avenue?

Well, I know the intersection, I say. But I didn't know there was a Christmas tree lot there.

And then comes the money ball.

Officer Campisi, the IAD guy says, at approximately 9:30 a.m. on December 13, 1978, did you drive your NYPD scooter number three-eight-three-oh onto the Christmas tree lot at Greenwich and Seventh and intentionally remove from the premises without paying for it one approximately six-foot-tall noble fir Christmas tree?

The question is so unexpected, so out of left field, that it takes me a moment to answer.

Absolutely not!

Later I get the story. It seems that a citizen had filed a complaint alleging that an NYPD cop on a Department scooter had driven onto the lot, hoisted a Christmas tree onto the back of his scooter, and taken off. The only description he had was that the suspect was wearing a blue NYPD uniform and that the number on the scooter started with three-eight; the last two digits had been obscured by the branches of the Christmas tree. So Internal Affairs is calling in every scooter cop with a three-eight scooter series number who had been in the area—about a dozen of us—under suspicion of having stolen the Christmas tree.

Well, if it had happened the way the complainant said it did—maybe it did, maybe it didn't—it was a pretty stupid thing for a cop to do. Maybe the cop thought it was just a prank, something to show the boys back at the precinct—Hey, look, I got us a Christmas tree for the lounge! But what it was was petit larceny, and if that same cop had seen someone else do it he would have collared him for theft. It was the sort of thing that made cops look bad, so if it happened, I halfway hoped that IAD would catch the guy.

But I want these IAD guys to understand that it wasn't me.

I wasn't anywhere near Greenwich and Seventh, I tell them. And I certainly didn't steal a Christmas tree.

Can you prove that, Officer Campisi? they say.

Yes, in fact, I can. So I show them my memo book, with the notes on the found briefcase and the patrol sergeant's scratch by the time and date. I tell them about the DO's time and date entry in the precinct's Interrupted Patrol Log, and about the call to the briefcase owner, and the sergeant seeing me back on post. It's all there in my memo book. Unless I'm in two places at once, there's no way I could have been stealing a Christmas tree at the corner of Greenwich and Seventh at 9:30 a.m.

But while I'm telling them all this, I notice that the two IAD guys are exchanging looks. They're almost yawning. They're bored! It's pretty obvious to them by now that they aren't going to crack the Great Christmas Tree Caper of 1978 with me. They're done with me.

That's fine, Officer Campisi, the young IAD guy says. You can go now. We'll let you know—but we're pretty sure this will come back unsubstantiated.

There are several ways an Internal Affairs investigation against a cop can come out: "Substantiated" means the cop did it; "unsubstantiated" or "unsub" means the cop may or may not have done it but there's insufficient proof either way; and "unfounded" means the cop is innocent.

Maybe the young IAD guy thinks he's doing me a favor by telling me it would be unsubbed, so I wouldn't worry about it. But I don't see it that way. An "unsub" is like being found not guilty in a criminal trial; you might actually be guilty as hell, but they just couldn't prove it. An "unsub" stays on your permanent record, and it carries a taint. An "unfounded" doesn't stay on your record; it's like the allegation against you had never been made.

Well, I'm not going to have an unsub on a theft allegation hanging around my neck for the rest of my career. Hey, I'm the guy who paid a dollar for a cup of coffee! And I'm especially not going to take an unsub when all it would take is a phone call or two for the IAD guys to determine that it was a solid unfounded. And I tell them so.

No way, I say. I don't want an unsub. This is an unfounded. Call the patrol sergeant. Check with the precinct DO. Call the lady with the briefcase. Call the cabbie. The phone numbers are all right here.

Then the young IAD guy gives me another bored look and says: We really don't have time for that, Officer. We're very busy around here.

I'm of Sicilian heritage; all four of my grandparents were born in Sicily. And while I don't want to shock anybody, people of Sicilian extraction are occasionally capable of displays of temper.

So when this IAD guy tells me they're just too busy to make a couple of lousy phone calls to protect the record and reputation of another cop, I go Sicilian on them.

You're too busy? I say, standing up from my chair. You're going to give me an unsub because you're too busy to do your jobs?

Now see here, Officer, the IAD sergeant says. You can't talk to us like that.

I don't care who you are! I say, waving my arms in the air—the Sicilian thing again. Make the calls! Do your jobs! If you unsub me on this I'll sue you! I'll see you in court!

And so on.

At this point, the PBA rep is tugging on my arm, saying: C'mon, kid, we're outta here. He's gone pale. A PO doesn't talk to a sergeant like that. And no sane cop gets up in IAD's grill.

The IAD guys, meanwhile, look shocked, even a little afraid. It's as if they've got an EDP (emotionally disturbed person) in an NYPD uniform on their hands. But I don't care. It's a matter of principle.

Finally the PBA rep drags me out of there. A few weeks later I get another written notice from Internal Affairs about the theft investigation of me.

It's marked "Unfounded."

I don't know if the IAD guys actually made any calls, or if they just marked it unfounded because they were afraid I'd go crazy on them again. I guessed it was the latter. And as far as I know, they never cracked the Great Christmas Tree Caper of 1978.

But even months later, it still rankled. It was bad enough that the Internal Affairs guys went after other cops. But what was almost incomprehensible to me was that when they'd had a chance to prove another cop innocent, those IAD guys hadn't wanted to lift a finger.

One thing the experience taught me: No matter what happened, I would never work for Internal Affairs. Never.

That just wasn't the kind of cop I wanted to be.

In March 2014 I retired from the New York Police Department after almost forty-one years on the job—the last seventeen of them as chief of the NYPD Internal Affairs Bureau. In fact, I was the longest-serving Internal Affairs chief in NYPD history.

A lot had happened during those forty-one years. By the time I left the NYPD it was a far different police force than the one I'd known when I was walking a foot post in the Seven-Three. And Internal Affairs was a far different unit than it had been when I got into the beef with those IAD guys in the 17th Precinct. During those four decades, both Internal Affairs and the NYPD had been fundamentally transformed.

And I strongly believe that the transformation in Internal Affairs was a major contributing factor to the transformation of the NYPD.

From the time I joined Internal Affairs in 1993 as an inspector in charge of the Corruption Prevention and Analysis Unit—I was named chief of the Internal Affairs Bureau three years later—I and the men and women in my chain of command did everything we could to fundamentally change the way we policed the police. We fought for and got new authority, new methods, new equipment and resources, new people, with new attitudes. We transformed Internal Affairs from a demoralized, ineffective, and widely unrespected unit of the NYPD into a modern, efficient, successful anticorruption force, one that has been emulated by police departments around the country and around the world. If the new Internal Affairs Bureau was not loved within the NYPD—it never will be—it certainly was feared, by corrupt and brutal cops and those thinking about becoming corrupt and brutal cops. And fear is simply respect in another form.

In creating the new IAB, did we wipe out corruption and misconduct within the NYPD? Of course not. There was corruption and misconduct before my time at IAB, there was corruption and misconduct while I was IAB chief, and there is corruption and misconduct now.

It's different than it used to be, though. The old-style, systemic corruption of the pre–Knapp Commission days, when entire precincts were on the pad, is probably gone forever; so is the kind of almost casual brutality applied to suspects who ran or were uncooperative in an interrogation room. The new corruption and misconduct is more opportunistic, more secretive, more limited in scope, and thus harder to detect.

But it's there. And any mayor or politician or high-ranking police official who says he's going to completely eliminate corruption and misconduct from any big-city police department is kidding himself. As long as police departments continue to recruit human beings, as opposed to cyborgs, they will have to deal with the same problems among cops that other human beings have: greed, hatred, violence, jealousy, drug and alcohol abuse, mental instability, laziness, incompetence.

Sure, you can try to reduce corruption and misconduct, to control it, manage it. And we did that at IAB. While I was chief we reduced corruption and misconduct cases by more than 50 percent, even as the NYPD expanded in size. Even the harshest NYPD critics, if they're honest, would have to admit that in terms of honesty and professionalism, the

NYPD is a far better organization than it was in the 1970s and '80s and early '90s.

But it's not perfect—and it never will be. It's a simple question of numbers.

Whenever there's a police corruption or misconduct scandal, people who support cops will always point out that 99 percent of cops do their jobs honestly and correctly. Actually, based on my experience in the NYPD, I think it's a little higher—99.5 percent.

But do the math on that. In a Department with thirty-six thousand cops, one half of one percent is one hundred eighty cops. Which means that as chief of IAB, at any given moment, I had a hundred eighty seriously bad cops out there on the streets of New York City, armed with guns and shields and the enormous power of the law, who were willing to rob, cheat, abuse, and even murder people.

They were the ones who kept me up at night.

During my years as IAB chief more than two thousand NYPD cops were arrested for various crimes, and we investigated thousands more for other serious misconduct. Some of those cases made national and even international headlines: the cops who fired forty-one times at a man who was standing on his front doorstep, and who turned out to be unarmed; the sadistic cop who savagely assaulted and sodomized a man with a broom handle; the so-called Cannibal Cop who fantasized about cooking and eating women. There were others, less sensational but still deadly serious: cops who stole millions of dollars from drug dealers; cops who trafficked in illegal guns; cops who beat up suspects after the cuffs were already on; cops who "flaked"—planted drugs on—innocent people; cops who sold their souls to make a few hundred bucks ripping off Manhattan street peddlers; the cop who stalked young girls online until he made the mistake of stalking an IAB undercover; the cop who robbed banks on his lunch hour. And on and on.

This book is partly about them, the one half of one percent. But it's also about the hard realities of being a cop on the streets of New York City, about the challenges of enforcing the law while at the same time obeying it, about how hard it is for some cops to maintain their honor when others around them have abandoned theirs. It's about battles won and lost on the street corners in Brooklyn and the Bronx, and battles won and lost in City Hall and the top floors of One Police Plaza. It's about politicians like Rudy Giuliani and Mike Bloomberg and the disastrous—in my opinion—Bill de Blasio, and how they handled crises, and it's about police commissioners like Ray Kelly and Howard Safir and Bill Bratton, and how they shaped the vast, diverse, and often fractious standing army that is the NYPD. This book is about judges and prosecutors, lawyers and reporters, bureaucrats and union leaders; it's about killers and drug dealers, undercovers and informants, about good cops posing as bad civilians and bad civilians posing as bad cops.

It's about all that and more. But the real heroes of this book are all the good cops of the NYPD—and the small group of men and women who stand between those good cops and a few criminals in uniform who would bring them down.

It's often said that police are the "thin blue line," the narrow bulwark standing between the public and uncontrolled chaos and crime. And that's true. Can you imagine New York City, or any city, without police? But within that thin blue line there's an even smaller, thinner line of cops whose job it is to protect the public from bad cops, and to protect the good cops from the bad ones. They're the men and women of Internal Affairs.

Their work is often misunderstood, by the public and by other cops. It is racked with uncertainties and ambiguities, not simple black and white but varying shades of gray. Even their successes are in a sense failures, because every time they catch a bad cop, that bad cop represents a betrayal of the public and of the Department's values.

And yet, without them, without that small group of cops who operate in the shadowy gray corners of the cop world, the thin blue line would rot from within and ultimately collapse.

They are the police who police the police—the brave, honest, dedicated cops of the NYPD Internal Affairs Bureau.

Chapter 2

SHIELD NO. 791

I'm standing outside the old 83rd Precinct house, at the corner of Wilson and DeKalb in Brooklyn, when I see my buddy Mike coming out the front door. Mike is one of my favorite cops, a tall, good-looking guy who always looks sharp when he's on post—buttons and shield polished, shoes and belt and holster shined, his hat just so. He's like an NYPD recruiting poster. So I fall into step beside him, and we trade a little friendly banter.

Caught any bad guys today? I ask him.

Not yet, he says, laughing. But I'm going to. You wanna help?

I'm young, eager, ready to put crooks in jail. And Mike would be a perfect partner.

You bet! I tell him, and he laughs again.

Okay, let's go get 'em, Mike says. So we set off down the sidewalk, looking for crooks, and as we're walking Mike takes off his NYPD hat and puts it on my head—and I'm thinking: I'm a policeman! I'm a policeman!

Of course, I'm going to have to wait a while before I can really help Officer Mike put bad guys in jail, because I'm still in the first grade. I barely reach up to Mike's belt buckle, his hat is hanging down almost to my chin, and I have to take two steps to his one just to keep up. But someday . . .

There are basically two stories you'll get if you ask a cop why he joined the NYPD. One is that he never gave being a cop even a second thought until one day, on a whim, or a dare, he went down and took the test. The other story is that he wanted to be a cop ever since he was five years old.

I wanted to be a cop since I was five years old.

I grew up in the Bushwick section of Brooklyn, a mile-square working-class neighborhood of row-house homes and apartment buildings and small breweries and textile factories and a commercial district on Broadway and Knickerbocker Avenue. It was the kind of neighborhood where everybody's dad was a bus driver or a city sanitation worker or a barber or a maintenance man—working people. The comedian Jackie Gleason grew up in Bushwick, and later he used a Chauncey Street address for bus driver Ralph Kramden and his wife, Alice, on the TV show *The Honeymooners*.

The Honeymooners—that was Bushwick in the 1950s.

All four of my grandparents were born in Sicily, and were part of the flood of Italian immigrants who came to New York in the early 1900s. They all died before I was born, so I never got a chance to know them, but I always thought it was funny that both of my grandfathers were barbers—and both were bald. Both my mom, Josephine, and my dad— he was born Ignacio, but he changed it to Charles, and his friends called him Chappy—grew up speaking Italian as well as English, although sadly I didn't. The only time my parents spoke Italian in front of me was when they didn't want me to know what they were saying.

My dad worked for most of his life as an assistant engineer at the Hotel McHenry, later the Hotel 123, on West Forty-Fourth Street in Times Square, fixing plumbing, repairing plaster, rewiring switches, you name it. A small man with big, rough hands, he could fix anything—and at the Hotel 123 there was always plenty to fix. Although once elegant and grand, a haven for New York's elite, like so much else in Times Square the hotel had started to decline in the '50s and '60s, and by the 1970s it was described in the *New York Times* as a "sanctuary for thieves, pimps, prostitutes and muggers." (Times change. After a renovation in the early 2000s, the hotel is now the posh AKA Times Square residential hotel—and once again home to millionaires.) My mother worked a variety of jobs—in a luncheonette, a yarn factory, an old folks' home.

So we obviously weren't rich, but we weren't poor, either. We lived in a four-room apartment on the second floor of a six-unit building on Suydam Street; the rent was fifty bucks a month. My parents never had a car, and never took vacations, but there was always food on the table, and love in the house. In the summer there was stickball on the street until the streetlights came on and day trips to Coney Island; Sunday mornings there was mass at St. Brigid's Catholic Church and then in the afternoon a bus ride to downtown Brooklyn for movies at grand old movie theaters like the Albee or the Paramount. There were baseball games at Ebbets Field in Flatbush—although when I was six my heart was broken, along with almost every other heart in Brooklyn, when the Dodgers moved to Los Angeles—and later at the Polo Grounds and Shea Stadium with the Mets. All in all, it was good to be a kid in Bushwick in the 1950s and '60s.

Unusual for an Italian family, I was an only child. My mother had had a series of lost pregnancies, and by the time I came along my parents were both in their forties, so I was a pretty big surprise. But I still had a large extended family, with aunts and uncles and more cousins than I could count to play with. Six of those cousins lived at my aunt Kitty's house, which was two doors down from the 83rd Precinct, a late-nineteenth-century building with a turret and parapets and granite columns at the front entrance—which is where my fascination with cops began. I'd see these guys going in and out of the precinct, uniformed cops like Mike, detectives in regular clothes with guns under their jackets, and I realized from an early age that they were respected, that people looked up to them.

There were two Eight-Three cops that I particularly remember, Ed Kearney and Harry Schroeder, both Community Affairs officers who worked with local residents and the neighborhood kids, trying to fix problems, encouraging the kids to join the Police Athletic League, trying to steer them away from the bad elements. Harry, a solid, broad-shouldered man, and Ed, an African American, a big guy with a bigger smile, were both brave, tough, and thoroughly decent guys. Both would later retire as detectives.

I was in awe of those guys and many others from the Eight-Three. In fact, when I was a kid the only other thing I wanted, besides being a cop, was to someday stand in the cleats of Dodgers (and later Mets) center fielder Duke Snider—although I figured out pretty early on that that wasn't going to happen.

My cop dreams were fine with my parents, even though unlike a lot of New York families, particularly the Irish ones, we didn't have a long tradition of cops in my immediate family; I would be the first. Being an NYPD cop was considered an honorable profession, a step up for a kid from Bushwick. (I did have a distant cousin, Anthony Campisi, a Marine Corps veteran of the Korean War and an NYPD vice cop, who was stabbed to death by a pimp while making an arrest on West Thirty-

Eighth Street in 1966. I'd never met Tony, but I remember my parents talking about it—and as tragic as it was, it didn't for a second make me rethink my desire to be a cop.)

But my parents had one precondition to me becoming a cop: no matter what, education came first. My father had had to drop out of school after the sixth grade and go to work, my mother the same after the eighth grade. They were determined that I would do better, that I'd get a college degree. To that end, they spent money they really didn't have to send me to Catholic schools, first St. Brigid's for grammar school and then high school at St. John's Prep in Bedford-Stuyvesant.

In those days, Bushwick was about 90 percent white, while Bed-Stuy was largely African American—which meant that for Bushwick kids to venture into Bed-Stuy to go to school was a little dicey. I always thought it was more a matter of turf—Hey, what are those Bushwick boys doing in Bed-Stuy?—than it was about race. At least it was for me. I never heard my parents utter a single racial epithet, in English or Italian, and I didn't do it, either. Still, the St. John's kids from Bushwick always traveled to and from school in groups of four or five, and while there were a few scuffles with the local kids, it was nothing serious—unlike now, back then kids didn't routinely shoot other kids.

(That would change, in Bushwick as in so many neighborhoods. In the 1970s and '80s Bushwick became increasingly black and Hispanic, but while most of the white families moved out, my parents stayed; they had no problem with minority people. Neither did I, but I did worry about the increasing crime rate. That hit home one day in 1991, when I was a deputy inspector in the Sixth Precinct and I got a call from a cop who had responded to an Aided call at my parents' apartment. My mother had found my dad in his easy chair, dead of a massive heart attack at age eighty-one. When I rushed over to help my mother the street was swarming with cops and patrol cars and ambulances; there'd been a drug-related shootout on the corner by my parents' building that left three young men DOA. The shootings didn't have anything to do with my father's death, but it was only then that I finally convinced my mother to move out to my neighborhood in Queens.)

Maybe it was the Catholic school environment, but the things that for most young people defined the 1960s—marijuana, LSD, long hair, acid rock, antiwar protests—pretty much passed me by. My most prominent act of rebellion was a mustache that I started growing when I was sixteen. Like the other guys I hung out with, I was into sports—baseball, football, roller hockey—and while I wasn't particularly outstanding in any of them, I was enthusiastic. (In roller hockey, for example, I was a third-line defenseman, but only because the team didn't have a fourth line; if it had, I would have been a fourth-line defenseman.) Our idea of a great time was going to Knicks and Rangers games at the old Madison Square Garden, which was a fifteen-cent subway ride away. Except for a few illicit beers in the park—which I never really developed a taste for—I didn't drink or smoke, not even cigarettes, much less joints; a couple guys in my crowd who did start smoking dope were quickly shunned. As for Vietnam, when I was seventeen a Marine recruiter almost got me and some of my buddies to sign up—he told us we might even be officer material!—and I actually talked my dad into signing the enlistment papers. But then my mother got wind of it and he changed his mind. A high draft lottery number ensured that I wasn't called up.

And I still wanted to be a cop. Even though you couldn't join the Department until you were twenty-one, at age eighteen you could sign on as a paid NYPD "trainee"—no gun, no shield, and you weren't a sworn officer; you'd do clerical work, or answer phones at a precinct. I figured I could work as a trainee and go to college at the same time.

So on a Saturday morning when I was seventeen I went down to George Washington High School in Brooklyn to take the NYPD written exam so I could get my name on the hiring list. Something like twenty-five thousand people took the NYPD test that year, of whom about fifteen thousand passed—all of them vying for about three thousand openings a year in the NYPD.

(I also took the tests for New York Housing Police and Transit Police—back then they were both separate from the NYPD—and the Fire Department and the Sanitation Department. The idea was that if the NYPD wasn't hiring, I could take a job in another city agency and then "roll over" to the NYPD, with the time in Fire or Sanitation being added to my NYPD retirement pension. When you work for the city, you think about angles like that.)

I scored pretty high on the NYPD test and wound up Number 440 on the waiting list. I also had to pass medical and psychological tests—two arms, two legs, no heart murmurs, uncorrected vision 20/30 or better, not demonstrably crazy. Check, check, and check. I also had to take a physical fitness test—chin-ups, lift sixty pounds with each hand, get through an obstacle course, get over a seven-foot wall. For me it was easy. The background check was a little harder. You had to fill out a form, some twenty pages long, listing almost every place you'd ever been, every person you'd ever known, every job you'd ever had, every school you had attended (with documentation to match), every traffic or parking ticket you'd ever gotten, with an explanation as to why you'd gotten it and proof that it had been paid. It was pretty extensive.

Unfortunately, as I was going through this months-long process the NYPD eliminated the trainee program, which meant I had to wait until I was twenty-one to be hired. In the meantime, with a couple of small scholarships and money I'd saved up I had enrolled at Long Island University–Brooklyn as a psychology major. I guess the idea of getting into people's heads appealed to me.

It was at LIU that I first realized that not everyone shared my admiration for cops in general, and the NYPD in particular. This was at the height of the anti–Vietnam War, anti-establishment protest era, and while LIU-B wasn't exactly a hotbed of activism, it wasn't unusual to hear the word "pigs" being applied to cops. As part of my NYPD application process I had to supply reference letters from people in responsible positions, so I asked one of my professors, Douglas Stafford, to give me one. Professor Stafford, a Harvard PhD, was a great guy, a great teacher, an African American who wore his hair in cornrows and sometimes wore a dashiki to class, and I admired him. But when I asked for a reference letter, he tried to talk me out of it. Why would anyone with a college education want to be a cop? A job like that was beneath me, he said. He finally relented on the reference letter, but it struck a nerve. Of course I'd known people who didn't like cops, but I'd never known anybody I respected who actually looked down on them.

Throughout high school I had always worked at a variety of part-time and summer jobs, and I continued that in college—driving a truck, working in a warehouse, even driving the "morgue wagon" for a local hospital, transporting dead bodies from the hospital to the Kings County morgue.

One of the best jobs I had was as a "pin chaser"—technically, a mechanic's apprentice—at the Hart Lanes bowling alley on Hart Street. I mopped floors, conditioned the alleys, oiled the automatic pin-setting machines, manned the front desk. The pay wasn't great, but there were certain fringe benefits. Bowling was a big thing with young people back then, so every Friday and Saturday night the place would be packed with girls, all wearing their best dresses, and more interested in flirting with the boys than in knocking down pins. One shift in February 1971 stands out in my memory. A group of young girls came in to go bowling, among them a beautiful girl named Arlene. Seven years later Arlene and I got married, and while you never know about youthful marriages, I think this one is going to work out. We've been married for almost forty years now.

And then, finally, in October 1973, a couple of weeks after my twenty-first birthday, I got the call.

Hey, kid, the voice on the other end of the line says, you still want to be a cop?

Yes!

Good, the voice on the phone says. Report to the Academy at nine a.m. Monday morning. Click!

I was still about ten credits short of graduating from LIU, but that was no problem. The university would give me some academic credits for getting through the Academy, and I could take PE or something to accumulate the rest. Becoming a police officer was also going to cost me some significant money. The only thing the Department gave you was your shield; everything else—summer and winter uniforms, hat, belt, handcuffs, nightstick, even your gun—you had to pay for yourself, at a total cost of about a thousand dollars. And those were 1973 dollars.

But none of that mattered. The important thing was that my childhood dream was coming true.

Finally I was going to get out there and catch bad guys with Officer Mike.

It's my sixth week at the Academy, test day, and I'm hunched over a battered desk in a classroom, trying to remember the ten court-approved exceptions to the search warrant requirement. I know I know this, I just have to think for a minute—and then it comes to me.

SPACESHIPS!

That's right, the ten court-approved exceptions that allow a police officer to conduct a search without a warrant are: Search incidental to lawful arrest; illegal items in Plain view; the Auto exception that allows searches of vehicles that may move contraband away from the scene; Consent of the person or owner of the property to be searched; Emergency; Stop, question, and possibly frisk if there's reasonable belief a person has a weapon; Hot pursuit; Inventory of property in a vehicle or structure that must be secured; Public place such as a park trash can or a storm drain; and of course, Special circumstances, which means you use your best judgment and take your chances.

Or how about this one: What constitutes grand larceny? Easy. Under New York law in 1973, grand larceny is C-GRAPES—that is, Credit card, theft of; Gun, theft of; theft of government Records; theft of Amount over $1,000; theft of any amount from a Person; Extortion; and finally, theft of Secret scientific material. C-GRAPES!

The acronyms just keep coming. The seven circumstances under which a police officer must file separate complaint reports for an incident involving two or more victims is A-SHARK. The six conditions that require an immediate search for a missing person is, predictably, MISSING. The six basic elements that must be contained in every incident report is NEOTWY. And on and on. Any illusions we recruits might have had that our days in the Academy would be primarily devoted to cool stuff like shooting and learning how to put handcuffs on bad guys is quickly dispelled when we're first issued our personal copies of the Patrol Guide, a four-inch-thick, single-spaced, double-sided loose-leaf binder containing thousands upon thousands of rules, regulations, and procedures. Looking at the Patrol Guide, one of the recruits asks the instructor: Sir, how much of this will we be expected to know? And the instructor says: All of it.

He's dead serious. The Academy motto is "Enter to Learn, Go Forth to Serve," but it's pretty clear there's a lot of learning to be done before there's going to be any going forth.

At the time, the Academy was housed in an eight-story building on East Twentieth Street in Gramercy Park that from the outside looked more like a corporate headquarters than a training ground for new cops.

(The NYPD has since built a new Academy in Queens.) On our first day, dressed in light blue shirts and blue knit pants we bought at Macy's, we take the oath as PPOs—probationary police officers—swearing to uphold and defend the constitutions of the United States and the State of New York, this in return for a salary of $229 a week, before deductions. (Previous generations of male recruits were called "patrolmen," and female recruits "policewomen," but earlier in 1973 the titles were changed to the non-gender-specific "police officer.") Although technically we now have the same authorities and powers that regular cops have, it's only technically. We aren't given NYPD shields, and certainly not our guns, and our recruit uniforms bear no insignia that might identify us as police officers in the making. The last thing the Department wants is for some citizen on the street to mistake us for real cops and ask us to intervene in some dispute; the liability potential could be enormous.

It's been said that the Academy is a cross between boot camp and kindergarten. I don't know about the kindergarten part—I never heard of four-year-olds having to memorize SPACESHIPS—but the boot camp part is accurate, especially for the first couple of months. Stand at attention, brace against the wall, wipe that silly smile off your face—the Academy instructors are on us all day long.

Every day at muster time we assemble by companies on the roof for inspection, each company comprising about thirty recruits, with a dozen companies in the class. (The twenty-five men and five women in my company, Company 61, are all from Brooklyn, while other companies are composed of recruits from Queens, Staten Island, and so on; it makes it easier for carpooling and outside training.) The company sergeant, usually a recruit with military training, calls us to order— Company, ATTEN-HUT! Dress right, DRESS! and so on—and then an instructor slowly walks through the ranks, handing out the demerits known as "gigs." Shoes not shined—gig! Out of uniform—gig! Sideburns too long—gig! Too many gigs and you get a command discipline, the first step to being shown the door.

There's this one instructor, Officer Fahy, who is maniacal on the subject of recruits being close shaven. He likes to take out a business card and rub it across your cheek and if it makes a scraping sound—gig! On the first day Officer Fahy takes me aside and warns me that the mustache I'm so proud of is going to be trouble, that the regulations on mustaches are particularly strict and detailed, and that I will almost certainly suffer gigs as a result; he makes it sound like I have a time bomb on my upper lip. Save yourself some trouble, kid, he says, lose the mustache. That very night I shave it off. That's how much I want to be a cop.

Training is divided into four basic disciplines: Law, which covers state and city criminal and civil codes; Police Science, which is basically the procedures and regulations in the Patrol Guide; Social Science, which covers race relations, psychology, how to deal with EDPs, and so on; and the Physical School, also known as "Gym," which in addition to physical fitness covers first aid, water rescues, firearms training, baton tactics, takedown methods, and basic self-defense. Today they teach recruits a form of martial arts, but back then it was boxing. The boxing instructor was an Academy legend, an officer we called "Mr. Clean"— never to his face, of course—because he looked just like the guy in the household cleaner ads: shaved head, muscles bulging out of his shirt, everything but the earring. Mr. Clean couldn't turn us into a bunch of Sonny Listons, but he taught us a few tricks.

For me the physical demands of the Academy are a breeze; sometimes I'd get home from a long day in class and run a mile or two on my own, just to stay sharp. But others find the running, push-ups, sit-ups, and climbing over eight-foot-high walls a little tougher, especially guys who struggle with their weight. In typical Academy fashion, these unfortunates are given an acronym, SUMOs, like the massively obese Japanese wrestlers, which stands for Students Under Maximum Observation. The instructors are merciless on them.

One thing almost everyone enjoys is firearms training. I had fired a rifle before, but like most kids in New York, which has strict laws regulating handgun ownership, I had never fired a handgun. We were allowed to choose either a Smith & Wesson or Colt .38-caliber six-shot revolver with a four-inch barrel. I chose the Smith & Wesson—it cost me a hundred dollars—and I carried it for more than twenty years, until like most other NYPD cops I switched to a 9-millimeter semiautomatic. (NYPD cops are required to be armed while off-duty as well as on, so for my off-duty gun I bought an S&W .38 with a shorter, two-inch barrel.)

Our shooting training mostly takes place at the NYPD's Rodman's

Neck Shooting Range, a sprawling outdoor facility in a far-flung and isolated section of the Bronx. We spend two weeks there, starting with the basic mechanics of shooting stationary targets at ranges of seven, fifteen, and twenty-five yards; pretty soon I'm scoring 100 percent. Later we move on to more complex elements of tactical shooting—cover and concealment, combat tactics, shoot/don't-shoot scenarios.

One bit of training advice that made an impression on me was that if we were confronting a perpetrator with a handgun, when taking a combat stance we should shift a half step to the left, the theory being that an untrained right-handed shooter will usually pull the gun slightly to his left, sending the bullet safely past you on your right. Of course, if the perpetrator happens to be among the 10 percent of Americans who are left-handed, this would mean we'd be stepping directly into the bullet's path—in which case, the instructors cheerfully assured us, the Department will give us a really nice funeral.

In general I thought the academic and physical training we got was about as good as it could be when you only had six months to absorb so much material. Most of the instructors were excellent, cops who really knew their stuff and felt passionate about making sure we knew it, too. But strangely enough, given the fact that it had only been a couple of years since the Knapp Commission held its public hearings, the one subject that I thought got relatively short shrift was police corruption.

It wasn't that the Academy ignored the subject. Instructors often lectured us on integrity, our duty as police officers to be honest, the laws concerning bribery and extortion as they applied to police. A guy from the Internal Affairs Division comes out and warns us that if we take even so much as a free cup of coffee, we'll be on a slippery slope toward worse corruption and eventual dismissal and disgrace. He tells us that when we get out to the precincts we shouldn't listen to the old guys who'll tell us that it's okay to accept a "tip" from a tow-truck driver or a free bottle of Scotch from a store owner at Christmastime. He shows us an old black-and-white training film called *I Used to Be a Cop*, about a former police officer who got caught taking a bribe and how it cost him not only his freedom and his job but the loss of his wife, his family, his self-respect; the "star" of the film was reportedly an actual corrupt former cop who had agreed to appear in the movie as part of a plea deal.

So yes, they talk to us about corruption. But even with the IAD guy, it doesn't seem as if their hearts are really in it. It seems as if the instructors are embarrassed, that corruption in the NYPD is an impolite subject, like venereal disease, and while they have to warn us about it, the less said the better. Certainly we recruits don't talk much about corruption. We have other, more exciting things to think about.

One of them is finally getting our NYPD shields.

NYPD police officer shields have numbers that range from one to five digits; the lower the number, the older it is. Although the shields themselves are periodically retired and melted down when they get too scratched and banged up, the numbers are constantly being recycled. Whenever a PO retires or is promoted—detectives and sergeants and above have different-styled shields—his or her shield number (and the shield itself, if it's still serviceable) goes back into a pool, to be more or less randomly handed out to a new police officer. Cynics in the Academy claim that a five-digit shield number is preferable to a two- or three-digit one, because the five-digit number will be harder for a citizen to remember if he wants to file a complaint against you.

But I never bought into that. I wanted a number with some history to it, and I got it—Shield Number 791. Later I found out that the number had first been worn by Patrolman William O. Jennings in 1898, shortly after Manhattan consolidated with the surrounding boroughs to become the modern New York City. Later the number had been worn by a cop who died while in service (although not in the line of duty), by another cop who was promoted to sergeant, by a cop in the 1940s whose name was followed by the racist parenthetical notation "(Colored)," and, most recently, both the number and the actual shield itself had been worn by a policewoman—or rather, a female police officer. The number made me feel connected to a lot of NYPD history—some of it good, some of it bad.

(When I become a sergeant, I will turn in that 791 shield for a sergeant's shield. But NYPD policy allows you to reserve a shield number for a family member if it's available, so in 2001, when my oldest son graduates from the Academy, he'll be wearing that same shield, number 791, that I had worn a quarter century earlier.)

But perhaps the biggest day for recruits at the Academy, next to graduation itself, is the day just before the end of our training when we get our duty assignments. The instructors put up a sheet on the bulletin board with all of our names on it, each name followed by a precinct number or command designation that will determine our fates for at least the next few years.

The assignments aren't completely random. Recruits who had served as company sergeants are usually rewarded with their choice of precincts. Or if you have a "hook," a connection within the Department or high up in City Hall, strings could be pulled to get you the precinct you want. In fact, one of the most coveted precinct assignments, Midtown North in Manhattan, which covers the Theater District and Radio City Music Hall, is nicknamed "Fort Hook." (To this day, the Department will officially deny that there is such a thing as the hook. The longstanding joke is: The hook does not exist; long live the hook!)

As for the rest of us, the Department generally tries to put us at least relatively close to where we live. If you live in the Upper Bronx, they usually won't assign you to a precinct across the city on Staten Island. But the biggest demand for fresh police bodies is always in the high-crime precincts—the Seven-Three, the Four-One, the Seven-Five, and so on—and that's where a lot of the recruits go. Some of them are eager to get into high-crime precincts on the theory that they'll learn a lot very quickly—which they will. But others aren't so sure.

So a recruit might look at the assignment list and say to an instructor: Sir, it says I'm going to the Seven-Three, what's that like? If the instructor is feeling merciful he might say: Oh, it'll be okay. And if he isn't feeling merciful he might say something like, The Seven-Three? Too bad, kid. It was nice knowing ya.

For me it's different. I don't get a precinct. The words after my name on the list are "Manhattan Traffic Area."

It isn't a complete surprise. Unlike a lot of recruits who hadn't gotten their driver's licenses until they entered the Academy—most city kids didn't have cars—I've been driving since I was seventeen. (At the time I had a beautiful 1969 red Oldsmobile Cutlass convertible that I'd bought with money saved from part-time and summer jobs.) Even more unusual, I have a motorcycle endorsement on my license that I'd gotten after I bought a 1970 Triumph 650cc motorcycle from my cousin. So I was one of the recruits called in when a lieutenant from Manhattan

Traffic came out to the Academy to talk to us about applying for the Manhattan Traffic Area Scooter Task Force.

It sounded like fun to me—and as it turned out, it was.

So I'm happy with my assignment—almost as happy as I am a couple weeks later when eight hundred recruits assemble at the National Guard Armory on Lexington Avenue, resplendent in our new blue uniforms and white gloves, our shields shining brilliantly on our chests. My mother and father are there, proud as could be, along with thousands of other proud mothers and fathers and aunts and uncles and cousins. The mayor gives a speech, and then the police commissioner gives a speech, and then we throw our white gloves in the air and that's it.

We are cops.

The very first words my training officer, Officer Lenny Swindell, says to me are: I guess they told you at the Academy that us older guys are all corrupt, that we're all on the take, right? I guess they told you rookies that we're all a bunch of hairbags and not to listen to us and pick up our bad habits, right? ("Hairbags" is the term for cynical and lazy veteran cops.)

Well, uh, not exactly, I tell him. Actually, they had warned us about exactly that, but I'm not about to admit it to Officer Swindell.

Don't believe it, Officer Swindell says. Out here we do the job the way it's supposed to be done, got it? I'm going to teach you how to do that.

And he did. Lenny was a great guy, and a good, honest cop, and he taught me a lot. In fact, whenever I think about what epitomizes the NYPD, I don't necessarily think of a squad detective tracking down a killer or narcotics guys kicking down a door in a raid. I think of cops like Lenny, walking a beat in the cold rain, giving first aid to an injured pedestrian until the EMTs arrive, breaking up an argument on a sidewalk, telling a double-parked driver to move it along—the day-to-day, unglamorous police work that keeps the city running.

Keeping Manhattan running was what Manhattan Traffic was about. Sometimes I'd be on foot patrol, sometimes in bad weather they'd put a couple of us in a patrol car. A few months after I got there I went through training for the Scooter Task Force, a group of two dozen cops who rode around on Lambrettas or Cushmans, taking radio calls, responding to traffic accidents, working traffic at sports or entertainment events—and yes, writing tickets.

Believe it or not, most cops hate writing parking and traffic summonses; sometimes it's because they'd rather be arresting real criminals, and sometimes it's just because they're lazy. Either way, they'll write as few tickets as they can get away with. But in Manhattan Traffic, writing tickets is a big part of the job—and as Lenny says, If ya got a job, do the job! I wrote a lot of tickets.

No, we didn't have quotas. Requiring cops to meet ticket quotas is specifically prohibited under state law. However, the Department is allowed to set "performance goals," and although the sergeant or the lieutenant will never say precisely how many tickets per month he wants out of you, he will let you know if the number of tickets you are writing fails to measure up to expectations. But I never had a problem meeting my quo— I mean, achieving my performance goals.

Drivers will often try to talk their way out of tickets, and if they have a good story, convincingly told—Officer, I'm on my way to the hospital, my wife's having a baby, here's the phone number, you can check it out—they could get a break from me. Same thing for a grandma on Social Security driving a ten-year-old beater on her way to church. Like they taught us at the Academy, a good officer uses discretion.

On the other hand, a guy could also talk his way *into* a ticket. If, as often happened, a driver would curse at me—You mother-effer, why don't you shove your ticket up your ass?—I'd be sure to write "M/F, shove ticket" on my copy of the summons so if he went to court I could tell the judge what he said. And while I didn't do it, some cops would bend the license of a cursing driver to signal the next cop who stopped him that the guy was a jerk. A cop might say: Yeah, the guy called me an asshole, so I bent him. Of course, that's against Department policy—but cops are human, too.

While trying to talk your way out of a ticket is fine, trying to buy your way out is not. Usually it wasn't an outright bribe attempt, but instead something like, Officer, can I just pay the fine right now? How much is it? Absolutely not, I'd tell them—and at that point, any chance they had of me giving them a break on the ticket went out the window.

But I remember one guy who wouldn't take no for an answer. He's a young guy from Colombia, and he speaks good but heavily accented

English. I pull him over for blowing a red light, and when he hands me his license there's a ten-dollar bill wrapped around it. What's that? I say. It's so I don't get the ticket, he says. Take it back, I say, and I proceed to give him a stern lecture about how maybe that's the way they do things in Bogotá, but not here in New York City—at least not with me. But when I step back to the scooter to write out the ticket, the guy gets out of his car and comes toward me, waving the ten and saying, Don't give me a ticket, take this!

That's it, buddy. You're getting the ticket—and you're under arrest. I take him to the precinct and process him for attempted bribery of a public official, a felony, and then I head back out on patrol. The funny thing is, a little later the guy's uncle shows up at the precinct, red-faced and waving his arms, demanding to know why his nephew is in jail. The desk sergeant explains that the nephew tried to bribe a police officer— and the uncle says: So what's the problem? He didn't offer him enough? The desk sergeant throws him out.

The next day I had to appear at the bribery perp's arraignment, but I was never called to testify at trial, so I assume that as usual the legal system let him off on a reduced charge, or maybe no charge at all. That kind of attitude ticked me off. A cop would suffer serious consequences for taking a bribe—dismissal from the Department, maybe even jail time—so why shouldn't a citizen suffer serious consequences for offering one?

Still, the attempted bribery arrest worked out for me. After the Knapp Commission the Department started making a big thing out of rewarding cops who arrested people for trying to bribe them—See? Our cops don't take bribes!—so I was called down to headquarters by the Integrity Review Board, an ad hoc group of senior commanders who reviewed integrity cases. Since the attempted bribe was only ten bucks they weren't going to give me a promotion or a transfer to a better assignment, as they sometimes did in bigger attempted bribery cases; I guess they figured that turning down a lousy ten-dollar bribe showed a little less integrity than turning down a thousand-dollar one. But they did give me a medal for "Excellent Police Duty," the Department's lowest-level commendation. I accepted it—it was worth something like an eighth of a point on promotions—but I always thought it was kind of strange that the Department gave you a reward for not taking a bribe.

It seemed to me that not taking bribes was the minimum standard for a police officer, and thus nothing special.

Of course, working Manhattan Traffic wasn't as exciting as working one of the high-crime precincts—although "high-crime" was a relative term. Today a lot of people have forgotten what it was like in Manhattan and the rest of New York City in the mid-1970s, just how bad crime was back then. In 1975 there were just under 1,700 murders in the city, more than 600 of them in Manhattan alone, and more than 90,000 robberies. (By 2014 the number of murders citywide had dropped to 335, and robberies to about 16,000.) The point is that back then there were plenty of opportunities for a cop to make good collars, no matter where he worked.

I made some. Once I was on scooter patrol on the Bowery and this old guy runs up to me, crying, and says: Officer, officer, they robbed me! He tells me he just cashed his Social Security check at a check-cashing place and when he came out two guys had strong-armed him and taken his money, about forty bucks. He'd seen which way they went, so I put him in the three-wheeled scooter and as we pass a side street we see three guys standing there, two of them of normal height but the other one a really tall skinny guy, maybe six-four or -five. That's them! the old guy says. Not the tall one, the other two!

So I radio for backup and park the scooter and the old man in a safe place. Then I walk up the side street with my gun unholstered and at my side, just in case. To the two shorter guys I say: You and you, against the wall! To the tall guy I say: You, get outta here! and he takes off. As I'm searching the two robbers one of them says: Hey, man, how come you let him (the tall guy) go? For a moment I think about telling him that the Department has a new policy, that we aren't arresting tall people this month, and then waiting to see how long it takes for that rumor to get back to me. But then I decide that, given the limited intellectual capacity of your average perp, a rumor like that might result in a wave of crimes committed by gullible tall guys who actually think they're immune from arrest. So what I say to the robber is: Shut up!

The backup arrives and we take the robbers to the precinct for processing. Later I heard that the two robbers disappeared after they were ROR'ed—"released–own recognizance," meaning no bail was required. In a city with ninety thousand robberies, that's how seriously the courts took robbing an old man of his Social Security money. Still, it was a solid felony collar, and a satisfying one. Two bad guys had been taken off the street, at least for a few hours, and the old man got his money back. That collar and others were the reason I had wanted to become a cop.

The job had its dangers. Although today it's still dangerous to be a New York cop, in the mid-1970s it was even more so. In 1974 and '75 fourteen NYPD cops were killed in the line of duty, all but two of them killed by gunfire; hundreds of others were injured by guns, knives, clubs, fists, car accidents, vicious dogs—you name it. (In 2013, by comparison, except for 9/11-related illness deaths, no NYPD officer died in the line of duty. Sadly, in 2014 four NYPD officers died in the line of duty, two of them shot and killed while they sat in their patrol car on a Brooklyn street.)

You never knew if a bullet might be waiting for you around the corner—literally. One night I'm on patrol with my partner, Bill, both of us riding Lambrettas. We're eastbound on Thirty-Fourth Street approaching Lexington when Bill asks me if I want Chinese food for meal. (It didn't matter if it was breakfast, lunch, or dinner, in the NYPD it was and is always called "meal.") I figure, no, I'm going to spend meal back at the precinct, studying for the sergeant's test, but I'll meet up with Bill back at the station house. I peel off left and Bill goes straight. And then it couldn't have been more than a couple minutes later that I hear the call over the radio from dispatch—Ten-thirteen, corner Three-Three and Two, shots fired, officer down! A 10-13 or "Signal 13" means "officer needs assistance"; it's the one call that will make every cop in the area drop whatever he's doing and race to the scene, which is exactly what I do. When I get to Thirty-Third Street and Second Avenue Bill's sitting on the ground, bleeding from a gunshot wound in the shoulder.

It turns out that after I peeled off, Bill drove on a couple of blocks and then stopped at a red light by a drugstore on the corner. An armed robber walks out of the drugstore after holding up the clerk, sees Bill, thinks he's responding to a robbery call from the drugstore, and pegs a shot at him, hitting him in the shoulder and knocking him off his scooter. An off-duty NYPD cop who happens to be passing by sees what happens and immediately chases down and collars the shooter. Fortunately, the shooter had a small-caliber handgun, a .22, and the bullet missed any major arteries; Bill was shaken up, but he was okay.

Like I said, there could be a bullet waiting for you around any corner.

All in all, then, being a cop was everything I'd hoped it would be: interesting, rewarding, exciting, and dangerous enough to keep you focused. I'd been able to finish the last couple of courses at Long Island University–Brooklyn to get my bachelor's degree, and had started on my master's degree in criminal justice at John Jay College of Criminal Justice in Midtown Manhattan, taking two night classes a week. Things were looking pretty good.

And then, suddenly, in the space of a half hour, I'm not a cop anymore.

It's 11:30 p.m.—2330 in cop time—on June 30, 1975, and I'm standing in the muster room at the 73rd Precinct in Brownsville, the Seven-Three, getting ready for the midnight-to-eight shift. It's hot, humidity about 80 percent, muggy in the way New York summer nights are, especially in a crumbling, dilapidated, un-air-conditioned building like the Seven-Three precinct house. We haven't even hit the streets yet, and we're sweating already.

Then the sergeant walks in and starts calling out names. Alvarez! Burroughs! Campisi! Donahue!—and so on, about a dozen names in all, all of us with one or two or three years on the job. He hands each of us a piece of paper that has just been spit out of the Teletype machine, and except for names and shield numbers, they all say the same thing: As of 12:01 on July 1, thirty minutes from now, the start of the fiscal year, our services will no longer be required by the New York City Police Department. We're laid off.

Shock, fury, despair; it's like a nightmare. The sergeant tells us to line up and turn in our shields—and since we aren't cops anymore, we also have to turn in our service revolvers and off-duty guns—bullets, too—because even though we had paid for our guns with our own money, as civilians it's illegal in New York for us to have handguns. The desk sergeant, a real hairbag, is tossing our shields and guns into boxes like they're trash, and barking out orders for us to count our bullets before we turn them in. One cop takes a handful of bullets and throws them in the sergeant's lap, telling him: Count them yourself, asshole! If I'm not a cop anymore, I don't have to take orders from you! There's pushing, shoving, shouting; it's a near mutiny breaking out in the Seven-Three muster room.

It's the same story in precinct muster rooms across the city. Just like that, more than fifty-five hundred men and women who were cops at 11:30 p.m. are not cops at one minute past midnight. Nothing personal about it, the city tells us. The city can't afford to pay us anymore, and they're laying people off in other departments, too. As required by the PBA contract, the rule is "last in, first out," so it doesn't mean we are—were—bad cops, they tell us. We'll take you back if the city ever starts hiring cops again.

Maybe we should have seen it coming. For several years the city of New York has been on a downward slide, financially and otherwise. The population is shrinking, businesses are moving out and taking their taxes with them, partly because of rising crime and assorted other social ills. Hookers and muggers fill Times Square, it's worth your life to go into Central Park after dark, transient camps flourish in the subways, garbage piles up on the streets. It seems like New York is turning into a Third World city—a bankrupt Third World city.

Meanwhile, with crime growing, the NYPD is shrinking. The Academy stopped taking in new recruits in 1974, and as older cops retire or resign there's nobody to replace them. With no fresh bodies coming out of the Academy, the Department starts stripping away cops from other commands and sending them to the high-crime precincts—the Seven-Five, the Four-One, the Seven-Three.

Manhattan Traffic Area is one of those commands. On a Friday afternoon in early 1974, one hundred of Manhattan Traffic's one hundred fifty cops are told to report to various high-crime precincts on Monday. I'm one of them. My orders are to report to the Seven-Three in Brownsville—Fort Z.

Actually I'm not too unhappy about it. I'd enjoyed working in Manhattan Traffic, and it had made it easy to work on my master's degree at John Jay. But I'm still living at my parents' apartment in Bushwick, just five minutes away from Brownsville, which makes for an easy commute, and I figure working a high-crime precinct will be a good learning experience. And for the most part it is.

That spring there are persistent rumors about layoffs in the NYPD; thousands of us are officially informed that we face termination at the end of the fiscal year. But nobody really believes it; everybody figures that the new mayor, Abe Beame, is bluffing, talking about layoffs to gain concessions from the police unions and to goad the federal government into bailing out the city. The NYPD had reduced the numbers in its ranks before, but it had always been through attrition; in the history of the NYPD, even during the Great Depression, there have never been layoffs. The old-timers all say: Don't worry about it, kid. It's all political bullshit. They ain't gonna lay off cops.

But now, on the last day of June 1975, they do.

About half of the fifty-five hundred laid-off cops, the ones with the most seniority, are rehired by the city after a few days. The rest of us are put on a preferred rehire list, and repeatedly told by the PBA and almost everyone else that it won't be long, that any day now we'll be back on the job.

Any day now. I'll hear that same story for the next twenty months.

I tried to keep it in perspective, to keep in mind a lesson that one of my Academy instructors, Officer Fahy, the one who'd advised me to shave my mustache, had taught us. We're sitting in law class one day, early on in our training, and Officer Fahy says to us: What is the one four-letter word that should never, ever be associated with your service in the NYPD? I'll give you a hint, he says, it starts with an *F*.

Profanity was seriously discouraged among recruits back then, so we're all looking down at our shoes; none of us wants to say the *F* word out loud. So finally Officer Fahy turns to the chalkboard and writes out, in big block letters, *F-A-I-R*.

Fair! he says. That's the four-letter word you should never associate with your work in the NYPD. Life isn't fair, the Department isn't fair, the job of police officer isn't fair—and the sooner you accept that, the better off you'll be.

It was a good philosophy. But it's hard to look at it that way when after a lifetime of wanting to be a cop, and working so hard to make it happen, I'm unceremoniously stripped of my shield and gun and told to hit the road.

(The layoffs would haunt the NYPD for years to come. Later, after Ed Koch was elected mayor in 1977 on a pro-cop, law-and-order platform, the NYPD rushed to refill its depleted ranks, often lowering standards and cutting corners to take in thousands of recruits at a time. Some of those recruits should never have been cops, and they would later cause a lot of problems for the Department in general, and Internal Affairs in particular.)

I don't have it as bad as some of the other laid-off cops. In June 1975,

I'm single, no kids, no mortgage, living in my parents' apartment. Still, I have to do something. I thought about applying to another police department, maybe in Nassau or Suffolk County, but somehow I just couldn't see myself working in the suburbs. I don't just want to be a cop, I want to be an *NYPD* cop, New York's Finest. And besides, with twenty-seven hundred fully trained ex-cops suddenly dumped onto the market, police jobs are hard to get.

I finally take a job as a security guard with a Brooklyn tobacco and confectionary wholesaling company, J. Rosenberg & Sons, escorting delivery trucks around the city to keep them from being hijacked, which was a big problem back then. One of the Rosenberg sons, Stanley, a really good guy, told me that he would pay me more than I had been making as a cop—and he did. The Department had paid me $229 a week; Stanley pays me $230. Since guarding trucks is a high-risk job, I manage to get a civilian handgun permit and carry my off-duty revolver with me on the job. But it isn't like being a cop.

Finally, in May 1977, after more than a year and a half of "any day now" from the Department and the PBA, I'm rehired by the NYPD. After a week of "retraining" at the Academy, they send me back to the Seven-Three.

It's the same old Brownsville as when I left—piss-bags raining from the rooftops, misery and despair, crime and drug addiction. It's the same . . . except now it's worse.

In 1977 it seems like City Hall and the New York City Police Department have just thrown up their hands and given up, not only in Brownsville but across the city. There are fifteen hundred murders in the city that year, double the number from a decade earlier, with rising rape, robbery, and assault stats to match. No one is enforcing what would later be called "quality-of-life" crimes—public drinking, loud music, aggressive panhandling, pissing on the sidewalk, and so on, all those small crimes that can and did make life in the city almost unbearable. Attacking those small crimes would later become a big part of the Department's successful effort to turn the city around in the mid-1990s, but in 1977 the politicians in City Hall don't want us to enforce those laws, especially in the minority neighborhoods, because they might seem like harassment— and with the long, hot summer coming, it could spark a riot.

And as for drug enforcement, forget about it. As a uniformed NYPD police officer, I'm not allowed to arrest a drug dealer, even if I catch him in the act. This goes back to the Knapp Commission in 1972, which decided that since drug arrests were a corruption hazard, with too many uniformed cops shaking down drug dealers, from then on only narcotics cops could make drug arrests. The idea was that since detectives have closer supervision than uniformed cops—in the NYPD, one sergeant had ten uniformed cops under him, while a narcotics team had a sergeant and just four or five plainclothes cops—that would reduce drug-related corruption.

Well, maybe so. But what it means for me as a uniformed cop in the Seven-Three is that the drug dealers barely look up when I drive by in a patrol car. I can bounce them off the corner, but I can't arrest them—and they know it. Sure, I can fill out an "intel card," noting I have observed a known drug dealer named Pee Wee pitching heroin at the corner of Livonia and Stone, and eventually it will get passed up to the cops from the Narcotics Division. Maybe they'll get around to working a buy-and-bust on Pee Wee, and maybe they won't.

In fact, sometimes we even have to ride shotgun for the drug trade. The city had set up a methadone program in Brooklyn North—the theory appeared to be that if you gave heroin addicts methadone, they wouldn't have to rob and steal so much to buy heroin—and since methadone has street value, one of our regular jobs is to follow the methadone delivery truck as it makes its rounds to the clinics to make sure it doesn't get hijacked and the methadone sold on the street. (In fact, a lot of addicts in the methadone program will hold their doses in their mouths without swallowing, then sell it on the street—it's called, for obvious reasons, "spit-back"—and use the money to buy real heroin.) It seems kind of strange to me that here we are, cops, and we're riding shotgun on drug deliveries for dope addicts. As we'll see, we aren't the only NYPD cops who ever rode shotgun for drug shipments—except that we were doing it legally.

Like I said. In 1977 the drug dealers and the addicts have won.

As always, it's the kids who suffer most. I remember once I caught a job to accompany a woman who had a court order to reclaim custody of her one-year-old son from his grandparents. I meet the woman outside the apartment building, and it's obvious she's a user. She has the dull eyes, the infected tracks, the wasting-away body—the whole picture.

And I'm thinking, wow, if the court is giving this drug addict custody of the kid, what must the grandparents be like?

So I leave the mom in the hallway and I knock on the door and the grandparents let me in. The apartment building is typical for Brownsville—peeling plaster, the smell of piss in the hallways, graffiti on the walls—but this particular apartment is immaculate, the grandparents well-spoken and polite; they're poor people, but they're good people. The grandparents know why I'm there, and they're crying and begging me not to take the little boy—Please, Officer, don't give her that child, she's our daughter but she's a heroin addict, she can't take care of him, please, please. And I'm thinking, there's gotta be a mistake here. What social services system would take a baby away from these people and give him to a skell? The judge who signed the order must not fully understand the situation.

So I radio my patrol sergeant to find out what to do. He shows up and takes one look at the court order and looks at me like I'm stupid, or crazy, or both. What, you can't read? he says. A court order is exactly what it says—an order! So give her the kid! And I have to tell the weeping grandparents that I'm sorry, but I have no choice, I have to take the little boy—and I did.

It breaks my heart—and it's not the first or the last time that my heart gets broken over a kid in Brownsville. But there's a word you should never associate with your job as a police officer.

It starts with an *F*.

Brownsville is bad, all right; so bad, in fact, that it seems impossible that it could get any worse.

And then the lights go out.

It's July 13, 1977, just after 8:30 p.m., and since I'm working midnights this week I'm at home in Bushwick. The city is still in financial crisis, we're in the middle of a brutal heat wave, the Son of Sam serial killer is out there shooting people with a .44-caliber revolver—and suddenly the power fails and the lights go out all over the city. In Brooklyn and the Bronx, the looting begins almost immediately.

So they call us all in, every cop in the Seven-Three, and we head out into the streets with our riot helmets and nightsticks and guns. On Pitkin Avenue, the commercial district, virtually every store has the security gates pried off, the windows broken, people running out with TVs and stereos and pieces of furniture balanced on their heads. Everywhere you look there's a felony being committed; some looters are standing outside stores, stealing stuff out of the hands of other looters, who then turn around and go back in the store to loot some more. Groups of cops wade into the stores and chase people out; other cops stand at the doors with their nightsticks raised, telling people coming out to drop the stuff, and if they don't—whack!—they get a nightstick on the arm. And this is all in the dark, no streetlights; the only light comes from the arson fires that have started breaking out.

Within minutes I collar three guys—two adults and a juvenile—who are lugging a couch out the broken front window of a furniture store and I take them to the precinct. We're arresting so many people that we can't spend time processing them into the system or even take down their names; we have to get back on the street. So instead, the desk sergeant takes a Polaroid of each perp with the cop who arrested him and writes the cop's name on the back; later we'll have to match the photos with the perps and process them then. Meanwhile, the holding cells are jammed with perps like Vienna sausages in a can; eventually we'll have to start putting the overflow in an old wooden garage out back. So I pose for my Polaroid with each of the furniture store perps—Smile!—and then I cram the two adult thieves into a cell and put the kid in the "juvenile room" and head back out into the chaos.

There's no stopping it. The power finally comes back on at about 10:30 p.m. the next night, but it's too late. By the time it's over, virtually every store on Pitkin is an empty blackened shell, broken glass covers the streets, haggard cops and firemen are walking around exhausted and dazed; I wind up working fifty-four hours straight, making arrests, standing guard on buildings, processing prisoners. Citywide, but mostly in Brooklyn and the Bronx, more than 4,500 looters are arrested, 500 cops injured, almost 2,000 businesses looted, 1,000 buildings set afire.

Remember I said earlier that Brownsville was an urban catastrophe? After the blackout, it's beyond catastrophe; it looks like Berlin at the end of World War II.

There's one interesting epilogue to this. Those furniture store looters I collared early on? Sometime later that night I'm passing by one of the packed holding cells and one of them, a guy in his mid-thirties, is wailing and crying from the back of the cell. Officer, officer, he says to me, please, I gotta go to the bathroom! Well, I'm pretty busy—Brooklyn is burning down around us—so I tell him he has to wait, but he keeps pleading, Please, help me, I really gotta go!

All right. So I pry him out of the cell and take him to the bathroom, and on the way back he stops and looks at the water fountain, and he says to me: Officer, I'm really thirsty. Can I please have a drink? Perps aren't allowed to use the water fountain, which may sound a little harsh, but hey, if you saw some of the skells who passed through the Seven-Three precinct, you wouldn't want them drooling over your water fountain, either.

But this guy seems all right, for a perp, probably not a career criminal but, like a lot of the looters we arrested, just a guy who got caught up in the moment and the lure of free stuff. And he's going to be in that holding cell for a long time. So I tell him okay, and he takes a long drink and then I cram him back into the cell.

And then I don't give it another thought until years later, when my wife and I are on vacation in the US Virgin Islands. We're having dinner in a restaurant, and I notice that the waiter keeps looking at me in kind of a strange way. And finally he says to me—I remember you, you're from New York; you're the cop who arrested me on Pitkin Avenue back in '77. You were kind to me, you let me have a drink of water, I've never forgotten it, and I want to thank you for it.

So I look at the guy, and yeah, it comes back to me now. He's the guy who stole the couch during the blackout. And he's probably being sincere about wanting to thank me, he probably really is grateful. But you never know. Maybe some other cops weren't so nice to him that night, and he's looking for some payback, even if it's only spitting in the food. After all, a cop is a cop is a cop.

So what I say to him is: Friend, you've made a mistake. I'm from Pittsburgh; I've never even been to New York. Sorry. He didn't seem to believe me, but that was my story, and I stuck to it.

That may sound overly suspicious, even paranoid. But it illustrates something about cops that people should know: In a social situation with civilians—a party, a PTA meeting, at a restaurant in the Virgin Islands, wherever—most cops won't tell anybody that they're cops. And

I won't, either. If somebody asks what I do, I say I work for the city. And if they press, I just say that I push papers around a desk—and then I move away from them as soon as possible.

It's not that we're not proud of being cops. We are. But if you tell people at a party that you're a cop, there's always going to be at least one guy who'll buttonhole you and start chewing your leg about some bad experience he had: I didn't run that red light but the cop gave me a ticket anyway, I was only double-parked for thirty seconds and that cop had my car towed, that cop was rude to me just because I called him an asshole. Whatever the beef, it's going to be a half hour out of your life. And if they don't have a beef, sometimes they'll just ask you dumb questions: Did'ja ever shoot anybody? How long does it usually take to beat a confession out of a guy? Did'ja ever take a bribe? And on and on.

Most civilians seem to think that cops as a group are insular, clannish, that we hold ourselves apart from everybody else. To some extent that's true, and necessary. It's hard for anyone who hasn't been a cop to understand what the job is like, and it's harder still for us to try to explain or justify it.

So if you're a stranger at a party, or a perp I arrested four years ago, I'm not an NYPD cop. I just push papers around for the city.

The city of Pittsburgh.

There are two ways to advance in the NYPD. You can go the supervisory route—sergeant, lieutenant, captain, and so on—or you can try for a detective's gold shield.

Carrying the detective's gold shield is probably the most coveted job in the NYPD, one that many, maybe even most, ambitious young cops dream about. You get better pay than in patrol, you're working serious crimes, you're never walking a foot post in freezing weather, no one is hounding you to write more tickets. To become an NYPD detective first grade, the highest detective rank—in a Department with thirty to thirty-five thousand cops, there are only about two hundred first grade detectives—is the pinnacle of a police career. They're the guys they make movies and TV shows about.

There are no written or oral tests to become a detective. Under the

rules, a police officer who works for eighteen months in an investiga-
tory assignment—say, making drug buys and arrests in the Narcotics
Division—is entitled to a detective third grade gold shield. (In recent
years the NYPD has created two detective titles—detective-investigator
for those who actively investigate crimes, and detective-specialist for
those who have special skills or work noninvestigatory assignments.)
You can also be given the gold shield as a reward for some conspicuous
act of bravery or outstanding police work. And although everyone at
NYPD headquarters will swear it isn't true, you can also get your gold
shield if you have a "hook" within the Department.

Carrying the detective's gold shield is a great job, and I thought
about going that route. But for me it had one major drawback: Detectives don't command anything. They are supervised by sergeants and
lieutenants and captains. In terms of rank within the chain of command,
detectives are the same as uniformed patrol cops.

So if you want to command, if you want to lead, you have to take the
supervisory career route.

And from the time I entered the Academy, I wanted to lead.

I stayed in the Seven-Three for a couple of months after the blackout and then transferred back to Manhattan Traffic. I took the sergeant's
test in 1978, and although I did pretty well, a lawsuit against the city
concerning police promotions essentially froze promotions for several
years; I finally made sergeant in 1982. I'd been teaching law at the Academy for the previous two years, which I enjoyed, but then they sent me
back to Manhattan Traffic as a training sergeant, teaching rookies fresh
out of the Academy the job. Later, as a lieutenant, I became the coordi-
nator of special events for Manhattan Traffic, and after I made captain in
1985 I took over as commanding officer—CO—of Manhattan Traffic
Area, managing traffic issues and coordinating presidential and other
VIP events, parades, demonstrations, and so on.

During all that I somehow managed to attract the attention of the
famously gruff and demanding Chief of Department Robert J. Johnston
Jr., the highest-ranking uniformed member of the NYPD—or at least, my
physical appearance attracted his attention. I was a marathon runner back
then, and consequently I was pretty thin, so while Chief Johnston didn't
know my name—there were hundreds of captains in the NYPD—when

there was a special assignment the chief would say things like, Where's that skinny captain? Put the skinny captain on it! Being skinny must have paid off, because in 1989 I was named commander of the Sixth Precinct, which covers Greenwich Village and the West Village.

I always thought being a precinct CO was the best job in the NYPD. You're in charge of a hundred to two hundred cops, depending on the precinct, which is a force that's big enough to make a difference but small enough that you can know everyone in your command by name. There's a lot of administrative responsibility, but if you have a good XO (executive officer) he or she can take care of some of that, leaving you free to get out on the street and get to know the precinct.

I walked every street in the precinct, and rode around in an unmarked car on almost every shift. I loved being out on the street, on patrol or walking foot posts with the C-POPs, the cops in the Community Patrol Officer Program, who introduced me to the businesspeople and residents on their beats, or riding with the precinct ACU, the Anti-Crime Unit, plainclothes cops who work crimes-in-progress. I'd work my regular daytime shift as precinct CO, then change into civilian clothes and ride along with the ACU cops for a four-to-twelve—cruising along Bleecker and MacDougal streets in an unmarked Chevy, staking out the corner of Eighth Street and Sixth Avenue, looking for robberies, muggings, purse snatchings, whatever, then chasing down the perp and putting him in cuffs. It was good old-fashioned police work, and for a guy who by necessity had to spend most of his time on administrative stuff, it was great fun.

That's the thing a lot of people don't understand about being a cop, how much fun it can be. Sure, a lot of times it's dull, routine, and frustrating, and sometimes it's more dangerous than you want it to be. But to see a crime in progress and chase the crook down a sidewalk and tackle him and hook him up and bring him to justice—there's a joy in that, a sense of exhilaration. It's cops and robbers, good guys versus bad guys, and it's the reason most cops, me included, became cops in the first place.

And even during my regular duties as a supervisor, sometimes I got to help with arrests. One in particular I remember. It's a seven-to-three shift, and I have "the duty," meaning I'm the senior supervisor on call to respond to any serious incidents not only in my own precinct but in all ten precincts in Patrol Borough Manhattan South. An officer-involved shooting, a fatal traffic accident, a barricaded suspect—anything like that happens, I have to go there and take command of the scene.

So anyway, I've got the duty, and I'm in a car on Allen Street, just riding around with one of my POs at the wheel, when I see these two Transit cops chasing a guy down the street, guns drawn. The Transit Police patrol the subways, but the sidewalks belong to the NYPD, so I jump out of the car and join the chase. And then I see that the Transit cops have caught the guy, they're on the sidewalk, struggling with him—and there's a gun in his hand.

But the Transit guys aren't doing it right. These two Transit guys haven't secured the perp's gun hand, so the gun is waving all around— this on a crowded Manhattan street. If this keeps up, either the cops or an innocent bystander, or both, are going to get shot. So I barrel into the perp, knocking him to the ground, and start pounding his gun hand onto the pavement until he drops the gun and it goes skittering away. Meanwhile, the Transit guys are just standing there, watching the unusual sight of an NYPD whiteshirt—lieutenants and above wear white uniform shirts instead of blue—grappling with a gun suspect on the sidewalk.

Finally we get the guy cuffed and searched; he has a second gun on him as well. Turns out the two Transit cops had been taking a smoke break outside a subway entrance when they saw this guy shoot a man, and they gave chase. Which was fine, except their tactics were lousy, and even though they aren't in my chain of command, I start telling them so. But while I'm chewing them out, and they're standing there looking sheepish, I realize that I've seen one of them before. I look at him, he looks at me, and I say: Steve? And he says: Charlie? Turns out he's a guy I went to high school with at St. John's Prep—and you really can't ream out an old high school buddy. Steve and his partner later got Transit Police medals for capturing the murderer, which was fine with me, even if their tactics were a little shaky. I was just glad that nobody else got killed.

The Sixth Precinct was an "A" house, a low-crime precinct compared with others. In 1990 there were just two murders in the precinct—one of the victims was a local TV executive who was shot and killed in a phone booth—this out of more than twenty-two hundred murders in the city as a whole. But as a relatively affluent area with a lot of bars and clubs, robberies and assaults were a serious problem. Still, we managed

to cut overall crime in the precinct by 15 percent, which earned my officers a Department Unit Citation.

Crime stats were and are important for any NYPD commander, and
although commanders don't have quotas to meet, like patrol officers they
do have "performance goals" for everything from summonses to arrests.
Meeting those goals is usually a matter of hard work, for you and the cops
under your command, but sometimes luck helps. For example, once when
I was CO of the Sixth Precinct there was a "wilding" incident in the adja-
cent Tenth Precinct, with seventeen young men swarming into a bodega,
knocking the owner to the floor, grabbing beers and cigarettes, and then all
seventeen of them piling into a van and driving away. When the call went
over the air, my patrol officers and ACU guys caught them coming through
the Sixth Precinct and pulled them over, blocking the van's doors with their
cars and trapping all of them inside like Spam in a can, preventing them
from scattering like they usually would. All of which left the Tenth Precinct
CO a little annoyed. He had to eat another robbery on his weekly precinct
crime stats, while I got seventeen easy robbery collars on mine.

Bringing down crime stats in a precinct isn't just about good police
work, though. It also involves working with community programs like
COP—Citizens on Patrol—which was one of the "community watch"
programs we instituted in the Sixth. Of course, you can take the community policing concept too far. Some police commanders and departments put too much emphasis on the "community" part and not enough
on the "policing" part. Muggers and armed robbers are never going to
show up at a Community Council meeting to discuss their problems,
and drug dealers aren't going to help you organize a Clean Up the Park
Day. Citizens can't put bad guys in jail; that's the cops' job.

But working with the local community is important. And in the Sixth
Precinct that meant working with the LGBT community.

Greenwich Village was the center of New York City's gay community, which presented some unique situations. Generally the cops and
the gay community in the Sixth Precinct got along pretty well; the days
when undercover vice cops would linger in parks or public bathrooms
and arrest gay men for violation of antiquated state sodomy laws were
long gone. But this was at the height of the AIDS epidemic, and there
were frequent marches and demonstrations on the streets and in Wash-

ington Square Park to demand more action on AIDS. Most of the demonstrators were good guys, and I sympathized with their cause. Once, at a candlelight march for AIDS victims, someone handed me a lighted candle, and even though I was working I carried it along with me.

But as in any group, there were some elements that were more radical, people who let their anger get the best of them and threatened damage to people or property. One incident I remember was when I almost lost the former mayor of New York to an angry mob.

It's a Saturday night, and there's a big AIDS awareness march coming down Fifth Avenue on the way to a rally at Washington Square Park. I'm out there with my sergeant, Jeff Nolan, and dozens of other Sixth Precinct cops, trying to make sure things stay peaceful. And then, just as the hundreds of marchers are passing by, a black limousine rolls up to the corner of Eighth Street and Fifth Avenue and out steps former New York mayor Ed Koch, who left office a few months earlier and still has an NYPD security detail. With three NYPD detectives from the Intelligence Division trailing behind him, Koch starts walking the half block from the corner to the front door of the apartment building where he lives at 2 Fifth. The former mayor isn't there to observe the march; he's just going home.

As commanding officer in the Sixth Precinct, which covered Greenwich Village, I maintained a good relationship with the LGBT community. But sometimes things could get out of hand. Here, I'm helping to escort former New York City mayor Ed Koch away from demonstrators angry at his administration's handling of the AIDS crisis. (John Penley)

Koch has had a stormy relationship with the gay community, which believes he hasn't done enough to fight AIDS; they're especially incensed because Koch himself is widely rumored to be gay. (Koch always said his sexual orientation was nobody else's business—and he was right.) So when Koch unwittingly steps out in the middle of the AIDS march, someone shouts: There's Koch! Get him!

There are two sets of words that no sane precinct commander ever wants to hear juxtaposed in his precinct. Those words are a former mayor's name and "Get him!" And seeing this, I can hardly believe it. Koch has always made a point of not being afraid to confront hostile citizens at community meetings. But this isn't a meeting at the senior center; it's a street demonstration that's getting out of control. I can hardly believe that his security detail would drop the former mayor off in the middle of a crowd of angry marchers instead of going around the back or waiting until the marchers had passed by. In fairness, it's possible that Koch insisted on it, and his security guys were afraid to say no. But still.

So Sergeant Nolan and I go bulling through the growing crowd surrounding him, grab Hizzoner by both arms, and frog-walk him through the protesters to the front door of his apartment building; his feet are barely skimming the pavement. We shove him through the door, not particularly gently, and then stand there, keeping the howling crowd at bay while the former mayor gets into the elevator. I was certain—and as I learned later, so was Koch—that if the crowd had gotten to him, he would have suffered some serious damage. They were just that angry.

(Later I had words with the head of the Intelligence Division, who was in charge of the mayor's security detail. He's a deputy chief and I'm only a deputy inspector—I'd been promoted from captain a few months earlier—but I was hot, and I made it clear that if his guys want to let the former mayor of New York get beaten up or lynched by an angry crowd, I would certainly appreciate it if they would do it in someone else's precinct. He was apologetic. Soon thereafter Koch showed up at the Sixth Precinct muster room to thank what he called "the brave police officers of the NYPD" who rescued him from the mob. Koch didn't recognize me as one of the cops who had thrown him through the door, and given the rough way we handled him, I thought it best not to mention it.)

Like I said, being a precinct CO is one of the best jobs in the

Department—and if it had been up to me I might have stayed a precinct commander for the rest of my career. But the Department had a policy of rotating precinct COs out after a couple of years, whether they liked it or not. So in late 1991 they put me in charge of the NYPD Cadet Corps. True, it wasn't as exciting as running a precinct, but it was considered a high-profile assignment—especially since the soon-to-be police commissioner, Ray Kelly, had not only started his Department career as a Cadet, but during his rise to the top he had once commanded the Cadet Corps program, and thus had a personal interest in its continued success.

The Cadet Corps was similar to the trainee program I had hoped to join when I was eighteen. We would take kids in their junior and senior years of college and give them paid civilian jobs in the Department—part-time or full-time, depending on their college class schedules—while they continued their college studies. The Department would also provide tuition financial assistance that would be forgiven if they actually became NYPD officers.

It was a great program, for the Cadets and for the Department—and for me. We'd put the Cadets through a shortened version of the military-style NYPD recruit training at the Academy—Stand at attention! Tuck in that shirt! Shine those shoes!—and teach them about basic police procedures. After that they'd go out to the precincts or other commands in Cadet uniforms—no guns, no shields—where they would answer phones, work the computers, process paperwork, that kind of thing. For them it was a chance to see police work close up and decide if a cop's life was for them—and if it was, they would have both experience and seniority when they graduated from college and went into the Academy to become full-fledged police officers. For the Department it was a chance to fill regular NYPD recruit ranks with college-educated young men and women with a demonstrated aptitude for police work and an eagerness to serve. And for me it was a chance to continue my interest in educating young people. By this time, in addition to my work as a cop, I was an adjunct professor of law and police science at John Jay, and I was just a dissertation away from completing my PhD in criminal justice at City College of New York.

The Cadet Corps was a popular program—almost too popular. We ran the Cadets through the Academy in ninety-person classes, and when

I first took over we had ten thousand applicants for those ninety slots. Cadets had to pass the same physical and psychological tests as regular recruits, which narrowed the applicant field somewhat, but we had to keep raising the minimum requirements for the program just to keep the number of qualified applicants at a manageable level. Pretty soon it was harder to get into the Cadet Corps than it was to get into the Police Academy as a regular NYPD recruit.

Running the Cadet Corps program was an important and rewarding job for me. But I figured that once I got the program where I wanted it to be, say in a couple of years, I would do something else—maybe go back to the Patrol Services Bureau, maybe as a supervisor in the Detective Bureau or Organized Crime Control Bureau. There were plenty of things to do.

Then on a Thursday morning in March 1993, I get a phone call at my Cadet Corps office at the Academy. It's a sergeant calling from Department headquarters at One Police Plaza, and he tells me the police commissioner wants to see me.

And from that moment on, my career as a cop would never be the same.

Chapter 3

THERE'S A NEW IAB IN TOWN

Police Commissioner Ray Kelly is sitting at his desk on the fourteenth floor of One Police Plaza, the same carved mahogany desk once used by his distant predecessor, Teddy Roosevelt, with his back to a window that looks out onto the Brooklyn Bridge.

Kelly's not a big man, but he carries himself like one, ramrod straight, hair cut short, looking every inch the Marine combat commander he once was in Vietnam, and the Marine Corps Reserve colonel he still was in 1993. A milkman's son, he's got almost thirty years in the Department, from patrol officer to commissioner. And as I walk into the office and snap a salute, I notice that his face looks drawn, almost haggard, as if he's in pain.

I hardly know Kelly—before this I'd only met him in passing—but I will serve under the man for fourteen years of my NYPD career, and I will come to recognize that drawn, haggard look.

It's the look he always has when one of his cops is killed in the line of duty.

In this case that cop is Detective Luis Lopez, age thirty-five, an eight-year NYPD veteran assigned as an undercover in the Manhattan South Narcotics Division (MSND). The day before, March 10, 1993, Lopez was working a gun- and dope-trafficking case against some dealers operating out of a T-shirt silk-screening shop on East First Street in the East Village. One of the suspects agrees to sell Lopez $10,000 worth of drugs, and when Lopez comes back to the shop with three cops from his backup team to make the arrests, the suspects start firing. Undercovers posing as drug buyers can't wear protective vests, for obvious reasons, and one of the suspects' bullets catches Detective Lopez in the chest. An hour later he dies on the operating table at Bellevue Hospital. It's only March, and Detective Lopez is already the fifteenth NYPD officer to be shot so far in 1993, and he is the first to die. Fifteen cops shot in a little over two months; that's what it's like to be an NYPD cop in the early 1990s.

Although I was commanding the Cadet Corps program, as a deputy inspector I had the duty that day, meaning I had to respond to any serious incident in Patrol Borough Manhattan South. So when the officer down call comes in I grab a car and a driver and race to the shooting scene. Detective Lopez has already been transported, three suspects are in custody, but the area is swarming with crime scene investigators and detectives from the Borough Shooting Team, taking measurements, collecting evidence, interviewing potential witnesses. Commissioner Kelly and other Department top brass show up briefly on their way back from the hospital, where the news is not good. My job is to take control of the scene, make sure everyone who isn't part of the investigation is kept away—always a problem in a situation like this, when so many cops want to help—and to collect as much information as possible for a preliminary report. Almost twelve hours later, at three a.m., I finally get things wrapped up and head home for a couple hours' sleep before going back to work. Then I get the call that the commissioner wants to see me at eleven a.m.

Kelly takes my salute and then gets up and walks around the desk and shakes my hand, then we move over to some chairs and sit down. I assume that the commissioner wants to talk about the Detective Lopez shooting—he already has my report on his desk—and we do talk about it. We talk about Detective Lopez's wife, now a young widow, and his thirteen-year-old daughter and his sixteen-year-old son, Luis Jr., who later will become an NYPD cop himself. We talk about how hard Detective Lopez's fellow MSND cops are taking it, how tough cops at the unit's headquarters at the Seventh Precinct on Pitt Street are walking around red-eyed, almost unable to speak. We talk about the upcoming funeral, which will be held at Sacred Heart Church on Staten Island, not far from the Lopez home, and which will draw seven thousand people, including thousands of cops.

We talk about all that for about five minutes, and then Kelly tells me why he called me in.

I'm transferring you, he says.

It's out of the blue, completely unexpected, but that's the way it is in the NYPD. So I ask him where I'm going.

I need you in Internal Affairs, Kelly says.

Kelly tells me that there's a transformation going on in Internal Affairs, that he wants me to be a part of it, that he wants me to head a new Internal Affairs group called the Corruption Prevention and Analysis Unit, which will track and analyze new patterns of corruption within the NYPD and help devise new strategies to combat it. It's an important assignment, he says, and I'm the man for it. I'm to report to my new assignment first thing Monday morning.

And my first thought is: No way.

Internal Affairs is the last place I want to go. Internal Affairs is the last place anybody wants to go. Oh sure, everybody agrees that it's important to fight corruption and misconduct, that it's vital for the Department to police its own, and that Commissioner Kelly seems determined to fundamentally reshape Internal Affairs. Everybody agrees that Internal Affairs is an important job—as long as somebody else actually has to do it. The truth is that Internal Affairs is the most thankless, no-win assignment in the entire Department, the sort of assignment where, like I said, every success is also a failure. Yes, you can succeed by putting corrupt cops in jail or dismissing them from the Department. But every time you do that, you're also announcing to the world that the Department, your Department, failed the citizens of New York City by allowing a bad cop on the streets with a gun and a shield.

So I spend a couple of minutes trying to talk the commissioner out of it. I'm just getting the Cadet Corps program in shape, I tell him, we're really starting to make things happen, and I know how important the Cadet Corps program is to him. And so on. And the commissioner just nods and says, Yes, the Cadet Corps is important. But this is more important.

And that's it. Ray Kelly is the kind of commissioner who's open to advice and counsel from subordinates, but once he hears the advice and makes his decision, it's end of story. The NYPD is a military-style organization, and when you get an order, you salute and do your duty. Besides, even as I try to talk the commissioner out of sending me to Internal Affairs, I'm feeling more than a little sheepish about it. Less than twenty-four hours earlier, Detective Lopez died doing his duty for the city and for the Department. Compared with that, the personal career aspirations of a deputy inspector just aren't that important.

So I say, Yes sir! and we shake hands again. As I leave the commissioner's office I notice that the clock on the reception room wall reads precisely 11:11 a.m. It had only taken eleven minutes for my life as a cop to change forever.

I know I'll do the best job I can. As Officer Lenny Swindell told me so long ago, If ya got a job, do the job!—and I will. And as the commissioner had assured me, it will only be for two years and then I'll rotate out.

Of course, as I leave Ray Kelly's office, I don't know that those two years will actually stretch to almost twenty-one. All I know is that our mission now is to transform Internal Affairs—and I know that's not going to be easy.

Because anybody who thinks he's going to change the way the NYPD handles corruption and misconduct within its ranks has a lot of history to overcome first.

I love the New York City Police Department; anybody asks me, I bleed NYPD blue. But you can love something while at the same time acknowledging its faults and problems.

And the NYPD had a corruption and brutality problem from the day it was born.

The NYPD was created in 1845, replacing the motley collection of city marshals, night watchmen, and "Sunday officers"—who enforced the Sabbath laws—with a full-time force of about eight hundred patrolmen, supervised by captains and "roundsmen" who made the rounds to ensure that the men were on post. (One trick used by roundsmen on winter days was to touch a patrolman's badge to see if the metal was cold; if it was warm, it meant the patrolman had been off sleeping or staying warm in a fire station or saloon, a practice later known as "cooping." A century and a half later, the touching-the-badge trick would still be used by patrol sergeants making the rounds of foot posts.)

From the start, payoffs from gambling operations and saloon and brothel owners were considered part of the job, which made police positions, particularly in the upper ranks, highly sought after. By the 1870s, when patrolmen were being paid twice the average workingman's salary—

about $1,200 a year, not including the so-called sugar from graft—the Tammany Hall political machine demanded a $300 payment for promotion to sergeant and as much as $15,000 for promotion to captain. Often that money was provided by saloonkeepers and gamblers in the sergeant's or captain's district as a kind of bribe in advance. Being a cop, especially a high-level cop, was a moneymaking proposition.

(By the way, despite what you've heard, the word "cop" is not derived from "constable on patrol." One story has it that before policemen had formal uniforms they wore star-shaped badges fashioned from common roofing copper—hence "coppers," and then simply "cops." Another theory is that in the early nineteenth century the slang word "cop" meant to take or seize something, so when someone was arrested he was "copped"—and from there came "coppers" and then "cops." There are a lot of other theories if you want to look them up.)

For the most part, the corruption was ignored or at least tolerated by New Yorkers. In the love-hate relationship between the public and the press and the NYPD that exists to this day, nineteenth-century newspaper accounts of the police usually centered on two other themes: cops gratuitously clubbing people over the head with their nightsticks, or heroic acts of derring-do by the men in blue—a cop stopping a stampeding horse or rescuing a child from a burning building or bringing a murderer to bay.

It's still that way. If you're an NYPD cop you have to get used to the fact that in today's headlines you may be a hero, but in tomorrow's headlines you're going to be a bum.

But periodically the corruption would become so pervasive and so brazen that it couldn't be ignored. Suddenly newspaper headlines would be screaming about it, clergymen would be denouncing it from the pulpits, reformers would be demanding change, and the politicians—who were always shocked, shocked, to learn that there was corruption in the ranks of New York's Finest—would appoint a committee or commission to investigate the problem. In the end, a few high-level Department heads would roll and some dirty cops might be sent off to prison—and everybody would forget about it until the next major scandal came along.

In New York City that happened every twenty years or so, almost as regular as clockwork. The Lexow Committee in 1894, the Curran Committee in 1912, the Hofstadter Committee in 1931, the Helfand Commission in 1951—they all revealed widespread corruption in the NYPD, ranging from bribery to extortion and even to murder. The 1970–72 Knapp Commission, prompted by the reports of Officer Frank Serpico, Sergeant David Durk, and others, called corruption in the NYPD— particularly payoffs by gambling operations but also low-level corruption like free meals and accepting bribes from tow-truck drivers—an "extensive department-wide phenomenon, indulged in to some degree by a sizable majority of those on the force." One of the Knapp Commission's star witnesses was a dirty cop named William Phillips, who called his police uniform a "money suit" and who got caught shaking down a Dutch-born Manhattan prostitute named Xaviera Hollander, aka The Happy Hooker. (Phillips was later sentenced to life for killing two people in a brothel.)

And after every one of those scandals, the Department brass announced that it was establishing new protocols to eliminate corruption from the NYPD ranks forever.

Before the Knapp Commission, corruption cases in the NYPD had been handled by a variety of different units: the Commissioner's Special Investigations Unit, the Bureau of Inspectional Services' Special Investigations Unit, and so on. After Knapp, the Department created an Internal Affairs Division of about a hundred fifty investigators to handle major corruption cases, and Field Internal Affairs Units of about ten investigators each in every command borough—the same guys I'd encountered in the Great Christmas Tree Caper of 1978 investigation—to handle lesser corruption and misconduct cases. Internal Affairs started planting anonymous "Field Associates," usually young cops fresh from the Academy, into the precincts to watch for and report corruption. The Department expanded integrity training at the Academy, and started showing recruits the *I Used to Be a Cop* training film. Precinct commanders were put on notice that any corruption within their commands would mean the end of their careers.

And for a while it worked—or at least it appeared to. The type of corruption that the Knapp Commission uncovered, in which almost entire units were "on the pad," extracting monthly cash payments from gambling operations that were picked up by police "bag men" and divided up along the line, from cops to sergeants to captains, virtually disappeared. Everyone seemed convinced that the Department finally had a handle on corruption.

And then, in 1992, right on schedule, twenty years after Knapp, the NYPD got hit with Officer Michael Dowd—a guy the newspapers called "The Dirtiest Cop Ever."

Dowd, a firefighter's son who grew up in suburban Suffolk County, always claimed that he was a good cop turned bad by a pervasively criminal NYPD culture, but I don't buy it. As far as I'm concerned, he was a bad cop from the day he graduated from the Academy in 1982. Dowd wasn't a victim of a criminal NYPD culture; he helped create that culture—at least on the midnight shift at the 75th Precinct, a high-incident precinct that covered the East New York section of Brooklyn.

Dowd and his corrupt buddies in the Seven-Five were real pieces of work. Dowd later admitted that while in uniform he routinely pilfered cash from DOAs and while responding to burglary calls; he and his partners later graduated to stealing cash and drugs from drug-dealing operations that fronted as neighborhood bodegas, and when that got to be too much like work, they started taking protection money from a Dominican gang that ran the drug trade in East New York. Dowd reportedly even "arrested" a rival drug gang member and delivered him to the Dominican drug gang he was working for—and the man was never seen again. Dowd and his pals were using cocaine as well as stealing and selling it; Dowd later admitted that he sometimes snorted cocaine off the dashboard of his NYPD patrol car.

The 1992 arrest of Officer Michael Dowd and other corrupt cops in Brooklyn's 75th Precinct rocked the NYPD and eventually led to a new, highly proactive Internal Affairs Bureau. (Getty Images)

Dowd and five other cops were finally arrested in May 1992—but not by the NYPD. Police and prosecutors in suburban Suffolk County, where Dowd was providing cocaine to a local drug ring, made the arrests, which of course were trumpeted in the newspapers. "COCAINE COPS!" the headlines said.

It wasn't the first NYPD corruption and misconduct scandal since the Knapp Commission of two decades earlier. For example, in 1986 eleven cops from the 77th Precinct in Bed-Stuy—the so-called Buddy Boys—were arrested on charges that they knocked down drug dealers' doors after sending in phony emergency calls and then stole money and drugs, which they later resold to other dealers. But the police brass had declared that the Buddy Boys case was an aberration, an isolated incident, not a symptom of a widespread problem. And initially they said the same thing about the Michael Dowd case. But there was one problem: It wasn't isolated. Eventually it would come out that other high-activity precincts had similar gangs of corrupt cops.

Perhaps even worse, people in the Internal Affairs Division had known for years that Dowd was corrupt, that there were problems in the Seven-Five, but nobody really did anything about it. The case fell to a single Field Internal Affairs Unit sergeant who got little if any backing from IAD in trying to build a provable case against Dowd and his fellow criminal cops. Instead, Dowd was transferred to some nothing jobs—guarding a police vehicle impound lot, that sort of thing—until finally, with the heat dying down, he was sent back to patrol in the 94th Precinct in the Greenpoint section of Brooklyn, where he resumed his drug-dealing activities.

The newspapers called it a cover-up by a Department that didn't want to admit that it had a corruption problem—which was about half right. It was clear that some high-level officials hadn't been enthusiastic about exposing the Department to corruption charges. As a former head of the Internal Affairs Division later admitted, "A message went out into the field that maybe we shouldn't be so aggressive [in pursuing corruption cases] because the department doesn't want bad press. . . . When I went [to top commanders] with the bad news that two cops would be arrested in the morning or that three cops would be indicted, I felt like they wanted to shoot me."

That fear of bad publicity affected lower-level commanders as well.

Corruption in your command was a career ender, whether you knew about it or not, so precinct commanders sometimes chose to simply reassign suspect cops—as had happened with Dowd—rather than call on IAD to investigate.

As for the Internal Affairs Division, the Dowd case made it plain that it had some serious problems. In the old days of the Knapp Commission, corrupt cops had been divided into two categories: the "grass eaters," cops who more or less openly took minor bribes and graft that came their way, and the "meat eaters," corrupt cops who were constantly on the prowl to make more serious criminal scores. IAD got a pretty good handle on the "grass eaters," but it failed to understand that the new model of corruption was the "meat eaters"—guys like Michael Dowd and his crew.

There were other problems with the old IAD. It was chronically underfunded and inadequately staffed. It was isolated from the police commissioner by multiple levels of bureaucracy. The bifurcated command and control system of the Internal Affairs Division and the various Field Internal Affairs Units in each borough command led to confusion and bureaucratic infighting. Corruption allegations against cops weren't being properly logged or processed; some sensitive allegations were relegated to a so-called tickler file, where they disappeared forever. IAD was also overly secretive, refusing to share information with other Department commands, let alone with outside agencies such as District Attorney's Offices and federal prosecutors—and in return, those agencies refused to share critical information with IAD.

The old IAD also seemed more concerned about the small stuff than with the major corruption problems like Dowd—with the SCAN program being a prime example.

I ran into SCAN—short for Stop Corrupt Activity Now—when I was CO in the Sixth Precinct. One day I started hearing the word that was spreading among my cops—Watch out, IAD's here, they're all over the precinct. It turns out IAD had flooded the precinct, which is only about one mile square, with half a dozen IAD teams, trying to catch cops taking bribes or committing other acts of corruption. (It wasn't just the Sixth Precinct; they were doing it to all the precincts on a rotating basis.) The problem was that these IAD guys—guys in suits—were driving around in IAD surveillance vans and unmarked cars that looked exactly like what they were—IAD surveillance vans and unmarked cars. My cops made them in an instant. And the IAD guys were doing this on the day shift, not the midnight shift, when most serious police corruption happens. After several days of this, the worst the IAD guys could come up with was three command disciplines against some of my guys for things like being temporarily off post or smoking in uniform while on duty and in public view. I honestly don't believe that any of my cops were guilty of corruption—but even if they were, these IAD guys never would have caught them.

Which brings up the biggest problem I think the old IAD had: its people. As I said earlier, there were some good investigators in IAD, but frankly they were the exceptions. Why would any good cop or investigator want a job that would brand him forever as a "rat" among his fellow cops? Why would any good cop or investigator join a unit that rightly or wrongly was despised as a dumping ground for incompetents and shirkers? The answer was, they wouldn't join such a unit.

And the result was that bad cops like Dowd and his buddies stayed on the street for far too long.

So in 1992, to stave off some of the political heat from the Dowd scandal, Mayor David Dinkins, true to historical form, appointed a special commission to investigate corruption in the NYPD. It was called the Mollen Commission, after its chairman, a former judge named Milton Mollen, but the commission's formal title left no doubt where it was headed. The title was "Commission to Investigate Allegations of Police Corruption and the Anti-Corruption Procedures of the Police Department." It was clear that the Mollen Commission was going to home in on the failures of IAD—and in the process make a case for an outside civilian agency to take over all corruption and misconduct investigations and enforcement within the Department.

The Department wanted no part of that, and with good reason. Civilians are not cops, they can never truly understand police work, they're not trained investigators, and thus they can never effectively understand and combat police corruption. Despite its troubled history with corruption, the Department was determined to prove that it could police itself.

So to steal a march on the Mollen Commission, Police Commissioner Lee Brown assigned his second in command, First Deputy Commissioner Ray Kelly—who a few months later would replace Brown as commissioner—to conduct his own investigation and come up with a plan to revamp and improve Internal Affairs.

Which he did. The changes Ray Kelly eventually made to Internal Affairs were dramatic, even revolutionary. For one thing, he did away with the old Field Internal Affairs Units and changed the Internal Affairs Division (IAD) to the Internal Affairs Bureau (IAB)—which was far more than just a name change. Before, IAD had been just one of three divisions in the Bureau of Inspectional Services, which reported to the chief of department, who in turn reported to the police commissioner; in other words, there were two levels of bureaucracy between Internal Affairs and the commissioner. As a "bureau," the new Internal Affairs Bureau was on equal footing with other enforcement bureaus—Detective Bureau, Organized Crime Control Bureau, and so on—and the IAB chief reported directly to the commissioner. And if you need something from the top guy, which is better? To ask your boss to ask his boss to ask the big boss—or to ask the big boss yourself?

The new IAB was a centralized command that was responsible for investigating all allegations of corruption and serious misconduct within the NYPD. For the first time, IAB also investigated all police shootings involving injuries or death and other serious but nonfatal "use of force" incidents involving cops. Minor violations of Department rules and policies—the "white socks" cases—were left to "Investigation Units" within the various NYPD Patrol Boroughs and to "Integrity Control Officers" within the precincts. To run IAB, Kelly brought in a civilian, Walter Mack Jr., a former federal prosecutor and, like Kelly, a former Marine combat commander in Vietnam, as deputy commissioner for internal affairs.

Commissioner Kelly also promised—and delivered—more money, more people, and better equipment for IAB, a promise that his successors would also honor. Eventually the IAB staff tripled from about two hundred fifty people to almost seven hundred fifty—making it the biggest police department internal anticorruption and anti–police misconduct operation in the world. We also had a $2 million annual budget (not including salaries) to pay for special equipment and other investigation expenses.

Of course, reorganizing a bureaucracy and throwing money at a problem is relatively simple. But Kelly understood that all that would mean nothing without a fundamental change in the culture, not only

within Internal Affairs but also in the Department rank and file's perception of Internal Affairs. Kelly knew that Internal Affairs would never be
loved—that would be too much to expect. Nor would it be enough if
Internal Affairs was simply feared, although that's a necessary part of it.
No, to be effective, the cops who work in Internal Affairs also have to be
respected within the Department.

But how do you accomplish that in a police department that had
always regarded Internal Affairs cops as a bunch of cheese-eating rats?

Some of us had an idea.

It's the fall of 1992, months before my meeting with Commissioner Ray
Kelly that put me into IAB, and news about the Seven-Five corruption
scandal and the newly created Mollen Commission is in the air. The
scandal has also spread to the Seven-Three, my old precinct, where a
gang of fifteen rogue cops known as "The Morgue Boys"—they would
meet during the midnight shift at an abandoned coffin manufactur-
ing factory to plan their scores—will soon be arrested for ripping off
drug dealers and stealing money and guns. And although it's not public
knowledge yet, the investigation has also spread to the 30th Precinct
in Harlem, the precinct that soon will be known as "The Dirty Thirty."

Like every other NYPD cop, I've been following all this in the papers
and on the TV news and through the usual Department gossip machine.
It's embarrassing to see these crooked cops paraded before the public,
to see my Department being humiliated this way. But I'm still happily
in charge of the Cadet Corps program, and I haven't been personally
involved in any of it.

Then one day I'm in my Cadet Corps office on the seventh floor of the
Police Academy when I get a call from Mike Farrell, the NYPD Deputy
Commissioner for Policy and Planning. I'd first met Mike at the Police
Management Institute, which is a kind of mini-MBA program offered by
Columbia University. Now Mike starts telling me about how amid all the
scandals, Kelly, who has just been named police commissioner by Mayor
Dinkins, is planning to remake Internal Affairs. They're putting together
an informal group to study the various issues involved—and will I help?

Mike is a brilliant guy, and I like him a lot, but I'm instantly wary.

This is just an advisory group, right? I ask him. I'm not actually going to be sent to Internal Affairs, right?

No, no, Mike says, nothing like that. We're just trying to develop some new ideas.

Well, in that case, okay, sure, I tell him. Glad to help out.

(Months later, after the commissioner sent me to IAB, Mike laughingly admitted that he'd sandbagged me. After I got over my initial urge to strangle him, I laughed about it, too.)

One of the tasks I have for the advisory group is to run some focus groups of cops to find out what their thinking is on integrity issues and Internal Affairs. So I ask the computer guys to start picking names out of the Department's personnel records—ordinary beat cops, detectives, sergeants, lieutenants, about six hundred in all, all chosen at random. Over the next six months or so I bring them in to the Academy in groups of twelve or fifteen and sit them down around a conference table. I introduce myself, and tell them that while I have my assistant here to take notes, it's all completely anonymous. We aren't videotaping this session, and no one will ever know what they say here—promise, Scout's honor. All we want to do is listen to what they have to say about integrity issues and Internal Affairs.

Of course, being cops, they're suspicious. Why have I been called in here? Is this some kind of IAD recruiting session? Am I under investigation for something? And who's this deputy inspector with the big mustache anyway?

So at first nobody wants to say anything. They're studying their shoes or staring up at the ceiling, as silent and motionless as an oil painting. But I've been teaching classes for years at John Jay, and I know how to nudge them along. I ask one young cop what he thinks about IAD, and of course he hems and haws and then he says: Well, I guess they're just doing their jobs.

And what else is he going to say to some strange DI he doesn't even know? But as soon as he says it, another young cop at the far end of the table will mutter under his breath: Bullshit! And then I'll bounce it over to him: What, you disagree? And he'll say: Well, uh, yeah, maybe they're doing their jobs—but why is IAD always trying to catch you for small stuff, like not wearing your hat or taking too long for meal? Don't they have anything better to do? And then I'll bounce it over to another cop, and he'll take it a little further: Yeah, those IAD guys don't know what it's like on the street. They just want to get other cops jammed up.

And once you finally get a bunch of cops talking, you can't shut them up. All I have to do is sit back and listen.

Yeah, those IAD guys really suck, they say. They're a bunch of losers, they say. As investigators they couldn't find their own asses with both hands. They're only in IAD because they're afraid to be on the street. Yeah, or they got jammed up and ratted out other cops to save their skins and IAD is the only unit that'll take 'em. With all the real criminals out there, why would any cop want to put other cops in jail? What a bunch of assholes!

And so on in every focus group we run. They really just document what everybody already knows: Everybody hates the Internal Affairs Division, just as they always have.

And the focus groups are equally unanimous when I throw out the question: Would you ever consider working for Internal Affairs? In virtually every case, the response is: Me? Work for IAD? I'd drop my papers first! In other words, they'd quit.

It's understandable. Traditionally, for a cop to volunteer to work for Internal Affairs is to be forever separated from the NYPD brotherhood. Once you voluntarily start investigating other cops, you're a rat—end of story. Old friends will turn their backs on you, and their wives will turn their backs on your wife. Cops who've known you for years will spit on the ground and walk away if you say hello. You aren't going to be invited to Christmas parties or retirement rackets—because hey, who wants a rat at a party?

And it's not like you can volunteer to work for IAD for a while and then go back to being a regular cop. IAD is like the roach motel—once you check in, you can never really check out. If you try to go back to a precinct or other command, once they know you were with IAD—which they'll find out before you even unpack your stuff into your locker—you'll be shunned, ostracized. Even scrupulously honest cops won't want to work with you, because, well, once a rat, always a rat—and how do I know this former IAD asshole isn't going to turn me in for some bullshit petty violation of the Patrol Guide? The other cops will start calling you "Ben" or "Willard," like the rat movies, and maybe they'll smear cheese over your locker, or hang a dead rat over it. That's been known to happen—more than once. Who wants to go through that?

So given all that, how do you get good cops to work for Internal Affairs when the good cops all tell you that they'd rather quit than work even one day for Internal Affairs? How do you get the best people into the new IAB?

The answer is simple: You don't give them a choice.

You draft them.

Which is exactly what the new IAB did. At the end of 1992, Kelly sends shock waves through the entire Department by announcing that as of January 1, 1993, the start-up date for the newly reorganized Internal Affairs Bureau, fifteen handpicked first grade detectives from the Detective Bureau and the Organized Crime Control Bureau, some of the best and most respected detectives in the Department, will be assigned to Internal Affairs for a two-year hitch. First grade detectives! Being sent to Internal Affairs! It's unheard of.

Of course, the other bureau chiefs go ballistic—You're stealing our best guys!—which is what Kelly intended. He knows that if he just asks the bureau chiefs to send some good people to Internal Affairs, who are they going to send? Sure, they'll promise to send their best people, and then they're going to cull out every incompetent, lazy burnout they can and cheerfully send him off to IAB. No way Kelly's going to play that game. He's sending a message: There's a new IAB in town.

And those fifteen handpicked detectives aren't going to be the last good cops that IAB steals, either. From now on, IAB will get first pick of all the sergeants and lieutenants who want to move into investigative supervisory positions. (Most IAB investigators are sergeants or lieutenants.) IAB will sit down with their personnel files and say: We're taking this guy, and that guy, and that gal, no, we don't want this guy, but this guy looks pretty good . . . And whether they like it or not, suddenly they're in IAB for the next two years or so. (Later, after years of complaints by other bureau chiefs, we finally had to change it so that IAB only got the first pick on a rotating basis, sort of like a pro sports draft system.)

And the new IAB's draft authority doesn't just cover those lieutenants and sergeants; it's Department-wide. If we need, say, an investigator who speaks Urdu, or one with accounting experience, or a cop who used to be a barber, we can search the Department's personnel records for someone with those skills and draft her, too. Or if we need some good instructors for the IAB training course, people who know how to teach, we'll draft them out of the Academy. The bottom line is that if IAB needs you, most of the time—unless you have a really, really good reason, or a really major "hook"—we get you. You're drafted. And the commissioner will back us up.

In fact, within a few years, as we gradually rotate out the old IAD guys, virtually everybody who works in IAB is a draftee—me included.

As you might expect, the people who get drafted into IAB bitch and moan about it; they try everything they can to wiggle out of it. Meanwhile, their fellow cops treat the news like there's been a death in the family—and then they thank God that they weren't drafted into the hated IAB.

I understood how they felt. After I was named Chief of the Internal Affairs Bureau in 1996, a three-star rank, I would meet with every new group of draftees. I'd commiserate with them about their fate—Yeah, I know you didn't ask to be here, but hey, I was drafted into IAB, too—and then I would explain what the new IAB is all about.

Forget what you knew about the old Internal Affairs Division, I tell them. We aren't going to send you out looking for cops who take a few extra minutes to go back on the air after finishing a radio run, or any other chicken-shit stuff; that's somebody else's problem. You're going to be working important, complex investigations against seriously bad cops, and you're also going to be protecting the good cops against false allegations. Think about it: If you're an honest cop and there's an allegation against you, who would you want working the case? Some burnout who's only in Internal Affairs because no one else wants him, and who's just counting down the days until he drops his retirement papers and moves to Fort Lauderdale? Or someone like you, someone who was handpicked by us because he's the best of the best? IAB is an elite unit, I tell them, because no one gets to choose to join it. We choose you. And we know you're going to act like professionals and do a professional job.

And then after the pep talk, I make them two promises:

First, I tell them, you're going to be better for having been here. You're going to undergo two weeks of special IAB training, which will teach you the unique skills you're going to need to conduct investigations of other cops—and if you can learn how to run a surveillance on a cop, someone who knows the same tricks you do, how much better are you going to be when you need to run a surveillance on some street mutt after you go back to the squad? And after that, we're also going to send you to specialized training classes—assault/homicide investigation classes, sexual assault investigation classes, narcotics, electronic surveillance, and so on—so that when you leave here you're going to have an impressive résumé that you wouldn't have gotten anywhere else. The bottom line, I tell them, is that IAB is going to be good for your career.

And second, I tell them, when you leave after two years, if you've done a good job, we're going to do everything we can to get you where you want to go. Detective Bureau? OCCB? Intelligence Division? We'll do our best to land you there—and in most cases, we'll succeed.

Of course, they're cops, with cops' natural suspicions, so most of them initially don't believe a word of it. The resistance is greatest among the draftees who come from cop families, guys whose fathers and grandfathers and great-grandfathers were cops, guys who've grown up hearing that any cop who would investigate other cops is a miserable cheese-eating rat. The other draftees have some of that attitude as well, but at least it didn't come to them through their mother's milk, so they're a little easier to convince.

But even though most of them will never stop bitching and moaning about being drafted into IAB—actually, it's when cops stop bitching and moaning that you start to worry—eventually most will come around and prove themselves to be first-rate investigators and supervisors. In fact, in all my time as IAB chief I only had one draftee who seriously bucked the system.

He's a sergeant, and on the very first day, after I make my speech, he stands up and says: I don't want to be here, and nobody can make me! I figure he's just sounding off, saying out loud what the rest of them are thinking. He's got a good record—we wouldn't have picked him if he didn't—and besides, it takes some stones for a sergeant to talk to a three-star chief that way. So I brush it off.

But as the IAB training course goes on, this guy is constantly dogging off, not paying attention, muttering under his breath; in the end, he intentionally fails the IAB training course exam. Who knows? Maybe he's one of those mother's milk cops who'll never see Internal Affairs as anything but the rat squad. Or maybe he's got some integrity issues of his own in his past, and he's afraid if he works for IAB they may come out. Whatever the reason, I don't want this guy in IAB anymore.

The problem is that if it gets out—and it will—that you can buck the IAB draft without any consequences, everybody's going to do it. So finally we bounce the sergeant out of IAB and into the new assignment the police commissioner has approved for him. The sergeant lives in south Brooklyn, and we all hope he's going to be very happy pushing papers on the eight p.m. to four a.m. shift in a precinct on the far side of the Bronx.

The sergeant was right. I couldn't make him become part of the new IAB—but I could make him wish he had. And if that sounds hard, well, we're in a hard business.

Some of the investigators we drafted into the new IAB stayed on long after their two-year commitments were up. Once they got over the emotional hurdle of investigating other cops, they found that pursuing smart and well-trained but crooked cops actually was a lot more challenging than locking up sixth-grade-dropout crackheads in the squads.

But most of the IAB draftees left after their two years—which meant that every year we'd lose about a third of our investigators as they rotated out. The high turnover was sometimes a problem, especially if a guy being rotated out was in the middle of a big investigation—in which case, he might have to stay a few months longer.

But the constant rotation had a positive corollary effect, one that we had intended from the start.

Over the years we rotated hundreds, even thousands, of IAB investigators and supervisors back into the regular ranks of the NYPD. When they get there, the other cops know that they've been with Internal Affairs for the past two years, but they also know that they hadn't volunteered for it, the Department made them do it—and thus they aren't rats. And they're good cops!

Back in the old IAD days, most cops never said the words "Internal Affairs" without adding the word "assholes." But when you're working with a gold shield detective or a sergeant or a lieutenant that you like and respect, and who just happens to have been shanghaied into IAB for a couple of years, it's at least a little harder to make that juxtaposition.

Of course, I'm not saying that IAB ever became beloved within the

NYPD. No cop ever stood up at a precinct Christmas party and pro-posed a toast to the Internal Affairs Bureau.

But the Internal Affairs draft system—a system that has since been copied by police departments across the country and the world—changed the perception of IAB and anticorruption efforts within the Department. IAB was no longer an isolated unit in the NYPD; it was a unit *of* the NYPD.

And the cops who work for IAB are just that. They're cops like every-body else.

It's a funny thing about the infamous Blue Wall of Silence, the code that allegedly prevents cops from reporting corruption or misconduct by other cops. What's funny is that the wall isn't quite as high and impen-etrable as a lot of people seem to think—and it's not always blue.

Actual case in point: Two FDNY firefighters at a fire station on Staten Island get into a beef, which ends with one firefighter whack-ing the other over the head with a folding metal chair. He hits him a little harder than he meant to, and the guy goes down unconscious and bleeding heavily from the head wound. The other firefighters transport him to the hospital, where a hospital worker reports it to the NYPD as a possible assault. But when the precinct detectives go to the firehouse to question the other firefighters about the fight, the response is: What fight? There was no fight. Eddie fell off a ladder. And after Eddie wakes up and the detectives try to question him, he's already gotten the word: There was no fight. I fell off a ladder. There's no complainant, no wit-nesses, and since the firefighters have already hosed the blood off the chair and the floor, no evidence—and thus no case.

So what is that? The Red Wall of Silence?

Another case in point: I'm teaching a police science class at John Jay and I decide to conduct an experiment on silences and walls. There's this young woman in class, she's my star student, she's aced every test so far, and she has expressed fascination with police undercover investigations. I call her into my office and tell her: Look, I'm going to give you an A on the final exam before you even take it, because I know you'd ace it anyway. All you have to do is . . . Then I lay out the scenario. She's more than game.

So final exam day comes, and the thirty students in the class are all at their desks, hunched over their test papers, when, as arranged, there's a knock at the classroom door. Professor Campisi, they need to see you in the dean's office right away. So I tell the class, I'm going to be gone for a few minutes, but you're on your honor here—no cheating. I'm not gone for three seconds before my star student makes a big show of grabbing a textbook out of her backpack and thumbing through it. Then she calls out: Anybody know the answer to number sixteen? Nobody answers, so she keeps thumbing through the textbook, then loudly says: Oh, here it is, and goes back to the test. I come back, collect all the tests—and then I wait. I wait for anyone in that class to call me or drop me a note or come by my office to tell me, Professor Campisi, I feel obligated to tell you that Ms. Star Student cheated on the test. And nobody does, ever, not one person, not even anonymously.

So what's that? The Ivy-Covered Wall of Silence?

I could go on. How often do lawyers inform on corrupt lawyers? It's the Pinstripe Wall of Silence. How often does a medical intern turn in a surgeon for botching an operation? It's the White Wall of Silence.

You get the point. Almost every profession tends to protect its own. And nobody wants to be a snitch, an informer, a rat.

Sure, you can argue that it's different with cops, that people's lives and freedom are involved—and you're right. One of the most disturbing aspects of the Dowd case and other police corruption cases was the fact that many of the other cops in their precincts knew or at least suspected what was going on. But none of those cops openly stood up and said so.

The Mollen Commission concluded that "the vast majority of police officers throughout the city do not engage in corruption," that serious corruption in the NYPD was generally limited to small pockets of corrupt and brutal officers in the high-crime precincts. But it also found that those groups of bad cops depended on the silence of honest cops to protect them from being caught.

Which sounds pretty bad. How can you be an honest cop and not report corruption by dishonest cops?

But try to look at it from a cop's point of view.

It's something that came up again and again in the cop focus groups I ran before and after I went to IAB. A dozen or so cops are sitting around the conference table, and they're saying, Look, we hate guys like Michael Dowd, we hate dirty cops, we won't work with them—and they don't want to work with us, either, 'cause they know we're straight. They don't want us to see what they're doing.

But even if we suspect they're dirty, the cops say, what are we going to do? Report our suspicions to the precinct CO, who's going to contact IAD? Do we contact IAD directly, call 'em up and say, This is Officer Krupke in the One-Five, and I want to turn in some dirty cops? Yeah, right. Even if we do it anonymously, maybe they have ways of finding out who we are. And the first thing IAD is gonna do is try to get us to wear a wire on other cops—and if we refuse, maybe the Department is gonna say we're impeding an investigation. If we do wear a wire, sure, maybe we can get close to the bad cops and help IAD build a provable case—assuming that the bad cops are stupid enough to talk about their scores in front of us. But remember, that wire's going to pick up everything else, too. Maybe one of our friends is complaining about his wife or his girlfriend. Or maybe he mentions he had a beer with his meal, which is a violation, or he was cooping on shift, and now it's on tape, and he gets jammed up, too.

And then what? the cops say. We get called in front of a grand jury to testify and authenticate the tapes, and maybe the assistant district attorney or one of the grand jurors asks us if we've ever witnessed any other acts of corruption. Well, what's corruption? A cop getting a free extra scoop of ice cream? A cop padding his overtime a little? So we say no, we've never seen any other corruption, and then later it comes out somehow, and now we're looking at a potential perjury charge.

Or maybe IAD arrests the dirty cops and turns 'em, gets them to cooperate. The dirty cops are looking for payback, so maybe they try to dirty us up, say that we're corrupt, too. Or maybe the case goes to trial, and some slick defense lawyer beats the shit out of us on the witness stand, he brings up every minor violation and bogus complaint we've ever got, he tries to make us look like bad cops—and the jurors, who don't like snitches any more than anybody else, believe him.

And then, these cops say, when we get back to the precinct, or even transfer to another precinct, who are we? Are we heroes who busted some bad cops? Hell no. We're rats, that's who we are. We're the cops who went undercover against other cops, including the innocent ones. The other cops are gonna think that the only reason we did it is because we got jammed up and we were trying to save our own asses—because why else would any cop wear a wire against another cop? And how does anybody know we're not still wearing a wire? That we're not trying to put some chicken-shit departmental charge on them? Sure, it's easy for the Department brass to say it's our duty to stand up and report corruption and misconduct. It's easy for the lieutenant and the captain to lecture us at roll call about turning in crooked cops. But once we do, our lives as cops are over.

So yeah, the cops say, we hate guys like Michael Dowd, but investigating corruption isn't our job. That's the job of Internal Affairs. Leave us out of it.

The cops have a point. Historically, NYPD cops who openly came forward with corruption allegations did not fare well. Most of the cops in the focus groups are too young to remember the Knapp Commission—it's ancient history to them—but some of them have caught the movie *Serpico* on late-night TV. They know that when Officer Frank Serpico tried to bring corruption to light, he was at first ignored and then turned into a pariah—and then he wound up being shot and wounded on duty under some possibly questionable circumstances.

Or maybe they've seen the film *Prince of the City*, based on a real-life corrupt NYPD narcotics cop named Bob Leuci who went undercover against other crooked cops and then openly testified against them in court. Leuci eventually was assigned to the Internal Affairs Division because no one else in the Department wanted him—which, as I've said, was another problem with the old IAD. Too often it was used as a dumping ground for corrupt cops who agreed to cooperate, or as an assignment of last resort for cops who really didn't belong there but couldn't be sent anywhere else.

Given all that, how can we reasonably expect cops to report corruption by other cops, even anonymously? In fact, under the old system, there was a time when cops were specifically prohibited from reporting corruption anonymously. They were supposed to stand up and give their names and shield numbers, just as they would if they were making an allegation against a civilian suspect; if somehow they were caught whispering an anonymous police corruption allegation into a phone, they could be in trouble. It's just too much to ask of cops—or of anyone, really. We had to set up a system where cops could report corruption without fear of ruining their careers and even their lives.

I called it the PRIDE line—1-800-PRIDE-PD. It was a special line for cops only at the IAB Command Center at the new IAB headquarters on Hudson Street. Unlike the regular IAB complaint line, calls to the PRIDE line were not recorded or caller ID'd. They were completely anonymous—again, we promise. And we made sure that cops in the precincts knew about it, putting up posters in every muster room and having the number read out at roll calls.

I'm not saying we had to bring in extra staff to handle the flood of phone calls from cops reporting corruption; in any given year we'd get about a dozen tips from cops on the PRIDE line. But as we'll see, the PRIDE line produced some good leads on significant corruption cases. And cops who tolerated corruption could no longer use the excuse that there was no avenue for them to safely report it.

The Command Center itself was an innovation. In the old IAD days, Internal Affairs was headquartered just across the Brooklyn Bridge from Manhattan, in a grimy old three-story building with bars on the lower windows that had formerly been the 84th Precinct headquarters; once IAD moved in it was known to cops as "The Rat's Nest." IAD had what it called an "Action Desk," a bank of phones manned by bored, sullen cops who took calls from citizens who had complaints—that cop beat the shit out of me, that cop stole my watch, that cop's on the take. The IAD "intake" cops were poorly trained, unmotivated, and often hostile to the complainants. A cop beat the shit out of you? they might say. Well, did you deserve it?

Every legitimate or even potentially legitimate complaint about police corruption that the IAD Action Desk received was supposed to be logged into the records, get a log number, be assigned to an investigator, and be forwarded to the appropriate borough District Attorney's Office. But as the Mollen Commission reported, that didn't always happen; in fact, it didn't happen a lot. Hundreds of corruption allegations disappeared, with sensitive cases being sent to the infamous "tickler file."

In the new IAB we changed all that. For one thing, we moved out of The Rat's Nest and into better quarters, on the third floor of an office building on Hudson Street. (Because of the nature of IAB's work, its headquarters are always kept separate from NYPD precincts or command headquarters; it wouldn't do to have cooperating cops or IAB undercovers walking in and out in front of other cops. But as bureau chief, my office was on the twelfth floor of NYPD headquarters at One Police Plaza.)

We get rid of the old Action Desk and introduce a new IAB Command Center as the initial contact point for reporting corruption. Again, that's more than just a name change. The Command Center is a state-of-the-art call center, manned twenty-four/seven by a half dozen or so police officers and a couple of supervisors. The "intake" officers are usually young cops who want to make detective but who need eighteen months of investigative experience before they can get their gold shields.

Answering phones may not seem like investigative work, but in IAB it is. We teach the intake officers how to interview people who call, what questions to ask, how to assess the information and write a report—which is what detectives do on the streets and in the squad rooms. Each call is logged—meaning a report is filled out—and given a log number; subsequent calls or actions on the initial case will also be logged and added to the file. In every case of alleged criminal behavior by a cop, we also notify the appropriate borough District Attorney's Office, and we work closely with the DA's anticorruption team throughout the case. In a way, the DAs and ADAs (assistant district attorneys) act as our legal advisers, guiding us through any potential legal snags as we build a case. In the old days the DAs and Internal Affairs barely spoke to one another—neither trusted the other—but in the new IAB we made it a point to partner up with them.

The Command Center takes in thousands of calls and e-mails every year, but not all of them, or even most of them, result in an IAB corruption or misconduct investigation. Some complaints involve cops who turn out not to be NYPD—say, the Port Authority Police—and those cases will be logged and then passed over to that agency. Or maybe a desk sergeant will call to report that a cop has lost some Department property, such as his shield; unless there's some unusual or suspicious circumstances—This is the fourth shield this guy says he lost!—that won't be an IAB case, but we'll log it anyway. A lot of calls from citizens concern rude behavior or excessive force by cops, which are handled not by IAB but by the Civilian Complaint Review Board, the CCRB. But they all get logged.

(A word here about the CCRB. Established in its current form in 1993, the CCRB is an independent civilian agency, not affiliated with the NYPD, that investigates all FADO complaints from the public—that is, Force (a cop roughed me up), Abuse of authority (a cop illegally searched my car), Discourtesy (a cop called me a "shithead"), and Offensive language (a cop used a racial or sexual slur against me). The CCRB has its own team of about a hundred fifty investigators who examine the allegations and the CCRB board then makes recommendations on discipline to the Department Advocate's Office, the NYPD's internal prosecutor. In serious or potentially criminal cases of alleged police excessive force—for example, if a suspect is injured, or if the individual officer has a series of complaints—IAB will also conduct its own concurrent but separate investigation. I should point out that in an average year the CCRB gets about five thousand complaints about cops—this in a city of eight million people—of which about half are fully investigated; only 1 or 2 percent of the complaints are eventually substantiated.

In any given year, the IAB command desk generates about fifty or sixty thousand logs, of which about a thousand will ultimately involve an IAB corruption or misconduct investigation—which has caused some confusion. At one point the head of the New York Civil Liberties Union (NYCLU)—and the press—took a look at the numbers and said: What? Internal Affairs is getting fifty thousand "logs" a year and only investigating a thousand misconduct allegations? They're ignoring tens of thousands of tips! It's a cover-up!

Well, I try to explain to them that a "log" is not a "tip," but simply a report of a call, or an action taken on a previous complaint; a single misconduct allegation may generate ten or twenty or more "logs" as the case progresses. I also try to explain that most of the calls the Command Center takes in do not involve corruption or misconduct allegations, or if they do, they're about other police agencies or they are outside IAB's area of primary authority. For example, of about two thousand civilian calls a year concerning alleged NYPD misconduct, about fifteen hundred are CCRB cases—That cop was rude to me! That cop put my handcuffs on too tight! Even though those complaints are referred to and investigated by CCRB, they still get a log number from us.

And I also try to explain that there are people out there like Barry from Brooklyn.

A call comes in to the Command Center and one of the POs on duty answers it the way he's been trained to do: Internal Affairs Command Center, Officer Smith speaking, how may I help you? But he barely gets the words out before the guy on the other end starts screaming.

He stabbed me in the eye! That cop stabbed me in the fucking eye! He was writing me a ticket and he took his pen and for no reason he stabbed me in my right eye!

We teach our intake officers to establish a rapport with callers, just as they'll have to do when they're interviewing witnesses or suspects as detectives. So Officer Smith says: Oh my goodness, that's terrible! Are you all right?

No, I'm not all right! the caller says. That cop stabbed me in my fucking eye!

Officer Smith finally gets him calmed down enough to get his name and address—he's Barry from Brooklyn—which he writes down in a log. He calls in a supervisor, a lieutenant, who sends a bus (an ambulance) to Barry's address, and calls the local precinct to have a patrol sergeant immediately respond to check on him. But when they get there, Barry's right eye is fine—and so is his left eye. There's no sign of any injury. Barry is still sticking to his story—That cop stabbed me in the eye!—but he doesn't have a name or a shield number or any other information. It's obvious that Barry is, well, a little mixed up.

And then a few days later the phone rings in the Command Center and it's Barry again. He stabbed me in the eye! That fucking cop took a pencil and stabbed me in my fucking right eye!

So just in case, we send a bus and a patrol supervisor again, and again, Barry's fine, physically, at least. And then a few days later Barry calls again, and then again a few days after that. Over the next six months, Barry calls the Command Center more than forty times—every call is logged—to report an eye-stabbing by a cop. The weapon allegedly used in each attack varies—a pen, a toothpick, a swizzle stick, a Popsicle stick—but Barry doggedly sticks to the basic story: That cop stabbed me in the eye! And then for some reason, Barry stops calling. Maybe he finally got back on his meds.

Or how about Mrs. Guzman in the Bronx? Poor Mrs. Guzman calls the IAB Command Center to report that every time a police car or ambulance goes by her apartment with its siren wailing, she loses bladder control—and she wants to know what are we going to do about it? We have to explain to her that as distressing and uncomfortable as we know her situation must be, there's really nothing the Internal Affairs Bureau can do, that emergency sirens are a public safety issue. We explain this to her more than thirty times over the course of a year—and each one of those thirty explanations becomes a "log" that the NYCLU thinks is a "tip" about police corruption and brutality.

Don't get me wrong. I'm not suggesting that a large percentage of the people who call IAB to complain about cops are EDPs. Most callers are people who honestly believe they have a legitimate complaint, and we'll help them as much as we can. And I'm not saying that the IAB citizen complaint system is perfect, either. We made some mistakes. But I can honestly say that while I was chief the Internal Affairs Bureau did its best to handle civilian complaints properly and effectively.

Like I said. There's a new IAB in town.

So that's how the new IAB is organized, and how it came to be. But maybe by now you're wondering, How do we actually do what we do? How do we keep honest cops honest? How do we protect good cops from false allegations?

And exactly how do we catch a crooked cop?

Chapter 4

TO CATCH A CROOKED COP

It starts with an accusation: There's this crooked cop . . .

The accusation may come in the form of a furtive, whispered call on our 1-800-PRIDE-PD line, and an anonymous cop will tell us, Look, I don't want to get involved, but there's these cops on midnights in the Nine-Nine, Smith and Jones and Alvarez, they're busting doors and ripping off drug dealers, that's all I'm gonna say, I won't call again—click!

Or maybe it's a woman who owns a bodega in Brooklyn, and she calls the regular IAB line and tells us, Hey, there's these two cops, they come into my store, and I didn't see them take it, but I've got money in a cigar box under the counter, and when the cops come in the money's there, and after they leave some of the money's gone, and no, I don't know the cops' names, but it happened on this day and at this time, and what are you gonna do about it?

Or maybe we get a call from another agency—the FBI, the DEA, another police department—and they tell us, Hey, we've got this informant who says he can give up some NYPD cops who did a hundred-thousand-dollar drug rip, are you interested? You bet we are.

Or maybe sometimes—actually, a lot—it's a cop's angry ex-wife looking to get even with a bad ex-husband, or a recently arrested perp looking for payback. We take those seriously, because who knows, they could be true.

But it's not just phone calls and tips that launch IAB investigations. Like I said, if the IAB really wants to fight police corruption and misconduct, we can't just wait for accusations against cops to come in over the transom. Sometimes we have to go out and look for corruption ourselves—and so we set up programs to do just that. And because everything in the NYPD has to have an acronym, we called those programs EDITs (Enforcement, Debriefing, Intelligence, and Testing) and AWAREs (Active Warrant Address Review and Enforcement).

Here's an example. In the NYPD, every arrestee being processed through the system is supposed to be "debriefed," meaning that squad detectives will ask him or her about other crimes they weren't necessarily involved in but that they may have information about: Do you have knowledge of any murders, shootings, robberies, illegal guns, drug dealing, police corruption or misconduct, rapes, assaults, and on and on—there's a long checklist the detectives go through. If a perp who's in for selling a couple of grams of crack knows who robbed that bodega on 164th Street the other day, the detective might offer to help him work out a deal for a reduced sentence on the crack charge in exchange for solid information that leads to an arrest on the armed robbery.

Which is fine. That's the way the system works, in the NYPD and in every other law enforcement agency in America. You may be a low-life, crack-slinging skell, but if you do something nice for us—which is to say, if you give us somebody who's a worse crook than you are—in return we'll do something nice for you.

The problem for us in IAB is that too often the precinct detectives will skip over the "police corruption or misconduct" part of the checklist. They'll say something like, You don't know anything about police corruption or misconduct, right? Good, let's move on. Being cops, they aren't looking that hard for misconduct allegations against other cops.

But we are. That's our job—and that's where EDITs come in. At least once a week, in every borough command, a team of IAB detectives goes out and debriefs perps who are being booked, or re-debriefs perps who have already been debriefed by the squad detectives. And if one of those perps says he knows about a cop ripping off a drug dealer or stealing money or beating people up, we'll work with the guy.

Yo, there's this cop in New Lots, the perp might say, I don't know his name, but I seen it, he banged Tay Weez and took his money.

Really? Tell us more.

Sometimes we won't wait for the perps to be arrested by other cops; we go out and arrest them ourselves. For example, a lot of our guys worked in Narcotics before we drafted them into IAB, and they know how to work a drug set. So they go out to a dope spot in Brooklyn or the Bronx, make some drug buys, make some collars, take the perps to the local precinct and go through the checklist: Do you have knowledge of any murders, shootings, robberies, illegal guns, drug dealing, police corruption or misconduct, rapes, assaults . . . If the perp gives up another criminal on a murder or a gun or a robbery or whatever, we'll hand him over to the regular squad detectives. If he gives us an allegedly crooked cop, he's ours.

Same thing with the AWARE program. Our IAB guys go out and pick up people who have outstanding warrants—usually for relatively minor stuff, like subway fare beating or a summons for public urination, stuff they forgot to show up in court for—and put them through the drill: Do you have any knowledge of . . .

Over the years we debriefed thousands of perps, and arrested hundreds more, and developed information on more than twenty-five hundred non-cop-related crimes that we handed over to other detectives. And while it didn't happen often, maybe a dozen times a year, every now and then one of those perps would tell us, There's this crooked cop . . .

So now we've got an allegation against a cop or cops—from a perp or a bodega owner or a nervous anonymous cop or another law enforcement agency or from our own EDIT and AWARE programs. But at this point, it's just that—an allegation, an accusation.

Now we have to find out if it's true.

Sure, sometimes we catch a cop corruption case with a nice neat bow on it, a case that's easy to make. For example, we once got a call on our PRIDE line from a nervous cop in a precinct in Queens. They've been having a string of bank robberies in the precinct, one-on-one "note job" robberies in which a bank robber confronts an individual teller and hands her a note that says: Give me the money in your cash drawer or else! This guy has hit four banks for a total of about $17,000, so they've posted a bank surveillance photo of the robber on a "Wanted for Bank Robbery" poster in the precinct muster room. The thing is, while the cop calling on the PRIDE line can't be sure, he says the surveillance photo looks a whole lot like another cop who works in the same precinct.

So we yank the suspect cop's official Department photo and compare it to the surveillance shot, and yeah, that's the guy. It also helps that we find out that at the exact time of every robbery the cop had checked out in civilian clothes to run a personal errand—the personal errand being to rob a bank. We pick him up, he confesses—I needed the money, he tells us, which is something we hear a lot—we kick him out of the Department, and he does five years in prison. (After he gets out, he actually lands another city job, driving a bus in Brooklyn.)

Unfortunately, most of our cases aren't that simple. Usually when we have an allegation against a cop, we can't just go out and scoop him up, take his badge and shield, and put him on desk duty while we investigate. That's especially true if the only thing we've got is an anonymous voice on the phone, or the uncertain memory of a victim, or an accusation from a perp who's trying to get out from under a charge. Again, our job in IAB is not only to catch crooked cops, but to protect innocent ones. We aren't going to put a cop on modified duty and damage his career unless we're pretty sure the allegation against him is true. Besides, if there is corruption, we also want to find out if any other cops are involved before we make any overt moves.

So unless the accused cop (or cops) poses an immediate danger, we'll leave him out there while we try to figure out: Who is this guy?

There have been numerous academic studies of police corruption and misconduct over the years—I've studied it a lot myself—and it would be nice if there were some consistent indicator, some reliable red flag in a cop's background to tell us if he or she is likely to be corrupt or brutal.

Yes, you can make a few generalities: better-educated cops are statistically less likely to be corrupt than lesser-educated ones; corrupt female cops are statistically less common than corrupt male cops; cops who were hired when the Department had to lower its standards to bring in enough recruits—the 1980s are an example—sometimes had incomplete background checks, and a few were criminals even before they became crooked cops, so there's a somewhat higher proportion of dirty cops in that cohort.

But to an IAB investigator those generalities are pretty much useless. An investigator can only safely assume that all corrupt cops are white, except when they're black or Hispanic or Asian, that they all grew up poor in the ghetto, except for the ones who grew up in middle-class suburbs, that they're all young, except for the old ones, or they're all males, except for the female ones . . .

Well, you get the point. There is no typical corrupt cop.

And there's no typical reason why cops decide to cross the line into corruption, either. Whenever we arrest a corrupt cop we always try to ask him why he did it, what made him steal from a DOA or shake down a drug dealer or whatever it was he'd been caught doing; on a few occasions it could even be a condition of a plea agreement with the prosecutor that the cop allow IAB to debrief him about his motives. As you might expect with cops caught for financial corruption, most of them say they simply needed extra money, like that cop who was robbing banks. But their underlying reasons vary as widely as they do in the civilian world: I'm going through a bad divorce, my child support payments are killing me, I'm a gambling addict, I just want a few of the little extras in life—a boat, a house in the country, expensive vacations with the wife, or with the girlfriend that the wife doesn't know about.

But whatever the reason, it's a fool's calculation. A crooked Wall Street hedge fund manager might be able to make tens of millions of dollars through his crimes, but no NYPD cop ever did; they just don't have the opportunities. For a crooked cop, it's a few hundred here, on rare occasions maybe ten or twenty grand there, on even rarer occasions maybe a hundred grand if they rip off a major drug dealer. But compared to what they're giving up, it's chump change. As chief of IAB, I would regularly go to the Academy and talk to the recruits about what I called "the Million Dollar Mistake." If you get caught up in corruption, I tell them, not only have you given up your honor, and your job, and your salary, and your freedom, but we're also going to take away your pension—a pension that over the course of twenty years can amount to well over a million dollars. I tell them, even if you can't think of another reason not to be a corrupt cop—and there are many—do yourself a favor and do the math.

So anyway, there is no hard-and-fast profile of a "typical" corrupt cop. Still, if you pull an accused cop's package, his personnel file—and that's one of the first things we do—and if you pore through other available records, there are some things that can stand out. None of them is proof of anything, but . . .

One of the things we'll look for is criminal associations in his background. Remember how I said that during my NYPD application process I had to list not only all my family members but almost everyone I ever knew? Well, maybe it's not relevant that a cop's second cousin or best friend from high school is now ganged up or Mobbed up or just got out of prison on a drug-dealing charge . . . but maybe it is. In New York City especially, ties to family and neighborhood are strong—sometimes strong enough to induce a cop to cross the line, or to continue in a family business that's already on the other side of the line.

For example, we had one cop under investigation for money laundering, taking the proceeds from a large-scale counterfeit sports apparel operation—fake NFL and Major League Baseball jerseys, that kind of thing—and making "structured" cash deposits in banks to avoid reporting requirements. When we pull his PA-15 (his Academy application) and run some names, we find that his father, his mother, and his brother have all done prison time for—you guessed it—money laundering and counterfeit goods trafficking. It's not always true, but sometimes the apple really doesn't fall far from the tree.

There are other things to look for. Has the cop in question bounced around from precinct to precinct? Okay, maybe he just likes a change of scenery—or maybe the other cops don't like to work with him, or his CO got suspicious and palmed him off on somebody else. Does the cop have a lot of Civilian Complaint Review Board complaints, even if most of them are unsubstantiated? It could just be that he's a hard charger, that he makes a lot of arrests, and everybody knows that the more arrests you make the more CCRB complaints you're going to accumulate. But it could also indicate there's a problem there.

On the other hand, is the cop a guy who used to make a dozen arrests a month and now makes zero? For a cop, an arrest usually means overtime pay, time-and-a-half, especially if he makes the collar near the end of his shift, because it takes hours, even a full day, to process a perp into the system. It's what's known in the NYPD as "collars for dollars." Some cops don't need or want the overtime, so they let their partners take the collars, but when a former hard-charger suddenly stops making arrests, it might mean something. It might mean he's got a new girlfriend who requires his attention. It might mean he's studying for the sergeant's exam and he just doesn't have the time, or it could be that he's taken a part-time moonlighting job for some extra income. Or maybe, just maybe, it means he doesn't need the arrest overtime because he's suddenly found an alternate method of increasing his income.

If there's a credible allegation against a cop you can also do a financial check. Does he have an off-duty job or side business, maybe a barbershop or a car repair place, that's in a high-crime or corruption-prone area? (All NYPD cops are required to register off-duty jobs or side businesses with the Department.) You can't get the guy's bank and credit card statements without a court order, and you aren't going to get a court order based solely on suspicions. But you can check public records. Does he drive a brand-new BMW or a ten-year-old Dodge Caravan? Does he have a nice house in Westchester, and a mountain cabin in the Catskills, and a beach place on Long Island? Well, maybe his parents are rich, or his wife is, but one thing's for certain: He's not paying for all that just on a cop's salary.

Depending on the case, maybe we'll also quietly reach out to the accused cop's CO, or to people we trust who used to work with him, or to the anonymous IAB field associate in the unit. (Field associates are regular cops recruited out of the Academy by IAB to let us know if they see or hear of corruption or serious misconduct problems within their units.) We ask them, what kind of cop is this guy? What's his reputation? Do other cops not like to work with him? Who's he tight with, and what kind of cops are they? What do the other cops call him? Does he have a nickname? Believe it or not, sometimes a cop's nickname can tell us a lot.

A lot of cops have nicknames—not nicknames like Charlie or Bobby or Bill, but street nicknames. Other cops will start calling them something based on their appearance or their personality or whatever and the name will just stick. They'll call one cop "Cheese," because his last name is Romano, and this one is "Too-Tall" because he's six-five, and this one is "Robo-Cop," because he's a policing machine, and this guy is "Pops," because he's a thirty-five-year-old rookie, or because his name is Popavich. And on and on.

Usually the nicknames are innocuous. But what if you have a cop that the other cops call "The Mechanic"? Is it because he likes to work on cars? Or is it because he gives "tune-ups"—beatings—to suspects?

If a cop's got a nickname that sounds aggressive or even just strange—
Killer, Thumper, Cuckoo—you have to ask yourself why.

Like the case of the cop known as "Psycho Sarge."

This is early on in my time at IAB. There's this sergeant in the 19th
Precinct in Manhattan, in a lot of ways he's a good cop, with tons of
arrests, medals, awards. But he's got an alcohol problem, and when he's
indulging his alcohol problem he also has a problem with women. One
night the sergeant gets drunked up at an Upper East Side bar and he sees
this young female rookie cop—the sergeant is her training officer—
come in, and he starts pawing her and making lewd comments, really
making a scene. She's understandably upset, so she files a sexual harassment complaint with the Department's Office of Equal Employment
Opportunity. When the sergeant hears about the complaint he grabs
the rookie's arm in the precinct station house, drags her up to the roof,
and tells her if she doesn't agree to drop the complaint he's going to
throw her off the roof! She believes him—and when she gets away she
calls IAB.

This is serious. So in this case we immediately go out and take the
sergeant's gun and shield and put him on modified duty in another unit,
answering phones or whatever, while the case is investigated. (He's later
fired.) Later that day I'm talking to the precinct CO, a deputy inspector,
about this sergeant, and the CO mentions, casually, in passing: Yeah,
the other guys all call him Psycho Sarge, I don't know why . . .

Wait a minute, I tell him. Psycho Sarge? *Psycho Sarge?* You've got a
cop, a supervisor, under your command that the other cops call Psycho
Sarge, and you never bothered to find out if the reason they call him that
is: (1) he's psychotically obsessive about proper paperwork; or (2) he's
the kind of dangerous nut job who threatens to throw another cop off a
freaking roof?

I can hardly believe it. It's a failure of command—and the kind of
thing that drives me crazy.

(By the way, except for "Charlie" the only nickname I ever had—that I
know of—was when I was CO in the Sixth Precinct, and my high expectations and attention to detail led some of my less motivated cops to start
calling me Captain Can't-Please-Me. Campisi, Can't-Please-Me, get it?
But I could live with that. At least they weren't calling me Psycho CO.)

So anyway, now that we've got a feel for who this cop is, we'll go out and shake the trees a little—and how we do it depends on the case.

Sometimes we might do a "lifestyle" surveillance on the cop or cops in question, follow them around, see where they go, on-duty and off. Do they head home to the wife and kids after work, or do they hit the bars and strip joints? Who are they hanging out with? Are they visiting known gambling locations or unlicensed social clubs? That's a violation of Department rules, and they can take an administrative hit for it, but it's not necessarily a crime.

You have to be careful when you put a tail on another cop. Our IAB surveillance guys are some of the best in the business—they have to be—and we certainly aren't going to tail a cop with two guys in suits in a stripped-down Crown Victoria; you do that, you might as well put a big flashing sign on the windshield that says "IAB." Like on any surveillance, when you're tailing a cop you use vehicles that fit into the background, with plates that won't come back as being registered to the NYPD. IAB has a fleet of available undercover vehicles—upscale "flash" cars, 200,000-mile beaters, yellow cabs, UPS-style step-vans, a city ambulance, you name it; once we even rented a boat.

But every NYPD cop has had at least some training in surveillance techniques, and cops notice things other people might not. So no matter how good you are, if you tail a cop too close, or stay on him too long, there's a chance that eventually you're going to get made—that is, recognized as being a tail. And at that point, the investigation is blown.

Again, it depends on the case, but we may also start looking for other victims of the accused cop—like what we do with the EDIT debriefing program, but focused on this particular cop. If, say, the allegation is that the cop is arresting low-level drug dealers and stealing their money, maybe we'll check the records, see who the cop has arrested recently, and then send some IAB detectives out to talk to them. We don't tell them we're IAB, or even the name of the specific cop we're interested in, because maybe the drug dealer will try to sell that information back to the cop in return for a get-out-of-jail-free card—and we don't want the cop to know that IAB is asking questions about him.

So maybe we'll tell the perp that we're with the NYPD Quality Assurance Division—there really is such a thing—and we're doing a survey of people who've had contact with the police, and would he mind answering just a few questions? More times than you might think, the perp will go for it. We know from this drug dealer's RAP sheet—Record of Arrests and Prosecutions—that he's been arrested twenty or thirty times in his career, by a lot of different cops. So after a series of innocuous questions, we'll ask him, casually: Did you ever have any problems with the cops who arrested you? You get ripped off? Kicked around? And maybe he'll say: Yeah, there's this one cop, Officer X, he ripped me for a couple hundred, ain't no big thing . . . And that will be our guy.

It's not enough to file a criminal case against the cop, of course; a street mope with thirty arrests on his record, a couple of felony convictions, and some prison time upstate isn't going to shine on the witness stand, even if we can get him to testify. And even if you line up three or four more drug-dealing street mopes with similar allegations against the cop, a jury's probably not going to believe them. To a jury, and a defense attorney, witnesses like that are just another way of saying "reasonable doubt."

That's a big problem with making cases against crooked cops. Let's face it, crooked cops aren't jacking up Wall Street hedge fund managers and stealing their Rolexes, or beating up suburban housewives in interrogation rooms in the Bronx. In most police corruption or misconduct cases—not all, but most—your witnesses are going to be drug dealers or gang members or junkies or prostitutes, or sometimes they're corrupt cops who get caught and make a deal to testify against other cops. They all have credibility problems.

The bottom line is that in a lot of cases, it's difficult if not impossible to convict a dirty cop for past acts of corruption. There's just not enough evidence. It's a lot better if we can catch the cop red-handed, in the act.

But how do we do that? Like I said, we can't tail a suspected cop every minute for weeks or months, because we're probably going to get made eventually—and even if we don't, what are the chances we're going to get close enough to actually see, and videotape, the cop or cops in the act of committing a crime?

For example, say we've got a crew of cops working midnights in the Bronx who are suspected of booming the doors of drug dealers' apartments—that is, knocking them down with sledgehammers or rams—and then going in to steal money or drugs. Leaving aside the obvious problems with trying to tail a bunch of cops on otherwise deserted streets at four o'clock in the morning, even if we watch these guys go into an apartment building, and watch them come out, what have we got? Maybe they found some money or drugs, maybe they didn't. If we stop them and they're clean, the investigation is blown, and we're never going to get these guys. Even if we go in afterward and find the drug dealer who got hit, what's he going to say to us? Yes, I'm an active drug dealer, and those cops took my stash, and could you please make them give it back? Not likely.

So sometimes we can't wait for the crime to come to us. We have to be proactive and creative. We have to set up a situation, a scenario, in which a cop can choose whether or not to commit the kind of crime he's suspected of committing. In other words, we have to do what's known as a sting operation.

And to do a sting, we have to have great undercovers.

There's a big difference between undercovers and informants. Informants are civilians, usually criminals, who are working with the police in return for money or for help getting out from under a criminal charge; in the NYPD they're known as CIs, or confidential informants. Sometimes informants only provide information, and sometimes cops will use them to get inside a criminal operation, to make drug buys, for example, or to gather intelligence. Paid informants have to be registered as CIs with the Department, but they definitely are not cops.

Undercovers (known in NYPD-ese as "uncles"), on the other hand, are cops, fully sworn like any other cops, who are acting the parts of drug users, street skells, Mob guys—whatever is called for. Their job is to get close to criminals, make drug buys, get intelligence on an upcoming score, secretly record their conversations, whatever the case requires—and because they're cops, they're a million times more cred-ible and more reliable than a CI. Most undercovers are new police offi-cers who want to get their eighteen months of investigative experience and earn their gold detective shields, but others are veterans who just like the work. (Undercovers shouldn't be confused with "plainclothes" cops, who wear civilian clothes but are instantly recognizable as cops by anyone with street smarts.)

Obviously, undercovers can't look like cops. Your best undercovers are going to look too young to be cops, or too emaciated, or too short, or too weak, or too whatever. In some cases your undercover can't smell like a cop, either. If an uncle is posing as a street skell junkie who sleeps in an alley, he'd better not smell like Irish Spring.

But it's not just looks; undercovers also have to talk and act the part. An undercover has to be able to twitch like a junkie who feels the sickness coming on, or chatter like a crackhead who's just hit the stem, or exude menace like a major drug trafficker. Undercovers have to be actors at heart, and in fact, we would often hire professional actors to come in and train our IAB undercovers in the finer points of the Stanislavski method—as in, Okay, I'm playing a crack slinger on the corner of Livonia and Stone in Brownsville. What's my motivation?

Obviously, being an undercover can be dangerous work. Unlike an actor, an undercover cop who flubs his lines or fails to play his role effectively isn't going to get a bad review in the Arts section of the *New York Times*; he runs the risk of getting a bullet in the head. An undercover can't wear a vest or carry a shield when he's working, and unless it fits in with his undercover character, he can't carry a gun, either. So in almost every case, an undercover will have "ghosts" backing him up, other undercovers who can blend into the background and move in if there's trouble. But the situation, the "set," in an undercover operation is always fluid, so on rare occasions an uncle might find himself on his own.

In IAB we had about two dozen undercovers on a permanent basis, and we could get more if we needed them. Some were drafted into IAB, while others were brought in by our detectives who worked with them in the past. In my opinion they were some of the best undercovers in the Department—again, they had to be, because they weren't going undercover against ordinary criminals; they were going undercover against other cops.

Undercovers come in all shapes. For example, we had a female officer whose parents were born in India; dressed in a sari, nobody was ever going to make her for a cop. Same thing with another female officer, who was in her mid-thirties but had prematurely gray hair; give her a little makeup, put her in a frumpy housecoat, hand her a leash with a miniature schnauzer at the end of it—she provided the schnauzer—and she was an old lady walking her dog, a perfect ghost. Another one of our uncles was a first grade detective with twenty years on the job; a few gold chains, a big pinky ring, and a flash car from the IAB garage and he could "dese" and "dems" and "doze" his way into making even streetwise cops believe he was a Mob wannabe from Jersey.

But on a sting operation against a corrupt cop, we don't want to just see the cop steal the money. We want to catch it on videotape. And for that we call in the tech geeks.

The NYPD's Technical Assistance Response Unit (TARU) provides equipment and expertise to any Department unit that needs recording devices, surveillance cameras, wiretaps, GPS tracking devices (known as "bird dogs," they usually require a court order), and other technical equipment. IAB had first crack at any TARU stuff we needed—the other bureau chiefs sometimes bitched about it, but the commissioner always backed us up—and we also had our own group of seven or eight IAB technical guys based in a warehouse complex in Queens, a sort of mini-TARU, who were experts in deploying surveillance equipment. If they saw some gizmo in a technology magazine that looked cool, and if TARU didn't have it, we could bypass channels and dip into our $2 million operations budget and buy it—making sure to get a receipt, of course.

When I started in IAB in the mid-1990s, and even more so now, the available surveillance technology—pinhole cameras, microrecorders and transmitters, and so on—was pretty amazing. Although putting a hidden recording device on someone is still known as "wearing a wire," the days of taping a bulky Nagra tape recorder to an undercover's body and hoping he doesn't get searched are long over; now you can put an audio recorder in a watch or put a camera in a button.

So anyway, if we've got a cop we suspect of corruption, we line up our undercovers, get our tech guys set up, and come up with a plan, a scenario. We plan it down to the last detail.

Then we put the cop to the test . . .

Chapter 5

TESTING, TESTING, TESTING . . .

It's a Friday afternoon on the Major Deegan Expressway in the Bronx, and even though the traffic is backed up for miles, the sergeant is feeling pretty good. He's heading home to Westchester, the weekend is ahead, time for barbecue and cold beers, and best of all, he's got three hundred twenty dollars in cash—tax free—sitting in his back pocket.

We can guess what he's probably thinking. He's thinking it's not the best score he ever made, but it's not the worst, either. He could have gotten more, but you don't want to get too greedy with these things. You wait for the right opportunity to come along, and when it does you don't take it all, just a little off the top, a few hundred here, a couple hundred there, not enough for anybody to get too excited about. As long as you're smart about it, as long as you're careful, there's no way you're ever going to get caught.

But if that's what the sergeant is thinking, he's wrong. Although he doesn't know it yet, he's already been caught. We watched him take that money that's in his pocket, and we're watching him right now.

And in just a few minutes, life as the sergeant knows it is going to come to an end.

The sergeant's trouble had begun two weeks ago, when we got an anonymous call on our PRIDE line, the one reserved for cops, and the unknown caller tells us there's this Conditions sergeant in a Bronx precinct, he's being funny with the money. Whenever they're on a call and there's money around he always wants to control it, he always personally vouchers it, or at least some of it, but it's weird, and we should check him out—click! The call has the ring of truth, and when we shake the trees a little, check around with people we could trust, we find that while there isn't enough there to make a corruption case against the sergeant, there is enough for us to believe that there might be a corruption case to be made.

And so the night before the sergeant heads home on the Major Deegan, this young Hispanic woman stands up at a Community Council meeting and starts complaining to the precinct CO about a guy selling dope in a park.

Like every precinct commanding officer in the NYPD, one night every month the CO has to go down to the Community Council meeting at the senior center or the Baptist church or wherever to meet with local citizens and talk about problems in the neighborhood; it's part of the community policing thing. At this meeting, the young woman is giving the CO an earful.

There's this guy selling dope by the park near my house! she says. Right by the park! He's got a light blue Chevy SUV that he parks right there and he stands there selling marijuana! In the daytime! Every afternoon! I'm afraid to even take my kids to the park! You're the police! What are you gonna do about it?

So the CO's aide takes down the information and the CO tells the woman: Yes, ma'am, I'll have my Conditions Team look into it. The precinct Conditions Team is half a dozen cops whose primary job is to respond to various quality-of-life complaints—teenagers hanging out and drinking in a parking lot, winos relieving themselves in an alley behind a bodega, some guy slinging reefer by a park. Whenever the CO catches a headache at a CC meeting, it's usually the Conditions Team's job to make the headache go away.

The sergeant is the head of the Conditions Team. So the next day the CO calls him in and tells him about the alleged drug slinger by the park and tells him to take care of it, get the guy out of there, and report back to him when it's done. No problem, boss, the sergeant says, and a few minutes later he grabs one of his guys and they head out for the park. The sergeant and his partner, a police officer, are both in plainclothes— jeans and a polo shirt for the partner, the sergeant in a Yankees jersey, No. 44, Reggie Jackson's old number, with their NYPD shields hanging around their necks—and they're driving a beat-up, unmarked black Chevy. No one could mistake them for anything other than cops.

They get to the park, and, sure enough, here's the guy, male, black, late twenties, sitting in a light blue Chevy SUV parked on the street. The sergeant walks up to the driver's-side window while his partner takes up a tactical position on the passenger side. The sergeant starts talking to the driver, and the more the sergeant talks to him the more nervous and evasive the driver seems. He's got an ex-con, cop-hating sullenness about him, and a career perp's darting eyes.

Excuse me, sir, the sergeant says, can I ask what you're doing here today? You're waiting for your friend? Yeah, what's his name? Ummm? Whaddaya mean, ummm? Your friend's name is Ummm? Oh, now you remember, it's Steve. Does Steve live around here? Yeah? Which building? What floor? Can't remember that, either, huh? Would you mind stepping out of the car, please? Would you mind showing me some identification?

So the guy gets out of the car, and while the sergeant is talking to him, his partner is looking through the passenger-side windows. And there, partially wedged into the crack of the backseat, but still in plain view, is an open black plastic bag full of smaller plastic bags containing what is obviously marijuana; it's weed packaged for sale. Contraband in plain view gives the partner the legal right to search the car—remember, from the Academy, SPACESHIPS—so he opens the door, grabs the bag of weed, and walks back over to the sergeant.

Yo, Sarge, the partner says, look at this. It was in the backseat.

That's it. More than two ounces of marijuana is an "A" misdemeanor, so this guy is no longer a citizen; now he's a perp. The sergeant rear-cuffs him and stands him up by the rear door of the SUV to search him, the perp protesting all the while: What are you arrestin' me for? I ain't done nothing! Fuckin' cops! He doesn't have any weapons, but as the sergeant is frisking him, he feels a large, soft bulge in the front pocket of the guy's pants. He reaches in the pocket and pulls out a big roll of cash, mostly twenties and tens.

Whoa! the sergeant is probably thinking. What have we got here?

While his partner watches the perp, the sergeant backs into the SUV's open door, almost into the driver's side of the compartment, his hands out of his partner's line of sight, and starts counting the money. As he's counting he calls out to the perp: How much money is this?

I dunno, the perp says, his back to the sergeant.

How much money you got here? the sergeant asks again.

I dunno, I just got paid, and my cousin give me some money he owed me and . . .

The sergeant's partner is watching all this with a kind of confused look on his face. He's probably thinking, What the hell is Sarge doin'? Why's he asking about the money? And why's he standing like that? Tactically, it's not the way you should do it. It's kind of weird. And it's not the first time, either.

How much money is this? the sergeant says again, and the perp finally says, Shit, I dunno, maybe seven, eight hundred dollars? How the fuck I supposta know how much money I got in my fuckin' pocket?

The sergeant smiles. This mutt doesn't even know how much money he has. The sergeant keeps on counting the money, which comes to exactly eleven hundred forty dollars. Then he splits it up into two separate rolls of cash, one bigger than the other, and puts them both in his left rear pocket.

Well, okay, it's not unusual during an arrest and search for a cop to put money or drugs in his pocket. He has to keep control of them, and he needs to keep his hands free to continue the search. But why did the sergeant split the money into two wads of cash?

Now, at this point, does the sergeant sense or suspect anything? Does he imagine that all of the bills in his back pocket have been photocopied and their serial numbers recorded by us, and then marked with a UV pen? Does he imagine that the sullen, perp-eyed drug dealer he has in cuffs is actually one of our undercovers, an IAB detective? Or that the marijuana is ours, too, evidence from an old case that was about to be routinely destroyed? Does he notice the young Hispanic guy riding the bike by the park, or the young black girl sitting on the park bench with a school book bag beside her, talking on a cell phone—and if he does notice them, does he realize that they are our "ghosts," our backup undercovers, put there to step in if anything goes wrong? Does he notice the empty parked car on the other side of the intersection with the Kleenex box on the deck under the rear window, or the gray van down the street with the tinted windows? Does he imagine that there's a camera in the Kleenex box, and another camera in the van? Does he know how many people are watching him?

Obviously he doesn't sense or imagine any of these things. Because a moment later, the sergeant turns the perp around, then reaches into his back pocket and pulls out the larger wad of cash. He holds it up in the air and makes a big show out of saying to the perp, Here, I'm giving you your money back! He shoves the larger wad of cash into the perp's pocket, while the smaller wad stays in his own back pocket.

It's a classic street skim, a traditional sleight of hand.

And now the sergeant belongs to us.

Yes, it's possible that before end of shift some twinge of conscience or creeping suspicion will cause the sergeant to suddenly "remember" that cash in his back pocket and voucher it at the precinct; we'll have to check on that. But we know in our hearts that's not going to happen.

The sergeant and his partner load the marijuana and the perp into their car and head back to the precinct. The partner takes the collar and starts processing the perp through the system. He vouchers the marijuana and then he runs the perp's prints through the database in Albany; we've already set it up so that our uncle's prints come back as belonging not to a cop but to a small-time dealer with a few priors, a short time upstate, and no current warrants. The sergeant probably notices that while the perp's personal belongings are being vouchered and bagged in front of him—keys, lighter, cigarettes, the remaining wad of cash, which comes to exactly $820—the perp doesn't complain about any money being missing. That's good for the sergeant, but even if the perp did complain, so what? Perps complain all the time—that cop hit me, he took my money, those aren't my drugs, that cop planted them on me, he flaked me, and so on. Nobody's going to believe him.

With the perp locked up the sergeant reports to the CO that the problem in the park is solved, they've got a good collar, drugs seized and vouchered—mission accomplished. The sergeant goes back to his desk and starts plowing through some routine paperwork. People are coming and going in the precinct all the time, so the sergeant probably doesn't notice the detective in a suit and tie who comes in and passes by the holding cells. The sergeant doesn't pay attention when the drug dealer in a cell calls out to the detective: Yo, you the boss around here? I gotta piss! Tell 'em to take me to the goddam bathroom! The detective ignores him and keeps walking. The sergeant doesn't realize that the detective is one of ours, and that the piss-call from the perp is a signal that the sergeant didn't voucher all the money.

Finally it's the sergeant's end of tour, and a few minutes later he's on the Major Deegan Expressway, thinking about cold beers and barbecue.

The sergeant is coming into Van Cortlandt Park when he notices that right behind him there's a blue-and-white NYPD patrol car with two uniformed cops in it. They turn on the lights and give him a single yelp on the siren and pull him over.

The sergeant probably isn't too worried; he doesn't associate the uniformed cops with the stolen money in his back pocket. Maybe he's got a burned-out brake light or something, in which case he'll just badge them, show them his NYPD shield, and be on his way. He knows that if he was really in trouble, they'd send detectives after him, not uniforms.

This is what we want him to think. The two uniformed cops are actually IAB detectives, temporarily back in uniform to put the sergeant's mind at ease. The sergeant has a loaded gun on him, and it's always possible that if he suspects he's been caught he'll resist, or as has happened before with corrupt cops who get caught, he'll eat his gun and blow his brains out. If he's going to freak out, we want to get his gun first.

The uniformed cops walk up to the car, one on each side, and the sergeant already has his shield out in the open window. The driver's-side cop is apologetic, soothing: Oh, gosh, Sarge, we didn't know you're on the job, but there's something wrong with your right rear wheel, could you step out for just a second and take a look? Maybe the sergeant doesn't really believe it, but he wants to believe it, so he gets out of the car and the two uniforms quickly move in close, not rough but close. They ease his gun out of its holster and pat him down and take the wad of bills out of his back pocket. The sergeant sees that there's another car parked behind the NYPD patrol car, an unmarked sedan, and two guys in suits and ties are walking toward him, and now he knows for certain. He knows who they are.

They're us. They're IAB.

And what the sergeant says is: Oh shit.

There's no shouting, no rough treatment. The IAB guys, a lieutenant and a detective, don't handcuff the sergeant, or even take his shield.

Instead they put the money in an envelope, then they ease the sergeant into the backseat of the sedan, and head back into the Bronx.

We can guess what the sergeant is thinking at this point. We've seen it before. The sergeant is trying not to panic; he's thinking there's gotta be a way out of this. Maybe he can insist that the cash in his back pocket is his, maybe all we've got on him is that after he left the precinct the perp in the holding cell started claiming that the cops stole his money—and who are they gonna believe, some drug-slinging skell or another cop with twelve good years on the job? Or maybe he'll tell us that it was a mistake, that he put the drug dealer's cash in his back pocket when he was making the arrest, and when he pulled the wad back out he accidentally left some of the bills in his pocket. In fact, he had just noticed that money in his pocket and was about to turn around and go back to the precinct and voucher it when the uniforms pulled him over! Yeah, he knows it's weak, he knows we won't believe him, but hey, it's not what we believe, it's what we can prove.

And besides, the sergeant may be thinking, what did he do that was really so bad? Take a few hundred bucks from a drug dealer? Big fucking deal. Everybody does it. They always have. And after all the years he's given the Department, the shitty hours, the lousy pay—you try paying off a mortgage and sending two kids to private school on a cop's pay—doesn't he deserve a little extra now and then? These guys are cops. They can understand that.

The sergeant starts to speak, to try to explain, but the lieutenant next to him in the backseat cuts him off, gently.

Look, Sarge, do us a favor and don't say anything, okay? Give us some time to figure out how we can fix this.

It's a glimmer of hope, a false one, but the sergeant seizes on it. He doesn't say anything more.

They bring the sergeant to the Bronx District Attorney's Office, to a windowless interview room on an upper floor, where we sit him down at a bare table. The ADA assigned to the case is already there. We read the sergeant his rights, and then we tell him: Don't say anything, just listen. We know you took the money. Now we want to give you an opportunity to help yourself.

There are some things we don't tell the sergeant, because he doesn't need to know. We don't tell him about the call to our PRIDE line, tipping us off that the sergeant was stealing, which set the investigation in motion. We don't tell him that the woman who complained at the Community Council about the drug dealer by the park is one of our undercovers, and that we knew the precinct CO would send him, his Conditions sergeant, to check out the complaint. (In most cases we would advise the CO if we were doing an undercover operation in his precinct, and ask him to cooperate with us, but for various reasons—nothing sinister—in this case we didn't.)

Although he's probably already figured it out, we don't tell the sergeant that from start to finish, this whole thing was carefully planned and orchestrated by us to see if he would do again what he was suspected of doing before.

It was a test. And the sergeant has failed it.

And there's one other thing we don't tell the sergeant. We don't tell him that while we feel sorry for his wife and family, for him we feel . . . nothing. We're not crusaders, or zealots, and we don't gain any particular pleasure—or pain—in catching another cop committing a crime. It's our job. Yes, it's embarrassing that there are cops like him in the Department, but there will always be a few cops like him, just as there will always be criminals. And as far as we're concerned, the sergeant isn't even a cop anymore, he stopped being a cop the minute he started stealing money. Now he's just another perp.

We don't tell him all that, but with the videos and the marked bills, we show and tell him enough for him to understand that it's over; he's done. The sergeant is a big guy, over six feet, maybe two hundred pounds, but in a small voice he says: Okay, yeah, I took the money.

So we take a run at him: We'll do what we can for you, Sergeant, you can't be a police officer anymore, but maybe we can ask the DA to go easy on you. But you have to tell us the truth. How many other times have you stolen money? How about drugs? Who else is in on it? Will you work with us against other corrupt cops? C'mon, Sergeant, we're trying to help you here.

But the sergeant hangs tough.

No, he says, he never took any money before; this was the very first time. We know he's lying; this can't be the first time he's ripped off a collar, or rifled the pockets of an Aided case before the EMTs arrived, or snatched a couple of twenties off a dresser during a domestic call. No corrupt cop ever gets caught the first time. But we don't have enough hard evidence to prove it in court.

And no, he says, he can't help us make cases against other corrupt cops, because he doesn't know any other corrupt cops—and in the case of his fellow Conditions Team cops, that's probably true. Why else would the sergeant hide his hands from his partner's eyes when he skimmed the money? Later we interview all of them, including the partner on the videotapes, and they all tell us: No, we never dreamed that the Sarge was skimming—and even if we don't completely believe them, we still don't think they were in on it. We understand that, cops being cops, they don't want to be rats. None of them admits to being the cop who called our PRIDE line, although one of them tells us, in a low whisper, that he's glad we got the guy. Good job, he says.

So after we get all we're going to get out of the sergeant, we suspend him from the Department—which immediately stops his pay—and take his shield. One of our detectives leads him away to be booked and processed like any other criminal. Later his lawyer works out a deal with the DA: The sergeant pleads guilty to a misdemeanor, no jail time, community service, dismissal from the Department, no pension, no benefits. And then the sergeant, the former sergeant, disappears to wherever disgraced ex-cops go.

And we move on to the next test.

We call them "integrity tests," but they're popularly known as "sting operations." Integrity testing is another thing that sets the new IAB apart from the old IAD. In the past, using sting operations to catch corrupt cops was rare, only used once or twice a year. In the new, proactive IAB, we run about five or six hundred integrity tests of cops every year, setting up controlled situations in which a cop will have the opportunity to do the right thing or the wrong thing. The key is to make the situation seem real, so real that, like the sergeant in the Bronx, the cop in question doesn't suspect he's being tested.

The test of the sergeant in the Bronx was one example of a targeted integrity test. Here's another.

We get a tip that a cop in the 33rd Precinct in Washington Heights is stealing money from drug dealers. We rent a run-down apartment in the cop's usual patrol sector and tech it up with video cameras; we also rent another apartment in the building so we can monitor the video. While the cop is on patrol, our IAB undercovers, posing as DEA agents—not a stretch, since a lot of them previously were with the NYPD Narcotics Division—call the precinct desk and say they need a uniform to come by to assist. Since it's in the targeted cop's sector, dispatch sends him to our location. When the cop arrives at the apartment, the "DEA agents" tell him that they've got an arrest warrant on the guy who lives there, but when they kicked the door to serve the warrant the guy was gone. They're pretty sure there's money and drugs in there, but now they need a search warrant to toss the place, so while they go get the warrant they want the cop to sit in the apartment and grab the perp if he comes back. No problem, the cop says.

So as we're watching on the hidden surveillance cameras, the undercover IAB guys leave, and they're not gone three seconds before the cop starts looking around and—lo and behold!—he finds some heroin (actually pancake mix) and about $20,000 in bundles of marked IAB money hidden in the dresser drawers. He ignores the drugs, but he skims $6,000 of the cash—like the Bronx sergeant, they almost never take it all—and stuffs it under his protective vest. The DEA agents come back waving a phony search warrant and thank the cop for the help. The cop leaves and at the end of his shift he goes back to the precinct and doesn't voucher the cash hidden under his vest. He's arrested.

That was a relatively easy integrity test; some are more complicated. Like this one:

Two cops in a precinct in Brooklyn go to their precinct CO and tell him they suspect that another cop has been stealing from perps. They can't prove it, but they don't like it, they don't want to be around this guy, they're afraid of getting jammed up. (So much for the Blue Wall of Silence.) Instead of hiding the problem, the CO does the right thing and calls IAB. We tell him to sit tight; we'll handle it.

We approach a bodega owner on the cop's beat and get him to cooperate with us, and he lets us put an IAB undercover in the bodega posing as a guy running a numbers game. Posing as detectives with the Organized Crime Control Bureau (OCCB), which handles illegal gambling cases, two IAB investigators approach the targeted cop while he's walking his foot post and show him a picture of the numbers guy. They tell him, Look, we're making a case on this guy in the bodega, he's making a lot of money, we don't want you to do anything, don't approach him, just keep an eye out, okay?

Sure, the cop says. Our undercovers give him a telephone number where he can reach them, and if the cop checks the NYPD directory he'll see that the number appears to belong to OCCB. In fact, the number goes to what's known as a "hello phone" in IAB headquarters. If a target calls the number, he's not going to hear "Internal Affairs, Detective Schmedlap speaking." Depending on the case, he's going to hear a simple "Hello"—or in this case, if the cop calls the number he'll hear, "OCCB, Detective Smith speaking."

Remember, we have to make this look real, so whenever the cop is in the area we send some of our undercovers into the bodega. Our guys go in, stay less than a minute, not even enough time for a cup of coffee, and they come out without buying anything. To anybody who's looking, including the cop, they look for all the world like numbers runners.

This goes on for a couple of weeks; we have to give the cop time to get comfortable with this. Then one day, while the cop is on post near the bodega, our OCCB detectives make a big show out of going into the bodega and arresting the numbers guy and hauling him out in cuffs. Naturally the cop runs over, and the detectives say: Thanks for the help, and could you do us a favor? Could you drive this guy's car to the precinct?

No problem, the cop says. The detectives hand the cop the keys to the perp's car that's parked down the street, and they load the perp into their car and disappear. The cop gets into the perp's car, an almost new Cadillac that's one of the "flash cars" we have in the IAB warehouse. The Caddie is fully equipped with our hidden videotape cameras.

So the cop heads for the precinct in the Caddie, and as expected, he starts checking the console box and glove box and under the seat, where he finds three stashes of cash we've put in there, about a thousand bucks in all, all of the bills photocopied and marked.

We can guess what the cop is thinking. He's thinking: Those OCCB guys didn't search the car, they don't know how much money's in here, if I take a little nobody's going to miss it, except possibly the perp—and screw him. The cop takes a couple hundred from each pile and puts it in his pocket—all clearly on tape. Again, we would have had a hard time proving past acts of corruption by this cop. But now we've got him dead to rights committing a current act of corruption. We arrest him, suspend him, and after he's brought up on criminal theft charges he's fired from the Department.

Okay, sure, there isn't much money involved. And we devoted a lot of time and resources to catching the guy. So is it worth it?

You bet it is. There's no such thing as small-time police corruption. And if we find a cop stealing, whether it's a few bucks or a hundred thousand—and we get both—we'll devote whatever resources are necessary to get him off the street.

We used the same basic principle to look for overly aggressive or violent cops as well. Here's how it worked:

We get a complaint against a cop for excessive force—I called that cop an asshole, the complainant says, and then he smacked me in the face for no reason! Well, maybe it happened that way, maybe it didn't. Since it's a FADO complaint and there's no serious injury we refer it to the CCRB, but when we pull the cop's package we see that he's had several excessive-force complaints. None was substantiated, but still, it's worth taking a look. So we open our own concurrent investigation, and we bring in our undercovers.

There's one, a young female officer who does a perfect crackhead, all skinny and jumpy and wild-eyed; she calls herself Millie the Crack Ho. We pair her up with another undercover, Marvin the long-haired, unwashed street drunk, and we put them on the cop's beat, surrounded by undercover ghosts and hidden surveillance cameras. When they see the cop coming, Millie and Marvin start to argue: You bitch! You asshole! You whore! So of course the cop comes over, and as so often happens in real life, Millie and Marvin suddenly aren't mad at each other anymore. They're mad at the cop.

Who the fuck asked you, you fuckin' cop! Mind your own fucking business! Get the fuck outta here! And so on.

During all this, Millie and Marvin are careful to keep their arms at their sides, hands in view, to do nothing that could be taken for physical aggression, or invite an arrest. They're just talking trash to a cop—and the question is, What does the cop do?

In one two-year period we ran dozens of these "force-related integrity tests" around the city, in various forms, and in almost every case the officer did what he was supposed to. He told them to break it up, move it along, and he ignored the curses and insults. In only four cases did the cops in question overreact, usually by sending the undercover participants an "asshole" or a "fuck you" back, in which case they got a little command counseling on the proper deportment of NYPD police officers. In only one case—the one with Millie and Marvin—did the officer physically overreact. As Marvin was walking away, still mouthing off, the cop took a run at him and pushed him from behind, almost knocking him to the ground, and threatened to kick his ass if he didn't shut the fuck up, and so on. That earned him a command discipline and lost vacation days.

Of course, those are just a few examples. As you'll see, we run other targeted integrity tests that are a lot more complicated, with informants, phone wiretaps, bugs, months-long surveillances, multiple targets. The targets aren't just uniformed patrol guys taking a few hundred here or there, either. But these examples give you an idea of how we do it.

Now, at this point I know what some of you are thinking, especially if you happen to be a criminal defense attorney or a Patrolmen's Benevolent Association union delegate. You're thinking: Hey, you can't do that! You entrapped those cops! Those cops wouldn't have, couldn't have stolen the money if you hadn't set up the whole thing and dangled it in front of their faces! It's not fair!

But it is fair. Cops use tricks to catch criminals all the time. Is there a rash of muggings of visiting Asian businessmen on the subways? The NYPD will put Asian American cops on the subways posing as businessmen, and when one of them gets mugged, the "businessman" and his backups will collar the muggers. Are old ladies getting their purses snatched in a certain neighborhood? A cop will put on a wig and a frumpy old dress and hobble down the street with a walker, and the next thing the purse snatcher knows the "old lady" has him up against a wall and under arrest.

Same thing with the integrity tests. In all the integrity tests we do, we run the scenario by the local DA's office beforehand to make sure we aren't coercing or encouraging the cop in any way to steal the money or drugs or to use excessive force. We simply set up situations in which a cop can choose of his own free will whether to do the right thing or the wrong thing. Calling that entrapment is like saying that a bank entrapped a bank robber just by being a bank.

But IAB integrity tests weren't limited only to cops that we already suspected of corruption or misconduct, though. We also did random integrity testing—and that was the most controversial anticorruption program we had.

In its simplest form, a random integrity test works like this: We send out our IAB undercovers posing as citizens, and they approach random cops on the street with a wallet or a purse containing cash and credit cards. Officer, officer, they'll say, I found this wallet (or purse) on the sidewalk. What should I do? Meanwhile, we'll have surveillance equipment filming the encounter.

And the question is, What does this cop do with the wallet?

Does he notify his patrol supervisor of "found property" and go through the proper steps to voucher it? If he does, he passes the test—although we won't ever tell him so, because we don't want to expose our integrity testing methods. On the other hand, does the cop tell the Good Samaritan that's he's too busy to take the wallet, that the Good Samaritan should just drop it in a mailbox and let the US Postal Service figure it out? In that case it's an administrative failure, a failure to follow proper procedures, and he'll probably wind up with a command discipline and loss of some vacation days. If the cop asks his sergeant what to do and the sergeant tells him to drop it in a mailbox, that's a supervisory failure, and the sergeant is going to take a hit.

But what if the cop takes the wallet, thanks the Good Samaritan, then ducks into an alley and takes the money? That's a criminal failure, and he's going to be arrested, suspended, and dismissed from the Department.

Again, that's the simplest form of random integrity test, one that we used a few times early on; most of the random tests we did were more elaborate. (Actually the random tests weren't completely random. Usually we would run them in precincts that had high rates of complaints against cops—missing property, excessive force, etc.—but we didn't have any specific cops identified.)

Here's one example of a random test. We get a city bus and stock it with IAB undercovers posing as passengers, another undercover as the driver (he has a commercial license), and still another undercover as a loud, unruly drunk with cash spilling out of his pockets. With our undercover cars trailing the bus, the driver starts down Broadway and puts "Call Police" on his destination sign, the signal that there's trouble on board. Naturally every cop the bus passes sees the sign and pulls it over and takes the obnoxious drunk off the bus. The question is, Will the cops take any of the money that's spilling out of the drunk guy's pockets?

Here's another. We rent a room in a sleazy hot-sheet motel and put in a male and a female IAB undercover posing as lovers having a loud argument—not violent, just loud, so the guy at the motel's front desk calls 911. When the cops show up, the female undercover is wailing— That bum! He lied to me! He didn't tell me he was married!—and she runs into the bathroom. The male undercover just wants to leave—That broad's nuts! I just wanna get outta here!—and since there's been no violence the cops let him go. The question is, With the guy gone, and the woman crying in the bathroom, do the cops take any of the money or jewelry that's lying on the dresser?

Some of the random integrity tests were a lot more complicated and lengthy. And sometimes they brought unintended results . . . like the Shop Right Collision auto repair shop scenario.

We're getting complaints from some tow-truck drivers that cops aren't following the proper rotation for calling tow trucks to accident scenes or breakdowns. Towing is a cutthroat business in New York, not so much for the towing fees but for the repair charges an auto shop can squeeze out of a customer if its tow driver gets the tow. In the old days, pre-Knapp, it was routine for drivers to pay cops ten or fifteen bucks to give them the tow—not much money, but still corruption. The practice had pretty much disappeared since then, but we're wondering if maybe it's coming back.

So working with the Brooklyn DA's office, we open Shop Right Collision auto repair on a grimy stretch of Georgia Avenue in the East New York section of Brooklyn. We staff it with IAB undercovers who have tow-truck operator licenses and experience in the auto repair business. Posing as tow drivers, our guys respond to about a hundred tow calls, and when they arrive at the accident or breakdown, they don't try to bribe the cop—we don't want our undercovers arrested for attempted bribery—but with a wink and a nod they suggest that they'd be really, really grateful if the cop gives them the tow. And in every single case, the cop does the right thing; he tells our undercover tow-truck drivers to buzz off and gives the tow to the next driver in the rotation.

But the hoods connected to the Gambino crime family aren't quite so ethically minded. We also put it out that in addition to towing and auto repair, Shop Right Collision is open for business in other fields—stolen cars, insurance fraud, loan sharking, bootleg cigarettes, anything to make a buck. Pretty soon some hoods from the Canarsie Crew of the Gambino family come calling, and after a seventeen-month investigation we bust thirteen members of the Gambino Mob on a host of fraud and racketeering charges. True, when we balance the books we find that Shop Right Collision lost $75,000 in business expenses—but hey, we're cops, not businessmen.

There were endless variations of random integrity tests, but the bottom line is that in each scenario we gave the cops—and the Gambino Mob guys as well—the opportunity to do the right thing or the wrong thing. And guess what? In almost every case, the cops did the right thing.

Take the year 2012, for example. That year we conducted five hundred thirty random and targeted integrity tests. Of those we had thirty-four "administrative" failures, meaning the cops failed to follow proper procedures, and two supervisory failures, meaning a sergeant or a lieutenant or other supervisor failed to follow proper procedures. But out of those five hundred thirty integrity tests, how many were criminal failures? How many times did the cop steal the money or the drugs?

The answer is, six cops stole the money or the drugs or committed another criminal act. That's right, six. Out of more than five hundred. That's about one percent.

There's good news and bad news in that. The good news is that in 2012 only six NYPD cops that we tested acted like criminals. The bad news is that six NYPD cops acted like criminals.

I know, there are people out there reading this, especially news reporters and cops who were never in IAB, who are saying: Those numbers are
bullshit, the cops you did your little integrity tests on saw you coming,
they made you, they knew you were IAB, you IAB guys are bumblers.

Well, I'm not saying our surveillance or undercover guys never got
made. In a few cases—very few—a cop might mockingly say to our
undercover: Oh yes, sir, thank you for returning this lost wallet, and
how long have you been with IAB? Or maybe the cop would take on a
stricken look, like he knew he was being watched, which he was. In cases
like that we'd have to reassess our scenario, or maybe send the undercover back to our in-house Actors Studio for some more Stanislavski.

But consider this: In the late 1990s a Columbia University professor
did a scientific survey of hundreds of NYPD cops. And one of the questions he asked every cop was: "Have you personally been the target of
an Internal Affairs integrity test in the past year?" Based on how many
cops answered yes to that question, the professor estimated that IAB
conducted about six thousand integrity tests every year.

When the professor told me that, I couldn't have been happier.
Remember, we actually only did about five or six hundred integrity tests
a year. But the professor's findings meant that six thousand cops out
there *thought* they'd been tested, they thought they had made us while
we were running a test on them. Not only does that indicate that the
tests have a deterrent effect—IAB is everywhere!—but it also means
that in most cases, the drunk on the bus or the Good Samaritan with
the wallet really was a drunk on a bus or a Good Samaritan with a wallet.
The cops just thought they were IAB.

Now, I realize that some people think that randomly testing cops for
honesty is, well, a little creepy, that it's a violation of their rights. Cops—
and the PBA—especially hate it. It's insulting, they say, and why is it just
cops who are being tested this way? Why don't you randomly dangle
cash or drugs in front of lawyers and judges and politicians and see what
they do? Ironically, even civil liberties types and journalists, who are the
first to complain about police corruption and misconduct, often think
the integrity testing is Big Brother–ish.

I can understand that. But what are we supposed to do? Corruption
undetected breeds more corruption—That cop is getting away with it,

so I can, too—and we're not going to passively sit back and wait for it to become endemic in the Department, like it was before the Knapp Commission. As for randomly testing politicians for honesty, I wouldn't necessarily be opposed to that, although it's not my call.

Besides, although the NYPD was the first big-city police department to institute a random integrity testing policy back in 1993—other departments have since followed suit—it's not like we invented the practice. Blame that one on the press.

In 1974, ABC investigative reporter Brian Ross, then a local reporter in Miami, set up a police integrity test of Miami cops. Role players turned over thirty-one wallets containing cash to cops while Ross's team filmed them. Nine of the thirty-one Miami cops were subsequently fired and/or criminally charged for stealing the money. Almost thirty years later Ross did the same thing in New York, turning over twenty cash-filled wallets to twenty randomly selected NYPD cops—and every single cop followed proper procedures and turned the wallet in with all the cash intact.

Like I said, the Officer-I-found-this-wallet routine had become pretty much old hat by that time. But I think it illustrates something about integrity testing. Random integrity testing isn't designed just to catch a few crooked cops. It's also a way to prove, to the public and to ourselves, that 99 percent of our cops are honest, that when given the opportunity to do the right thing or the wrong thing, they'll do the right thing.

But integrity tests and surveillance cameras and recording devices aren't the only tools we use to fight police corruption and misconduct.

Another important tool we have in the arsenal is a little plastic cup.

The NYPD has a simple policy when it comes to drug use by its cops, the same policy as the US military. The policy is zero tolerance. If you're caught using illegal drugs or steroids, you're fired. Period, end of story. It doesn't matter if you're a rookie or if you're two months away from your twenty years. You're gone, and your pension is gone, too.

Maybe that sounds harsh, or hypocritical, given that an NYPD cop with an alcohol problem can get Department-sponsored treatment, while a cop with an illegal drug problem can't. It's debatable. But what's not debatable is that every cop has seen what drugs do to a neighborhood, and to a city. And almost every cop has been to a Department funeral for another cop who was killed by a drug dealer or a drug user.

So every year 20 percent of the force, up to and including the chief of department, is selected at random by computer and ordered to report that day to the NYPD Medical Division in Queens to pee in a cup. Cops are also drug tested when they're promoted, or when they transfer to special units such as Narcotics and IAB. (In IAB and other special units, half of the cops are drug tested every year.) The cop's "contribution" is divided into three samples, and if Sample 1 tests positive for drugs, Sample 2 is also tested to make sure.

The failure rate is extremely low. Out of more than eleven thousand tests administered by the NYPD in 2014, there were only twenty-two cops whose tests came back positive for drugs or who refused to take the test, which is an automatic failure.

Still, no matter how relatively small the numbers, cops with guns and shields who are using drugs are clearly a danger to the public, and to other cops. It's also a corruption problem. They're either stealing those drugs from dealers, or they're buying them from dealers who they should be arresting, or, if it's an expensive drug like cocaine, they may be stealing money to buy the drugs. Or they may be getting them from other cops.

So when a cop's drug test comes back positive, Medical Division doesn't notify the cop. They notify the Internal Affairs Bureau.

As soon as we get notification of a positive drug test result we'll go out to the cop's house to take his gun and shield. At first they'll almost always deny they're using drugs—It's a mistake, the test was wrong!— in which case we tell them they have the right to order a third test from the same urine sample, at their own expense. But they almost never do. They know they're caught.

And sometimes they'll try to make a deal with us, like the cop with the Midtown North Street Peddlers Unit.

Pushcart vendors and street peddlers have been part of the New York City landscape since the beginning. There are thousands of them in the city, some licensed, most not. They sell everything from hot dogs and falafel to knock-off designer watches and clothing—"Rodex" watches, "Guci" handbags and scarves—to out-and-out counterfeits and pirated CDs and DVDs.

You might think they're harmless, but they're like musicians in the subways, or mimes in the park, or those guys who dress up like Disney characters or superheroes and pose for tourists in Times Square: When there's a few of them they're picturesque, but when there are too many of them they're a pain in the neck. The peddlers set up their carts or their folding tables or their blankets on the sidewalks, blocking foot traffic, aggressively soliciting passersby, blocking access to stores, and often getting in fights with each other over territory.

The street peddlers, many of whom are immigrants, are especially thick in the tourist areas of Manhattan and the commercial sections of Brooklyn. So precincts in those areas have special street peddler units, a sergeant and five or six cops in uniform or plainclothes who try to keep them under control. If they catch a street peddler without a license or committing some other violation, they can give him a summons and legally confiscate his wares.

Like any other assignment in the NYPD, 99 percent of the cops doing it do it honestly. But a few don't. Which brings us back to the cop from Midtown North.

Medical Division notifies us that the cop—in deference to his family, not to him, we'll call him Officer Constantine—has tested positive for cocaine. So we go out to his house and take his gun and shield, and then, because cops who are using drugs are often involved in other corruption, we take a run at him.

Look, we tell him, you can't be a cop anymore, but there are two ways to do this. We can suspend you right now, in which case your pay stops immediately, along with your benefits, and in thirty days you'll be fired. Or you can work with us, tell us about any corruption you and other cops have been involved in, help us with the investigation. If you do that we can keep you on for a few months, as long as the investigation takes, you'll still be getting your pay, and then maybe you'll be allowed to resign instead of being fired, and you can get a fresh start in another line of work.

Officer Constantine, who's got seventeen years on the job, is seeing his whole life crash down around him because of a few lines of cocaine— or more likely, many, many lines of cocaine. He thinks it over and says: Okay, I'll tell you, we've been ripping off the street peddlers. Constantine tells us that cops in the Midtown North Street Peddlers Unit are shaking down peddlers near Rockefeller Center for a hundred bucks a day, rousting the ones who refuse to pay, confiscating their stuff, and then selling it to other peddlers. It's been going on for months, he says.

So we take him down to the Manhattan District Attorney's Office to make a deal. The ADA on the case wants to put a recording device on Officer Constantine and send him back into the precinct to gather more evidence against the other cops. But I'm not so sure.

It used to be the standard practice to take a cop who's caught in corruption and then turn him, persuade him to work for us, and send him back to his unit wearing a wire. The Buddy Boys scandal in the Seven-Seven, the Morgue Boys scandal in the Seven-Three, the Dirty Thirty scandal—they all involved corrupt cops who agreed to work undercover against other cops in exchange for leniency.

Actually it's kind of ironic. A lot of otherwise good cops believe in the Blue Wall of Silence, and they'll never inform on a crooked cop. They may not like what the crooked cops are doing, they may not want to work with them, but unless it's something really horrendous they won't drop a dime on them to IAB. But often when really crooked cops get caught, and they're facing a long prison term, for them the Blue Wall goes out the window. They'll gladly wear a wire on other cops, including the good ones, to save themselves.

But putting a corrupt cop back into his precinct or his unit with a wire is risky. Most corrupt cops aren't trained as undercovers, and a lot of them don't have the temperament for it. For example, in the Dirty Thirty investigation, a crooked cop was caught, turned, and put back into the precinct wearing a wire. But his sudden change in behavior aroused suspicions, and when another cop accused him of being a rat, they got into a scuffle and the wired-up cop shot the other cop in the foot.

With the Midtown North Street Peddlers Unit investigation, I'm certainly not going to put a known drug user like Officer Constantine back on the job with a gun on his hip. What if the guy gets high and shoots somebody? Even setting aside the injury or loss of life, it would be a personal injury lawyer's dream come true. You can almost hear him in the civil trial: So is it your testimony before this court, Chief Campisi, that you knowingly allowed this corrupt police officer, this admitted drug addict, to walk the streets of this city, armed and under the full color and authority of the law, whereupon in a drug-induced psychotic rage he drew his service weapon and intentionally shot my innocent client in the foot?

I don't want to see anything like that happening. So putting Officer Constantine back in his unit with his gun is not an option. But if we send him back in without his gun, the other cops are going to know that he's jammed up, and they won't talk to him.

Then I get an idea. The regulations say that a cop can't carry his gun if he's physically incapable of drawing and firing it. So how about if we give Officer Constantine a broken arm?

No, no, we aren't going to actually break his arm. We'll just make it look like he broke his arm, so the other cops won't wonder why he doesn't have his gun. He won't be out on the street, he'll be on desk duty inside, but he'll still be able to talk to the other dirty cops and maybe record some incriminating statements.

So I call a friend of mine, a doctor in Medical Division, and without telling him why, I ask if he can put a cast on a human arm that isn't broken. The doc ponders the medical ethics of the thing for a minute and finally decides that, yeah, if the "patient" is willing, he can do that. Constantine is agreeable, so the next morning we pick him up at his house and drive him to Medical Division to get his cast. But on the way, Constantine says to us: Uh, guys? I talked to my PBA delegate, and he doesn't think I should do this, he doesn't think I should cooperate with you guys. What do you guys think I should do?

What? You talked to your PBA delegate? Geez, why didn't you just take out an ad in the *Daily News*? If the PBA knows about this investigation, the word is already out.

So the investigation is blown. We quickly search the unit sergeant's locker at the precinct and find a bunch of confiscated watches and handbags that hadn't been vouchered. We also find a victim, a peddler from Senegal who the cops were shaking down. The sergeant is indicted and fired, and so is Officer Constantine, since he's no longer cooperating. A couple of other cops in the unit are fired after refusing to take a drug test—Officer Constantine isn't the only one with a cocaine problem—and a couple others are transferred, but we've got no criminal evidence against them. End of case.

Now, so far I've talked mostly about the proactive side of IAB operations—debriefing perps, setting up surveillances, sending in undercovers, conducting integrity tests. But there are other cases that require us to be reactive, to investigate alleged crimes by cops that have already happened, to sift through conflicting reports and accounts and get to the truth, often amid the glare of publicity and the harsh scrutiny of a suspicious public.

Sometimes those alleged crimes by cops involve police brutality.

And sometimes they involve police bullets.

Chapter 6

OFFICER INVOLVED

It's the summer of 1991, a sultry night in Lower Manhattan, long before I'm in IAB, and I'm standing on a subway platform with my service revolver pointed at a guy with a bloody knife in his hand. And I'm shouting and praying at the same time.

What I'm shouting is: Drop the knife! Drop the knife! DROP THE KNIFE!

And what I'm silently praying is: Please, God, don't make me have to shoot this guy!

He's a white guy, late twenties/early thirties, brown hair sticking up in all directions, wearing dark pants and a white pullover shirt that, like the six-inch knife in his hand, is covered in blood—another man's blood. He's holding the knife at waist level, slowly moving it back and forth in a "stay back" kind of motion, and he's got his lips pulled back in a sort of weird, feral grin. He's not saying anything intelligible, just standing there, back to the wall, snarling and growling like a wild animal. I'm guessing that he's drunk, or high, or an EDP—emotionally disturbed person—or, worst-case scenario, all three at once.

I don't know this guy. I've never laid eyes on him before this happened. But I know that under the right circumstances, if the situation gets to a certain critical point, I'm going to shoot him. As a cop, under the right circumstances, shooting him won't just be my job, it will be my sworn duty.

But I desperately don't want to do it. Which is why I'm shouting and praying: DROP THE KNIFE! (Don't make me have to shoot this guy!) DROP THE KNIFE! (Don't make me have to shoot this guy!) *PLEASE* DROP THE KNIFE…

As so often happens in police work, this night had gone from dull to potentially lethal with astonishing suddenness. Just ninety seconds earlier I'd been sitting in an unmarked Chevrolet, looking forward to a nice cup of tea and a quiet end of shift. At the time I'm a deputy inspector (DI), the commanding officer of the Sixth Precinct, which covers Greenwich Village and the West Village, and on this night I had drawn the duty. Although the duty is mandatory for precinct commanders at least once a month, I actually would do it even if it wasn't. The duty is a chance for me to get away from the bureaucratic demands of being a precinct CO, to talk to my people, to simply get back to police work on the street for a while.

It's been a quiet night, no major incidents, so at about three a.m. my partner, a young African American police officer named Rodney, and I decide to stop at an all-night deli for some take-out coffee—well, coffee for him, tea for me. (Technically, Rodney is my "driver," but as far as I'm concerned, any cop riding in a car with me is my partner, no matter what the difference in rank.) Rodney parks the Chevy just down the street from the Christopher Street–Sheridan Square subway station and goes into the deli to buy the drinks, while I sit in the car, windows rolled down, listening to the soothing sounds of the radio chatter. A couple minutes later Rodney comes walking back out with two Styrofoam cups—and just as he does I hear angry words from across the street.

I look through the open driver's-side window and see two guys, white males, standing on the sidewalk a few steps from the subway entrance, yelling at each other. I can't understand exactly what they're yelling, but it's of the Fuck you! No, fuck you! variety. They're face to face, well within flying spittle range, but they're not in fighting stances, and nobody's throwing any punches.

Rodney walks up to the car and says to me: Hey, boss, what's up with that?

I shrug and say: I dunno, but I guess we better quiet 'em down.

So Rodney sets the Styrofoam cups on the hood and I open the car door and climb out. We aren't planning on arresting these guys. If you collared everybody who's having a loud argument on the sidewalk in New York, half the city would be locked up. All we want to do is separate them, quiet them down, send them on their respective ways, give them a chance to cool down a little. Routine police work.

And then, just as we start walking across the street, the guy on the left pulls a six-inch knife out from under his shirt, raises it over his head, and then plunges it to the hilt into the other guy, halfway between his neck and his shoulder.

Suddenly, this isn't routine anymore.

The victim just kind of stands there, caught in a momentary embrace with the stabber, until the stabber pulls the knife out and the victim staggers backward, blood spurting like a fountain from the wound—the knife must have punctured his subclavian artery—and then his knees buckle and he sags to the sidewalk. The perp—his status has now instantly changed from angry citizen to dangerous perpetrator—doesn't make another move on the victim, or try to stab him again. He just looks down on him, maybe with shock and horror at what he's done, maybe with triumph and satisfaction.

All this takes about a second and a half. As soon as we see the knife, Rodney and I start running, shouting: Police! Don't move! We're about twenty yards away when the perp looks up at us, then he turns, knife still in hand, and takes off running down the sidewalk. I stop briefly to check on the victim—he's sitting up, moaning, his hand pressed over the knife wound—and then I key my radio mic and call in—Central, this is Six CO, we're in foot pursuit at Seventh and Christopher, man with a knife, victim down, we need an eighty-five and a bus forthwith—meaning that we need backup units and an ambulance ASAP. A 10-85 isn't quite as serious as a 10-13, "officer needs help," which would cause every unit in the precinct to drop whatever they were doing and rush to the scene, but it still gets attention.

As I'm calling this in, the perp makes it to the subway entrance and disappears down the staircase. Our radios don't work well underground, so I let the dispatch center know we're going to be in the subway station and probably out of contact—Six CO to Central, Christopher–Sheridan Square station, we're going in the hole!—and then Rodney and I start running down the steps. The perp hops the turnstile, and so do we, then he runs down onto the platform. Even at three a.m. there are still a few citizens on the platform, waiting for a train, and as the guy runs past them, bloody knife in his hand, with two cops in pursuit, they start running, terrified, in the other direction. The perp runs to the far end of the platform, but now there's nowhere to go, so he turns with his back to the wall, still holding the knife, and starts with the snarling and growling.

At this point I draw my gun and take up position behind one of the steel ceiling support columns a few feet from the track. Rodney, about ten feet to my right, is against the wall, his gun in his right hand, his baton—they're better-known as nightsticks—in his left. We both have our guns pointed at the perp, who's about fifteen feet from us. My gun is a Smith & Wesson Model 10 .38-caliber revolver with a four-inch barrel, which weighs a little over two pounds—but right now, as it's pointed at this perp's chest, it feels like it weighs a hundred. I'm in good physical shape—just a few years earlier I'd finished a New York City Marathon— and during the foot pursuit I'd only run, what, less than a hundred yards? But my breathing is rapid and shallow, my skin is clammy, and my heart rate is about 160 beats a minute. The adrenaline is surging.

It's not from panic, or fear, at least not fear for myself. I'm in a good defensive position, and I'm confident that my training and experience will allow me to resolve the situation one way or another. But I am concerned for my partner, who's in a more open and vulnerable position.

Drop the knife! Drop the knife! Drop the knife!

At this point, the perp has three options. He can drop the knife and submit to arrest. He can jump down onto the tracks and run into the tunnel and maybe get electrocuted or smashed by an oncoming train. Or he can charge at us and hope that he can somehow make it past us and escape.

If he chooses Option 1, that's fine. Even if he just stands there, not surrendering but not making a move, that's okay, too. We'll wait for backup to arrive, maybe use some of the specialized nonlethal takedown equipment that patrol sergeants have in their car trunks: a handheld water cannon to knock the guy down, a long-handled shepherd's hook to try to pull his feet out from under him. If the Emergency Service Unit (ESU) guys are called in—they're the NYPD equivalent of the SWAT team—they'll have beanbag shotguns that shoot a painful but less than lethal soft projectile, and net guns that can wrap the guy up. As long as he stands still, there's no hurry. In a standoff, time is on our side.

If the perp chooses Option 2 and runs into the tunnel, that's still manageable. We'll get the Transit guys to shut off the power and divert the trains—hopefully before the perp gets fried or squashed—and then send ESU in to get him.

But if this guy chooses Option 3, if he charges at us with the knife, there's going to be trouble.

Because for us, Option 3 is not an option. This guy has already stabbed one person, possibly fatally, and if he makes a move toward us with the knife, if he tries to close the fifteen-foot gap that separates us, which will take him less than a second, he's an imminent threat to me and my partner, and we will have to stop him.

Here's how we're not—repeat, not—going to stop him.

If he has that knife in a stabbing or slashing position, we're not going to tackle him or use some fancy jujitsu moves to get the knife out of his hand. We're not trained for that, we're not Jackie Chan, and even if we were, in a close quarters struggle there's still a good chance that with that knife waving around one or both of us is going to get slashed or stabbed. Yes, we're both wearing soft body armor under our shirts, which offers some protection, but Kevlar is designed to stop bullets, not knives; under the right circumstances, a knife can penetrate it. And besides, the vest only covers the torso, which means a lot of our important parts—really important parts—are unprotected.

We're probably not going to use a baton if he charges at us, either. I left mine in the car, and even though Rodney has his, we're probably not going to let the guy get close enough for Rodney to try to hit him with it. We're not going to spray him with Mace. By the time the charging perp gets close enough for us to use it, even assuming we can hit him directly in the face, it most likely won't even slow down his momentum, much less stop him; it might only make him madder. (Mace, which is essentially tear gas, was later replaced by OC, oleoresin capsicum, or pepper spray.) We're not going to Taser him, because at the time Taser guns have hardly even been invented yet—and even if we time-traveled the incident ahead a couple of decades, we probably still wouldn't have Tasers. Because of concerns about their potential lethality—unfounded concerns, in my opinion—in 2014 the NYPD only had about six hundred Tasers, and they were only issued to specialized units like ESU and to some patrol sergeants and lieutenants.

So no, if the perp with the knife charges us, and we believe we have no other reasonable option, we're not going to wrestle him or club him or spray him or Taser him.

We're going to shoot him.

We're not going to fire warning shots—that is specifically prohibited by NYPD regulations. We're not going to try to shoot him in the leg, or the arm; Lord knows we aren't going to try to shoot the knife out of his hand. That only happens in movies—bad movies. Instead, following our training and Department policy, we're going to aim for the center of his chest, his "center mass," and we're going to shoot. If he still keeps coming we're going shoot again and then again, until he no longer poses a deadly threat or until our revolvers are empty and the hammers go "click"—and even then, if somehow he still poses a deadly threat, and there's no other way to stop that threat, and if we have time, we're going to reload and shoot some more. We're not "shooting to kill"; NYPD policy is "shoot to stop." But if the only thing that stops the threat is this guy dying, that's what's going to happen. I know that sounds cold, even brutal, to a lot of civilians, but that's the reality.

But I don't want that to happen. *Please don't make me have to shoot this guy.* For a lot of reasons.

One is that I have a natural aversion to putting a bullet into another human being. A lot of people might not believe it, but just about every cop feels the same way. There may be a few exceptions, like Officer Romeo, that cop in the Seven-Three who almost shot the teenaged burglary suspect in the back, but they really are the exceptions. More than 90 percent of NYPD cops will never fire their weapons at another person during their entire careers—and they're glad of it.

Another reason that I don't want to shoot this perp is that I know if I start shooting, some of my shots are almost certainly going to miss.

I'm a good shot. I routinely shoot a 100 percent on my semiannual firearm requalification tests at the NYPD firing range at Rodman's Neck in the Bronx, which means I put fifty out of fifty shots into the critical area of a stationary paper human silhouette target at distances of seven, fifteen, and twenty-five yards. I also do well on the FATS machine (Firearms and Tactics Simulator), which has officers respond to amazingly realistic "shoot/don't shoot" video screen scenarios by shooting wax "bullets." (Later they switched to laser guns.)

But I've read the annual NYPD Firearms Discharge Reports, which track every bullet fired by NYPD officers each year. I've seen the statistics. So I know that on average, year in, year out, only about one in three of the bullets fired by officers at a perpetrator will hit him; about two-thirds of the rounds fired will miss the perp completely. At close range, zero to seven yards, the averages go up a little, to about 40 percent hits, which still means 60 percent misses. It doesn't mean that NYPD officers are bad shots; the numbers are consistent with or better than national averages. It just illustrates how hard it is to hit a small target with a handgun, in the heat of the moment, and especially if that target is moving.

And for me, standing on the subway platform, any bullets I fire that don't hit the perp are going to hit something else—a steel support column, the concrete floor, the tile-covered walls, something. Those bullets are traveling at about a thousand feet per second, and there's a good chance they could ricochet, or fragment into little pieces of lead and copper that could go zinging every which way, including our way. It's certainly something to think about.

And there's another good reason why I don't want to shoot this guy. It's because I know that the instant I pull that trigger, my life is going to change.

After the shooting, my gun—and Rodney's, too, if he shoots—will be impounded and I'll be placed on administrative duty, meaning I can't go out on the street for at least several days, until a preliminary investigation is completed—and longer if there are questions about the shooting. The trajectory of every round I fire will be tracked and analyzed. My tactics will be reviewed and second-guessed at the highest levels of the police department. Not only will I have to show that I had no choice but to shoot, I'll also have to prove that I didn't unnecessarily put myself in a position in which shooting was the last resort.

Because I'm a DI, I'll probably get even more scrutiny than an average cop, not less; as a supervisor, I may also be held accountable for Rodney's tactics. I'll probably have to report to a shrink in the Department's Psychological Services Unit to have my mental health evaluated. And since it's not every day that a deputy inspector shoots somebody—it's not even every year—it will probably get big play in the papers: "NYPD COMMANDER SHOOTS MAN IN SUBWAY." Maybe the reporters will get it right, maybe they won't.

Don't get me wrong. I'm confident that our tactics are by the book, and that if we have to shoot it will be justified. But you never know. It could be that a "witness" will magically appear and claim that we cold-bloodedly shot the guy after he dropped the knife. It wouldn't be the first time that happened. Or maybe the perp will turn out to be the son of some politician or VIP, who'll tell the press that his boy was a really nice guy as long as he took his meds, and then demand to know why the cops had to kill him, why they didn't just shoot the knife out of his hand. It's not likely any of that will happen, but it's possible.

So the bottom line is that I've got only one good reason to shoot this guy—he poses an imminent threat of death or serious injury to me or another person—and about a million good reasons not to.

And in the end, thank God, I don't have to.

After a few more rounds of DROP THE KNIFE! DROP THE KNIFE! Rodney senses an opportunity. He calls out to me, You got me, boss?—meaning do I have him covered, and I nod to him. Rodney holsters his gun, takes a step away from the wall, and takes a two-handed grip on his baton, holding it over his shoulder like an MLB slugger getting ready to crush one out of Yankee Stadium. Then he says to the perp, in a low voice, full of menace: For the last time, buddy, drop the *fucking* knife!

It's mostly a bluff. I don't think Rodney will really wade in and hit the guy; for the reasons mentioned above, you don't take a stick to a knife fight. But Rodney is a big guy, six feet, intimidating, with biceps bulging out of his short-sleeved summer uniform shirt. The perp is probably imagining how much it's going to hurt when that stick meets his humerus. Still snarling and growling, he throws the knife on the floor and it skitters away.

So now the perp is an unarmed suspect, and we can treat him as one. I holster my gun and Rodney and I both rush him. We spin him around and throw him against the wall, then search him and cuff him. It's over. The standoff on the platform has lasted less than a minute, but it feels like an hour. I can feel the adrenaline draining out of my body, my heart rate slowing; an intense sense of relief washes over me.

Thank you, Lord. I didn't have to shoot this guy.

It turns out that the man he stabbed survived—apparently they were having some sort of lovers' quarrel—and eventually the perp will go down for attempted murder. Back at the precinct, Rodney takes the collar and starts processing him into the system, while I find another partner/driver and head back out on patrol.

Of course, that wasn't the only time I ever had to draw my gun on the job—although I'm pleased to say that during my almost forty-one-year police career I never had to shoot anyone.

But maybe it gives you some idea of what it's like for cops who find themselves in a potential shooting situation: the fear, the adrenaline, the terrible uncertainty, the inevitable repercussions.

And maybe it also helps you understand what every good cop knows: Those guns we carry are double-ended weapons.

They can kill and maim at one end.

And they can ruin a career, and even a life, at the other.

The most surprising thing about police shootings is not how often they happen, but how often they don't—especially in the NYPD.

As I said, the NYPD gathers detailed statistics on all shooting incidents involving NYPD officers, and assembles them every year in the annual Firearms Discharge Report. The report details how many shots were fired, how many officers fired them, how many civilians were killed or wounded, how many officers were killed or wounded, the rank, years of service, gender, and race of the officers involved, the race or ethnicity of the civilians involved—it goes on and on. The report is public. Anybody can take a look at it.

In 2013, my last full year on the job, the report listed 81 incidents in which NYPD officers fired their guns. Ninety-eight on-duty and off-duty officers were involved in those incidents, and a total of 248 shots were fired. Of those 81 incidents, 19 involved animals shot while attacking officers or civilians, all of them dogs, almost all of them pit bulls. (It's not always vicious dogs, though. In 1999, for example, cops shot and killed a rampaging bull named Roughrider that had escaped from an illegal parking lot rodeo in Queens. That's right, a rodeo in Queens.) Another 8 of those 81 shooting incidents were suicides or attempted suicides by cops, and 12 were "unintentional discharges"—the gun went off because of improper handling, or in a struggle with a suspect, or when a cop's gun hand got caught in a door during a search warrant. Two shooting incidents were "unauthorized use of a firearm"—one of them a cop shooting into the air, another an EDP who grabbed a cop's gun and shot him in the foot, and so on.

So that leaves 40 incidents in which NYPD cops intentionally fired their weapons at suspects in 2013—the Department calls them ID-ACs, or Intentional Discharge–Adversarial Conflicts. Fifty-five cops were involved in those shootings, and altogether they fired 162 rounds. During those incidents, two cops were shot and wounded; neither was killed. Two civilian bystanders, both women, were slightly wounded when cops opened fire at an EDP near Times Square. Meanwhile, 17 "subjects" were intentionally shot and wounded, and 8 were shot and killed.

Let me repeat that: In a city of 8.4 million people, in a Department of 36,000 armed cops, a Department that made about 400,000 arrests that year, including 5,000 gun arrests, NYPD officers shot and killed 8 people in 2013—all males, all of whom were carrying guns or knives, 7 of whom had serious criminal histories and one who had a history of violent psychiatric problems.

Yes, that's 8 dead people short of perfect. The NYPD would have been happier if those 8 suspects had wound up in prison or a psych ward instead of dead on the street. But keep the shooting numbers in perspective. In that same year that NYPD cops intentionally shot and killed or wounded 25 people, almost 1,300 civilians in New York City were shot and killed or wounded by people who were *not* cops.

The point is that anybody who claims that trigger-happy cops are the biggest danger to the people of New York City simply doesn't know what he's talking about. More people are killed by errant cabdrivers in New York City every year than are killed by NYPD cops—and the people killed by cabdrivers are innocent people minding their own business, not dangerous perps with guns or knives.

And compare the recent cop shooting numbers to the way it used to be. In 1973, when I came on the job, there were 118 people shot and wounded by NYPD officers, and 58 people shot and killed—seven times more people killed by cops than there were four decades later. In that same year, 7 NYPD cops were shot and killed.

That's partly because New York was simply a much more violent place back then, with almost 1,700 homicides and other violent crime rates to match. (In 2013, homicides had fallen to 335, a historic low.) More violent crime inevitably means more police shootings.

But the NYPD also made a number of changes in policy, training, equipment, and attitude over that forty-year period that I believe have helped drastically reduce officer-involved shootings.

For example, until the early 1970s NYPD cops were allowed to shoot at suspects fleeing from a violent felony—a robbery, a rape—even if they shot him in the back. That was changed to allow cops to shoot only if the suspect posed a clear and imminent threat to themselves or another person. (An exception to that policy, one that became known as the so-called Son of Sam rule after the famous serial killer, allowed cops to shoot a fleeing suspect if he was a known killer, there was reason to believe that he was armed, and there was a high probability that he would kill someone else. But even then, the cop better be damned sure he's got the right guy.)

Firearms training also improved over those forty years. When I was at the Academy we got just enough firearms training to pass the qualification on the stationary paper target range; they hardly even taught us how to clean our weapons. Later they started giving recruits more realistic shoot/don't shoot training, including sessions at the "Haunted House," in which range instructors acted out various scenarios—suspicious person with his hand in his pocket in a dark hallway, innocent bystander suddenly opening a door behind you, and so on—and the recruit had to make an instant decision on whether to shoot. That training improved with the introduction of the FATS machine and the "Tactical Village," a mock city street that allowed instruction in real-life situations. Unfortunately, because of limited facilities, most recruits and cops don't get nearly enough time on the simulators or other realistic firearms training.

NYPD nonlethal or less-lethal equipment like OC spray and Tasers have also helped reduce police shootings—although as I said, the NYPD has been reluctant to deploy Tasers very widely.

But in addition to all that, over the past decades I believe there has been a dramatic shift in the way NYPD cops on the street think about police shootings. Cops know that the Department is going to give a police shooting much more scrutiny than it might have gotten in the old days. Even the simplest officer shooting investigation—say, a gun is accidentally fired in a precinct locker room, no one injured—will eat up hundreds of man-hours; a complicated or controversial one will consume thousands. A shooting investigation can take months, or even years if there's a potential criminal or civil case, during which the officer will be locked in a legal and professional limbo. And even if the investigation determines the shooting was justified, cops also know that in today's social and political climate, that shooting can still get them seriously jammed up.

In any shooting incident involving an NYPD cop, on-duty or off-duty, a supervisor goes to the scene, impounds the fired weapon, and secures the scene. If anyone has been injured or killed, or if the shooting looks problematic, Internal Affairs is notified, and investigators from the IAB's Force Group go to the scene. (IAB investigators in the Force Group, also known as Group 54, are specially trained in weapons, ballistics, police use-of-force laws, and other investigation techniques.) They'll work with investigators from a Borough Shooting Team to collect evidence, interview witnesses, and prepare a preliminary report to be presented to the police commissioner, usually within twenty-four hours or less; ballistics tests and toxicological and medical reports take longer. The local DA's office will also conduct its own investigation, with our help, to determine whether to file criminal charges against the officer; if there's a criminal case, we'll hold off on our final report until the case is over. If the DA declines the case, or a grand jury refuses to indict, a final report will be reviewed by both a Borough Firearms Discharge Advisory Board and the chief of department's Firearms Discharge Review Board, an ad hoc group of senior supervisors that will make a recommendation on the shooting and what disciplinary steps to take, if any, against the officer. The police commissioner makes the final decision.

Police shootings in the NYPD officially fall into two basic categories. If the officer followed all the rules and procedures outlined in the Patrol Guide, the shooting is deemed "within guidelines"—or in cop parlance, a "good" shooting. If he or she didn't follow the rules, the shooting is "not within guidelines," or a "bad" shooting, and the officer can face discipline ranging from counseling and retraining to dismissal.

In my seventeen years as chief of IAB I was involved in the investigations of hundreds of police shootings, of which only a very small percentage were bad shootings under Department rules, which admittedly give police officers the benefit of the doubt. The rest were officially "good" shootings.

Sometimes the good shootings were easy calls. One example, out of many, happened in 2006, when two armed men in ski masks, both career criminals, robbed a bank in Queens of $15,000 and then tried to carjack a vehicle driven by off-duty officer John Lopez. Lopez starts chasing one of the robbers down Fifty-Fifth Avenue when the robber turns and shoots Lopez in the thigh. Lopez fires back, hitting the robber twice, and then, despite being wounded, pins him down until backup arrives. They caught the other guy, too. Mayor Bloomberg called Officer Lopez a hero, which he was. As you might expect, the Department investigation concluded it was a good shooting.

Bad shootings are sometimes pretty easy to call as well. For example, in 1998 we had an off-duty officer named William Morales who was moonlighting as a security guard at a Bronx sporting goods store. He's playing around with his authorized off-duty gun, a revolver, and as a joke he takes some of the cartridges out of the cylinder, points the gun at another employee, calls out "Russian roulette!," and pulls the trigger. The gun goes off, wounding the employee in the groin. Then this knucklehead makes it even worse by walking the wounded employee outside the store and trying to get him to say he'd been shot in a drive-by shooting. Predictably, the official Department shooting investigation determined that it was a bad shooting, but by then it was a moot point: Morales had already been convicted of felony assault and was fired from the Department.

But it's not always that easy. The truth is that a lot of "good" shootings aren't completely good, and even some of the "bad" shootings aren't completely bad. Police shootings often aren't clearly defined in black and white; instead, they come in varying shades of gray.

And one of the grayest—and saddest—"good" shootings I was ever involved in was the 1999 shooting of Amadou Diallo.

It's 12:44 a.m. on a cold February night in the Soundview section of the Bronx, a low-income, high-crime residential neighborhood. Four NYPD cops in an unmarked Ford Taurus, all in plainclothes, are riding by an apartment building at 1157 Wheeler Avenue when one of them sees a man standing on the sidewalk, then moving to a stoop at the entrance of the dark vestibule that leads to the apartment building's front door.

The cops are members of the NYPD Street Crimes Unit, the SCU, a citywide force of about four hundred plainclothes cops whose primary mission is to flood high-crime areas and make arrests, especially gun arrests. But tonight they're also on the lookout for a serial rapist suspected of attacking more than fifty women in Soundview as well as in other areas of the Bronx, Manhattan, and Westchester County. One of the rapist's MOs is to surprise women in dark hallways or apartment entrances, push them inside, and then rape them at gunpoint. The rapist always wears a mask or bandanna, so the only description of him is that he's a black man.

The man standing in the dark vestibule is black—but then, so are most residents of this part of Soundview.

The driver stops the unmarked police car and two officers get out of the right-side front and back doors; their shields are hanging around their necks. They walk toward the man in the vestibule, saying: Police! Can we talk to you? The man turns and seems to be trying to get inside the door at the end of the vestibule. The officers get to the stoop and call out: Stop! Let us see your hands! Without a word, the man turns to his left and with his right hand reaches into his jacket pocket—and then he pulls something small and black out of the pocket.

Gun! one of the officers shouts. He's got a gun!

Forty-five minutes later the phone next to my bed starts ringing. I look at the clock and already know what's coming. Good news can always wait until morning; the only kind of news you're going to get at 1:30 a.m. is bad news.

The Internal Affairs Bureau Command Center supervisor, a lieutenant, is on the line.

Chief, he says, we've got some MOSs (Members of the Service) involved in a shooting in the Bronx. The subject, a black male, is DOA. Four SCU guys involved. Looks like they fired a total of more than forty shots. And, Chief? It looks like the guy was unarmed.

Oh, Lord. It's important for me—for everyone—not to draw any conclusions before we get all the facts. But just from what I've heard so far—forty shots or more, man dead, no weapon—I'm guessing that this is going to be both a tragedy and a firestorm.

As it turns out, I guessed right.

I make sure the Command Center lieutenant has pulled the personnel records of the four officers involved and that he gives them to the investigators from IAB's Group 9, the Night Watch, to take to the scene. Already been done, the lieutenant says.

Ten minutes later I'm in my Department car, heading for the scene. I don't necessarily have to be there; my Group 54 Force Group guys and the Bronx Borough Shooting Team that responds to any shooting in the Bronx all know what they're doing. But I know this is going to be an important IAB case, and I want to get a feel for the scene.

When I get there the shooting scene is swarming with detectives interviewing neighbors, crime scene investigators and ballistic specialists collecting evidence, and patrol supervisors and senior borough commanders keeping things under control. Even though it's the middle of the night, there's a small crowd of spectators gathered behind the yellow police tape, staring silently.

The man's body has already been transported to the hospital, where he's been officially pronounced dead. The four officers involved in the shooting have had their guns impounded as evidence and been taken to the hospital for observation. That's SOP. There's a pool of blood in the vestibule, and the vestibule and the sidewalk in front of the apartment building are covered with clear plastic cups, each placed over an expended cartridge casing or bullet fragment by the crime scene investigators. There are literally dozens and dozens of clear plastic cups; it looks incongruously like the aftermath of a college kegger party. Investigators will soon determine that the four officers fired a total of forty-one shots, nineteen of which hit the dead man.

The IAB Night Watch Group leader hands me the personnel files on the four officers, and I go through them in the glow of the portable lights that have been set up to illuminate the scene.

Officer Edward McMellon, age twenty-six, with the Department for five years, has had five complaints against him with the Civilian Complaint Review Board, none of them substantiated; Officer Sean Carroll, thirty-five, also on the job for five years, has three unsubstantiated CCRB complaints; Officer Kenneth Boss, twenty-seven, who has seven years on the job, has three unsubbed complaints; and Officer Richard

Murphy, twenty-six, has four years on and no complaints. Three of the officers are relatively recent members of the SCU; only Carroll has been with the unit for more than two years.

One thing stands out: three of the four officers have been involved in shootings before. In 1997 Boss fatally shot a man who was brandishing a shotgun in the East New York section of Brooklyn; in fact, the Brooklyn DA's office still hasn't closed that investigation. McMellon shot and wounded a man holding a 9mm pistol seven months earlier, but the investigation found the shooting to be within guidelines. Carroll was cleared after firing a round at an unidentified suspect in the Bronx—the shot missed—the previous August.

As I said, the vast majority of NYPD officers will never fire their weapons at a person during their entire career, so this is pretty unusual. But these guys are in SCU, which is a highly active unit that makes about 40 percent of all the gun arrests in the city; it attracts cops who are aggressive and like to make arrests, and when you're making gun arrests the chances that you'll be involved in a shooting are far higher than if you're answering phones in a precinct house. Still, it's something to keep in mind.

And there's one other thing. In a perfect world it wouldn't matter, but in this world it does: While the dead man is black, all four officers are white.

According to the neighbors, who are already being interviewed by detectives, the dead man is Amadou Diallo, age twenty-two, an immigrant from the West African nation of Guinea who has been in the city for a little over two years. They say he's a pious Muslim who doesn't drink or smoke; a quiet, unassuming man who works as a street peddler in Manhattan, selling socks, gloves, videotapes, and imitation designer watches—"Rodexes"—on Fourteenth Street. His background check shows no criminal record.

The Borough Shooting Team detectives are fanning out to search for possible witnesses and my Group 54 investigators are doing the same. They don't find any eyewitnesses to the shooting, but they find several "earwitnesses," people who heard it happen. They distinctly remember hearing someone shout "Gun!" or "He's got a gun!" followed by a fusillade of gunfire; their statements are recorded. The next night our investigators will do an "anniversary canvass" at the same time of night to see if there are any witnesses who saw something but left before investigators arrived, and a week later, on the next Thursday, they'll do the same to see if there's someone whose job or routine puts them in the area at that time. Before it's over, IAB and Shooting Team investigators will question hundreds of people in the case.

But four people we don't question are the four cops who fired the shots.

That's something that surprises, and sometimes outrages, people who don't understand how the legal system works. You've got four cops who fire forty-one shots at an unarmed man, hitting him nineteen times and killing him, and the NYPD doesn't even ask them any questions? You're protecting those cops! It's a cover-up!

No, it's not. As investigators, we'd like nothing better than to question the officers who fired the shots. And we certainly have that authority. We can sit those cops down at a so-called GO-15 hearing—the same kind of hearing I had with the Field Internal Affairs Unit after the Christmas tree incident back in 1978—and order them to tell us what happened. And if they refuse to answer, or if they lie, we can suspend them from the Department and ultimately dismiss them.

But remember what I said about GO-15 hearings? According to the courts, those are compelled statements, given under threat of termination, which means that anything the cop tells us can't be used against him in a criminal case. And if anything he tells us leads prosecutors to new evidence against him, they can't use that, either, because it's what lawyers call "fruit from the poisoned tree."

In fact, in every police shooting or serious misconduct case that could result in criminal charges, I always call the District Attorney's Office and ask if they want us to GO the officer. And every time they say: Good Lord, no! That's the last thing we want you to do! That could totally screw up the case!

Yes, I know it's inconvenient. But there's this thing called the Fifth Amendment—and it applies to cops like anybody else.

Still, even though we can't interview the cops involved, we find out what happened to Amadou Diallo. The ballistics guys track the bullet paths and the bullet fragment paths, and figure out which bullets came from which cop's gun. The earwitnesses tell us what they heard, or didn't hear. The supervisors who immediately came to the scene tell us what the officers said and did after the shooting—and we can legally use those statements.

And even the four cops tell us their side of the story—indirectly. Within a few hours, the officers' lawyers or PBA reps will come up to us and say something like, It could be that Officer A thought the man had a gun, and it could be that Officer B said that he was in fear for his life, and it could be that Officer C was trying to protect his fellow officers from being shot . . . We can't use any of that against the officers, and neither can prosecutors if it comes to a criminal trial, which in this case it will. But it gives me the information I need to write a preliminary report on what happened.

This is what happened.

Officer Carroll, at the top of the stoop, shouts, He's got a gun! Carroll thinks the gun is pointing at McMellon, and almost simultaneously he and McMellon start firing; the vestibule lights up with muzzle flashes. McMellon is stepping backward as he fires, and then he tumbles backward down the stoop steps to the sidewalk; from the ground he keeps firing into the vestibule, emptying his 9mm semiautomatic—sixteen shots in all. Bullets are ricocheting off the metal front plate of the apartment building door, making it seem as if rounds are being fired out from the vestibule, not just into it. Carroll, seeing McMellon fall backward, thinks McMellon has been shot by Diallo. He backs away from the vestibule, also firing his 9mm semiautomatic until it's empty—another sixteen shots in all. Meanwhile, Officer Boss is out of the car, hears the gunfire, sees McMellon fall, thinks he's been shot; he sees Diallo in the dark vestibule with his arm extended, and then Boss fires five shots. Officer Murphy also sees McMellon fall; he runs toward the vestibule and fires four shots at Diallo. All of this takes less than ten seconds; nineteen of the shots hit Diallo.

It's a clear case of what experts call "contagious shooting," the tendency of cops in a confused shooting situation to start firing their weapons because their partners are firing their weapons, and then their partners keep firing their weapons because their partners are now firing their weapons. As I said, police policy is to continue firing until the threat is stopped, and in a cop's eyes, if your partner is still firing, the threat must still exist. Often a cop in an officer-involved shooting won't even know how many rounds he fired. When we eventually talk to him, he'll swear that he only fired three or four rounds, but when you check the gun you see that every round is gone, that he fired until the gun went "click!" The cop isn't lying; he knows you've got his gun and the expended cartridge casings, that the ballistic guys have been able to look at the extractor marks on the casings and match them to his gun. He knows we know exactly how many rounds he fired, and that lying would be both pointless and stupid. He just truly doesn't know how many shots he fired.

We try to train "contagious shooting" out of them, on the FATS machine and other training scenarios, try to teach them how to stay calm, assess the situation, stay in control—which is easy enough on the shooting range. The problem is that the FATS machine isn't shooting bullets back at them—and no cop ever gets shot at enough on the job to get used to it.

As the sound of gunfire drifts away, Carroll approaches Diallo, who is lying on the floor of the vestibule; he's still moving but close to death. Carroll reaches down to pick up the "gun" lying near Diallo's right hand—but it's not a gun, it's a wallet, a black wallet. It could be that Diallo, who spoke halting English, brought out the wallet to show his ID, or maybe he thought the cops weren't cops at all, but robbers, and he was giving up what little cash he had. We can never know.

Seeing the wallet where he expected to find a gun, Carroll kneels next to Diallo in the vestibule, saying: Oh my God! Please don't die! Boss radios for "a bus and a boss, forthwith!"—meaning he needs an ambulance and a supervisor immediately.

When the ambulance and the backup units arrive, Amadou Diallo is already dead, and all four officers are in a state of near shock. Carroll is crying, Murphy, too; Boss sits in the back of a sector car, unable to speak.

That's not unusual. I've seen cops after shootings who cried, screamed, beat their fists on the pavement, gone catatonic. Once when I was in Manhattan Traffic, I got flagged down by a truck driver who says there's a guy with a gun on Lafayette Street, he's sure it's a .45, he was in the military, he knows guns. Sure enough, it's a guy in a wheelchair who's waving a .45 around, obviously an EDP, and a cop is drawn down on him, screaming at him to drop the gun, knowing that if the guy in the wheelchair points the .45 at him or at a citizen, he's going to have to fire. Finally the guy tosses the gun—it's a replica .45, not a toy but a plastic replica, it looks absolutely real—and after it's over I find the cop sitting on the curb between two parked cars, throwing up between his knees into the gutter. And between spasms he's saying: I almost shot him, I almost shot him. He's saying it over and over.

One thing I've never seen cops do after they've shot somebody is laugh, or cheer. Sure, maybe later, when it turns out that the guy they shot was an armed murderer-rapist who shot at them first, and after the police commissioner has pinned an NYPD Combat Cross or Medal for Valor on them, maybe then, being cops, and to show how tough they are, they'll laugh and high-five it with their buddies at the bar. But most won't. No cop will ever shoot and kill enough people that it becomes routine, and if they ever entertained any Walter Mitty–style fantasies about heroically shooting down bad guys, those disappear before the echoes from the last shot of their first shooting fade away. As I said, in any shooting there are just too many things that can go wrong—for the cop.

So are the cops on Wheeler Avenue crying for Amadou Diallo, or are they crying for themselves? I can't tell you what's in their hearts at that moment. But they know that they've all fired multiple shots at a man who did not have a weapon, leaving him dead. And soon enough they'll know that the man they killed wasn't a rapist or a perp lurking in a strange doorway, that he wasn't a drug slinger with a long record, that instead he was simply a decent man with no criminal record who was standing on his own front steps, and they'll know that no one's ever going to pin a medal on their chests for what happened this night. They'll know that even if they did what they thought they had to do to save their partners' lives, the bottom line is that in a city already racked with racial divides and tension, they have shot and killed a completely innocent black man.

And they've all been cops long enough to understand what that means.

Controversial shootings with ethnic or racial overtones have been part of the NYPD ever since cops started carrying guns. In 1857, for example, when German immigrants rioted after the police started enforcing the "Sabbath laws" against German beer halls—apparently the Germans weren't handing over enough "sugar"—cops allegedly shot an innocent German man who was out for a walk with his wife, further enraging the German community. Later that year, a cop shot an Irish longshore-man who he said had attacked him, causing outrage in the growing Irish community; a coroner's jury indicted the cop and had him thrown in jail at the Tombs, but he was later released.

In more recent times, in 1973 two plainclothes cops in South Jamaica, Queens, stopped a man and his grandson, ten-year-old Clifford Glover, for questioning about a robbery, and when the man and the boy ran, one of the cops shot the boy twice, later saying he thought the boy had a gun. The cop was charged with murder but acquitted, sparking several days of rioting. In 1976 a white cop named Robert Torsney confronted a fifteen-year-old black kid named Randolph Evans at a Brooklyn housing project and apparently without any provocation fired a single shot to his head, killing him. While his partner screamed in shock, Torsney ran back to his patrol car and drove to the 75th Precinct, where he was subsequently arrested; charged with second-degree murder, he successfully presented an insanity defense, saying he had suffered a psychotic episode, and he was sent—briefly—to a hospital for the criminally insane. In 1984, an ESU cop who was part of a team serving an eviction notice shot and killed a sixty-six-year-old black female EDP named Eleanor Bumpurs, who had lunged at them with a knife; the cop was later acquitted by a judge.

And then there was the Jose "Kiko" Garcia case.

As the duty supervisor in Manhattan North that night, July 3, 1992, I caught the case—34th Precinct, officer-involved shooting, subject down, apartment building on 162nd Street in Washington Heights. When I get there the scene is chaotic—patrol cars, emergency lights flashing, a crowd starting to gather—although not yet a violent one; that would come later. The Borough Shooting Team detectives—at the time, the old IAD did not roll out on officer-involved shootings—are already there, and when the detectives fan out to talk to the other cops and interview witnesses I try to piece together what happened.

What happened is that three plainclothes cops in an unmarked car spot Garcia, twenty-three, a Dominican Republic immigrant who's on pro-bation on a cocaine sales charge, with what appears to be a gun. Officer Michael O'Keefe gets out and chases Garcia while the other two cops in the car circle around to head him off. O'Keefe catches Garcia, they strug-gle and stagger into the vestibule of the apartment building while O'Keefe screams for help into his radio. Garcia pulls out the gun, a .38, and O'Keefe then shoots him twice. Garcia dies later at the hospital, the same hospital where O'Keefe is treated for bruises and cuts suffered in the fight.

That's what happened, but it's not the story on the street. The story on the street is that O'Keefe beat the hell out of Garcia outside the building and then dragged him semiconscious into the vestibule and stood over him and shot him three times in cold blood while Garcia begged for his life. By the next day, people we had interviewed the night before, people who had told us they hadn't seen anything, suddenly recalled that they'd seen everything, and that the cop had murdered that young man, who by this time is no longer a convicted drug slinger with a gun but a pleasant young man who may have had some trouble in the past but was turning his life around and wouldn't hurt a fly. And the press and the TV news stations buy that story line, repeating it again and again until it sounds like truth.

That routinely happened in officer-involved shootings and excessive-force incident investigations in which I was involved. Veteran reporters would assume that everything the cops said was a lie, part of the inevitable police cover-up to protect their own. But when some street mope they'd never seen before and would never see again sidled up to them at the yellow crime scene tape and whispered in their ears—You know, those cops didn't have to shoot that boy, I seen it all, they shot him down like a dog while he was beggin' for mercy!—the reporters would treat it like gospel. They would write it in their stories or broadcast it over the air, something like, Despite police denials, a witness said the officers shot the man while he begged for mercy . . . And from that point on the facts wouldn't matter.

And that's exactly what happened in the Kiko Garcia case. Several days of rioting follow—cars burning, windows broken, rocks and bottles flying. Mayor David Dinkins tries and fails to calm the unrest by having the city pay for Garcia's funeral in the Dominican Republic, and succeeds in infuriating almost every cop in the NYPD. Dinkins becomes known to cops ever after as "the mayor who paid for a drug dealer's funeral." Two months later, in front of a grand jury, two alleged eyewitnesses who claim to have seen the cop stand over Garcia and shoot him in cold blood see their stories crumble in the face of the facts—bullet impact marks, the medical examiner's report, tapes of radio transmissions, evidence gathered not just by us but also by the FBI. The grand jury declines to indict the cop, and even the DA has to admit that there's absolutely no basis for a criminal case. But the alternative story line is the one that lives on—They shot him while he begged for his life!—just as the "Hands up, don't shoot!" story line about a young man named Michael Brown in tiny Ferguson, Missouri, is the one that lives on, despite all the evidence to the contrary.

But the Amadou Diallo case is different. In the Diallo case, everyone— the police, the press, the public—agrees on the basic facts: Four cops who are white fired many, many shots at an innocent unarmed man who was black. The only question is, Was it a tragic accident? Or was it a crime?

There are demonstrations, of course, beginning with one of about a thousand people on Wheeler Avenue led by the Reverend Al Sharpton. I'd met Sharpton a number of times when I was a captain in Manhattan South and he was organizing periodic demonstrations in front of City Hall or One Police Plaza against police brutality, racism, whatever was the outrage of the day. I would go up and introduce myself and he would shake my hand and say: Gonna have a lot of people here today, lot of people, but don't you worry, we're gonna keep it peaceful! The guy couldn't have been more pleasant and cooperative—and then he'd get in front of a microphone and start shouting about how every cop in New York, presumably including me, was a racist thug who woke up every morning just itching to get out and shoot innocent black people. Sharpton was, and is, a charlatan and a race-hustler—but he's a personally charming charlatan and race-hustler.

Later there are daily demonstrations against the Diallo shooting in front of Police Plaza featuring appearances by former mayor David Dinkins, Jesse Jackson, Congressman Charles Rangel, and numerous others, all denouncing the police, many intentionally getting themselves arrested as an act of civil disobedience.

But it isn't just the black community that's infuriated by the Diallo shooting. The reaction throughout the city, and even the entire country, is one of anger and disbelief—How can the cops shoot an unarmed man forty-one times? (Of course, while forty-one shots were fired, Diallo was actually hit nineteen times—but to most people, maybe understandably, that's a distinction without much of a difference.) The *New York Post*, usually the most pro-cop of the city's papers, leads the Diallo shooting story with a screaming headline, "IN COLD BLOOD"—which it wasn't; it was a heat-of-the-moment tragedy, nothing cold about it. The *New Yorker* publishes a cover cartoon showing a fat NYPD cop cheerfully plinking away at black human silhouettes in a shooting gallery. Bruce Springsteen writes a song about it called "American Skin (41 Shots)"—"No secret my friend / You can get killed just for living in your American skin." To a public that has no real conception of what it's like to be a cop on the street, Diallo becomes a symbol of everything that's wrong with cops in general, and the NYPD in particular.

For the NYPD, the Diallo shooting, coming on the eve of the trials in the Louima police brutality case—more on that later—is a disaster. Throughout the early 1990s, crime in the city had dropped precipitously, people could walk the streets again, everybody talked about the "New York City Miracle"—and the NYPD rightly got most of the credit for making it happen. But with Diallo, that's forgotten; for a lot of people, the NYPD isn't solving a problem, it *is* the problem.

Like I said, it's the eternal cop truth: One day you're a hero, and the next day you're a bum.

I never heard a single NYPD cop describe the Diallo shooting as anything but a tragedy, a terrible mistake, something that could have happened to any of them. Although cops hate it when civilians second-guess them, cops certainly aren't reluctant to second-guess other cops about their tactics, so there was some talk about how the SCU cops should have done this, or could have done that. But I also never heard a single cop say that what the four SCU officers did was a crime.

But as you might expect, the Bronx District Attorney's Office doesn't . . . can't . . . see it that way.

On their lawyers' advice, none of the four cops testifies before the grand jury. Given the public reaction, it's almost certain they will be indicted, and they'll probably testify in their own defense, so from their lawyers' point of view, why give prosecutors an early bite at the apple that could later be used against them at trial? As expected, seven weeks after the shooting DA Robert Johnson announces that the grand jury has indicted the four cops for second-degree murder, alleging that they had acted with "depraved indifference to human life"; the charge carries a possible twenty-five-to-life sentence. They are also charged with "reckless endangerment" of people who lived inside the apartment building.

Johnson was the city's only black district attorney, and as IAB chief I'd often worked with him and his staff on police corruption cases. And I think that deep in his heart he knew that it was going to be difficult, maybe impossible, to prove that under the law the four cops had acted with "depraved indifference to human life"—especially if the cops went to a bench trial in front of a judge instead of a Bronx jury. The law says that police officers have a right to shoot if they have a "reasonable" belief that their lives or that of others are in danger—not an absolute belief, not a certain belief, only a reasonable belief. It's part of the deal that society makes with cops: Here's a badge and a gun, now go out there and protect us from dangerous people who may also have guns—and if you make an honest mistake, even a fatal one, we'll give you the benefit of the doubt.

But DAs in New York are elected officials, and as a politician as well as a prosecutor, and given the public outrage, Johnson feels he has to do something.

After various legal maneuvers in the case, including a change of venue to Albany, the case goes to trial, and all of the officers testify, sometimes emotionally, that they'd been in fear for their lives and their partners' lives. In February 2000 a jury of four blacks and eight whites finds them not guilty.

There is anger over the verdicts, of course, with some people claiming that cops who shot citizens, even innocent ones, always got off, which wasn't exactly true. In 1995 a Housing police officer was convicted of criminally negligent homicide after shooting a man while searching for a burglary suspect; he was sentenced to one to four years in prison. In 1997 a Transit police officer was found guilty of second-degree manslaughter for fatally shooting an unarmed man in the back on a Bronx subway platform; he served three years in prison. In 2003 an NYPD undercover officer who shot and killed an innocent African immigrant named Ousmane Zongo during a botched raid on a Manhattan warehouse was convicted of criminally negligent homicide; he was sentenced to probation and automatically dismissed from the Department. In 2016 former rookie cop Peter Liang was sentenced to five years probation and community service for felony negligent homicide in the accidental shooting of Akai Gurley in a Brooklyn public housing building.

But despite those cases, and others, it's true that while cops involved in controversial shootings are often indicted, convictions are rare, for the reasons I already mentioned. It's hard to prove beyond a reasonable doubt that a cop doing his job in a high-stress situation in a dark alley in Brooklyn or on a bad corner in the Bronx is guilty of criminal behavior when he or she makes a mistake, even an egregious one. Civil liability is another issue, and in almost all of the cases I've mentioned, the city wound up paying the dead person's family hundreds of thousands or even millions of dollars. (Diallo's parents eventually received a $3 million settlement.) It goes without saying that no amount of money could ever bring the dead person back to life—although it's also true that sending a cop to prison for making a mistake wouldn't bring them back to life, either.

And people forget that the justice system runs two ways, that civilians have beaten the rap after shooting cops as well. In 1974 a jury acquitted a man charged with shooting and killing Officer Phillip Cardillo during a scuffle at a Nation of Islam mosque in Harlem two years earlier. In 1986 a guy named Larry Davis became a folk hero in the Bronx after shooting and wounding six cops and eluding capture for two weeks; a jury found him not guilty of the shootings. In 1999 a Bronx jury acquitted a man of shooting and permanently injuring an NYPD captain while he was serving a search warrant; one juror was quoted as saying the captain "got what he deserved." There were other, similar cases. When it comes to the court system, one man's justice is another man's judicial travesty.

After the acquittals in the Diallo case there were some demands that the four cops be prosecuted under federal law for violating Diallo's civil rights, just like the four LAPD cops in the Rodney King case in LA were charged in the federal system after being acquitted in state court. (Two of the LAPD cops were convicted in the federal case.) I'm a cop, not a Supreme Court justice, but I could never understand how that isn't double jeopardy—especially since in virtually every case it's only used against cops. But eventually the US attorney passed on prosecuting the case.

And now the question was, What is the Department going to do with these four cops?

Just because a cop is acquitted in a criminal trial doesn't mean he automatically gets his gun and shield back and goes back to work. We still have to decide if the cop broke any Department rules. In the Diallo case, after the not-guilty verdicts, and after the US attorney declined to prosecute, our Group 54 investigators were finally able to GO-15 the four officers, sitting them down and requiring them to tell their versions of events. It was mostly a formality, since the cops had already told their stories and been cross-examined at trial—and the stories they told us matched in every detail their court testimony and the stories their PBA lawyers had conveyed to us immediately after the shooting. We wrote up our final report, and the Firearms Discharge Review Board ruled that the Diallo shooting was "within guidelines."

In other words, in police parlance the shooting was technically a "good" shooting. But in practical terms, no one in the NYPD, perhaps including even the four officers themselves, would ever use the words "good shooting" and "Amadou Diallo" in the same sentence.

In the NYPD carrying a gun is a privilege, not a legal right or even a union contract right. The police commissioner at the time, Bernie Kerik, chose to keep the four officers on "modified duty," meaning they couldn't carry firearms, and his successor, Ray Kelly again, upheld it. Although the PBA didn't agree, at the time it was an obvious call.

After all, what would the public reaction be if one of those cops went out and somehow got involved in another officer-involved shooting? Even if the shooting was totally justified, the press—and the personal injury lawyers—would pounce: "DIALLO SHOOTING COP KILLS AGAIN!" Or what if one of those cops found himself in a violent situation and hesitated to shoot when he should have, putting his partner or someone else in danger?

Maybe it wasn't fair to the cops. But remember what I said about the word "fair" and the NYPD?

For most of the cops involved, not getting returned to full duty was a moot point. Two of them, Murphy and McMellon, joined the New York Fire Department—although even that was controversial—and Carroll retired not long afterward. Kenneth Boss was assigned to Floyd Bennett Field in Brooklyn, where he worked in an equipment repair shop at the ESU training headquarters; his NYPD ID card was stamped "No Firearm." While on military leave Boss served a combat tour in Iraq with the Marines in 2006; he also waged a decade-long legal fight to get his gun back, arguing that as a member of the so-called Rubber Gun Squad he was a pariah in the Department. He lost every court case, but in 2012 Commissioner Kelly returned him to full duty with the Special Operations Division, which handles emergency situations like water rescues. As far as I know, Kelly never told anyone why he returned Boss to duty. Maybe it was simply because he decided that after thirteen years, the Diallo shooting cops had suffered enough.

I know what you're probably thinking. These cops shot an innocent man, and they never spent a day in prison, and you're telling me they suffered?

That's exactly what I'm telling you. Amadou Diallo and his family suffered far more, but those cops suffered, too.

And no, I really don't expect you to believe that, or to understand it. But every cop will.

The Amadou Diallo shooting wasn't the last controversial police shooting I would be involved in as IAB chief—sadly, it was far from it.

In March 2000 a Brooklyn man named Patrick Moses Dorismond was standing outside a club in Midtown Manhattan when an undercover narcotics cop tried to buy drugs from him. There was an argument, a scuffle with the undercover and his backups, and then one of the cops' gun fired, killing Dorismond. A grand jury ruled it an accident.

In January 2004 a Housing cop named Richard Neri Jr. was checking a rooftop at a public housing project in Bed-Stuy when a nineteen-year-old unarmed black man named Timothy Stansbury suddenly appeared in a rooftop doorway. Startled, the cop fired his drawn weapon a single time, mortally wounding Stansbury. The cop told a grand jury that it was an accident, that he was sorry, and the grand jury declined to indict him. Later, after our investigation, the shooting was ruled "out of guidelines" and Officer Neri was suspended for thirty days and placed on modified duty, with no gun.

There were other controversial shootings, too many of them, including the Ousmane Zongo case I already mentioned. But the most controversial, the one most often compared with the Diallo shooting, was the Sean Bell case.

In November 2006, Bell, who was to be married the next day, is holding a bachelor party at a Queens strip joint called Club Kalua that was being investigated by NYPD undercover detectives and their backup team for alleged prostitution and drug dealing. One of Bell's friends gets into an argument, and a black undercover detective inside the club, Detective Gescard Isnora, says he heard the friend tell someone else to "get the gat"—meaning a gun. As Bell and his two friends leave, Isnora steps out of his undercover role, retrieves his gun and shield from his car, and follows them to Bell's car, a Nissan Altima that's parked nearby. Isnora says later that when he tries to stop the car, Bell tries to run him over before crashing into a fence. As Isnora approaches the car, he shouts out "Gun!" and starts firing. Four of his backups also start shooting; together they fire fifty shots, leaving Bell dead and his two friends wounded. No gun is found in the car.

As expected, the Bell shooting prompts outrage and demonstrations and denunciations of the trigger-happy NYPD in the press. Most of the protesters and commentators compare it to the Diallo case, another example of an unarmed black man shot down in a barrage of police bullets.

But the Sean Bell case isn't the Amadou Diallo case. Although the results were the same—an unarmed man shot dead—from a police standpoint, the Bell case was worse. The Diallo tragedy occurred because of some cops' misjudgments in a few brief seconds; the Bell shooting occurred because of some cops' misjudgment over the course of minutes.

I was on vacation when the Bell shooting happened, but my XO called and told me that the shooting didn't look good from a Department policy point of view. I immediately flew back and when I looked at the reports the IAB Force Group had put together, I saw what he meant. Not only had an unarmed man been killed and two others wounded, but the cops involved had made some serious procedural mistakes— starting with Detective Isnora stepping out of his undercover role.

Isnora and two other detectives were indicted by a grand jury on charges ranging from first-degree manslaughter to second-degree assault, but they were acquitted of all counts in a nonjury trial. After the US Justice Department decided not to prosecute on federal charges—

which took months—seven cops, including the lieutenant who was supposed to be supervising the undercover investigation at the club, were brought up on Department charges that the shooting had violated Department policies. After a trial before the Deputy Commissioner for Trials, the shooting was declared "out of guidelines," and Detective Isnora was fired and three others were forced to retire or resign.

It's like I said: Police guns are double-ended weapons: They can kill and maim at one end, and they can end careers at the other.

I wish I could tell you that someday there will be no more fatalities from officer-involved shootings, in New York City or anywhere else. And maybe someday we will have *Star Trek*–style "phasers" that will reliably put a suspect down without killing or seriously injuring him—although even then I suspect there will be some deaths, just as there are with the Tasers we have today.

But until then, as long as criminals have guns, cops will have to have guns, too. And sometimes they'll have to use them.

When they do, when cops do have to fire their weapons, in most cases it will be a trained reflex, a decision made in a half-second or less, with no time to think about it or consider the terrible potential consequences. But if any good cop does have time to think before he fires his gun, if he has time to consider what can happen in even an officially "good" shooting, in virtually every case I can tell you what that cop will be thinking.

He'll be thinking:

Please, God, don't make me have to shoot this guy.

Chapter 7

EXCESSIVE FORCE

It's four o'clock on a Saturday morning in August 1997, but the crowd outside the Club Rendez-Vous in the Flatbush section of Brooklyn still isn't ready to give up on Friday night. The music and dance club is a popular spot with Brooklyn's tightly knit Haitian community, and hundreds of people have shown up to hear a Creole pop band called the Phantoms play the Haitian dance music known as compas. But when the music stops and the club closes at three a.m. the crowd streams out onto the sidewalk in front, still pumped up and rowdy.

Two women in the crowd get into a screaming fight—it's a "You slut! Stay away from my man!" kind of thing, rendered in Creole, a combination of French, English, Spanish, and African languages—and other club patrons crowd around them, some trying to intervene, some just to watch. Fights are not an uncommon occurrence at the Club Rendez-Vous, and neither are gunshots; six months earlier a sudden spray of gunfire through the front window killed one of the club's bouncers. As the fight between the two women escalates, one of them gets her dress torn off, and she stands there almost naked, screaming.

Then the cops wade in.

The half dozen cops at the scene are from the midnight shift at the 70th Precinct, the Seven-Oh, and they're all wearily familiar with the Club Rendez-Vous. Several of the cops start pushing their way through the crowd to break up the fight and disperse the spectators. While the crowd jeers, one of the cops pushes a man to the ground, which angers a thin, thirty-year-old Haitian immigrant named Abner Louima. Louima, who has a wife and a child and who works as a security guard at a water and sewage treatment plant, thinks the cops are being too rough. Louima starts shouting at the cop, and the two get into a shoving match. Then somebody—not Louima—sucker punches the cop in the head. He goes down, briefly, the crowd starts to scatter, and some other cops grab Louima and take him to the ground and put him under arrest. They rear-cuff him and then two cops put him in the back of a patrol car and start heading back to the precinct.

On the way they meet up with the cop who got hit in the head outside the Club Rendez-Vous, who's in another two-man car. He gets out, looks at Louima lying in the back of the other patrol car and mistakenly identifies him as the man who hit him. Enraged, he starts beating the handcuffed Louima with his fists and a police radio; Louima later says the other three cops also beat him with their fists.

At the precinct, Louima is charged with disorderly conduct, obstructing government administration, resisting arrest, and third-degree assault. While he's being searched his belt is removed, and his black pants start slipping down as he's standing at the front desk. After they finish processing the arrest, one of the cops starts walking Louima toward the holding cells. His pants have slipped down around his ankles now, so he's shuffling, still rear-cuffed. But instead of taking Louima left toward the cells, the cop turns right, heading toward the bathroom, where another cop is waiting.

Forty-two hours later, at eleven p.m. on Sunday, I get a call at home from the supervisor of the IAB's four-to-midnight call-out team, a captain. The call-out teams respond immediately to any serious incidents, twenty-four hours a day, and the captain is calling from Coney Island Hospital. He and his team have been investigating a report that came into the Command Center that afternoon.

The captain tells me they've got an arrestee from the Seven-Oh that the EMTs brought in early Saturday morning, a guy named Louima—pronounced Loo-EE-ma. He's got severe internal injuries, with punctures in his small intestine and bladder and a perforated colon.

And, Chief? the captain says. The guy's in a lot of pain and pretty heavily sedated, but he's saying that the cops did it. He told the nurses that some cops at the Seven-Oh took him into the bathroom at the precinct and rammed a stick, a toilet plunger or something, up his rectum.

I'm not sure that I'm hearing him right.

Wait a minute, I say. He's saying that cops did that to him?

Yeah, Chief, the captain says. We're still talking to people, we'll know more in an hour or two. I'll call you back.

Well, I've been a cop for a long time, and in IAB for several years now. So if you tell me that some cops are involved in what looks like a bad shooting, or that some cops are accused of beating a prisoner, giving him a tune-up in an interrogation room, or that cops have been shaking down drug dealers, I can believe it. I don't like it, but I can believe it.

But when you tell me that NYPD police officers engaged in a brutal, sadistic, almost medieval torture of a prisoner inside a precinct house, that they shoved a stick up a prisoner's rectum and inflicted massive internal injuries, I'm going to need some pretty good evidence to convince me. Like I said, I've been a cop a long time, and I've never, ever heard of anything like this.

Then a couple hours later the captain calls back.

Chief, the captain says, I know this is hard to believe. But it looks like this really happened.

Before I head into the office—no sleep tonight—I make sure we've got enough people on the case. We've got an IAB team at the hospital, another on its way to the Club Rendez-Vous. And there's another team of a half dozen IAB investigators on their way to the 70th Precinct, a drab, three-story granite building on Lawrence Avenue.

Except that as far as IAB is concerned, the Seven-Oh Precinct isn't a precinct anymore.

It's a crime scene.

Police work is often brutal. But there's a big difference between brutal police work and police brutality.

Case in point: It's the summer of 1982, I'm a sergeant in Manhattan Traffic, and my driver/partner and I catch a call over the radio about an EDP on Thirty-Fourth Street near Herald Square. When we get there we see this guy on the sidewalk, a white male, six-three or -four, maybe two hundred forty pounds, completely naked except for boxer shorts. The guy is covered in a sweat-sheen, and he's literally got foam coming out of his mouth; it's pretty clear that he's dusted, meaning he's on angel dust, PCP, which can cause bizarre and violent behavior.

One other unusual thing about this guy: He's got a uniformed foot post cop hanging onto each arm—and he's swinging those two cops around like they're on the Tilt-a-Whirl at Coney Island.

So I run up and Mace the guy square in the face—Mace is just a form of tear gas—but it doesn't even faze him. He keeps swinging around and around and finally one of the cops on his arms goes flying backward onto the sidewalk.

So I grab the now-free arm and my partner grabs a leg, but the guy's so sweaty and slippery that it's hard to hold on; it's like one of those greased pig contests at the old county fair. All we want to do is get this mope down so we can put handcuffs on him, but he's not having it. He's not fighting us, exactly, he's not throwing punches or kicks, he's just resisting, squirming and twisting and grunting. Now the cop on the sidewalk has crawled over and grabbed the guy's other leg, so we've got a cop on each arm and each leg. Then another patrol car with two more cops shows up, and one of them jumps on the guy's back. Five cops we've got on this guy, and we still can't control him. Meanwhile, a crowd is gathering to watch, and we can hear them start: Five cops! On one guy! Why don't you cops fight fair?

So finally the sixth cop, the only one who doesn't have a piece of this guy, because there's no more pieces to grab, takes out his baton. He side-strokes the guy across the shins—whack!—which makes a sound like a baseball bat hitting a tree trunk, and then again—whack! We can hear the onlookers gasp at the sound of it.

And that does it. The guy cries out in pain and then sinks to his knees—he's hurting, but not seriously injured—and we get him face-down on the sidewalk and cuff him, then we roll him over on his side. You don't want to leave a cuffed suspect facedown, because with some people, particularly heavy ones with underlying medical conditions, it can cause asphyxiation. Then we all stand there, bent over, exhausted, gasping for breath, eyes burning from the Mace, two of the cops bleeding from being scraped on the sidewalk, while people in the crowd are muttering: Why'd ya have to hurt him? That's police brutality!

Well, yeah, it was brutal. It was brutal on the perp, and it was brutal on us. But like I said, morally and legally it wasn't police brutality.

The law allows—in fact, it requires—a police officer to use reasonable force, including the intentional infliction of pain, to gain compliance to a lawful order or to stop a threat of bodily injury or death to another human being, the cops themselves included. Depending on the circumstances, the level of force can range from simply touching a suspect—grabbing him by the arm—all the way up to shooting and killing him. Of course, the key word here is "reasonable." A cop can't shoot a guy just because he won't turn around to be handcuffed; just as obviously, you can't expect a cop to gently grab the arm of a guy who's waving a knife.

The law also demands that once compliance and control have been achieved, or the threat to human life has been stopped, all use of force against the suspect has to stop—immediately. Any additional use of force, whether it's to punish a suspect for his resistance or just because the cop is having a bad day, is excessive force, and it's illegal, and it can get a cop seriously jammed up.

All of which sounds very neat and tidy and easy to understand. But when a cop is confronting a violent EDP on a sidewalk, or a wife-beating husband on a domestic call, or even a guy with an open warrant who has decided he just doesn't want to go to jail tonight, it's a little harder to determine exactly where the line is between "reasonable" and "unreasonable," or whether the perp on the ground has really ceased resisting or if he's just resting up to take another run at you.

What many people don't seem to understand is that in almost every instance, it's the suspect, not the cops, who determines the level of force that's used against him. For example, a compliant suspect who follows orders to turn around and put his hands behind his back can probably expect the minimum level of force—that is, a cop puts on the cuffs and searches him and puts him in the back of a sector car, being careful to shield the suspect's head so he doesn't bump it. If every suspect did that, if everyone involved in a confrontation with a cop did exactly what the cop told him to do, excessive-force cases would drop to virtually zero.

But too often they don't do that. Sometimes they're drunk, sometimes they're high, sometimes they're just pissed off. So they fight, they spit, they claw, they bite, they kick, they punch. And even if, like the dusted guy on the sidewalk by Herald Square, they're only resisting—

twisting, squirming, refusing to give up—the cops still have to make the arrest. The only alternative is to say: Well, okay, sir, it's apparent that you don't really want to go to jail tonight, so we're just going to let you go— but please do us a favor and don't beat the hell out of your girlfriend again tonight, okay?

But the public doesn't want us to do that. The public—and the girlfriend—wants us to take that guy to jail.

So how do we do that? How do we make a guy go to jail when he really, really, really doesn't want to?

Every NYPD cop has had training in using his or her hands and feet and police baton against a resisting suspect. At the Academy they teach recruits various self-defense and compliance moves—the wrist hammer lock, the thumb in the armpit move, the side-stroke with the baton or, more recently, the telescoping baton known as an ASP, and so on. They also teach recruits what not to do: never baton-stroke a suspect in the head, never leave an unresisting handcuffed suspect facedown, never use a chokehold or sleeper hold that can deprive a suspect of oxygen or blood to the brain and possibly cause death. There's a lot of emphasis on when, how, and how much force a cop can use.

But we have to be realistic. We don't have thirty-six thousand Chuck Norrises out there. We can't turn every cop into a professional-level martial artist, able with one deft move to flip a suspect facedown on the floor, ready for cuffing. Maybe Mr. Spock on *Star Trek* can use the Vulcan Nerve Pinch to gently render someone unconscious, but if Spock tried that on a violent suspect on the streets of New York City he'd probably wind up getting beaten to death—or at the very least he'd get sued, since sleeper holds are prohibited.

Of course, there are other ways to subdue a resisting suspect. The NYPD and other police departments across the country have adopted various types of specialized, nonlethal or less than lethal takedown equipment to get barricaded or resisting subjects under control: net guns that can wrap a suspect up, handheld water cannons to knock him down, beanbag shotguns, pepper spray or OC (oleoresin capsicum), Tasers.

And all that specialized equipment is fine, if you have the time to use it and if it's available—which it often isn't. As I said earlier, because of concerns about their potential lethality—unfounded concerns, in my opinion—in 2014 the NYPD only had about six hundred Tasers, and they were only issued to specialized units like ESU and to some patrol sergeants and lieutenants.

But the truth is that most of the time, if a suspect is resisting arrest, it winds up in a flat-out brawl, with one or two or three cops rolling around with a flailing suspect on a sidewalk or in a filthy stairwell in a high-rise. Later, from the perspective of a nice, clean, air-conditioned courtroom, with the "victim" all spiffed up in a new suit with his attorney at his side, it may be easy for civilians who've never been in a fight before to decide that, yes, the cops used too much force, that they gave the guy one too many baton strokes after he stopped resisting. But it's not so easy when you're in the stairwell or on that sidewalk.

Of course, there's a big difference between a cop who honestly misjudges the amount of force to use on a perp and a cop who intentionally uses force on a nonresisting suspect for payback or intimidation. But most excessive-force cases in the NYPD involve the former, not the latter.

Yes, there was a time in NYPD history when a perp who ran from the cops, or who fought with the cops, could expect some pretty comprehensive "street justice" at the end of the chase. Remember that teenaged burglar in the Seven-Three we caught in the abandoned building after a foot pursuit? He was terrified of what was going to happen to him—and in the old NYPD he might have had reason to be. Same thing went for a perp who was wanted for shooting or seriously injuring a cop. In the old NYPD, he was well advised to turn himself in at another precinct, with his lawyer at his side, if he expected to come out of NYPD custody in the same condition as when he went in. I'm not saying it was right, I'm just saying what it was. I never personally witnessed any serious abuse of a prisoner or what I considered excessive force in an arrest; when I was a young cop the other cops wouldn't do anything illegal in front of me, and after I became a supervisor, the cops under me knew better. Still, I knew that it happened.

But it's different now. There are too many cell phone cameras, too many surveillance cameras, too many police brutality lawyers, too many reporters looking for a police brutality story, too much Department supervision—not to mention the many IAB investigators standing by to pursue cops who intentionally cross the line. Today every cop in America knows that if a perp is seriously injured or dies while he's wearing your handcuffs, whatever the cause, you're in a lot of trouble. Just ask those six cops in Baltimore who were indicted for manslaughter in 2015 after a suspect died in the back of a police van.

The bottom line is that despite what you may think from watching the news, bona fide intentional excessive-force cases in the NYPD are actually pretty rare.

But do they happen? Of course. During my time at IAB there were a number of controversial and highly publicized "excessive-force" cases in which people died in confrontations with the cops. But one of the most controversial lethal "use of force" cases in recent NYPD history occurred after I retired. In July 2014 cops in Staten Island attempt to arrest Eric Garner—forty-three, six-three, three hundred fifty pounds—for selling illegal "loosie" cigarettes on a sidewalk; Garner had been arrested thirty times previously. Garner resists, and eventually five cops get him to the ground and handcuff him. After saying "I can't breathe" several times, Garner stops breathing and is declared dead at a hospital an hour later. The ME rules that Garner died of compression of the neck and compression of the chest, with asthma, heart disease, and obesity as contributing factors. The case sparks nationwide antipolice demonstrations, although a grand jury declines to indict Officer Daniel Pantaleo, who allegedly used an illegal chokehold while subduing Garner. As of this writing, a federal investigation is continuing.

There were also numerous less than lethal excessive-force encounters that made the news and angered the public. There was the rookie cop—the guy had eleven days on the job—who violently pushed a bicyclist off his bike at a rally in Times Square. The veteran cop who, also in 2008, hit a handcuffed suspect ten times with an ASP, paused to take a cell phone call, and then hit the guy ten times more, all caught on a surveillance camera. The deputy inspector who, for questionable reasons, pepper-sprayed Occupy Wall Street protesters in 2011. The list could go on and on—and when you stack them up like that it may seem like the NYPD has a chronic and frequent excessive-force problem.

But consider these numbers.

In 2013 the New York Civilian Complaint Review Board received about 5,300 allegations of excessive force by NYPD cops, everything from people who said they were beaten in a patrol car to people who said the cops roughly pushed them on a sidewalk to arrestees who said their handcuffs were too tight. Admittedly, that sounds like a lot of allegations, and it's the number that anticop activists and reporters home in on.

But let's look a little deeper. About half of those allegations were dropped for various reasons, usually because the complainant didn't follow up on the complaint. Maybe the complainant thought it was too much trouble. Or maybe it was a perp who figured that just filing the complaint was enough payback against the cop who arrested him. Or maybe the complainant was someone like Barry in Brooklyn—That cop stabbed me in my fucking eye!—who made excessive-force allegations two or three times a week.

Whatever the reason, that takes the number down to roughly 2,200 excessive-force allegations that were investigated by the CCRB that year. Of those, about 900 were ruled "exonerated," meaning the cop in question used the force the complainant described, but that use of force was legal and justified. Another 200 force allegations were ruled "unfounded," meaning that the alleged use of force never took place. In about 200 of the cases the CCRB investigators were unable to identify the officer, and in almost 800 cases the allegations were ruled "unsubstantiated," meaning there was insufficient proof either way.

So how many allegations of excessive force against NYPD cops were ruled "substantiated" by the CCRB, meaning that in the CCRB's opinion the cop in question had, in fact, gone too far in using force? To put it another way, how many allegations of "police brutality" were found by the CCRB to be true?

The answer is 40. In a Department that made about 400,000 arrests that year, and out of the thousands of allegations of excessive force investigated by the CCRB, only 40 of those allegations were substantiated by the CCRB. And remember, this is the *Civilian* Complaint Review Board, not the NYPD, that investigated those excessive-force allegations. (About half of those 40 cases resulted in Department discipline against the officers, up to and including dismissal; in the other cases the Department trial advocate—also a civilian—decided that there wasn't enough evidence to proceed with a Department trial. None of the CCRB cases resulted in a criminal indictment.)

Obviously, that number doesn't represent every instance in which a New York City cop gave a resisting suspect or even an ordinary citizen one punch too many, or one push too hard, or otherwise exceeded the regulations for the lawful use of force. A lot of alleged instances of police excessive force don't get reported.

But the numbers demonstrate that despite the perception of the NYPD as an excessively violent institution—a perception fueled by antipolice community activists, police brutality lawyers, and the press—the truth is that most NYPD cops do their jobs in a professional manner. Again, at times they may have to be rough, even brutal. But in the vast majority of cases, it's not police brutality.

But if that's true, if the NYPD is not inherently an excessively violent institution, how can I reconcile that with what happened to Abner Louima?

The answer is that I can't reconcile it. I couldn't reconcile it then, and I can't reconcile it to this day. And neither can most other NYPD cops.

The truth is that when they first heard about the Louima case, almost every cop I knew, me included, couldn't believe that it really happened.

But it did happen. And it was IAB's job to prove it.

It's eight o'clock Monday morning, nine hours after I got the first call about Louima, and I'm waiting in the oak-paneled foyer outside the police commissioner's office on the fourteenth floor of One Police Plaza. Commissioner Howard Safir steps out of the elevator, and as he makes his way to his office he's smiling and offering morning greetings to the aides and secretaries as he passes their desks. And then he sees me there, waiting, and suddenly he's not smiling anymore.

That's something you have to get used to if you're chief of the Internal Affairs Bureau. On a personal level, you can have great relationships with the people you work with, but on a professional level, nobody is ever happy to see you coming through their office door or waiting outside to see them. They know you aren't there to give them good news.

Commissioner Safir is no exception.

This isn't good, is it? he says, and I tell him, No, it's not. He can probably see in my face that it's not ordinary bad news.

So we go into his office and I start laying it out for him.

I tell him we've got a thirty-year-old victim—Louima is a victim now, not a perp—arrested for dis-con (disorderly conduct) at a club in Brooklyn early Saturday morning by cops from the Seven-Oh. We've confirmed that when he was arrested and booked there was no sign of serious injuries, but he's now in intensive care at Coney Island Hospital with massive internal injuries—so obviously the injuries occurred while he was in our custody. We got the first call about it at the Command Center Sunday afternoon from some of his relatives, and we rolled out on it immediately and talked to the victim and some of the medical staff.

I have to pause for a second at this point. I can hardly believe what I'm about to say to the commissioner. But I have to say it.

What the victim is saying, I tell the commissioner, is that two cops took him into the bathroom at the precinct, and one of them rammed a stick, maybe a toilet plunger, into his rectum, and then the cop waved it in his face and told him he'd kill him if he told anybody. The docs say his injuries are consistent with assault with a blunt object. The victim also says that on the way to the precinct four cops beat him while he was handcuffed in the car. From the precinct desk records, it looks like they left him bleeding in a holding cell for a couple of hours before an ambulance finally came and took him to the hospital. He hasn't ID'd the cops yet—he was still heavily sedated last night—but we've got an IAB team at the precinct, and from the arrest report and desk logs it looks like four officers and two sergeants were involved in the arrest and booking. Our guys at the hospital are going to try to show him a photo array to see if he can pick them out. We've got an IAB team at the precinct, they've got it locked down, and the crime scene guys are there.

Now, Safir's a tough guy, and he's been in law enforcement for a long time, starting with the old Federal Bureau of Narcotics (forerunner of the DEA) and later the US Marshals Service, where he headed a program to pursue dangerous fugitives around the world; he's seen his share of the seamy side of crime and law enforcement. But as I'm telling him all this, the look on his face is first one of incredulity, and then, after he hears what we've got so far, genuine horror.

Oh my God, the commissioner says. Are you sure about this?

Yes, Commissioner, I'm sure.

I show him the personnel file photos of the four targeted officers and two sergeants who were directly involved in the arrest, and I tell him what we know about them so far.

Officer Justin Volpe, twenty-five, four years on the job. A graduate of St. John's University, Justin Volpe lives in Staten Island with his mother and father, retired NYPD Detective Robert Volpe, who was known throughout the Department as "The Art Cop" for his investigations and recoveries of stolen Picassos and Byzantine artifacts. Justin Volpe has four EPD medals (Excellent Police Duty) and two MPDs (Meritorious Police Duty) for some gun arrests. He's got one CCRB complaint, unsubstantiated. But from what we're hearing, Justin Volpe is known in the Seven-Oh as an aggressive, sometimes reckless young cop with a short temper; a burly, buffed-up bully that other Seven-Oh cops don't like to work with.

Officer Thomas Bruder, thirty-one, Volpe's partner that night, joined the Transit Police in 1991 and transferred to NYPD three years later. Lives with his mother in Hicksville, Long Island, and was planning to take a new job with Nassau County police in a couple of weeks. Two civilian complaints, one unsubbed, one administrative discipline.

Officer Charles Schwarz, thirty-one, six years on the job. In 1992 he was suspended for fifteen days for hitting a guy in the face on St. Patrick's Day while he was off-duty. He lives in Staten Island with his wife and helps take care of his paralyzed younger brother. A six-foot-two former Marine, he was the driver of the car that took Louima to the precinct station house.

Officer Thomas Wiese, thirty-three, eight years on the job, two excessive-force complaints, both unsubbed. A karate expert, he's the PBA delegate on the Seven-Oh midnight tour, and he was Schwarz's partner on the night Louima was arrested.

The two targeted sergeants are Michael Bellomo, thirty-five, ten years on the job, no civilian complaints, who was the patrol supervisor that night; and Jeffrey Fallon, thirty-two, nine years on the job, two unsubbed excessive-force complaints, who was the desk officer.

Except for Schwarz's fifteen-day hit, there's nothing in the officers' or sergeants' backgrounds to indicate a serious excessive-force problem—

certainly nothing to indicate any of them would be capable of something like this. And yet it had happened.

And there's another issue enveloping this case like a foul mist. There
were dozens of cops who passed through the precinct that night, many
of whom had to have noticed Louima bleeding and moaning in the holding cell. But as far as we know now, none of them did anything about it.

And one other thing. Again, in a perfect world this wouldn't matter,
but in this world it does: The victim, Louima, is black, and all of the
targeted officers are white.

The commissioner and I talk a little bit more about how the investigation is progressing. I tell him we've got an expanded IAB team, about
a dozen investigators, at the Seven-Oh to freeze—secure—the arrest
and command logs, and the roll-call rosters. The Brooklyn DA's office
has been notified, I tell him. We're pulling out all the stops on this one.

The briefing over, I leave the commissioner's office, but an hour later
he calls and says we have to brief the mayor. So Safir, First Deputy Commissioner Pat Kelleher, and I walk over to City Hall. On the way, Pat,
himself a former IAB chief, keeps saying: I can't get my arms around
this, I just can't get my arms around this. Intellectually he knows that
something horrible has happened, and that cops did it. But emotionally
he's having a hard time believing that other cops could do such a thing.

Inside the mayor's office we sit down around a conference table.
Outside of a few official functions, it's the first time I've met Rudy
Giuliani. The commissioner has already given him the basic information over the phone, and I can tell that, like the rest of us, the mayor
is having a hard time with it. Although known for his tough anticrime
and pro-cop stands as mayor, as a young assistant US attorney Giuliani
had been a prosecutor in the NYPD corruption scandal that became the
movie *Prince of the City*, and he knows a lot about bad cops. But this?
He's never heard anything like this.

But as I explain what we've got, the prosecutor in him takes over. He
starts asking tough, hard questions—have we done this, have we done
that, do we have enough manpower on it? It's almost like he's building
the case himself.

There's one other thing I notice. Despite his aggressive, confronta-
tional, take-no-prisoners personal style and his frequent outbursts of

almost volcanic temper—most people who cross Rudy Giuliani soon have reason to regret it—the mayor seems genuinely concerned about the victim, Abner Louima, and the pain he went through. He keeps saying, over and over, The poor man, the poor man. Sure, the mayor has an election coming up in a couple of months, and something like this is bound to hurt him politically, so you'd expect him to act concerned in public. But this is just him and us and a couple of aides sitting in his office. He doesn't have to act concerned now, but he is.

We talk for about forty-five minutes, and at one point the mayor asks us: Does the press have the story yet?

That's a prosecutor's question, not a politician's question. No matter what the political fallout, no one in the room thinks for a minute that this case can, should, or will be kept secret indefinitely. To try to cover up something like this would be not only unethical but completely and totally stupid and bound to fail.

Still, the longer it is before the story breaks, the better it is for us.

Yes, the public has a right to know. But from a prosecutor's or investigator's viewpoint, the public doesn't have a right or a need to know right this minute—for obvious reasons. As with any controversial case, once it hits the papers and the TV news, reporters are going to swarm around the same places we are—the hospital, the precinct, the club, Louima's home, and so on—and start asking people questions. And in any criminal case, it's important that we get to those people first and get their stories locked in before they read in the papers what other people are saying about the case. For us, the perfect time to bring the press and public in on this investigation—or any investigation—is after a grand jury has already returned an indictment and the DA or the US attorney has called a press conference.

Unfortunately, it often doesn't work that way—and it doesn't work that way in the Louima case. Within a couple days, the late *Daily News* columnist Mike McAlary breaks the full story, with a hospital interview and photograph of Louima, under the headline "TORTURED BY COPS." A lawyer for Louima also publicly claims that Internal Affairs had been out to talk to Louima and had then done nothing, which is a dumb thing to say, even for a lawyer.

Eventually the spin will be that but for the doggedness of the press, the Louima case would never have seen the light of day, that IAB would have ignored it, that it would have been covered up by a Department desperate to protect its reputation. Which is flat-out ridiculous. Anybody who believes that either doesn't know or doesn't care about the facts.

The fact is that by the time the story of Louima's ordeal breaks in the press, we have already had hundreds—literally hundreds—of IAB investigators and specialists working the case for the past two days.

And we're ready to start arresting some cops.

By the early-morning hours on Monday, the Seven-Oh precinct is swarming with what cops call "suits"—IAB investigators—who are seizing arrest reports and other records from the desk. They're also guarding the bathroom—a narrow, tile-walled room with a couple of sinks, a couple of urinals, and two toilet stalls—while waiting for the crime scene techs to arrive.

Meanwhile, the four cops—Volpe, Schwarz, Wiese, and Bruder—are trying to get their stories straight. A little after four a.m. Monday, Wiese and Schwarz, who are on patrol, come into the precinct for a meal break, see the suits, and hear that IAB is conducting an investigation into a sexual assault against a prisoner. Shortly thereafter they drive to a pay phone and call Volpe and Bruder at home, and a couple of days later the four cops meet in the basement at the precinct. Volpe initially says that it's all BS, that if anything happened to Louima he inflicted it on himself; later his lawyer will suggest that Louima was injured while engaging in rough gay sex at the Club Rendez-Vous.

But it's not going to fly. Not only do we have Abner Louima, a family man with no criminal record, as a witness. But pretty soon, the Blue Wall of Silence notwithstanding, we're also going to have other witnesses in blue.

IAB Sergeant William Hargrove had been the first of our investigators to interview Louima on Sunday even though he was recovering from surgery and was still groggy. Louima gave us enough to launch the investigation, and for us to identify from the records the four cops who probably were involved, but he hadn't been able to positively ID them yet.

By Tuesday Louima, although he's still in the ICU, has recovered enough to talk to us at length. IAB Lieutenant Reinaldo "Ray" Daniels, one of our best Force Group investigators, who has already established a rapport with Louima, shows him four "photo arrays" of the suspected officers. Each photo array has six photographs, including the cop in question and five other cops who bear a resemblance to him but have nothing to do with the case.

(In any photo array or lineup, you can't use people who don't look at all like the suspect. For example, if a victim has described a suspect as a white guy, you can't surround him with five black guys; even the dumbest, greenest defense lawyer in America could get an ID like that thrown out of court, which could also taint any evidence you discovered that was based on the victim ID. On the other hand, you don't want to use photos that too closely match the suspect's. As an obvious example, you wouldn't put a photo of a suspect's identical twin brother in a photo array. You have to find a balance.)

When Louima looks at Justin Volpe's picture in the photo array, Lieutenant Daniels will later testify, his reaction is one of pure fear. His eyes get wide, and the vitals on his bedside monitoring machine—blood pressure, heart rate, respiration—suddenly spike.

Don't be afraid, Ray tells him. Nothing is going to happen to you or your family.

He did it, Louima says, indicating Subject No. 4—Officer Justin Volpe. He's the one who stuck the stick in my butt.

Louima can't ID the second officer he says was in the bathroom, the one he says held him down in the stall while Volpe assaulted him. All he can say is that the second cop was the driver of the patrol car that took him to the precinct—which the patrol logs indicate was Schwarz. He can't pick out Wiese or Bruder as two of the officers who he says beat him on the way to the precinct, but radio logs and desk reports have already told us they were there.

There are some inconsistencies in what Louima tells us. For one thing, he believes that the "stick" used to assault him was the handle of a toilet plunger; in fact, it will turn out to be the blunt end of a broken broom handle. He also claims that the second officer in the bathroom—"the driver," later identified as Schwarz—held him down while Volpe assaulted him; later he will testify that he wasn't certain what the second officer was doing.

But the biggest inconsistency in Louima's story will come a few days later, when he testifies from his hospital bed for a grand jury—and later repeats at a press conference—that while he was being assaulted, Volpe had said to him "This is Giuliani time, not Dinkins time"—a reference to former mayor David Dinkins's liberal policies versus Giuliani's hard line against criminals and in favor of cops. Louima never mentioned that in his earlier tape-recorded interviews with IAB's Ray Daniels, and later he will admit that he made it up. But while the lie isn't crucial to the case, it makes it a lot harder for some cops to believe that the assault really happened.

But in IAB we need no convincing.

In 1999 former officer Justin Volpe pleaded guilty to sodomizing Abner Louima with a broken broom handle and was sentenced to thirty years in prison. I was determined to get at the truth of what occurred, and was proud of IAB's work on the case. (Getty Images)

As expected, when the story breaks on Wednesday morning the public reaction is one of both horror and revulsion—not only in New York City but across the nation. Excessive force by cops is one thing—New Yorkers have heard that many times before—but this is sadistic, psychosexual torture of a handcuffed prisoner inside a police precinct. The Seven-Oh is immediately besieged by reporters and protesters, many of them carrying toilet plungers. Later the crowds outside the precinct will swell to four thousand people, with another fifteen thousand marching on City Hall.

Giuliani and Safir hold a press conference at City Hall to confirm the news reports—Giuliani calls what happened to Louima "shocking" and "reprehensible"—and I have to be there, too, standing in front of a roomful of reporters not only from New York but from around the world. The mayor and the commissioner handle all the questions, but for me it's tough to have to stand there and tacitly admit that a member of the New York Police Department, the Department I had loved and served for so many years, could do something like this.

Rudy and the commissioner both later visit Louima in the hospital to express condolences. They're followed by a steady stream of politicians and community activists—including Reverend Al Sharpton, who's running for mayor in the Democratic primary—who denounce the attack in particular and the NYPD in general.

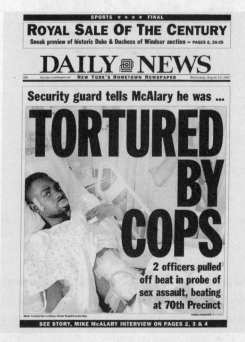

The vicious assault by some NYPD cops on Haitian immigrant Abner Louima in a bathroom in Brooklyn's 70th Precinct shocked not only the public but also the Internal Affairs Bureau, which assigned hundreds of investigators to the case. (Getty Images)

Also on Wednesday we order Volpe, who we've already relieved of his gun and shield, to report the IAB Brooklyn Borough offices, where we formally arrest him for aggravated sexual abuse and first-degree assault; he's arraigned the next day and is released on $100,000 bond. A couple days later he and Schwarz are both indicted by a grand jury. On Thursday Safir suspends, reassigns, or transfers ten cops from the Seven-Oh, including the precinct CO, the XO, and the two sergeants on duty the night Louima was attacked.

Meanwhile, we're continuing our IAB investigation. After the DA gets search warrants we search the lockers of every cop on the midnight tour and other areas of the precinct, looking for the stick used in the assault; we also search every Dumpster in the vicinity, and we even have the city Sanitation Department dredge the sewers, but we can't find the stick. We also interview witnesses who saw the arrest at the Club Rendez-Vous—for help with that we draft into IAB two young, Haitian-born cops who speak Creole, both of whom turned out to be excellent investigators—as well as the EMTs who transported Louima and medical staff at the hospital who treated him. We also try to talk to other cops who were in the precinct that night, but the precinct PBA delegate has been appearing at roll calls, telling the cops to keep their mouths shut. For the first few days, at least, nobody in blue is talking. Except for Louima, we have no eyewitnesses to what happened in the precinct that night.

And then at 3:30 a.m. on Friday, IAB Captain Barry Fried, who had spent the previous twenty-four hours working nonstop on the Louima case, gets a call at home from a friend, another NYPD captain, who's at the Seven-Oh. The captain tells Barry there's a rookie cop at the Seven-Oh who's ready to talk—but he's kind of shaky, and the precinct PBA delegate is trying to get him to shut up. Barry calls the IAB Command Center, and they call me, and we agree that Barry should go to the precinct immediately, and take a couple of IAB lieutenants with him, to grab this kid before anybody gets to him.

The rookie cop is Eric Turetzky, a shy, diffident kid who lives with his mother and grandparents in the Canarsie section of Brooklyn. Turetzky is one of the cops who was at the club the night Louima was arrested, and although he didn't see it happen, he was in the precinct when the assault took place. Disgusted by what happened to Louima, and troubled by the PBA's attempts to cover it up—some PBA delegates are buying the story that Louima was injured during rough gay sex at the club—he decides, after talking it over with his family, to come forward.

At two o'clock Friday morning, while taking his meal break, Turetzky sees a police duty captain—Barry Fried's friend—and a couple of "suits" in the CO's office. The young cop thinks the suits are IAB—they're not, they're actually investigators from another unit who aren't involved in the Louima case—so he goes in and starts telling them what he saw. While he's talking to them a PBA delegate bursts into the room, demanding to know what Turetzky is telling them. The duty captain kicks the PBA guy out, but it's pretty clear that the entire precinct knows what's going on—and the kid is scared. So the captain calls Captain Fried at home, and when he and the two IAB lieutenants arrive they take Turetzky back to the IAB Brooklyn Borough offices at Nazareth High School—we rented office space there from the Catholic church—and turn on a tape recorder. And what the young cop tells them is this:

After Louima was booked, Turetzky saw Officer Schwarz lead him, rear-cuffed, with his pants down around his ankles, away from the holding cells and toward the bathroom. Fifteen minutes later he saw Volpe, his uniform disheveled and his shield number and nameplate covered up, taking Louima, his pants still down around his ankles, into a holding cell. In his right hand Volpe had a two-foot-long piece of a broken broom or mop handle, dark green or blue in color, that he was swinging like a sword, waving it in the air and hitting the wall with it. What Officer Turetzky tells us not only confirms Louima's ID of Volpe; it puts the stick in Volpe's hand. Although we still haven't found the stick—we never will—we do find the bottom half of a broken broom handle that matches Turetzky's description.

Turetzky is the first Seven-Oh cop to come forward, but not the last. With the word out that Turetzky is cooperating with IAB, other cops who were in the Seven-Oh that morning start to talk.

Officer Mark Schofield tells us that before the attack, Volpe had borrowed a pair of leather gloves; afterward, when he gave them back to Schofield, they were covered in blood and feces. Disgusted, Schofield threw them behind some lockers; we quickly recover them. Officer

Kenneth Wernick tells us that shortly after the attack, Volpe bragged that he "broke a man down" by putting a stick in his rectum and had showed Wernick the broken broom handle. Although Officer Michael Schoer initially lies to us—I didn't see nothin'—later he says that he, too, saw Volpe waving the feces-stained stick. In the end there are four cops ready to testify against Volpe—which, coupled with Louima's testimony and forensic and medical evidence, will make a very strong case.

As horrible as the Louima case is, the NYPD—and specifically the IAB—can take pride in the way it handled the investigation of its own. (In fact, IAB later received an award for investigative excellence in the Louima case from the US attorney general.) Within a week, two cops—Volpe and Schwarz—are indicted for the assault in the bathroom, and in another week two more officers—Bruder and Wiese—are charged with assaulting Louima during the ride to the precinct. Numerous other Seven-Oh cops are facing Department discipline for failing to do their duty to help Louima or report what happened. We put together a solid case in record time.

In fact, there is only one significant mistake in our handling of the case—but it's a bad one.

We had always said that we first became aware of the case at about four p.m. on Sunday, about thirty-six hours after the assault on Louima, when a Louima family member called the IAB Command Center. But throughout the case there were persistent reports that the first call to IAB about Louima had been made at about ten p.m. Saturday night—eighteen hours before the call on Sunday.

That didn't seem possible, because I checked the records and couldn't find any log of the call—and remember, all calls to the Command Center are logged. But then I listened to the actual tapes—and there it was.

What happened was that the Command Center was short a body on the phones that night, so they brought in a detective from another IAB unit who'd never been trained on Command Center intake protocols. And of course, he's the one who caught the call from Coney Island Hospital on Saturday night.

The female caller was actually a Haitian-born nurse at the hospital, but for some reason she had said she was calling about her husband, who she said had been beaten and brutalized by police. She was nervous, anxious, and she kept pronouncing her "husband's" name differently—Low-ma, Lee-ma, Loo-na. The IAB detective on the phone couldn't make much sense of it. Finally she asked if she could call back, and the detective said exactly the wrong thing. Instead of keeping her on the phone and trying to get more information, he told her: Sure, call us back. And then he compounded the mistake by not logging the call and not telling the supervisor. Not until four o'clock the next afternoon, Sunday, did a member of Louima's family call the IAB Command Center to alert us to Louima's injuries—at which point we rolled out immediately.

It was a major screw-up in one of the worst and most shocking police brutality cases in American history—and my unit was responsible for it, which meant that I was responsible for it. It was only going to give ammunition to the anticop conspiracy theory that we tried to cover up the Louima assault, which we did not.

So as soon as I unscrewed myself from the ceiling, I called the commissioner and the Department immediately issued a statement admitting that IAB had "mishandled" the initial call, which probably was a little too generous. The press used the word "bungled," which was closer to the truth. We established new protocols at the Command Center to make sure nothing like it happened again.

Did the eighteen-hour delay make any difference in the long run? I don't think so. Louima was still too groggy and disoriented from his surgery on Saturday to ID any of the officers until Monday. And we developed information that Volpe had taken the broom handle out of the precinct soon after the attack occurred, so I doubt that our extensive search for the weapon used in the assault would have found it, even if we had started earlier. But I'll never know for sure. And it remains one of my greatest professional regrets.

Still, as I said, we had built a solid case for prosecution in state court. And then someone decided to make a federal case out of it.

Whenever there's a controversial police use-of-force case, and especially when there's a racial element involved, the US Justice Department and the local US Attorney's Office follow the case closely to see if there's a potential civil rights case against the officers involved. Sometimes the feds will let the state case run its course before getting actively involved—the Rodney King case in LA is an example—but sometimes they'll step in and take over.

Often there are practical legal reasons for that. Rules of evidence in federal court generally favor the prosecution more than in state court, and potential punishments are stiffer, increasing the odds that a defendant will make a plea deal or "flip" and testify against other defendants in the case. That certainly was true in the Louima case. In state court, Volpe and Schwarz were looking at a maximum of twelve and a half to twenty-five years; in federal court, they'd be looking at life in prison.

Brooklyn District Attorney Charles J. Hynes, a tough prosecutor and an outgoing politician of the old school, didn't necessarily want to give up the Louima case to federal prosecutors, but I think that from the beginning he saw the writing on the wall. Two weeks after the assault on Louima, Hynes and US Attorney for the Southern District Zachary Carter agree that the case will go federal.

For IAB, the switch poses some problems. During our investigation we had granted limited immunity and interviewed almost a hundred Seven-Oh cops who hadn't been directly involved in the assault but who might have seen or heard something, even secondhand. For legal reasons, some of the information that was given under a grant of immunity couldn't be passed along to federal prosecutors and the FBI because they were concerned it might compromise the federal case. So although IAB continues to investigate the case along with the FBI, we have to bring in a new team of IAB investigators who hadn't worked on the initial investigation.

It's complicated in the way that real-life criminal cases, as opposed to TV criminal cases, often are. But in the end, there is justice—or at least partial justice—in the case of Abner Louima.

In February 1998 a federal grand jury indicts Volpe and Schwarz on civil rights charges in the bathroom attack on Louima; Wiese and Bruder are charged with beating Louima in the police car; and Sergeant Michael Bellomo, the patrol supervisor that night, is charged with covering it up. Later the grand jury adds conspiracy and obstruction of justice charges against Schwarz, Wiese, and Bruder.

When the trial finally begins in May 1999, Officers Turetzky (then a detective in IAB), Schofield, Wernick (then a sergeant), and Schoer all testify against Volpe. In the middle of the trial, with his defense falling apart, and confronted with the other cops' damning testimony, Volpe suddenly decides to plead guilty. It isn't a plea bargain; Volpe simply decides to throw himself on the mercy of the court.

When Assistant US Attorney Alan Vinegrad, the lead prosecutor in the case, calls to tell me about the planned guilty plea, I'm worried. The last thing I want is for there to be any doubt that Volpe had done exactly what he was accused of doing.

Throughout the Louima investigation, and right up to the trial, Volpe had maintained publicly that he was innocent, that whatever had happened to Louima, he didn't do it; his lawyer and the PBA were still alleging that Louima was the victim of rough sex at the club. Some of the PBA delegates in the Seven-Oh, like the PBA rep who tried to intimidate Eric Turetzky when he came forward, were so aggressive in their defense of Volpe that it bordered on obstruction of justice.

So there was a feeling among many of the Department rank and file that Volpe and the other cops were being railroaded by IAB and the feds, that what happened in that bathroom hadn't happened the way prosecutors said it did, that political pressure had been brought on the cops who testified against Volpe. Even some senior chiefs had stopped me in the hallways at One Police Plaza to ask me about the case—Hey, Charlie, did this thing really happen?—and though I couldn't talk about the case, I could tell that they really couldn't believe a cop would do such a thing.

So I don't want Volpe to simply stand up in court and plead guilty to some vague assault charges. I want him to admit exactly what he did, and I strongly urged Alan Vinegrad to make sure that happened. Vinegrad didn't have a lot of leverage—again, it was a straight guilty plea, not a plea bargain—but he promised to do what he could. And it must have worked.

The next day a shaken-looking Volpe stands up in court and formally pleads guilty, telling the judge that when he attacked Louima he was in "shock," that he was "mad," and that he wanted to "humiliate" Louima for disrespecting him. And then he says the words:

"While in the bathroom," Volpe tells the judge, "while in the bathroom at the precinct . . . I sodomized Mr. Louima by placing a stick in his rectum. I then threatened to kill him if he told anybody."

The judge later sentences him to thirty years in prison.

Meanwhile, the trial continues for the other four cops. In June 1999 the jury convicts Schwarz of civil rights charges—he is sentenced to up to fifteen years—but acquits the other three cops. The trial and appeals and retrials of the Louima case cops went on for several years, with Schwarz being released from prison in 2007. In 2001 the city and the PBA settled a civil lawsuit by Louima for $8.75 million.

The Abner Louima case was finished. But for the NYPD it would never be over.

It's not fair—that *F* word again—to the vast majority of NYPD cops who end every shift with their honor intact. But that's the legacy that Volpe and the other cops who were involved left the NYPD.

After Louima, people assume that NYPD cops are capable of anything.

Chapter 8

IF THEY'VE GOT THE BLONDE, WE'VE GOT A PROBLEM

It's often said that a cop is only as good as his informants. The cop who has good informants will make a lot of arrests, he will shine in the eyes of his supervisors, and his career will flourish. Without good informants, a cop will barely have a clue as to what's going on in his patrol sector or in his particular field of investigation—narcotics, organized crime, gangs, whatever—and as a result he will not make a lot of arrests, he will not shine, and instead of earning a gold shield, or moving up in the supervisory ranks, he could end his career living on Staten Island and pounding a beat in the Bronx.

Which is kind of ironic. After all, most—not all, but most—police informants are criminals: cokeheads, meth-heads, potheads, junkies, low-level drug dealers, prostitutes, petty thieves, gang members, Mob wannabes—in short, people who swim in the shallow end of the crime pool. But cops often need the cooperation and assistance of those criminals not only to fight crime, but to advance their careers.

Of course, that cooperation and assistance comes with a price. As I said earlier, most police informants are people who've been arrested and are trying to work their way out from under the charge. And it's usually a onetime thing: They give up information on a more serious criminal and in return they get a break on their current crime.

But sometimes informants will agree to work for the cops on a more permanent basis. In that case, if the cops follow proper procedures, the informant will be photographed, given a code name, and be vetted for past criminal history; you don't want a convicted rapist or other serious criminal as an informant. After that, they'll be officially registered with the Department as a "confidential informant," or CI. In return they'll be paid with Department funds for providing information or other assistance—maybe thirty or forty bucks for making a "controlled buy" from a crack dealer on a street corner, which allows narcotics cops to swoop in and bag the dealer, maybe a hundred for giving up an illegal gun that some perp has stashed in an empty apartment in a public housing development. It's all negotiable, and all payments to CIs are carefully recorded. And while a cop can't officially give his CI a get-out-of-jail-free card, it's usually understood that if the CI gets jammed up on some minor beef—emphasis on "minor"—the cop will at least try to help.

Cops handle their CIs in different ways. Sometimes a cop may play the role of a benign, understanding uncle who listens patiently to the CI's problems, of which almost every CI seems to have an almost inexhaustible supply. Sometimes a cop will be the stern and demanding authority figure who pounds his fist on the desk and tells the CI that he's a lying scumbag who's taking him, the cop, for a chump and that he better start producing cases or there's gonna be trouble. Sometimes a cop will be the buddy who likes to talk to the CI about Rangers and Knicks games before they go out and work a drug set on a corner. Cops will do whatever works best to keep the CI productive.

But it's always an act—or at least it should be. No smart cop will ever tell a CI about his wife and kids, or about his new house on Long Island, or about what a jerk his CO is, or anything else the CI doesn't need to know. A smart cop will always remember that a CI is just that— a professional informer, and a criminal to boot, and if given a better opportunity, he or she will turn on the cop in a heartbeat.

The bottom line is that no wise cop will ever trust or get personally close with his CIs. And it almost goes without saying that a cop shouldn't have sex with one of them.

You'll notice that I said it "almost" goes without saying.

Which brings us to the case of The Blond CI and Brooklyn South Narcotics.

It starts with a cop who forgot to turn off his tape recorder.

It's September 2007 and two cops assigned to the Brooklyn South Narcotics Unit, a group of about two hundred fifty plainclothes cops and detectives who handle drug investigations in the patrol borough's thirteen precincts, are riding in an unmarked NYPD car. One of them, a detective, starts talking about a bust he'd made the night before, when he and another Brooklyn South narcotics cop had arrested a drug dealer at his Coney Island home with twenty-eight small plastic bags of cocaine. But after the arrest, the detective says, they had only vouchered seventeen of the bags. They held back the other eleven bags of cocaine, the detective says, to give to their CIs as payment for information.

There's only one problem with this conversation—a problem for the detective, anyway. He's forgotten that the recording device he's been wearing during another drug arrest is still running, capturing every word he's saying about paying his informants with confiscated cocaine. After the detective turns in the tape as part of the evidence in the drug arrest, a supervisor listens to it—and he can hardly believe what he's hearing. He does the right thing and calls us, IAB, and the investigation is on.

Now, narcotics cops paying off informants with confiscated narcotics has been around as long as there have been cops and narcotics. You may remember that scene in the film *Prince of the City*, where Treat Williams, playing a corrupt NYPD Special Investigation Unit (SIU) narcotics detective based on Robert Leuci, chases down a small-time heroin dealer/user in the rain, robs him of his heroin stash, and gives it to one of his informants. Back then, in the late 1960s and early '70s, it was a common practice in NYPD narcotics units.

And in the old days, some cops even privately defended it, arguing that with the limited funds the Department had for paying informants, paying off their CIs with drugs allowed them to make more cases at less cost to the taxpayers. Besides, they argued, even if they did use Department funds to pay their CIs, the CIs were all addicts who would just use the money to buy more drugs anyway. So why not eliminate the middleman and just give them the drugs? Some cops even described it as a form of "noble corruption"—that is, breaking the rules to accomplish the greater good of more drug arrests.

But there are several problems with that argument. Here's the biggest one:

Giving illegal drugs to informants or anyone else is against the law, and it always has been. When a cop gives somebody narcotics, he's breaking the same drug distribution laws that he's putting other people in jail for violating. The NYPD is in the illegal drug control business, not the illegal drug distribution business—and every cop knows it. There's nothing noble about it.

Here's another problem: Once a cop steps over the line of illegality, it makes it easier to take another step, and then another—especially in narcotics enforcement, where at the higher levels a cop may have to deal with money or drugs measuring in the hundreds of thousands of dollars. Call it the slippery slope, or call it the in-for-a-dime-in-for-a-dollar theory, but a cop who steals dope from a doper to give to another doper, for whatever reason, is just a degree or two of separation away from banging a major dealer's door and stealing a hundred grand in cash. I mentioned Bob Leuci and the SIU, and how they routinely gave drugs to informants? Well, of seventy detectives in SIU, two-thirds of them were indicted for ripping off drug dealers or other acts of corruption.

And there's another big problem with cops paying CIs with drugs: The minute a cop does it, that CI owns him. That hyped-up, methed-out, doped-up junkie CI now has information that can put the cop in jail. And as far as I'm concerned, a cop who's stupid enough to put his career and his future and his family's future in the hands of someone like that is too stupid to be a cop.

So anyway, after listening to the detective's inadvertent tape recording, we notify the Brooklyn DA's office and open an IAB investigation into the Brooklyn South narcotics detective and the other cop. But we don't immediately arrest them or put them on modified duty. The tape recording in itself isn't enough for a criminal case—and as always, we want to see how far this thing goes. Because of the long history of narcotics-related police corruption, there are strict Department procedures concerning the disposition of confiscated drugs, including a requirement that a supervisor, usually a sergeant, makes sure that all the drugs confiscated during an arrest are vouchered. If no one's doing that at Brooklyn South Narcotics, then there's not only a command and supervision problem, but there's a good chance that other cops in the unit are doing the same thing. Eventually our investigation targets every cop in the two ten-person narcotics "modules" or teams that work the Coney Island–Red Hook–Bay Ridge section of southern Brooklyn.

Based on arrest records, which show how much narcotics were vouchered in each arrest, we start quietly tracking down as many perps as we can who've been recently arrested by the Brooklyn South narcotics cops. Of course, we don't tell them we're IAB; we don't want that on the street, because it will get back to the narcotics cops we're investigating. Instead, we use the same gambit that I mentioned earlier. We tell them we're with the NYPD's Quality Assurance Division and we're conducting a widespread and completely anonymous survey of people who've recently had interactions with the police, and we just have a few questions: Were the officers who arrested you polite? Did they use any offensive language? Did they behave in an overall professional manner? Oh, and by the way, did any of the officers happen to take anything from you during the arrest—say, for example, money or drugs that weren't mentioned in your arrest report?

As you can imagine, it's a ticklish question. Ordinarily it would not be in a drug dealer's best interests to admit that, yeah, he actually had more drugs on him than what he was charged with. But we assure them—Scout's honor!—that nothing they tell us is going to bring a heavier charge on them. And some of these mopes are smart enough to know that if the cops who arrested them are caught breaking the law by stealing drugs or holding back drugs for their own purposes, the criminal case against them goes out the window. No jury is going to believe the testimony of an arresting officer who's been caught stealing drugs; the DA wouldn't even take a case like that to trial—and as we'll see, that's going to become a major issue in the case against Brooklyn South Narcotics.

So some of the perps we track down are willing to talk to us about the narcotics cops who arrested them, and how some of their money or drugs went missing—including the Coney Island drug dealer whose arrest sparked the investigation. But their allegations alone aren't enough to make a prosecutable criminal case—remember, these are drug dealers we're talking about—and none of them is too interested in working for us in any kind of sting operation to catch the cops in the act.

And then we find The Blonde. That's what the cops who know her call her—The Blonde.

I guess every crackhead's story is sad in its own way, but The Blonde's seems even sadder than most. She came from a good home, a decent family, had a husband and some kids, and she looks like she was once an attractive woman. But now she's in her late thirties, totally cracked-up, emaciated-looking, trading herself for money or drugs. Yeah, she tells us, she got arrested for possession a while back by two cops from Brooklyn South Narcotics—and she's seriously pissed off about it.

She's not so mad about the arrest itself. For a crack addict, getting arrested is part of the job description. No, The Blonde is mad because one of the plainclothes cops who arrested her, Officer Jerry Bowens, age forty-one, twelve years on the job, is being a jerk. After he arrests her he tells her that he wants her to work for him as an informant—not an official CI who's registered with the Department, but as an off-the-books informant. In return, Bowens tells her, he'll give her some of the coke he takes off the crack slingers she helps him to arrest.

The Blonde says okay, and later she fingers a crack dealer for Bowens and other cops from the narcotics module. After the dealer is arrested, Bowens meets with The Blonde in his car and gives her a couple of twenties and some coke that he took off the drug dealer.

But Bowens isn't quite finished. He starts talking to her, telling her how nice-looking she is, or whatever, and she's thinking: Well, I know where this is going . . . And that's exactly where it goes. She has sex with Bowens in the car.

Now, I'm no Dr. Ruth, but a few words here about cops and sex.

Is it a bad idea for a cop to have sex with a crackhead or a hooker or any other kind of criminal, petty or otherwise? The answer is, no, it's not a bad idea, it's a *terrible* idea. At minimum it's conduct unbecoming and criminal association—which can cost a cop his job—and if the cop is coercive about it, if he says: Give me sex or I'll put you in jail . . . then it's rape, and it can cost a cop his freedom. Like I said, when you get personally involved with a criminal, you're putting your career and even your life in that criminal's hands. And yet it happens all the time.

Case in point: IAB gets notified that a rookie cop in Brooklyn has lost his shield; he says it fell out of his pocket while he was off-duty on the subway. Okay, losing a shield isn't good, but it's not a capital offense. But then a street hooker gets arrested, and when they're processing her at the precinct, what do they find in her purse? The cop's shield. To get out from under the prostitution charge, she gives up the cop, saying that while she was servicing him, and his attentions were elsewhere, she lifted the shield out of his pants pocket. But has the cop learned his lesson from having his shield stolen by a hooker? No. A day or two later we put a tail on him and he goes to Coney Island and picks up another hooker. He's fired for criminal association and lying about the lost shield.

Another case in point: We've got a veteran detective in the Bronx who arrests a young woman on a credit card fraud case. He takes her to the precinct, where she signs a confession, but then the detective tells her that he will make the charge go away if she will "take care of" him. She doesn't want to do it, but she's afraid the arrest will cost her her job at a hospital, so she agrees to meet him later in her car, where she performs oral sex on him and then uses a Kleenex to clean up. Next day she's understandably feeling used and angry about this, so she calls us, IAB—and fortunately she's still got the Kleenex with the detective's DNA on it in her car. We put a tail on the detective, who's a smoker, and when he tosses a butt we snatch it up, send it to the lab, and yeah, the DNA on the cigarette butt matches the DNA on the Kleenex. (That's all perfectly legal. We don't need a warrant to grab somebody's DNA off something they've discarded, like a cigarette butt or a soft drink straw.)

Of course, when we pick him up, the detective claims the sex was consensual, and since it's a he-said/she-said thing, the DA won't file criminal charges. But for us it's simpler: A cop can't have sex with someone he has arrested, period; there's too much opportunity for coercion. And he's certainly not allowed to dump a case in return for sex. Eventually the detective is forced to resign from the Department after nineteen years and eleven months on the job—thirty days short of his twenty years. Talk about the Million-Dollar Mistake.

I could go on and on. During my IAB career I saw hundreds of cases where cops got jammed up over sex—sex with hookers, sex with drug users, sex with other cops who were not their husbands or wives, or with other cops who ranked far below them in the chain of command. Next to alcohol and greed, inappropriate sex is probably the number one killer of cop careers.

So anyway, to get back to The Blond CI, she does a couple more deals with Bowens and his supervisor on the module, a sergeant, point-ing out crack dealers and getting paid with money and cocaine taken from the dealers. Which is fine with her, but the problem is that Bow-ens also wants more sex from her—and after the second or third time, frankly she's tired of this guy. This cop is always calling her up, stop-ping her on the street, demanding sex—the guy is insatiable. It's like he's stalking her or something.

So when we get to The Blonde in our debriefings of recent drug arrestees, she's ready to flip. Sure, she says, she'll work for us against Bowens and the other narcotics cops. So we sign her up as an official Department CI—which is kind of strange when you think about it. Here IAB has an official CI who's also working as an unofficial CI for a cop who IAB is investigating. She's like a double agent.

Of course, unlike Bowens, we're not paying The Blonde with drugs or money that has been ripped off from a drug dealer. We're paying The Blonde with Department money from the "confidential funds" cash that's kept in a safe at IAB headquarters; eventually, over the course of the investigation, it will come to about fifteen hundred bucks, a hun-dred here, a couple hundred there. Also unlike Bowens—and this time it really does go without saying—no one in IAB is having sex with The Blonde.

So with The Blonde working for us, we set up a sting.

The Blonde sets up a meet with Bowens and tells him there's this dealer she knows, she's bought from him lots of times, and she'll point him out, so Bowens and his supervisor, a plainclothes sergeant, pick her up in an unmarked car. The Blonde is wearing a recording device hid-den in a wristwatch we've given her from our IAB tech unit, and she's searched by a female IAB investigator to ensure she isn't carrying drugs when she gets into the car. She spots the crack dealer on a corner in Coney Island and points him out. Bowens and the sergeant dream up some probable cause and then they move in with other members of the team and arrest the dealer.

Except the dealer The Blonde fingered for them isn't really a dealer. He's one of our IAB undercover cops who can take an arrest—meaning that if he's arrested and processed into the system his ID won't come back as a cop. He's got $250 in marked IAB bills on him, and forty small plastic bags of cocaine; he's also got a couple of IAB ghosts backing him up, and a surveillance team is videotaping it. After the arrest, the sergeant tells Bowens to give The Blonde forty bucks and two of the bags of cocaine that they took off our undercover dealer—which she later turns over to us. The sergeant vouchers the remaining $210 and thirty-eight bags of cocaine.

(Ordinarily, in a sting operation involving drugs, we use "beat" drugs—that is, phony drugs like pancake flour for heroin or powdered lactose for cocaine. But experienced narcotics cops will know the difference, and they may chemically field test the drugs, so in those cases we have to use the real thing.)

So now we've got Bowens and the sergeant on tape stealing money and drugs and giving some of them to an informant—and the fact that they were stolen from an undercover cop doesn't make any difference, legally. If they'd been stolen from a real drug dealer, that wouldn't make any legal difference, either. It's distribution of a controlled substance and larceny.

Still, as I explained earlier, ordinarily we wouldn't make an immediate arrest. We would leave these guys out there to see how far this goes.

But in this case, we can't—for two reasons.

One is that while we're investigating these cops, they're still arresting drug dealers—and every one of those drug cases is going to be dismissed by the District Attorney's Office, because the DA can't ethically proceed with a criminal case in which the arresting cop's actions are themselves criminal. They'll also have to go back and look at every past case in which the suspect cops were involved and possibly have to dismiss them as well. We're talking hundreds of cases here.

And the other, even more important reason we have to wrap up this investigation is that these cops aren't just using confiscated drugs to pay informants. We have reason to believe that at least some of the cops are using confiscated drugs to "flake" people—that is, they're planting the drugs on people to frame them for crimes they didn't commit.

During our debriefings of perps who've been arrested by the suspect cops, a lot of them are telling us: I swear to God, man, I didn't have no drugs on me when they arrested me, those cops flaked me! In another variation, perps tell us that an undercover narcotics cop intentionally dropped some marked drug buy bills on the ground and then busted them when they picked up the marked money, claiming they had sold the cop some drugs.

Of course, you have to remember that most of these guys are chronic criminals with long arrest records, and in that world, the allegation that they were flaked by the cops is a pretty common lie. It's right up there with the check is in the mail. But when we start hearing the same cops' names over and over, we have to wonder. It's not enough to criminally charge the cops involved—an accused cop's defense attorney would have a field day with witnesses like these guys—but it's enough for us to put these cops under scrutiny.

And in one case, the flaking allegation isn't from a career criminal. A man and his girlfriend, neither of whom had been arrested before, claim that earlier in 2007 a cop from Brooklyn South Narcotics had approached them in front of their home on Neptune Avenue in Coney Island, searched their car, and planted a small bag of crack in it, after which they were arrested. They spent about twelve hours in jail while being processed, and their case is still pending.

Of course, legally and ethically it doesn't matter if the flakee is a known drug dealer or an innocent young couple in Coney Island. Cops planting evidence on suspects, any suspects, is unforgivable. It's one of the worst things a cop can do, and we can't let innocent people, or even not-so-innocent people, wind up in jail because of it. We've got to put these cops on ice.

So three months after the Brooklyn South Narcotics investigation began, we arrest the detective who, without realizing he was being recorded, had bragged about holding back drugs, and we also arrest the other narcotics cop who helped him bust the drug dealer in Coney Island. And once they're publicly arraigned in court, the word is out in Brooklyn South Narcotics: IAB is in the house. From that moment the heat is on, and no one in Brooklyn South Narcotics is using confiscated drugs to pay informants or flake people.

At the same time, we hit Bowens, at home, telling him what we have on him, and giving him the usual speech: You can't be a cop anymore, and you're going to be arrested, but maybe you can help yourself with the DA if you cooperate . . .

He quickly folds, and he agrees to make a taped call to his sergeant. Bowens calls him up and says something like, Hey, I'm worried about this IAB thing. I can't find The Blonde, but I think maybe she's been talking to IAB . . .

And what the sergeant says in response is exactly this:

If they've got The Blonde, he says, we've got a problem.

Well, we do have The Blonde—she's now safely stashed away out of the neighborhood—and yes, these two cops do have a problem. Shortly thereafter we arrest them both for official misconduct and stealing money and drugs from our IAB undercover. Later we also arrest another Brooklyn South narcotics cop for flaking the couple in Coney Island. At the same time, we put more than a dozen narcotics cops in the unit on modified duty pending Department discipline, and Commissioner Kelly transfers the three top commanders of Brooklyn South Narcotics and the deputy chief in charge of the entire Narcotics Division for their failure to supervise the unit.

Eventually four of the five indicted cops either plead out or are found guilty, and because there is no evidence that they kept any of the confiscated drugs or money for themselves, their court-imposed punishments are light—probation and community service. Even the cop who flaked that innocent couple in Coney Island escapes jail after he cries and begs for forgiveness. But in a tragic twist, Bowens, who like the other accused cops is out on bail while awaiting sentencing, somehow gets his hands on an illegal gun and, in a jealous rage, shoots and kills an ex-girlfriend in her apartment in the Greenpoint section of Brooklyn; he's later sentenced to forty years to life in prison.

Meanwhile, although I hate to look at it this way, the IAB investigation of Brooklyn South Narcotics makes a lot of drug dealers and drug users happy. The Brooklyn DA's office has to dismiss almost two hundred past or pending drug cases that involved any of the cops implicated in the scandal; you can't prosecute a case when one of your primary witnesses is a crooked cop. In some cases, the city pays people who were wrongfully arrested a thousand dollars for every hour they spent in jail.

Are we happy that drug dealers are back on the street? Of course not. Is Brooklyn DA Charles Hynes, who's been in on the investigation from the beginning, happy about having to toss so many cases? Again, of course not. And we could have avoided it. We could have just popped the detective who made the inadvertent tape recording and let it go at that instead of conducting a widespread investigation. But that's not how the new IAB works. Which is why it always astonishes me when critics accuse the NYPD and the IAB of covering up corruption to avoid making the Department look bad. They simply don't know what they're talking about.

As for The Blonde, we encouraged her to seek treatment for her drug problem, but apparently she didn't listen. More than a year later, when she testifies in a Brooklyn courtroom against one of the cops, a newspaper reporter describes her, not very charitably, as "a gum-chewing motor-mouth Brooklyn drug addict" who talks so fast that the court reporter can't keep up with her.

After that, I don't know. I hope she got out of the crack life before it killed her. But when it comes to drug addicts, after more than forty years as a cop it's hard for me to be optimistic.

So did the IAB investigation of Brooklyn South Narcotics do any real good? Did it permanently eliminate the practice of paying informants with narcotics, or rogue cops flaking people? The answers are yes and no.

As I said earlier, with the heat on not only in Brooklyn South but throughout the Narcotics Division, and with supervisors looking over everyone's shoulder to make sure confiscated drugs were handled properly, the practice of paying informants with drugs virtually disappeared, at least for a while. And in our periodic follow-ups we didn't find any credible evidence that Brooklyn South narcotics cops were flaking known drug dealers, or anybody else.

But cops are people, and people tend to forget. As time goes by, supervision loosens up, cops get lazy and cynical, and think they can cut corners. So no, I can't say there aren't some cops out there who are breaking the law in order to arrest other people for breaking the law.

But while it's not my business to give advice to crooked cops—except to advise them to find another line of work—I do know there are some things that cops like that should never do.

They should never forget to turn off the tape recorder.

And they should never trust an informant.

*   *   *

Che Che wants to make a deal.

It's early 2001 and Che Che—it's pronounced "Chee-Chee"—a low-level drug dealer and drug money courier from the Bronx, is sitting in a cell at the Mohawk Correctional Facility in Rome, New York, looking at a ten-year jolt on a state drug conviction. And even though Mohawk is a medium-security prison, and thus at least marginally less dangerous and brutal than a max-security hellhole like Attica or Dannemora, Mohawk is unpleasant enough that Che Che has no desire to spend the next decade there.

So Che Che calls his lawyer and says he's got some information about a crime that he wants to sell; in effect, he wants to trade someone else's freedom for his own. Okay, fine, the lawyer says, what have you got to offer?

Of course, Che Che can't just offer up some low-level mutt he did a drug deal with back in the day; nobody's going to make a deal with one low-level drug dealer just to put another low-level drug dealer in prison. It'll have to be something better than that.

Which it is. According to Che Che, he can give up a couple of dirty NYPD cops, one of them a detective, one of them a high-ranking officer within the Department, who helped him rip off a Dominican drug dealer he was working for five years ago.

Now that's something a lawyer can work with. The lawyer calls the FBI, and since it's NYPD cops who are involved, the FBI calls us—IAB. (Because the case comes to us through the FBI, it's technically a federal case, even though we handle most of the investigation. More on that subject later.)

So we send a couple of IAB investigators up to Rome, one of them a Spanish-speaker—although he's lived in New York for more than a decade, Che Che's English isn't that great—to sit down with Che Che and see what he has, and what he wants in return for giving it to us. There's some back and forth between his lawyer and the US attorney, but eventually there's a deal: Che Che will give us what he's got in return for no additional prison time and a recommendation for early release on his current sentence. And what Che Che's got is this:

It's the summer of 1996, Che Che says, and he's working for this

Dominican drug dealer in Washington Heights. He's supposed to drop off $60,000 in buy money to a supplier, but when he gets out of a gypsy cab at the busy corner of Grand Concourse and East Tremont Avenue in the Mount Hope section of the Bronx, two plainclothes cops in an unmarked car come screeching to a halt next to him. They jump out of the car and one of them shouts: Freeze, Che Che!—and then, while numerous passersby look on, they arrest him, handcuff him, put him in the car, and drive off. But it's a bogus arrest, a rip-off, and Che Che is in on it. The two cops drive Che Che to a nearby park, take the cuffs off, hand him a wad of money, and let him go, keeping their share of the cash. Che Che later tells the drug dealer he's working for that some crooked cops grabbed him and ripped him off.

As you can imagine, this is a pretty high-risk strategy—for Che Che. Maybe his bosses will believe him, especially if they had their own tail on him, as drug traffickers sometimes do with their money couriers, who can independently verify the "arrest." It wouldn't be the first time one of their couriers had been ripped off by corrupt cops. On the other hand, it wouldn't be the first time a dealer or a courier had staged a phony rip in collusion with corrupt cops, either. And if the courier's bosses come to that conclusion, things will not go well for Che Che. But apparently he is believed, because nobody murders him.

Anyway, that's what Che Che is telling us. He's also telling us that one of the cops is an old friend of his, a guy named Robert, a detective who at the time was with the elite Bronx Homicide Narcotics Task Force, which worked drug-related homicides; Che Che had worked for Robert as an unofficial, off-the-books informant, and they had gotten tight—another case of a cop getting too close to his snitch. Che Che says he doesn't know who the other cop was, just some cop friend of Robert's, but later he heard from Robert that the other cop had become a high-ranking guy in the NYPD, like a captain or something, but he doesn't have a name. Che Che says that he and Robert did one other similar drug money rip in 1999, a few years after the first one, and got $30,000.

So that's what Che Che tells us. The question is, Is it true?

Che Che manages to pick Robert out of a photo array, which indicates that yeah, at least he actually knows the guy. Robert had grown up in Washington Heights, where four of his uncles had been involved with Dominican drug gangs—a family connection that in the old days would have been a disqualifying factor for appointment to the NYPD, because having a father in prison or an uncle in the Mob or any other similar connection was considered a corruption hazard. But by the time Robert came on the job in 1990, the Department had decided that the sins of the fathers should not be visited on the sons, and that, plus the fact that the Department was having a hard time finding enough fresh bodies to fill the ranks, allowed him to get through.

Other than that, he's been under our radar. He worked for a while in the 50th Precinct, a low-incident house in the far northern Bronx, then the Narcotics Homicide Task Force; currently he's working as an undercover with the FBI/NYPD Joint Narcotics Task Force, where, we're told, he's highly regarded. And we've got nothing on him but the word of a convict.

So we take a run at him. We hit him at home, and the minute our guys flash their shields and say IAB, Robert starts to fold. It's basically like, Oh my God, you got me! Without telling him that his old friend Che Che gave him up, we let him know that we know everything, even though we don't, and he says yes, he'll cooperate. So we take him to the US Attorney's Office, across the plaza from NYPD headquarters, provide him with a lawyer, and work out a deal: He can't be a cop anymore, but if he tells us everything, and if he's willing to testify against any other co-conspirators, he won't go to prison.

So Robert walks us through the 1996 rip in Mount Hope, and everything he says—date, time, place—matches exactly what we got from Che Che. He adds a couple of details, including the fact that he and the other cop were both off-duty, and that after the rip, when they went to Robert's apartment to split the money, the bills were so heavily dusted with cocaine they had to wash their hands to get it off. Robert says he blew his share of the money paying off some long-overdue bills and taking his girlfriend on a vacation to Mexico.

But the big question we have for Robert is this: Who's the other cop? And when he tells us who it is, we can hardly believe it. We don't even want to believe it.

It's Dennis Sindone, Robert says. Deputy Inspector Dennis Sindone. There are a little over a hundred deputy inspectors in the NYPD, and of all of them at the time, Sindone is probably the one thought most likely to be on track to make senior chief. On the force since 1983, the son of a retired NYPD detective, Sindone, thirty-nine, is a water walker, a guy whose climb through the ranks has been meteoric. As a sergeant with Bronx Narcotics Homicide Task Force, he was credited with helping make cases against two drug gangs that between them had committed more than forty murders; later, as a lieutenant and CO of the Bronx Special Victims Unit, he and his guys tracked down a notorious rapist who had attacked fifty women. Promoted to captain and assigned as CO of the 60th Precinct in Coney Island, Sindone compiled such impressive crime-reduction stats that after just thirteen months as a captain he had recently been promoted by Commissioner Bernie Kerik to deputy inspector. In fact, just two weeks earlier I had attended his promotion ceremony and had shaken his hand and wished him well. Outgoing and gregarious, with dark good looks, he's popular with both subordinates and superiors.

It seems impossible. And yet . . .

Robert tells us that he had been friends with Sindone since they worked together in the 50th Precinct—they were drinking buddies—and that when he approached Sindone with his plan for the Mount Hope rip Sindone had eagerly signed on. Robert says he also approached Sindone about helping with the second rip-off of Che Che in 1999, but that Sindone, then a lieutenant, had wanted more time to set it up, and a bigger score, so Robert had done it on his own. We will also find out that at the time of the first Bronx rip, Sindone was having money troubles, this after an earlier bankruptcy, and that he was dropping money that he really didn't have at the $250-minimum blackjack tables in Atlantic City.

And there's another piece of evidence that we get. After Robert gives up Sindone, we put together a photo array to show to Che Che, who's still in prison up north, to see if he can pick him out. Like I said earlier, a photo array is made up of a headshot of the suspect and five photos of other people (in this case, other cops) who look similar to him—not exactly the same, but not too different, either.

So we put Sindone's Department file photo in an array and show it to Che Che, who doesn't know that Robert has fingered Sindone as the second cop. Che Che immediately IDs Sindone's photo as the second cop who "arrested" him.

All of which is persuasive. And both Robert and Che Che have good reason not to lie. For example, if when we check the records we find out that Sindone was actually on an extended vacation in the Caribbean on the same day Robert swears his old friend was helping him do a rip in the Bronx—in other words, if Robert lies to us—then Robert's deal goes out the window and his admissions can be used against him in a criminal case, in which case he's looking at forty years in the joint. Same thing with Che Che.

But even though they have an incentive to tell the truth, Che Che is still a convicted drug dealer with a long criminal history, and Robert is still an admitted corrupt cop who has turned informer to save his own skin. These guys are not going to shine on the witness stand. We need more.

So we have Robert make a phone call.

After some rehearsals, we put Robert on the phone and have him call Deputy Inspector Sindone at his office at the Six-Oh. At first it's all, How ya doin', haven't talked to you in a while, heard about the big promotion, congratulations, that's really great—and so on. Sindone is happy to hear from Robert—he calls him "Bubula," which is New York-ese for little buddy—and they talk about the old days for a while.

Then Robert makes the pitch. He can't be too specific, because any cop gets suspicious if another cop starts openly talking on a phone line about a score. So what he says is basically this:

Robert says to Sindone: Look, I got this thing, like we used to do, it could really work out for the both of us, are you interested?

And what does Sindone say? Does he say, Whaddaya talkin' about? What kind of a thing we used to do? What's this about?

No, what Sindone says is simply this: Nah, I don't do that stuff anymore.

Anymore?

It's not a legally incriminating statement in and of itself. A defense attorney could certainly raise some doubt about what Sindone meant.

But I've been doing this a long time, and I've heard dozens, even hundreds of wiretap and recording device tapes of corrupt cops talking about scores they've made or plan to make. And after listening to the tape, and considering all the other evidence, I still don't want to believe it, but I have to: Deputy Inspector Sindone, the guy whose hand

I shook a couple weeks before, did exactly what he's suspected of doing. For a relative handful of cocaine-dusted bills, which he mostly pissed away anyway, he put his freedom and his career into the hands of a low-life drug dealer and a weak cop who gave him up with hardly a second thought, and then he went on with his life as if it had never happened.

I never could really understand how any cop could do that. I couldn't understand it then, and I still can't understand it now.

But whatever the reason behind it, it's time to let Deputy Inspector Sindone know that his past has caught up with him.

We don't want to just arrest him. We want to put him in a position in which he'll agree to cooperate, to tell us about other scores he made, if any, and if other cops, maybe even other former or current high-ranking ones, were involved.

So instead of taking a run at him at home, or in the 60th Precinct, we have an administrative aide call him and tell him that First Deputy Commissioner Joe Dunne needs to see him first thing in the morning—nothing major, just routine. The next morning, Sindone, in a suit, not his DI's uniform, shows up on the fourteenth floor of One Police Plaza and is escorted into the first deputy's conference room. I'm already there, along with IAB's Deputy Chief John Moakley and Lieutenant John Donnelly, the CO of IAB's Group 25, which coordinates IAB investigations with the feds.

The minute he walks in, Sindone can tell that something's wrong. None of us is smiling; none of us is enjoying this. But before he can react I walk over to him and shake his hand—and then I don't let go. At the same time, Deputy Chief Moakley moves in and gives him a quick pat-down. We're looking for his gun—not because we're afraid that he'll use it on us, but because we're afraid he might use it on himself. That has happened more than once with NYPD cops caught up in corruption scandals, and we don't want it to happen again. But he doesn't have a gun on him.

Where's your gun, Dennis? I say.

It's in my car, Sindone says, and we send someone down to get it. We've also arranged for some IAB investigators to take his on-duty gun out of his locker at the 60th Precinct.

Meanwhile, Sindone is looking like the world is collapsing around him. It's painful to watch. He keeps saying: What's going on, am I in trouble? And we keep saying the standard IAB line: Look, Dennis, don't say anything, just listen, we're trying to help you here . . .

So we take him across the plaza to the US Attorney's Office and sit him down in a small conference room. We tell him a little of what we've got, without mentioning Robert or Che Che by name—although he has probably already figured out who gave him up. We explain how he can help himself by cooperating, but by this time Sindone has regained his composure, and he's not buying what we're selling. He wants to see his lawyer, he says—and the interview is over.

We take his shield and put him on modified assignment, pending his indictment by a grand jury, so he's not going back to the 60th Precinct. Police Commissioner Bernie Kerik transfers Sindone to a holding spot in the Property Division; a few days later he busts Sindone back to captain, the biggest demotion that civil service rules allow. Kerik is furious that a guy he just promoted and publicly praised is now the highest-ranking NYPD cop ever caught up in a drug-related corruption scandal—which is kind of ironic since Kerik, as we'll see, has some secrets in his own background that are going to come back on him.

Later Sindone is indicted by a federal grand jury for violating the civil rights of the unnamed drug dealer whose money he and Robert and Che Che stole—yeah, I know it sounds kind of strange, but that's the way the federal law is written. He's formally arrested and booked at that point. At his trial, Robert and Che Che are the prosecution's main witnesses, and as expected, his defense attorney argues that Robert and Che Che are self-serving rats and snitches who can't be believed—and the jurors agree. Faced with two admittedly unsavory witnesses, and bound by the "beyond a reasonable doubt" burden of proof, they acquit Sindone on the federal charges.

But his troubles aren't over. Despite the acquittal, he's brought up on administrative charges at an internal Department trial, where the standard of proof is simply a "preponderance of evidence." By that standard, after a hearing the deputy commissioner of trials finds Sindone guilty and he is dismissed from the Department. Sindone never stops maintaining his innocence, and although he files a number of appeals with the courts, the dismissal stands. Meanwhile, Robert resigns from the

Department and gets probation, and Che Che gets a "cooperation letter" from the US Attorney's Office that eventually helps him win parole.

So is that fair? A lot of cops don't seem to think so—not then, and not to this day. The Sindone case remains a kind of cause célèbre within the ranks, with a lot of cops—especially those who don't know all the facts—arguing that Sindone was railroaded out of the Department solely on the word of a drug dealer and a crooked cop who ratted out another cop to save his own skin, which to cops is the worst kind of low-down, cheese-eating rat there is. But again, there's an irony there. Every day, cops use drug dealers and informants and snitches to make criminal cases against civilians. But they get angry, some of them, when those same kinds of informants and snitches are used to make criminal cases against cops.

There is one unusual postscript to the sad story of Deputy Inspector Dennis Sindone. In 2007, five years after being dismissed from the NYPD, he bought a lottery ticket at a convenience store in Rockland County, and when he scratched it off in the parking lot it was a winner—a big winner.

" 'CROOKED' COP WINS $1 MILLION LOTTO," the headline in the *New York Post* announced. The story quoted Sindone as calling it "poetic justice."

And maybe that's about half right.

Maybe it was poetic.

It's the day before Thanksgiving 2003, and the cops and federal agents from the El Dorado Task Force are staking out a money courier at the corner of Ninety-First Street and Astoria Boulevard in the East Elmhurst section of Queens. The mutt they've got under surveillance is a twenty-eight-year-old from the Dominican Republic who's working for a Colombian drug dealer named Calvo, and inside the black backpack he's carrying on his shoulder is $169,000 in cash.

The task force guys know this because it's their money.

The El Dorado Task Force—which includes NYPD detectives, US Customs agents, IRS agents, other federal agents—has been on this investigation for months, trying to make cases against "remitters," guys who take large sums of cash from drug sales in New York City, hundreds of thousands of dollars at a time, then break them down into smaller amounts and wire-transfer the funds offshore, usually to Colombia. The idea is to evade cash reporting requirements by making it look like the wire transfers are small remittances sent by immigrants to their families back home.

In other words, it's money laundering, and the task force cops are following the money. One of their undercovers inside the drug operation gave the $169,000 in the backpack to the unsuspecting courier, who's supposed to make a drop at the corner, and then the task force guys will see where it goes. They've got a surveillance camera running to film the money drop.

But then suddenly two guys in a silver Toyota Avalon come to a screeching stop beside the drug courier and jump out of the car. One of them is Hispanic, average height, the other a big white guy with silver hair—and they're both wearing Department "raid" jackets, blue windbreakers with the Department patch and "NYPD" in big white letters on them. They grab the courier, and the bag, and then the Hispanic guy unzips it, looks inside, and gives the big white guy a thumbs-up sign. They handcuff the courier and start to load him, and the bag full of cash, into the Toyota.

And the task force guys, watching this happen, can't believe it. What the . . . ? Who the hell are these guys?

So they run over, badges out, and without saying who they are— they don't want to blow the fact that this is a surveillance—they ask the guys in the raid jackets what's going on. The Hispanic guy flashes an NYPD detective's gold shield and says it's okay, they're with a special NYPD/federal narcotics unit.

I'm on a wire, he tells the task force cops, which could mean that he's working a wiretap case, or it could mean that the courier, or the cop himself, is wired with a recording device. Either way, it still doesn't make any sense.

But then, before the task force cops can say anything else, the guys in the raid jackets get in the Toyota and take off, with the courier and with the $169,000 in cash, while the task force guys stand there, mouths agape, stunned. And it's all caught on the task force guys' surveillance camera.

So now the task force cops have to call their bosses and tell them that their surveillance target and their money are both in the wind, taken from right under their noses by two unidentified guys who appear to be other cops. I can only imagine just how unpleasant that conversation was. And then they have to try to figure out what just happened.

They're pretty sure that the guys in the raid jackets were actual cops. Sure, anybody can buy a knockoff NYPD detective's gold shield, but these guys talked like real cops, and moved like real cops. One of the NYPD detectives on the task force even vaguely remembers the big white guy as an NYPD narcotics detective he'd known back in the day. And when they run the plate on the Toyota Avalon it comes back as being leased by the NYPD.

But even if those guys are real cops—especially if they're real cops—this kind of thing isn't supposed to happen. Whenever a law enforcement agency in the New York City area, federal, state, or local, wants to open an investigation of a drug location or a drug dealer or drug informant, they're supposed to check the DECS computer system—Drug Enforcement Coordination System—to see if any other federal, state, or local narcotics unit has already targeted that person or location. If anyone has, they're supposed to back off, or at least call the unit and ask permission to get involved. The whole idea behind DECS is to keep one group of narcotics cops from stepping on other narcotics cops' cases—or worse, to keep one group of narcotics cops from raiding a location and maybe shooting another narcotics group's undercovers who are working the case.

But now these guys in the NYPD raid jackets haven't just stepped on the El Dorado Task Force's case. They've stomped on it and left it for dead.

Funny thing, though. When the task force guys check the records, they find out that nobody from the NYPD has tried to open a file or run a DECS check on their case. If anyone had, it would have left a computer footprint. The only NYPD unit that can run a DECS check without leaving a footprint is us—the Internal Affairs Bureau.

So now the task force guys, especially the ones from the NYPD, start to wonder: Were the guys in the NYPD raid jackets part of some IAB sting? Had IAB targeted members of the El Dorado Task Force for an integrity test? So the task force supervisor calls IAB and asks us, discreetly, if we just happened to have run an IAB integrity test operation that afternoon at the corner of Ninety-First and Astoria in Queens.

In a way, it's flattering that they would think we were involved—IAB is everywhere! But this isn't something that IAB would do. We wouldn't run an integrity test on a joint NYPD/federal task force without the federal agency's higher-ups knowing about it. And we certainly wouldn't have two IAB guys just grab $169,000 from other cops and run away with it to see what the other cops will do. If we do that, one of our guys could wind up getting shot.

No, as soon as the task force supervisors tell us what happened, we know what we've got here. We've got two bad cops doing a drug money rip.

Well, with the Toyota Avalon's license plate and the surveillance tape, it doesn't take a lot of superior detective work to ID these two guys. The Hispanic guy in the raid jacket is Detective Julio Vasquez, age forty-three, on the job seventeen years, used to work in the now-defunct Northern Manhattan Initiative antinarcotics unit, which had been created during the '90s to flood drug-plagued Harlem and Washington Heights with hundreds of narcotics cops. Vasquez is now assigned to the elite Firearms Investigation Unit in Harlem, which concentrates on getting guns off the street; the NYPD-leased Toyota used in the drug money rip is assigned to him. The big white guy is Thomas Rachko, age forty-five, retired in 2002 after twenty years with the Department, including a stint as a detective in the Northern Manhattan Initiative, where he worked with Vasquez.

Now, ordinarily we might have let these guys stay out on the street for a while, put a tail on them, maybe get a wiretap up, listen to what they're saying, see if other cops are involved. But that takes time, and this case is a red alert. After the confrontation with the task force guys, we have to assume that Rachko and Vasquez know they've been made on the money rip. They probably won't run—cops who know they're under IAB investigation almost never go on the lam—but they might get rid of the stolen cash. And the El Dorado Task Force would really, really like to get its money back before that happens.

True, federal agencies like the FBI and the DEA and the ATF (Bureau of Alcohol, Tobacco, Firearms and Explosives) and US Customs and all the rest are the envy of every NYPD cop for the vast amounts of cash they can bring into an investigation for drug buys, to pay informants, and so on; for every dollar the NYPD has for such purposes, the feds have ten, maybe twenty. But even the feds don't want to have to eat the loss before their very eyes of $169,000 in cash.

So we immediately scoop up Rachko at his home in the Riverdale section of the Bronx; the next day, Thanksgiving, we grab Vasquez at his home in Brooklyn. We make the usual run at them, to see if they'll cooperate—Look, detective, we're trying to help you here—but neither one of them bites, at least not yet. They want to talk to their lawyers. Later they're arraigned on charges of grand larceny, money laundering, obstructing governmental administration, and coercion, and they're both released on $50,000 bail each.

But their lawyers are talking to our lawyers—"our" lawyers being the Queens District Attorney's Office and the US Attorney's Office—and eventually they both agree to talk in return for lighter sentences. And what they tell us and the prosecutors is what we already suspect: This isn't the first drug or money rip they've done. And they aren't the only cops they know who've done the same.

This particular rip of the drug money courier had been Rachko's idea, and the courier, the twenty-eight-year-old from the DR, was in on the plan. He had been one of Rachko's unofficial off-the-books CIs back in the Northern Manhattan Initiative days, and he had always provided good information about drug houses and money drops and so on— and after Rachko's retirement they had kept in touch. The plan was for Rachko and Vazquez to make a big show of arresting the courier in a busy public place—the corner of Ninety-First and Astoria—and then they'd drive off and split the money, after which the courier would breathlessly inform his bosses that he'd been grabbed and handcuffed by two corrupt cops who stole the money and then kicked him out of the car.

As I said earlier, this is a pretty high-risk strategy for the courier; it's the sort of thing that can get a guy killed. In fact, the day before the rip at Ninety-First and Astoria, one of Vasquez's unregistered informants from the old days in the Northern Manhattan Initiative had been found handcuffed and duct-taped and extremely dead in the backseat of a car on East 205th Street off the Grand Concourse in the Bronx, a victim of multiple gunshots in the neck. We checked it out, of course, but we never found any reason to link that killing to Vasquez. After all, being a narcotics CI who's working for the cops and the dealers at the same time is a situation fraught with mortal peril, and the list of people who might want such a person dead can be long indeed. And we really don't think Vasquez is a killer; we think he's just a thief.

So anyway, Vasquez and Rachko tell us that on the day of the rip at Ninety-First and Astoria, Vasquez told his boss at the Firearms Investigation Unit that he was going out for lunch, then he picked up Rachko in the NYPD's Toyota and they headed out to "arrest" the courier. And everything went according to plan until the guys from the El Dorado Task Force stepped up and asked them what's going on.

As they sped away from the scene, Vasquez and Rachko knew they were done, that it was over. Vasquez and Rachko didn't know who those other cops were, and they didn't know for sure that they had the courier under surveillance—the courier obviously hadn't known that, either—and they didn't yet know the whole thing was on videotape. But they knew those other cops didn't just happen to be on that corner; they knew that much from the stunned looks on their faces as Rachko and Vasquez sped away; and they knew those stunned-looking cops probably got the plate number on the car. And they knew that if anybody asked why a detective assigned to the firearms unit in Harlem and a former detective who retired last year were arresting a drug money courier on a street corner in Queens . . . well, it was going to be a little hard to explain. Vasquez and Rachko knew that unless they were the two luckiest crooked cops in the world, the hammer was going to come down.

So after they made sure they weren't being tailed, they pulled over and quickly split the cash without even counting it. Rachko wound up with exactly $68,680, Vasquez a little less, the courier still less than that. They split up, but on his way home Rachko panicked; as we had expected, he wanted to get rid of the evidence. He stuffed his sixty-eight grand and change into a bag and tossed it into a Dumpster near the Hudson River, a few blocks away from his house in Riverdale. (Later, working with the feds, we'll track the garbage pickup and disposal records and, amazingly, we'll find the bag and the cash in a dump in the Bronx.)

Vasquez, meanwhile, kept his cool. He stashed his share in a secured storage locker facility near his home, then went back to the Firearms Investigation Unit office acting as though nothing had happened. He and Rachko were arrested hours later. Shortly thereafter, the courier, who was still alive and well—either his bosses bought his story, or else they just hadn't gotten around to murdering him yet—was picked up, too, and charged with money laundering and drug offenses.

And now, after the arrest, Rachko and Vasquez, separately, with their lawyers present, sit down with the prosecutors to make a deal: leniency in return for cooperation. As usual in situations like this, the rule is that they have to give up everything, and hold nothing back. If later we find out they've lied, or withheld critical information, if some other crooked cop later fingers them in a rip they forgot to mention, then the deal will be off, the prosecutors will go for the maximum sentence, and any evidence they've already given us can and will be used against them. But if they're completely truthful, and they agree to testify if necessary against other corrupt cops, the prosecutors will ask the judge to go easy on them. Although sentencing judges aren't bound by any agreements between the defendants and the prosecutors, they usually go along with prosecutors' recommendations.

So Rachko and Vasquez start to sing, and name names. They tell us and the feds that sometimes together, sometimes with members of a small group of other cops from the Northern Manhattan Initiative, they've done dozens of drug and money rips. In almost every case, one of their off-the-books CIs would tell them about a drug or money drop, and they would hit the dealer or the courier and steal the money or the drugs, then split the cash with the CI. If they stole drugs, they'd sell them to another dealer and then split the cash. Most of the time the dealer or courier they robbed would be one of their CIs, like the courier in the Queens rip, and if they weren't, they knew the dealers or couriers they robbed would never report the thefts; they were just happy that instead of arresting them the cops let them go, since the money or the drugs would be gone in either case. All told, over the years, Rachko and Vasquez figure they stole about $2 million from the dealers they hit.

And where did the money go? Rachko claims that he's got a gambling addiction, that he pissed away every dollar of his share of that $2 million—about $800,000—at OTB (off-track betting) parlors, betting on the ponies. We're not sure we completely believe that, but we can never prove otherwise. Vasquez was a little more frugal. He tells us he's got a huge stash of stolen and ill-gained cash in that storage locker in

Brooklyn—$744,370 to be exact—which is quickly seized and deposited into government coffers.

During the debriefings, Rachko is remorseful, emotional, ashamed to be exposed to his kids and to the world as a crooked cop. He's a broken man.

But Vasquez is different. At one point I'm personally debriefing him, and unlike Rachko, he's not showing even a hint of emotion. He's got a wife and kids, too, but if he feels any shame about being exposed to them as a dirty cop, I can't see it. He's cocky, even arrogant—a lot more cocky than a guy looking at years in prison should be.

No, he tells me, he never engaged in small-time acts of corruption, never pilfered a few bucks from a drunk or a DOA or anything like that; there was no slippery slope. It wasn't until he confronted the big money in narcotics that he got greedy, he says; he saw an opportunity and he took it—and then he took it again, and again. And unlike Rachko, he didn't piss the money away. He and his wife, who works in a bank, have a nice town house in Boerum Hill, a gentrified neighborhood in Brooklyn, but he's not living a flashy lifestyle. That three-quarters of a million in cash in the storage locker? He says that is, or was, for his retirement, sort of like an off-the-books 401(k).

Like I said, it's a fool's calculation. Because now not only is that three-quarters of a mil gone, but after seventeen years on the job, so is his pension, and his freedom. Once again, it's the Million-Dollar Mistake.

Anyway, while I'm talking to Vasquez about his many crimes, I'm wondering: Over the years IAB has done dozens of investigations and prisoner debriefs and integrity test stings in the Northern Manhattan Initiative's area of operations in Harlem and Washington Heights, and we've arrested a lot of crooked cops. How did we miss this guy Vasquez and the others?

So I ask him, wasn't he worried that IAB would find and turn one of his informants against him? Wasn't he ever afraid that one of his rips would turn out to be an IAB sting? And he says, no, he never worried about that. At first I take this as a kind of professional insult—I'm not afraid of IAB!—but then Vasquez explains why.

He says he'd never been afraid of an IAB sting because he never did a rip that he or Rachko hadn't set up from beginning to end. He had served warrants on drug dealers' apartments with a million in cash sitting on a table, and pulled over cars with hundreds of thousands in the trunk, and he never took a dollar. Any one of those could have been an IAB sting operation.

Instead, Vasquez tells me, he only did rips with people he knew and trusted, people who would never give him up, or in situations that he knew from his most trusted informants were legit. As for the Queens rip of the courier, well, that was just bad luck. How were they to know that out of the dozens, even hundreds of drug money couriers carrying millions of dollars in dope money around the streets of New York on any given day, their guy would be the one who just happened to be under surveillance by the El Dorado Task Force?

And that's the new face of major corruption in the NYPD. It's not the Buddy Boys or Dirty Thirty scandals, with gangs of cops randomly banging down doors every night without really knowing what's inside, or shaking down drug dealers for a few bucks at random on the street. The new face of major corruption in the NYPD is what we call "familiar corruption." It's one or two cops, working with people they trust— longtime informants, family members with criminal associations, people they've known for years—who are executing carefully planned rips of large amounts of cash or drugs. In familiar corruption cases, we can't wait for the victims to report the crimes, because they won't. We can't wait for honest cops to come forward and report the crimes, either, even anonymously, because the honest cops don't know about them. Instead, we have to try to work them from the inside, debriefing perps—drug dealers, money couriers, and so on—and hope that eventually we'll find one who's sufficiently jammed up to make him turn on his corrupt cop accomplices.

The point is that catching crooked cops who are involved in familiar corruption like that takes a lot of hard work, and a lot of patience. But it never hurts to have some luck as well—and in the case of Rachko and Vasquez, we had some.

Eventually Rachko and Vasquez both plead guilty to state and federal charges, and are sentenced to six years in Vasquez's case and seven years for Rachko—an amazingly light jolt, considering that they could have been put away for life; it illustrates the wisdom of post-arrest cooperation.

At his sentencing, Rachko cries as he apologizes for his crimes, blaming them once again on his gambling addiction. And as so often happens, Vasquez seems to be a different man on sentencing day than the cool, cocky crooked cop I'd seen during his debrief. As his wife weeps behind him in the courtroom, he, too, gets teary-eyed as he apologizes for his crimes, blaming them on "greed, avarice, and an egotistical attitude." I'm sure his wife's tears were real.

Meanwhile, we're investigating the other cops from the Northern Manhattan Initiative who Rachko and Vasquez had fingered during their debrief as being in on various drug and money rips—ten current or former cops in all, which is actually a pretty small number when you consider that some seven hundred cops were assigned to the Northern Manhattan Initiative.

The problem is that a lot of those rips happened six or seven years ago, and Rachko's and Vasquez's memories have faded. They remember doing this rip with that cop, and another rip with that other cop, but the dates and times are vague. Like Rachko and Vasquez's rip of the courier in Queens, most of the rips were committed off-duty or on meal breaks, they weren't part of any official investigation, and no one was arrested, so it's hard to reconstruct them based on any activity logs or arrest records. It's not like the cops who did the rips were writing them down in their logbooks.

Still, after months of debriefing perps and other cops, and going through what records are available, we're able to give federal prosecutors enough evidence to charge two former members of the Northern Manhattan Initiative. One is a retired lieutenant, Rachko and Vasquez's former supervisor, who agrees to cooperate with the investigation and later pleads guilty to stealing $110,000 in drugs and cash; he gets fourteen months in prison. The other is an NYPD detective, also a former member of the initiative, who admits in court that he stole $45,000 from a drug dealer and used it to remodel his home on Long Island; he gets two years.

In the cases of two other former initiative detectives, including one who earlier had moonlighted as a driver for a New York real estate mogul named Donald Trump, there isn't enough evidence for criminal charges. But Department administrative trials require a lower burden of proof, so we bring Department charges against them and both are fired—although Trump's former driver later successfully appeals his dismissal.

In the end, I guess you could argue that the entire Northern Manhattan Initiative corruption investigation was just a fluke, that it never would have come out but for the chance encounter between Rachko and Vasquez and the team from the El Dorado Task Force on that street corner in Queens. And maybe that's so. Like I said, we had some luck on that one.

But who knows? Maybe it would have eventually come out anyway, because secrets are hard to keep forever. After all, as the Rachko and Vasquez and Sindone and Brooklyn South Narcotics cases demonstrated, corrupt cops are often quick to turn on their former comrades when they get caught and are looking at a long stretch in the joint. As for confidential informants, ratting people out is their job, and no matter how much you might trust them today, when they get in trouble tomorrow and need to work their way out from under a prison sentence, they will happily give you up.

Which is why I always wondered: How can corrupt cops sleep soundly at night, knowing that at any moment the crimes they committed long ago, and the people with whom they committed them, can suddenly come back to haunt them?

The answer is: They shouldn't.

Corrupt cops should never sleep soundly at night.

Chapter 9

WAIT A MINUTE—THOSE GUYS AREN'T COPS!

The woman on the phone from Pennsylvania is angry and distraught, and with good reason. The man who fleeced her out of thousands and thousands of dollars is an NYPD cop—and what is the Internal Affairs Bureau going to do about it?

The story she tells us is an old and familiar one. The woman—we'll call her Betty—is middle-aged, a bit overweight, divorced, and lonely, and she has a thing for cops. So she goes on a chat room website called ILoveNYCCops.com and she meets this great guy, Angel Gonzalez—his online name is "Archangel"—who's a detective in the 70th Precinct in Brooklyn. They trade messages back and forth for a couple of weeks, something clicks between them, and finally she invites him to visit her in Pennsylvania, which he does, and well, nature takes its course. Now she's totally smitten with this guy. He's young, early thirties, a good decade younger than her, in fact, and he's sort of good-looking. An added attraction is the NYPD detective's gold shield he carries, and the reassuring bulge of the Glock 9mm he carries in a hip holster; he makes her feel safe.

So later he invites her to visit him at his home on Long Island, which is to say, the basement of his parents' home on Long Island, where he's been living since his divorce. When she gets there, she sees that the closet is crammed with NYPD uniforms and gear, and the walls are covered with awards, plaques, and framed attaboy letters, all praising Detective Angel Gonzalez for outstanding police work. He's Police Officer of the Month, Detective of the Year, winner of the New York City Police Commissioner's Award for Conspicuous Valor, and on and on. This guy isn't just a cop, he's a supercop.

But there's a problem. In a moment of postromantic bliss, Detective Gonzalez tells Betty a long and complicated tale involving his angry ex-wife, a legitimate but off-the-books moonlighting job, a bank account in Puerto Rico, and certain sums of money owed. The bottom line, he tearfully tells her, is that if he can't come up with $15,000 in two days, his ex-wife is going to call the NYPD Internal Affairs Bureau and falsely accuse him of corruption, and his career will be in ruins. If Betty could just loan him fifteen grand—in cash, please—for a week or so, he'll pay her back as soon as he can get his money out of the bank in San Juan. It will save his life, he says. And then he says: Betty, will you marry me?

Betty is swooning. He wants to marry her! As for the money problem, she's not worried. She trusts him. After all, he's a cop.

So Betty goes back home to Pennsylvania and rounds up the cash from her savings. Detective Gonzalez joins her there, and together they buy an engagement ring—on her credit card. The next day, Detective Gonzalez leaves with the fifteen grand—and then it's like he drops off the face of the earth. He doesn't write, he doesn't call, he won't answer her tearful telephone messages. And finally it dawns on Betty that this NYPD cop has not only broken her trusting heart, he has also fleeced her out of her hard-earned money.

Betty remembers what Detective Gonzalez had said about Internal Affairs, how afraid of IAB he seemed to be, so she calls us. Of course we're sympathetic. We don't like our cops taking advantage of vulnerable women, and we especially don't like our cops stealing their money. We open an IAB investigation on Detective Gonzalez for suspected fraud, and while there are some jurisdictional issues involved—the alleged crimes actually occurred in Long Island and Pennsylvania, not in New York City—we start building a case. Working with the Suffolk County DA's office and the Pennsylvania police, we collect enough evidence to file fraud charges against Detective Gonzalez and get a search warrant on his house.

And then we find out that Betty isn't the only victim of this crooked cop; in fact, as Detective Gonzalez's victims go, Betty is actually small change. After the Suffolk County DA announces the indictment, nine other people come forward to tell us that they gave money to Detective Gonzalez as well—a total of close to $700,000—to help him out of some jam or other, and then he started ducking them and never gave them their money back. Some of the victims are lonely-heart types like Betty, some are just casual friends and acquaintances. And when we ask them why they would trust Detective Gonzalez enough to give him that kind of money, they all say the same thing: We trusted him because he's an NYPD cop.

But the truth, as you may already have guessed, is that Detective Gonzalez isn't an NYPD cop, or any other kind of cop; we figured that out within a couple hours after Betty first called us. When we search his house, we find the phony detective's gold shield and the NYPD uniforms and gear that he bought on the Internet, and the awards and plaques that he had made up at a trophy shop, and the attaboy letters he wrote for himself. Angel Gonzalez is a con man, but he's definitely not a cop, and never has been.

Instead, Angel Gonzalez is, or was, a police impersonator. And he's not alone. At any given time there are hundreds, even thousands of them out there across the country.

And in New York City, if they're committing a serious crime, it's IAB's job to catch them.

It's easy to become a fake cop.

Fifteen minutes on the Internet can get you decked out with a uniform, handcuffs, a police radio and scanner, emergency lights and sirens for your car, a realistic-looking fake ID with any name and law enforcement agency you want on it, and a badge that's an almost perfect knockoff of an NYPD shield or any other local, state, or federal law enforcement agency badge. True, New York law prohibits the sale of NYPD uniforms and replica shields, and federal law prohibits the sale of FBI or other federal agency badges—but when did that ever stop people from buying stuff over the Internet? (In fact, even though it's against NYPD rules, most NYPD cops carry "dupes"—duplicate shields— because they're worried about losing their real shields, which have to be turned in when they leave the Department or are promoted.) There are also bounty hunter and security guard "schools" that, for a hefty fee, will outfit you with a phony badge and ID and also teach you how to do cop stuff, like how to slap handcuffs on somebody. Or you could save your money and just watch some crime shows on TV.

Some of the people who buy police badges and gear are collectors or police buffs who don't do any harm. Others are more serious wannabes, guys who like to carry badges or dress up as cops, who derive some psychological satisfaction from the power and authority the badge and the uniform project, which is fine as long as they only do it in the privacy of their own homes. But unless it's Halloween, if they go out in public in what appears to be an actual police uniform, or carry what appears to be a real police officer's badge, and if there's any intent to deceive others into believing that they're real cops or to exercise authority over them, under New York law it's criminal impersonation, and they can be arrested.

Same thing with the cars. You'll sometimes see cop buffs drive around in stripped-down old Crown Victorias with multiple antennas, listening to calls on a police scanner and then showing up at crime scenes to gawk from behind the yellow tape. Nothing illegal about that, but if they also outfit the Crown Vic with a siren and emergency lights in the grille, that's a Vehicle and Traffic Law violation—and if they actually turn on the siren and the emergency lights to get somebody to pull over or whatever, now we're back into criminal impersonation.

Sometimes police impersonators are just trying to impress somebody—a girl they've met in a nightclub, someone at a party. They'll puff themselves up, flash a badge, and say: I'm a cop . . . or better yet, an undercover cop, which sounds much more dangerous and glamorous. Most people won't question them, or look too closely at the badge.

Other impersonators actively try to intimidate people who annoy or anger them. It's especially common in "road rage" incidents. Somebody cuts them off in traffic, and suddenly they're waving a phony badge out the window and trying to get them to pull over.

For example, in 2007 a forty-nine-year-old rabbi from a Manhattan temple was arrested after repeatedly pulling up beside slow-moving drivers on suburban highways, flashing a badge inscribed with "Triborough Bridge and Tunnel Authority—Officer 1338" on it—a complete fake—and shouting: Police! Pull over! A couple of drivers actually did, after which the rabbi got out of his car and started screaming at them for holding up traffic. After his arrest he explained that he hated people who drive too slowly; his lawyer said he had bipolar disorder. Except for the rabbi part, this wasn't unusual; it happens all the time.

Some police impersonators are simply trying to save a buck. If they get pulled over for a traffic stop they'll flash a phony badge they got over the Internet—Junior G-Man, Honorary Fire Marshal, whatever—in the hope that the cop will just wave them on without actually looking at it. But cops are wise to that dodge, and if the guy actually claims to be a police officer—if he says, Yeah, I'm a cop—then it's criminal impersonation and he's under arrest. Same thing with fare beaters. To add extra security and encourage cops to use public transportation, New York City allows NYPD officers to ride free on subways and city buses. These days NYPD cops are given Metro pass cards they swipe through the machine, but in years past guys would quickly flash some shiny silver thing at a bus driver or token booth operator and try to skate by. If the driver or operator was paying attention, he'd call a cop, but if not, it was a free ride.

Usually police impersonators are loners, guys who act out their cop fantasies on their own. But sometimes they're members of shadowy "police" organizations that hand out badges and ID cards and whose members actually think they're cops.

A case in point is the now-defunct Kings County Society for the Prevention of Cruelty to Children. (Kings County encompasses Brooklyn; this group should not be confused with the New York Society for the Prevention of Cruelty to Children.) Incorporated under an archaic 1875 state law that allowed certain private groups to enforce child abuse laws, these SPCC guys—there were about fifty of them, many of them doctors, lawyers, accountants, and so on—had set up their own little police force, complete with uniforms, badges, cars that made them look like NYPD cops, and their own "headquarters" in the Sunset Park section of Brooklyn; in fact, their equipment was actually newer and better than ours. Some of them even had gun permits. Although the group claimed to have conducted a number of child abuse "investigations," it was actually more of a wannabe social club, with the top guy calling himself the "commissioner" and most of the members holding the rank of "chief" or "deputy chief." It might sound harmless, but the last thing anybody wanted was for guys with no police training whatsoever to interfere with ongoing child abuse investigations, or to draw a gun on somebody and shout: Freeze! SPCC Police! We raided the SPCC headquarters with a warrant in 2005 and later arrested nine members—including a Manhattan doctor and an attorney—who had actively passed themselves off as NYPD officers. The New York State Attorney General's Office finally shut them down in 2006.

Sometimes police "impersonators" are actually law enforcement officers who are just straying out of their lane. New York has an endless array of quasi–law enforcement agencies—the Department of Citywide Administrative Services Police, NYC Transit Authority Property Protection Officers, City Marshals and City Sheriff's deputies who enforce evictions—and on and on. I once had a neighbor who told me that he was "on the job," meaning he was a cop, and when I asked him where he worked he showed me a gold badge that identified him as a Poultry Inspector for the New York City Department of Agriculture and Markets. It was a beautiful badge, and a real one; the guy was a bona fide chicken policeman, although he wasn't allowed to carry a gun. In most cases the people who work for these agencies only have authority within their own fields of enforcement. Officially, they are "peace officers," not "police officers"—although occasionally they forget that.

For example, at one point we start getting complaints at the IAB Command Center about "cops" who are working off-duty as repossession men for a large furniture rental chain. When someone falls behind on the payments, these cops are showing up at their homes, flashing their shields, identifying themselves as police officers and threatening to arrest them if they don't either pay up or turn over the rented furniture. This is a serious matter for us, because with a very few exceptions, NYPD cops are not allowed to moonlight as security officers—or as repo men. And they certainly aren't allowed to flash their shields and tell people they'll wind up in jail if they don't give up the La-Z-Boy. So when we look into it, it turns out that the repo "cops" are New York City Department of Correction officers who are getting more than a little overzealous. We turn that one over to the DOC's internal affairs unit.

So far the police impersonators I've talked about have been the relatively low-threat types—wannabes, traffic stop badge flashers, fare beaters, and so on. And most of those cases—there are hundreds of them every year in New York—are handled by regular patrol cops or precinct detective squads.

But there are other, more sinister police impersonators who pose a real danger. Those cases come to IAB—specifically, Group 51, the IAB Police Impersonation Group, which was and is the only police department investigative unit in the country tasked exclusively with investigating serious police impersonation crimes.

Group 51 began with the creation of the new IAB back in 1994. At the time the Department was having a big problem with bogus cops who were hitting bodegas, travel agencies, or other small businesses, primarily in immigrant communities. They'd flash police badges, identify themselves as cops, steal the money from the cash register or the cigar box under the counter, and then warn the victims not to report it. It was an effective MO for the robbers. Most of the victims came from countries where corrupt cops were the rule, not the exception—and where they came from, to report to the police a crime committed by other police would usually result in a beating, or worse.

The problem was that the robberies were "pattern crimes," crimes committed by the same individuals or crews across precincts and even borough boundaries, and there was no centralized detective squad assigned to track dangerous police impersonators citywide. Also, sometimes it was unclear at first if the robbers were real crooked cops or ordinary crooks posing as crooked cops.

The result was that from 1994 on, IAB was tasked to handle all serious crimes committed by people who appeared to be or claimed to be cops—whether they turned out to be real cops or not. Which only made sense. If they were real crooked cops they'd come under IAB's purview, and if it turned out they weren't real cops, it didn't make sense for an ongoing investigation to be turned over to regular detectives. Within IAB, any case that involved crooks who were clearly police impersonators would go straight to Group 51.

(Group 51 was easily the most coveted assignment among investigators drafted into the IAB for a couple reasons. One is that cops generally despise criminal police impersonators; they're like a personal affront, and they make real cops look bad. And the other reason is that, given the choice, cops would much rather arrest cop impersonators than arrest real cops.)

Although small in number—only about a dozen investigators are permanently assigned to Group 51—every year Group 51 arrests about a hundred police impersonators who are involved in serious crimes. On the lower end of the serious scale are guys like Angel Gonzalez, who use people's trust in police officers to scam them out of their money but at least don't put them in fear for their lives. At the higher end of the serious scale are the guys who use badges to rob and rape people.

Rapes by police impersonators are a particularly widespread problem, not only in New York City but across the country. Rapists are by nature cowards who depend on intimidation to control their victims—and sometimes a badge, even a phony one, can be even more intimidating than a knife or a gun.

There are countless examples. Like this: A thirty-five-year-old man bangs on a woman's apartment door in Queens, flashes a Department of Sanitation badge in front of the peephole, says, Police! Open up! and when she does he beats and rapes her. He's tackled by neighbors as he tries to flee. Or this: A fifty-year-old child predator recently released from prison approaches a fifteen-year-old boy on a subway platform in Sunset Park in Brooklyn, flashes a fake badge, and "arrests" the kid for littering. He loads him into a van, drives to a remote area, and then sexually assaults him. Or this: A forty-year-old Staten Island man is standing in front of a subway station in Harlem wearing a full NYPD uniform and shield. (That's actually pretty unusual; most impersonators pass themselves off as plainclothes cops with their "badges" on their belts or around their necks.) When a young immigrant woman asks this uniformed cop for subway directions, he orders her to go with him to the roof of a sixteen-story apartment building—she obeys, because after all, he's a policeman—then he threatens to throw her off the roof if she doesn't take off her clothes and do what he wants. She screams and fights her way free.

In none of those cases was the perp a real NYPD cop, or any other kind of cop. And yet in each case the victim acquiesced, at least at first, because they were intimidated by a badge.

Like I said, cases like that are all too common. But more common are police impersonators who prey on prostitutes.

The guy in East New York is a good example. This guy is driving around the known prostitution strips, picking up hookers, and when they get in his car he tells them he's a cop and then calls in the "arrest" over a police-style radio. Then he drives them to a dark alley or parking lot, handcuffs them, and tells them he wants sex with a "police discount"—in other words, free—and if they don't comply they're going to jail. In at least one case, when the victim resists he beats her up.

Yes, they're prostitutes, but it's still forcible rape. The problem is that in most cases like this the prostitute won't report it, either because she thinks the rapist is a real cop who could cause her trouble, or because she figures the real cops won't do anything about it. And it's true that we have had some cases in which real NYPD cops forced prostitutes to give them free sex.

With the East New York case, though, we catch a break. While those rapes are going on, we're investigating a real NYPD vice cop who's suspected of setting himself up as a pimp for some of the hookers in the same area. (He was later kicked off the force.) While we're debriefing some of the hookers for that case, one of them mentions the cop who threatened her for free sex. Several other hookers tell us the same thing. But when we hear what this guy said and did, he doesn't sound like a real cop to us. And it helps that in addition to being a rapist, this "cop" is also a moron. After forcing one of the hookers to give him sex, this guy tells her he wants to be her pimp, and he actually enters his cell phone number into her cell phone and later sends her several texts—which makes it pretty easy for us to track him down and arrest him. Turns out he's a Con Edison power company employee from New Jersey, and he has never been a cop. He gets ten years.

Like the Con Ed guy, in most cases serious criminal police impersonators target victims who are least likely to report the crime: undocumented immigrants, runaway street kids, prostitutes—in other words, people who generally want nothing to do with the police, even after they've been victimized. So it's not surprising that drug dealers are also a frequent target of phony cops.

Usually it's a case of two or three guys stopping a courier on the street or banging a door in an apartment complex, then flashing badges and taking off with the money or drugs. But some of the rip-off crews are more sophisticated.

For example, in one joint NYPD/FBI operation, sixteen members of the Latin Kings gang who were doing police impersonation drug rip-offs were caught with police tactical vests, handcuffs, police scanners, bolt cutters, a hydraulic battering ram for knocking down doors, and a Crown Vic with emergency lights and a special button that let the driver activate a retractable piece of steel to cover its rear plate.

Another police impersonation crew took a different tack. They used the same kind of equipment—Crown Vics, badges, scanners, and so on—but instead of hitting drug or money shipments, they would track major drug dealers, stop their cars or invade their apartments, and then beat and torture them or their family members until the dealers paid a ransom or revealed where they hid their drug and money stashes. In some cases, the crew would threaten a dealer's testicles with a pair of pliers. Prosecutors estimated the police impersonation gang hit more than a hundred drug dealers in New York City and other East Coast states, for a total take of about $4 million.

The victims of police impersonation drug rip-offs usually don't resist. Sometimes it's because they're in on the rip—like Che Che in the Dennis Sindone case—but usually it's because they figure there's no percentage in getting into a gunfight with guys who appear to be cops. And a drug dealer whose money or drugs get stolen almost never reports the crime, either, because whether the rip-off crew is composed of real cops or phony ones, either way the result is the same: The drug dealer isn't going to get his stolen money or drugs back. (I say they almost never report it because, as we'll see in a later chapter, there was at least one case where a dealer whose drug shipment got ripped off by some apparently corrupt cops actually called IAB to complain.)

In fact, for drug dealers it's actually better if the guys who rip them off *are* cops, or at least plausibly pretend to be, as opposed to members of a rival drug gang. For example, if members of the Trinitarios gang are getting ripped off by members of the rival gang DDP (Dominicans Don't Play), to maintain their reputations and street credibility they have to do something about it—which is to say, they have to kill the guys who ripped them off, or somebody close to them, which draws heat, invites retaliation, and is generally bad for business. But if they can say they've been ripped off by cops, well, that's just an occupational hazard. They're not going to kill any cops, even corrupt ones, because that would be really bad for business.

So the phony cop drug rip-off ploy can work to everyone's advantage—which is why so many drug rip crews use it. In fact, in the world of cop drug rip-offs, bogus cops far outnumber the actual ones. It's impossible to quantify crimes that don't get reported, but I would guess that for every case of a Rachko/Vasquez–style drug rip—they were the two crooked NYPD narcotics cops discussed previously— there are probably a hundred cases of phony cops doing drug rips.

But phony cops or not, they cause IAB no end of headaches. If they're real cops doing drug rips, obviously we want them. And if they're phony cops doing rip-offs, we want them, too, not only because they're drug dealers and thieves but also because they're giving honest cops a bad name. But sometimes we don't know for certain if they're real or phony cops until we have them in the bag.

Like the case of the cop rip-off crew in Long Island City.

We've got this perp in Queens, a career criminal who's been locked up on a drug distribution charge. He's a midlevel player in a Dominican drug-running crew in Washington Heights, and now he's looking at some serious time up north—so when our IAB investigators yank him out of a cell in Central Booking for a routine debrief, he's ready to make a deal.

He tells us he's been working as an informant for this crew of NYPD cops who are hijacking trucks carrying cocaine and stealing the drugs. This perp calls the cops and tells them when and where the trucks are transporting the drugs—he knows this because it's his own crew's trucks he's giving up—then the cops swoop in and grab the drugs and the perp gets a cut later. Yes, he's certain these guys are real cops, he knows a cop when he sees one—but no, he doesn't know their full names, just their first names. So we sign this perp up as an official Department confidential informant, in return for which the DA will give him a break on the outstanding drug charge. And we start figuring out how we're going to grab these crooked cops.

We don't want to try to tail them and then take them while they're ripping off an actual drug shipment. For one thing, it could be weeks or months before they do another drug rip, and in a surveillance like that we're probably going to get made. Also, the drug couriers are probably going to be armed, the crooked cops almost certainly will be armed, and we definitely will be armed—heavily armed. The last thing we want is a three-way gunfight breaking out on a busy street. Instead, we want to take them in a controlled situation—so we set up a sting.

We have our CI tell the leader of the cop crew that there's a shipment coming in, three kilos of cocaine hidden in a dresser in an old step van full of used furniture. On a Friday night when there won't be anybody around, the couriers will park the van in front of a warehouse on a narrow side street in the industrial section of Long Island City, and it will be picked up by the CI's crew a few hours later. (In a typical high-level drug deal, the buyers pick up the drugs at one location and then the sellers pick up the payment money that's been left at another location. That way the drugs and the cash are never in the same place at the same time.) But during that time frame, the CI tells the rip crew, the van will just be sitting there, unguarded, and they can just walk in and take the dope. Easy.

It's easy for them. For us it requires a lot of preparation. We park the step van in front of the warehouse with three kilos of "beat" cocaine hidden in the dresser and a surveillance camera inside to record the action. We set up an OP (observation post) in a rented warehouse across the street, also teched up with surveillance cameras, and put two semi-tractor trailers a few blocks away so when the arrest starts to go down they can roll up and block the street. Hidden in the back of each truck are a half dozen Emergency Service Unit A-Team cops—again, they're the NYPD's equivalent of a SWAT unit—in full combat gear: ceramic bulletproof body armor, helmets, assault rifles. The ESU guys also bring in an armored car and park it in a garage across the street from the step van, and we have a dozen IAB investigators hidden around the site. We're loaded for bear—or rather, we're loaded for armed cops-and-robbers.

That's assuming they are real cops. From the names and descriptions our CI has given us—again, he only knows their first names—we haven't been able to match any of this robbery crew to actual NYPD cops. But who knows? Maybe they're real cops from another agency. We have to prepare for the worst.

In any event, just before midnight two cars roll up the seemingly deserted street, with a total of five guys in them. They're all Hispanic, all have silver badges hanging around their necks. While three of them stand guard, the other two guys pry open the back door on the step van. With the surveillance camera inside the van filming, they go straight to the dresser and grab the three bags of bogus coke.

And then the wrath and voice of God descends on them.

The voice comes from a loudspeaker: POLICE! DON'T MOVE! NYPD! And when the perps fail to heed the voice and start to scatter, the ESU armored car bursts out through the garage door and an ESU guy jumps out and tosses a flash-bang grenade at the robbers' feet—*BOOM!*

Flash-bang grenades are exactly that: They make a bright flash and a loud—really loud—bang and they give off some smoke, but unlike military grenades they don't explode into potentially lethal fragments or create a potentially lethal concussion. They're designed to disorient suspects, not injure or kill them; it's sort of a shock-and-awe technique. (They were later effectively banned, by the NYPD, anyway, after a fifty-seven-year-old Harlem woman who worked for the city died of a heart attack after an ESU warrant team mistakenly raided her apartment and used a flash-bang grenade.)

With four of the robbers, the flash-bang does the trick. Their attitude seems to be, Well, if they're going to throw hand grenades at us, I guess we'd better give up. They meekly raise their hands. But the last robber takes off sprinting down the street, straight toward the ESU guys who've dismounted from the tractor trailer, and when in the darkness he appears to be pulling a gun one of the ESU cops squeezes off a round from his assault rifle. Fortunately, it only grazes the bad guy under the armpit, because he turns out not to be armed. In fact, none of the robbers is carrying a gun—and none of them is a cop, either. Their badges look like NYPD shields, except they say "Security Officer." These "cops" are just ordinary police impersonators—and not very good ones, at that.

Still, like so many other cop impersonators, these guys cause us a lot of trouble. Now not only do we have a robbery and criminal impersonation case to handle, but we also have to conduct an IAB officer-involved shooting investigation. That robber was just lucky that the ESU guy's aim was off—those guys aren't supposed to miss. And maybe that should serve as a warning to others like him: For robbers, it can be dangerous to play cops.

Except for the shot being fired, the IAB operation in Long Island City wasn't all that unusual. We do a couple of operations like that a year, in cases where we're dealing with a large number of cops or cop impersonators and there's a serious potential for violence.

But more often the IAB Police Impersonation Group tracks down criminal police impersonators the old-fashioned way—through solid detective work. Sometimes it's easy because the impersonators are dumb, like the rapist in East New York who gave his victim his phone number. But sometimes police impersonators can be ingenious and stupid at the same time—like the three cop impersonators who hit the Pay-O-Matic in Queens.

It's eight o'clock in the morning, Valentine's Day 2012, when the cop walks up to a female employee in the parking lot outside the Pay-O-Matic twenty-four-hour check-cashing store on South Conduit Avenue in Queens. He's a white male, big guy, early thirties, bald with a brown goatee, wearing sunglasses, gloves, a blue raid jacket with "NYPD" on it, and an NYPD gold detective shield hanging from his neck. Two other white males in similar NYPD raid jackets and shields and wearing New York Yankees caps are sitting in a black Ford Explorer nearby.

The detective asks the female employee if she works at the Pay-O-Matic and she tells him she does; she's a teller. The detective pulls some photographs out of his pocket and shows them to her, asking her if she recognizes any of the houses shown in the photographs, which she does. One of them is her house, and she tells him so. He asks her who's inside the Pay-O-Matic, and she tells him there's only one other employee, the night shift teller. Then he starts pushing her into the building, his hand on her back, while the two other men in the NYPD raid jackets follow close behind.

The female employee is confused and intimidated, but she has already figured out this much: These are not ordinary cops, if they're cops at all. But since they have a picture of her house, they know where she lives, so she'd better cooperate.

The detective with the bald head orders the night shift teller to open the double doors separating the customer area from the teller cage, the bulletproof-glass-enclosed area where they keep the cash—and now there's no question about it: This is a robbery. One of the men pulls a gun and orders the night shift teller and the female teller to the floor, while the big bald guy goes to the open safe and starts stuffing money into a black plastic garbage bag; another robber empties the teller drawer. Then one of the robbers pulls out a juice bottle full of bleach and starts splashing it over the teller counter, the safe, the cage floor— anywhere the robbers might have left some DNA evidence. After warning the prostrate employees not to move, the robbers flee with $200,755 in the black plastic bag.

By the time the first patrol units get there, the robbers and the Ford Explorer are gone.

Since the robbers presented themselves as cops, IAB catches the case, although we'll work on it with NYPD squad detectives and the FBI. (Check-cashing businesses, like banks, are federally insured institutions, and robbing one is a federal as well as a state crime.) And there's one thing that's clear to us from the very start.

These three guys almost certainly aren't real cops. Because why would they be?

After all, it's one thing for real cops to bang a drug dealer or a money courier, someone who's probably not going to report the robbery. But it's another thing entirely for real cops to rob a legitimate business of two hundred grand and make no secret of the fact that they're cops. They know the crime is going to be reported; no matter how intimidated the female teller may be, she's not going to be able to keep quiet about the $200,755 that's suddenly missing, and neither is the other teller. These guys also know that every check-cashing business in the city is equipped with multiple security cameras—and these robbers made no effort to disable or avoid the cameras, or to hide their faces. If they're real NYPD cops, it would take us about ten minutes to ID them; they might as well have left their NYPD business cards. So what's the advantage in letting everyone know they're real cops?

There is no advantage. So while we'll keep an open mind on it, we're almost certain these are impersonators—and therefore the case goes to Group 51, IAB's Police Impersonation Unit.

There's something else that we notice about this robbery. In some ways it seems like the perfect professional takeover. For one thing, the robbers had extensively cased the check-cashing store—employees had earlier noticed the black Ford Explorer parked nearby on several occasions—and they knew what time the teller shifts changed, so they could grab a teller outside and force her or him inside the building and then inside the locked cage. Since they had the photograph of the female teller's house, they'd probably followed her home after work one day. The robbers also were in and out in about three minutes, just under the silent alarm response time, and there were no acts of gratuitous violence of the sort that a lot of amateurs commit.

Like I said, they seem like pros. And yet there are also indications that these three mutts are just that—street mutts trying to act like a professional robbery crew.

Take the bleach thing. Sure, bleach will destroy DNA evidence, if there's enough of it. But a little juice bottle being splashed around isn't going to do the trick. And besides, why bother? They're wearing gloves, and unless they're spilling blood on the floor, or unless one of the robbers deposits a big gob of spit on the counter, the chances that the crime scene guys are going to find a usable DNA sample are between slim and none. Yeah, maybe it looks cool and professional, but it could also indicate that these guys have seen one too many bank heist movies—which, as we'll see, they have.

And there's another reason to think that maybe these guys are amateurs. That photograph of her house that the first robber, the big guy, showed to the female teller? As he's pushing her through the door, he accidentally drops the photo on the floor, and it's still there when the robbers leave. On the back of the photo is the word "Walgreens" and two numbers—one of them a store ID number for a Walgreens in Queens, the other a receipt number for photo printing. When IAB detective Michael Visconti, the lead investigator on the case, checks it out with the Walgreens manager, he finds a copy of the receipt with a phone number and the first initial and last name of the customer—"E. Byam."

In police work, this is what we call a clue.

True, as dumb mistakes by criminals go, this isn't quite on par with the bank robber who writes his "demand note" on the back of his own apartment electric bill or an envelope with his own address on it and then leaves it on the counter when he runs off with the cash. (That has actually happened, and more than once.) But it's pretty close.

There's one problem, though. The name and phone number on the photo receipt trace back to a twenty-four-year-old Queens man, Edward Byam, who is African American, and eventually we'll also connect the robbery to two of his friends, who are also black. But from the start, the victim tellers—both of whom got very close looks at these guys—have said that all three robbers were clearly white, and the surveillance tape bears that out. And all the press and TV reports about the heist have said that the three suspects were white. So all along we've been saying that we're looking for three white guys, and then suddenly we wind up with three black suspects? You can imagine what a defense attorney could do with that.

But we've got a pretty good explanation as to why the white robbers are actually black robbers.

Early on in the investigation we release some of the surveillance photos to the news media and put them on the NYPD's Crime Stoppers website. Most of the resulting tips don't pan out. One tipster says they're some guys he knows from Long Island. Another says he saw them on a TV show. Several tipsters say they are some real cops who they know, but while we check it out, we're still pretty convinced that these guys aren't real cops.

But there is one anonymous phone tip that's interesting. The caller says he recognizes one of the faces—and it's not a real face, it's a mask. Not one of those plastic Halloween masks with an elastic band around the back of the head to hold it in place, but a Hollywood-quality, full over-the-head silicone mask. And when we take another close look at the surveillance tapes, we see it. The earholes are a little too big, and the "skin" at the back of the neck bunches up in an unusual way. It's hard to believe we didn't see it at first, but then, the victim tellers who were standing just inches away from these guys didn't realize they were wearing masks, either. That's how convincing these masks were—so convincing that three armed black robbers could put them on and have everybody swear they were armed white robbers.

So these guys aren't just cop impersonators. They're also race impersonators.

Police impersonators were a big problem for the Internal Affairs Bureau. This armed robbery crew wore Hollywood-style masks so realistic that eyewitnesses swore the thieves were white, but when we caught them they turned out to be black.

There aren't too many companies that make these kinds of high-end masks. Eventually we find a company in Louisiana called CFX-Composite Effects that produces amazingly lifelike silicone masks—they made masks for the film *Abraham Lincoln: Vampire Hunter*, among others. They also sell stock masks in a variety of characters and ethnicities: black men, Asian men, white men, males and females. And yes, before the Pay-O-Matic robbery they had sold a Mr. Byam three masks for $1,800; the stock model name was "Mac the Guy," which was sort of a generic white man mask that could have facial and head hair added to it. In fact, Mr. Byam had actually sent the company some e-mails, praising the quality of the masks and promising them more business in the future.

The case comes together pretty quickly after that. The masks were shipped from CFX to the home of a friend of Byam's named Akeem Monsalvatge, who was out on bail awaiting trial for the armed robbery of another Pay-O-Matic store in 2010. (That robbery did not involve police impersonation.) Subpoenaed records of a company that sold police gear online showed that Byam's cousin, a guy named Derrick Dunkley, had ordered three NYPD raid jackets just like the robbers wore. Cell phone relay tower records showed that the men were in the vicinity of the Queens Pay-O-Matic on the day of the robbery. And when IAB investigators and FBI agents arrest the three men, they find three masks and a small bottle of bleach under Byam's bed. The only thing missing is the money, which has already been squandered on trips to expensive resorts and spending sprees on Gucci, Christian Louboutin, Ralph Lauren, and Louis Vuitton clothes and accessories—not to mention a $12,000 diamond-encrusted Rolex watch—for themselves and their girlfriends.

And there's another thing. We notice that the MO in the Pay-O-Matic robbery is similar in many ways to something we've seen before—in a movie. Specifically, the 2010 Ben Affleck movie *The Town*, in which guys in a professional robbery crew in Boston dress up as cops, put on silicone masks, splash bleach around robbery scenes, and gather information on victims and their families to intimidate them into cooperating.

From a police point of view, a lot of what Ben Affleck and his crew did was implausible, even ridiculous, the sorts of things you'd only see in a movie. But the Pay-O-Matic robbery crew had apparently used *The Town* as a kind of training film; in fact, Monsalvatge had a picture of himself posing in a T-shirt with *The Town* movie logo on it.

But there was one big difference between the movie and real life. In the movie, Ben Affleck got away—and these three mopes didn't. After a trial in federal court, they each got thirty-two years.

Again, these guys were more inventive than most cop impersonators. But they made the same mistake that other police impersonators make: They were living in a fantasy world, believing that just because they could look like cops they could also think and act like cops. But with no police or investigative training, they made dumb mistakes that real cops were quick to exploit.

So how can an average person tell real cops from police impersonators? I wish I could say there is some foolproof method, but there isn't. The good news is that with more than 900,000 local, state, and federal sworn law enforcement officers in the US, the real ones far outnumber the bogus ones.

Still, I can offer a few suggestions.

Have you noticed that your neighbor's high-school dropout son is suddenly walking around in a blue uniform and driving a Crown Vic with an antenna farm sprouting from the trunk? Does a guy you meet at a party announce right off the bat that he's a cop, or an undercover cop—which, as I said earlier, is something most cops don't do, and undercovers never do? Do you notice that one of your coworkers—or even your rabbi—is carrying what appears to be a badge of some sort?

Maybe it's harmless, simply a case of someone who likes to fantasize about being a cop. On the other hand, a lot of guys who start out as seemingly harmless wannabes eventually graduate to serious criminal police impersonators.

So if you see something suspicious, do the public—and us—a favor. Call the real police.

Chapter 10

OTHER AGENCIES

The Suffolk County police commissioner needs a favor. He wants to borrow some of our uncles.

He's got this cop, thirty years old, seven years with the Suffolk County PD, a onetime Cop-of-the-Month who has taken a wrong turn. Some other Suffolk PD cops, worried that this guy is going to get them jammed up, have dimed him, anonymously calling their own Internal Affairs unit and telling them that Officer Cop-of-the-Month and possibly some other cops are using and dealing cocaine and steroids. These cops are bodybuilders who hang out at a place called the World Gym, and when they aren't pumping up they're partying at the nightclubs and "gentlemen's clubs" on the East End of Long Island, acting like a bunch of junior Sopranos, Mob wannabes, always talking about the big scores they're making, the scams they're running; they're all about gold chains, waxed bodies, perfectly coiffed hair—and don't spare the cologne. Officer Cop-of-the-Month is also suspected of stealing some high-end camera equipment from this movie producer who has a place in the Hamptons; he'd been an extra in one of the producer's movies— ironically, the title of the film was *Wannabes*—and he apparently has dreams of Hollywood stardom.

So the Suffolk police commissioner wants to put some uncles— undercover cops—in with these guys, get to know them, find out where this might lead, how many cops are involved, and exactly what they're involved in. But while Suffolk County PD has its own very capable and efficient Internal Affairs unit, it's a relatively small department, about twenty-five hundred cops, and they don't have undercovers who won't be recognized if they try to put them next to this cop crew. So could the NYPD Internal Affairs Bureau help?

And my answer is the same as it always is when another law enforcement agency needs some assistance from IAB: No problem!

So after a full brief from Suffolk PD, we sit down with one of our undercover teams and start coming up with a plan. Our initial contact man will be an IAB undercover I'll call Dominick. Dominick is a veteran detective, big guy, comfortably padded around the middle but sleek, with salt-and-pepper hair, beautifully manicured nails, and a tanning salon glow. He's going to play a Mob-connected guy—not a made wiseguy, that would be too easy for a targeted cop to check, just a guy with some loose Mob connections—who runs a sham construction business and who's always looking for a score: drugs, untaxed cigarettes, insurance frauds, whatever can bring in a buck. Dominick is a "dese," "dems," and "dose" guy, a thug in a silk suit, just the sort of guy these wannabes might respond to. Another IAB undercover, Nick, who's in his mid-twenties but looks like he's about eighteen, will play Dominick's nephew and all-around gofer. The initial "meet" between Dominick and Officer Cop-of-the-Month is set for a strip club in Commack, Long Island, where a civilian who's cooperating with Suffolk PD and who knows Officer Cop-of-the-Month will make the intro. We'll also have IAB "ghosts" inside and outside the club.

Now, whenever we have to send our undercovers into bars or casinos or strip joints we make sure they fully understand the rules. To maintain their cover they're allowed to have drinks—at Department expense—ideally no more than two in an eight-hour period, never so much that they're physically impaired; uncles know how to nurse a drink and look drunk at the same time. They're never allowed to take drugs; if a target insists they snort a line to prove they're not cops, maybe they fake it or, depending on the character they're playing, maybe they get all indignant and say something like, Whaddaya kidding me? Do I look like some kinda fuckin' loser to you? I sell that poison shit; I don't use it! (If an undercover is forced at gunpoint to take drugs, he or she is immediately pulled out and placed under medical observation.) If an undercover's role takes him into a strip joint, the Department will pay the cover charge, but that's it. The New York City Police Department does not, repeat, does not, pay for lap dances.

Oh, and there's one other rule we make sure our undercovers understand: If while on undercover duty they win any money or other prizes in a lottery or raffle or game of chance, it's our money, not theirs.

You might not think that such a warning would be necessary, but it is. Back in the mid-1990s we had a female IAB undercover working another case in a bar in East Quogue on Long Island, and when she bought a beer—with Department money—she automatically got one of those tear-off tickets for a car raffle. When, at the end of the night, they pulled the winning ticket out of the jar, the undercover won the car—a shiny new red $14,000 Plymouth Neon. Our undercover's position was that the car was hers, and Walter Mack, then deputy commissioner for internal affairs, wanted to let her keep it. But the city Conflicts of Interest Board thought otherwise, and after a hearing the Department kept the Neon, and the precedent was set.

So anyway, we put Dominick and Nick into one of IAB's undercover cars from the warehouse in Queens, one with a plate number and VIN that won't trace back to the NYPD, in this case a three-year-old Mercedes; we want Dominick to look like a moderately successful crook, but not like a Mob boss with a brand-new Mercedes. Backed up by their ghosts, they go to the strip club, where they "accidentally" run into the cooperating civilian, who's there with Officer Cop-of-the-Month. And then it's, Hey, Dominick, how-ah-ya, how-ah-ya, hey, I want you to meet a friend of mine . . .

So does Dominick immediately start talking to Officer Cop-of-the-Month—who doesn't identify himself as a cop—about drugs or scores or anything else? Of course not. After a few words, Dominick barely even looks at the guy. He's just a businessman out for a good time. Dominick stays for a while, has a drink, looks at the girls—being an undercover can be a tough job, but somebody's got to do it—and then he's out of there. Officer Cop-of-the-Month doesn't see him again for a week, maybe two, until Dominick just happens to come into another club where Officer Cop-of-the-Month is hanging out, and even then Dominick acts like he hardly remembers the guy. Oh yeah, you're So-and-So's friend, how ya doin'?

This goes on for weeks, then months. (During this time, Dominick and the other members of the undercover team are working other, unrelated cases as well.) As in any undercover investigation, the idea is for Officer Cop-of-the-Month and his pals to get used to seeing Dominick and his nephew around, to feel comfortable around them—and eventually they do. At one point Officer Cop-of-the-Month invites Dominick and Nick to a party at his house, and Dominick gets into a conversation with a guy, one of Cop-of-the-Month's wannabe crew, who sounds like an NYPD cop; there's just something about the way he talks. Nephew Nick goes out and surreptitiously takes down the plate numbers of the cars parked outside, and when we run them, sure enough, one of them pops to a thirty-four-year-old NYPD sergeant who lives on Long Island and is on modified duty because of a domestic violence incident with his girlfriend. So now we're not only helping Suffolk PD make a case on one of their bad cops, they're also helping us make a case on one of our bad cops. We also find out that a couple of New York State Troopers are part of the junior Sopranos cop crew.

So how bad are these cops? Well, they're using and dealing drugs, cocaine and anabolic steroids, and they're making some money on it. Dominick vouches for a couple of other IAB undercovers who come in and make some hand-to-hand buys from these guys. But it's not major-drug-trafficker weight.

But as for the "scores" these guys are always bragging about, we finally decide that that's just the coke and the steroids talking. The only real scam we find Officer Cop-of-the-Month running is when he tries to talk Dominick into investing a million and a half dollars in a Hollywood movie project, an investment that he says will double in six months. There's really no movie, of course, but if you locked up everybody who tried to hustle investors for a bogus movie project, half the people in LA would be in jail.

So the bottom line is that these cops aren't the Sopranos. They're the Jersey Shore.

Still, they're cops, and the last thing we want is coked and 'roided up cops in our departments. Finally, after an investigation that stretches out over a year, the Suffolk County PD rounds up fourteen people on various drug-dealing charges, ten of them civilians, four of them cops: Officer Cop-of-the-Month, our NYPD sergeant, and two state troopers—all of whom are immediately suspended. One of the state troopers eventually beats the rap, but the other three cops are all convicted or plead guilty—and they aren't cops anymore.

Now, although by IAB standards this wasn't a particularly big case, it still required a lot of IAB time and resources. So why do we do it? Why spend NYPD time and NYPD money on somebody else's case?

There are two reasons. One practical reason is that a lot of NYPD cops live in Suffolk County, as well as in Nassau and Westchester counties, so we get a lot of cases involving those jurisdictions. I know that if they need our help on a case today, we're going to need their help on a case next month.

And the other, more general reason is that as far as I'm concerned, any law enforcement supervisor who doesn't go out of his way to maintain good working relations with other law enforcement agencies—local, state, and federal—simply isn't doing his job. Turf wars, interagency squabbles, personal feuds between agency chiefs—they may reflect human nature, but they're also a waste of time, efficiency, and the tax-payer dime. And if you ask them, almost all law enforcement officials will agree with that—at least in theory.

But actually putting the theory into practice can be a little tougher.

In his book *Crime Fighter*, the late, great Jack Maple, a onetime Transit cop turned NYPD deputy commissioner under Bill Bratton, and one of the primary architects of the NYPD's transformation in the mid-1990s, described what he called his "Fantasy Island" concept of cooperative crime fighting.

In Jack's vision, at least once a week representatives from every law enforcement and law enforcement–related government agency in an entire metropolitan area will sit down at a meeting. There'll be some-body from the metropolitan police force—like the NYPD—as well as cops from suburban police forces, county sheriffs, city marshals, state police, and highway patrol. The feds will all be there—FBI, DEA, ATF (Bureau of Alcohol, Tobacco, Firearms and Explosives), ICE (Immi-gration and Customs Enforcement), IRS, and even the Secret Service, which in addition to protecting the president and other officials also handles counterfeiting and financial fraud cases. Prosecutors from the local District Attorney's and US Attorney's Offices will be there to offer guidance on how criminal cases will be prosecuted in court. There'll be officials from the local housing authority and building inspector's office and the city fire marshal and child protective services, and even somebody from the US Department of Agriculture, which handles food stamp fraud cases. And when you got all these guys and gals around a conference table, they'll do one simple thing:

They'll share. They'll share with everybody else detailed information on what cases they're working on, and what they can do to help some other agency's case. They'll share intelligence on criminals who are on their radar, or who have dropped off their radar and maybe turned up on somebody else's. They'll agree to freely share resources and manpower and even funding. They'll do everything but hold hands in a circle and sing "Kumbaya," because hey, we're all in this together, right?

Wrong. And that's why Jack Maple called the idea of complete and unselfish cooperation between local, state, and federal law enforcement agencies a "Fantasy Island" scenario. Sure, you can create your various "joint task forces" pairing local cops with state and federal agencies, and at the street level cops and federal agents can work well together. But Jack understood that as long as law enforcement agencies are staffed and led by human beings, there are always going to be petty jealousies and simmering resentments and competitive egos at work, especially at the upper management levels. You can try to control it, but you can never completely eliminate it.

Still, in the new IAB I think we came pretty close to Jack's ideal. We had to. Because for us, cooperation with other law enforcement agencies was a matter of survival. If the NYPD was to continue to police itself, instead of having that function turned over to an outside agency with its own political agenda, the new Internal Affairs Bureau had to prove that, unlike in the old days, we were open, trustworthy, and capable of working with other law enforcement entities to clean up our own house.

We started with the prosecutors.

There's only one NYPD, but there are eight different chief prosecutors in New York City that the NYPD deals with—five district attorneys, one in each of the city's five boroughs; a special narcotics prosecutor for the city of New York, who handles high-end drug cases citywide; and two federal US attorneys, one in the Southern District (which covers Manhattan and the Bronx and some counties north of the city) and one in the Eastern District (which covers Brooklyn, Queens, and Staten Island as well as Nassau and Suffolk counties on Long Island). Each of the DAs has his or her own team of investigators—many of them current or retired NYPD detectives—who handle public corruption cases, including police corruption and misconduct, and each US attorney has a team of prosecutors who work with the FBI's Public Corruption Unit, known as Unit C-14.

And every one of those DAs and US attorneys loves to put crooked cops in jail.

The reason is simple: Crooked cops make news. I mean, if you're a DA or a US attorney and you call a press conference to announce that you've just charged some ordinary street mutt with beating up a bodega owner or moving a couple of keys of cocaine from Washington Heights to Brooklyn, how much ink are you going to get in the papers or airtime on TV? Zero. Because that kind of thing is a "dog bites man" story— that is, it happens all the time. But when you get a cop caught stealing a wallet off a DOA, or giving a handcuffed perp an extra baton whack within view of a surveillance camera, that's unusual, it's not something that happens all the time—in other words, it's a "man bites dog" story.

Now, I'm not saying that prosecutors like to go after crooked cops for the publicity alone. In my experience most prosecutors have a sincere and deeply held revulsion for public corruption and misconduct. Still, local district attorneys are elected officials, with a finely tuned sense of what attracts the voters' positive attentions. And while US attorneys are appointed by the president, not elected by the people, they, too, generally have a firm appreciation for the value of good publicity. So when they get an opportunity to stand up at a press conference and announce the latest dramatic victory in the relentless war against police corruption and misconduct, you can bet they're going to jump on it.

And in the old days before the new IAB, they wouldn't even tell the NYPD about it. Say, for example, that the Bronx DA had an informant who gave up some crooked cops. DA's investigators would work the case on their own, maybe arresting a crooked cop, turning him, and putting him back into a precinct with a wire to gather incriminating information on other crooked cops. This could go on for months, or a year, and the old Internal Affairs Division wouldn't even know about it, because back then nobody talked to the IAD—not the DAs and not the feds, either. Rightly or wrongly, the old IAD had a reputation for leaking like a sieve, and no outside agency was going to endanger its investigation by bringing them in on a case. And then when the investigation was complete, the DA or US attorney would call the NYPD police commissioner and tell him: Hey, we're indicting two or three or ten of your guys in the morning. And after the arrests the PC would have to stand there at the press conference, looking like a deer in the headlights, while the DA or the US attorney told the world how he—the champion of the people!—was cleaning out the rotten apples in the NYPD.

It was embarrassing—and worse, it was inefficient. Why have eight different prosecutors independently investigating police misconduct and corruption in the NYPD when the new IAB is doing the same thing? But at the same time, how does one law enforcement agency—which is to say, us, the IAB—overcome years, even decades of mistrust and suspicion and silence with another law enforcement agency?

First of all, as Jack Maple envisioned, we share. We share intelligence, we share strategy, we even share informants. As I explained in an earlier chapter, in the new IAB, every single allegation of possible criminal behavior by NYPD cops is immediately forwarded to the appropriate DA's office. It doesn't matter if it's cops allegedly mussing up a handcuffed suspect in the Bronx or a senior chief allegedly brandishing a gun in a parking dispute in Brooklyn, the Bronx DA or the Brooklyn DA knows about it from the start. If the DA decides that it doesn't rate a criminal investigation, fine, IAB will handle it administratively. And if the DA decides to open a criminal investigation, IAB investigators usually take the lead, with a couple of the DA's own investigators assisting. There's a practical reason for that. A DA might have a couple dozen investigators available to handle corruption or misconduct cases, while IAB has hundreds. The important thing is that the DA will be kept informed every step of the way—and no one can ever say that the NYPD is dumping police corruption cases or sweeping police misconduct under the rug.

The value of personal relationships between agency heads is another important factor, one that I can't emphasize enough. As I said earlier, most of the conflicts between law enforcement agencies originate not at the street level but at the boss level. But if my boss trusts and respects your boss, and vice versa, there's an extra incentive for people to cooperate all the way down the line.

So as IAB chief I made it a point to establish personal relationships with all the DAs and their Public Integrity Unit heads. I met regularly with all of them to discuss ongoing investigations, and part of the discussion always included this question: Are your guys having any problems with my guys? If so, I would find out why. And if my guys were having any problems with the DA's prosecutors or investigators, I knew that every one of those DAs would do the same.

Don't misunderstand. That sort of trust and cooperation doesn't happen overnight. It took months, sometimes even years. But eventually every DA in New York City was working with us, not around us, to investigate corruption and misconduct in the NYPD. In every nonfederal police corruption or misconduct case I've mentioned in this book, cooperation with the district attorneys played an important role.

True, there was one thing that never changed, and probably never will. We'd get a criminal case against some corrupt cops, spend hundreds or even thousands of IAB man-hours working it, then hand it on a plate to the DA to take to the grand jury. And then, at the postindictment press conference, the DA would stand there at a lectern bearing the great seal of the Office of the District Attorney and tell the assembled reporters how he and his dogged team of DA's investigators had relentlessly pursued and apprehended these blue-uniformed betrayers of the public trust. Sure, somewhere in there, usually near the end, the DA would throw in a line about how much the District Attorney's Office appreciated the invaluable assistance of the NYPD Internal Affairs Bureau in bringing these corrupt cops to justice. Which always left me rolling my eyes and thinking: Assistance? He's thanking us for our *assistance*? We handled the entire case!

That's a natural reaction. For one thing, I wanted the public and the press to understand that the NYPD, and specifically the Internal Affairs Bureau, was policing itself, that the Department was trying to cleanse itself of corruption, that it wasn't a case of the District Attorney's Office coming in and cleaning up the Department. And I also wanted my IAB investigators to get more credit for their hard work—which is what this book is all about.

Sure, I can understand why the DAs do it; they have to win an election every four years, and IAB doesn't. Still, it rankles a bit.

And it's the same thing when we're dealing with the feds.

The NYPD and federal law enforcement agencies, especially the FBI, have a long tradition of butting heads. Yes, the NYPD works with the feds in a variety of joint task forces—the Joint Terrorism Task Force, the NYPD/DEA New York Drug Enforcement Task Force, the aforementioned NYPD/ICE/IRS El Dorado Task Force, and so on. They generally work well together, but there are always tensions, usually coming from the top down—and especially with the FBI. That's because both the NYPD and the FBI are absolutely convinced that they are the premier law enforcement agency in the world—naturally I'm on the NYPD side of that argument—and that they can do any job better than the other guys can.

That's particularly true in the field of counterterrorism. After the 9/11 attacks, under Commissioner Ray Kelly the NYPD vastly expanded its counterterrorist efforts, including the creation of a new NYPD Counter-Terrorism Bureau, the expansion of the Intelligence Division, the training and equipping of special antiterrorism "Hercules" teams, and even the posting of NYPD detectives in a variety of foreign capitals to gather intelligence on terrorist activities. It's fair to say that this annoyed a number of high-ranking members of various federal agencies, including the FBI, who thought that counterterrorism activities in New York City and the rest of the US was their job.

Well, it's one thing for the NYPD as a whole to have turf battles with the feds. After all, if the FBI uncovers a terrorist plot directed at New York City, nobody's going to criticize the NYPD for not uncovering it first, because foiling terrorist plots is the FBI's job. On the other hand, if the FBI single-handedly investigates and arrests some NYPD cops for misconduct or corruption, everybody's going to say: Hey, why didn't IAB know about these corrupt cops? That's their job! What are they, asleep at the wheel?

So IAB had to cooperate with the FBI and the US attorneys—not the phony, forced-smile, grip-and-grin-for-the-camera sort of cooperation, but real cooperation from the top down. And we did that the same way we did it with the DAs—through free exchange of intelligence and the development of personal relationships.

Again, it wasn't easy, because in the pre-IAB days the FBI and federal prosecutors had never talked to the old IAD about an ongoing investigation; sometimes the first time that NYPD officials would know of an FBI corruption investigation of the NYPD was when they read about it in the newspapers.

But in the early 1990s, Deputy Commissioner for Internal Affairs Walter Mack, himself a former federal prosecutor, tried to address the problem. In discussions with the US attorneys, we came up with a system to handle federal cases of NYPD corruption and misconduct.

Part of the new operating procedure was that if a potential case involving NYPD personnel originated with the FBI or the DEA or some other federal agency—for example, if an FBI informant gave up some allegedly corrupt cops—the criminal case would remain federal, but the feds would bring in IAB to jointly investigate the case. Because IAB had far more investigators than the federal agencies' public integrity units, and far more experience in investigating corrupt cops, in practice IAB would handle most or all of the investigation, and the US attorney had the option of prosecuting the case in the federal court system.

But in any interagency effort, there also has to be cooperation and respect at the street level. And that's why we created IAB Group 25—the Federal Liaison Group.

Cops by nature are suspicious of almost everyone—including other cops. Before they'll completely trust each other they'll spend a long time circling around each other and sizing each other up: Is this guy a hairbag or a hard charger? Does he really know what he's doing, or did he get where he is because he's got a hook? Will he be the first guy through the door on a search warrant, or the last? Can I trust this guy to watch my back?

The sniffing-out period takes a lot of time. So if you're always randomly throwing together cops from different units—and especially different agencies—to conduct joint investigations, it's going to be a long while before they actually get to the "joint" part. On the other hand, if you have the same NYPD cops working with the same FBI or DEA agents on case after case after case, the sniffing-out period is quickly over with and the cops and federal agents will actually be working together. They develop a camaraderie, and pretty soon they'll be lined up together at the bar after work, trading war stories and arguing about whose top brass are the most screwed up. They become in effect a unit, not an odd collection of cops and agents who don't know or trust each other.

That was the theory behind Group 25. We took a dozen IAB investigators, commanded first by the late Lieutenant John Donnelly and later by Sergeant Joe Clarino, and made them the lead group on any IAB case with a federal component. They were specially trained in federal criminal laws and procedures, and they worked closely with the New York US attorneys and the FBI's Public Corruption Unit—the same people over and over again.

I've already mentioned a number of cases in which IAB and the feds worked together. The Louima case was one; the Dennis Sindone drug rip-off case was another; the Rachko/Vasquez rip-off of the $169,000 in El Dorado Task Force buy money still another. But there are numerous other examples. In one 2010 case, an FBI informant in Brooklyn gives up a cop in the 68th Precinct who's smuggling bootleg cigarettes. That may not sound like much, but when you can buy cancer sticks for six bucks a pack retail in Virginia—less for wholesale, and for nothing if you just hijack them off a truck—and then sell them for twelve bucks a pack retail in New York City, well, the possibilities are obvious. With the FBI we set up a sting on this cop and other Six-Eight cops, using wiretaps and IAB and FBI undercovers, and arrange for them to transport stolen slot machines and even some guns—which we render inoperable—across state lines. In the end, eight current and retired NYPD cops are arrested, along with four civilians, and convicted on federal charges.

In another 2010 case, a robbery crew led by three NYPD cops— one a former undercover cop in the elite Intelligence Division—stages a bogus raid on a warehouse in New Jersey, flashing their NYPD shields and tying up a dozen employees before loading half a million dollars in designer perfume into some rented trucks. Because they're NYPD cops, or claim to be, the FBI calls us in and we start a joint investigation. Actually it's a pretty easy case, since these knuckleheads left behind at the scene not only a paper printout that we traced back to an NYPD computer, but they also left behind one of the rented trucks—which one of these geniuses had rented in his own name. We quickly roll them up and they're prosecuted on federal interstate robbery charges.

Usually we helped the feds make criminal cases against bad NYPD cops in federal court. But sometimes the feds helped us make cases against bad cops in state court. Like in the case of the cop known as "Marty the Murderer."

It's 2001, and an off-duty NYPD sergeant named Martin Peters is having a violent argument with his ex-girlfriend, a newly hired federal Immigration and Customs Enforcement (ICE) detention officer who is the mother of his two children, at her apartment in Bedford-Stuyvesant. Enraged, Peters draws a gun—not his service weapon or off-duty gun— and shoots her three times in the head, killing her. During the melee

Peters also accidentally shoots and wounds his best friend, a guy named Nigel, a childhood friend from Peters's native Trinidad who was delivering some clothes for the kids when the argument started.

Being a cop, Peters knows he'll have to come up with a cover story to divert attention away from him. So while his friend Nigel is lying there bleeding on the floor, Peters orders him to tell the cops that an intruder broke in and shot him and Peters's ex-girlfriend—and if Nigel tells the cops otherwise, Peters says, he'll kill Nigel and his whole family, best friend or not. Nigel knows that Peters is serious, so even though Peters has almost killed him—the shooting leaves Nigel a paraplegic—that's the story Nigel tells the homicide detectives: a masked intruder broke in and shot him and the ex-girlfriend.

The homicide detectives don't believe the story, and neither do we—and neither do the dead woman's family and friends, who later tell us she was terrified of Peters, that he had physically abused her for years and used his position as a cop to intimidate her and her family into not reporting it. But with no physical evidence and the only eyewitness— Nigel—sticking by his story that an intruder shot him and the ex-girlfriend, the DA doesn't have enough evidence to charge Peters. And we can't even fire him from the NYPD. He's not charged with a crime, and under civil service rules all we can do is take his shield and gun and put him on modified duty escorting prisoners in the Manhattan Criminal Courts building, where he's shunned by other cops, who call him Marty the Murderer.

You can imagine how frustrating it is to have a cop like that on the NYPD payroll, but that's the law. In fact, this guy even has the gall to sue the Department for not promoting him to lieutenant while he's on modified duty!

But we never give up on the case. Finally, after almost four years of investigation, working with the NYPD Cold Case squad and ICE, we get enough evidence for the US attorney to file immigration fraud charges against both Peters and Nigel. It turns out that more than a decade earlier, shortly before he entered the Police Academy, Peters had obtained US citizenship through a sham marriage to a US citizen—a detail that somehow slipped past the Department background investigators. In other words, this guy should never have been a cop in the first place.

As for Nigel, when faced with time in federal prison and then deportation back to Trinidad, where the social services safety net for paraplegics leaves something to be desired, he suddenly remembers what really happened on the day of the murder and agrees to testify against Peters. The Brooklyn DA's office files state murder charges against Peters, who is later convicted and sentenced to forty-three years to life—and Marty the Murderer is no longer a cop.

Well, I could go on, but you get the point about our cooperation with the feds. It wasn't just lip service, or public relations. In IAB we really did work closely with the federal agencies.

I'm not saying that every single joint operation that IAB conducted with federal agencies went smoothly. In police work there's always a chance that things can go wrong—especially when some high-level supervisor decides that protecting his own bureaucratic turf is more important than getting the job done.

A joint IAB/FBI operation the feds called "Operation Bump-in-the-Night" is a case in point.

It starts like this:

The FBI has an informant who gives up a drug rip crew that's hitting drug dealers' apartments in Washington Heights, booming their doors and grabbing whatever cash or drugs are inside. The informant says that some of the guys in this crew are NYPD cops, that they're driving Crown Vics and waving NYPD shields when they do the rip-offs. So the FBI calls us in, and together we set up a sting.

First we rent an apartment on the top floor of a five-story walk-up apartment building in a seedy, weed-choked residential section of Washington Heights, tech it up with surveillance cameras, and also rent another apartment on the fourth floor where we can monitor the cameras.

Of course, when I say we rent the apartments, I don't mean that some FBI or IAB guys in suits simply knock on the apartment super's door and plunk down the first and last month's rent. At this point in the history of Washington Heights, chances are that if the super or the other residents in the apartment building aren't actually in the drug trade, then they have an uncle or a cousin who is—and in five minutes everybody in the neighborhood will know that the cops are in Apartment 5C. In an undercover operation, even renting an apartment is an undercover operation. So we send in some of our Spanish-speaking undercovers—IAB and FBI—guys who look like drug dealers, to rent the apartments, and then over the next weeks we have other undercovers posing as dealers and runners going in and out of Apartment 5C; we have to make it look like they're using the apartment as a drug and money drop.

The plan is to plant $50,000 in marked cash—half of it the FBI's money, half ours—in two bags in the apartment and then have the informant tip the rip-off crew that the money's in there. When the crew hits the apartment, we'll have them on the surveillance cameras and a joint NYPD Emergency Service Unit A-Team and FBI SWAT team will burst in, put them on the floor, and then we'll move in and cuff them and separately debrief them. (In cop talk, to "bump" somebody is to grab them unexpectedly, which is why the FBI is calling this Operation Bump-in-the-Night.)

Or at least that's the plan until the last minute, when a new FBI assistant special agent in charge (ASAC), who we've never worked with before, suddenly announces at our final tactical planning meeting that there's a change in the plan: The FBI SWAT team and FBI agents will handle the takedown and arrests by themselves, while our IAB guys will fall back and play a supporting role, and the NYPD A-Team won't be used at all. Last-minute changes like this are almost always a bad idea, but when we and the ASAC's own FBI guys start to protest, the ASAC gets his back up and says: Look, it's an FBI informant, which makes it an FBI case, and the FBI is going to handle it. End of story.

Well, technically he's got us there. That's the agreement; their informant, they're the lead agency. But hey, I work at One Police Plaza, so I know a little something about bureaucratic egos. And I know exactly what this ASAC is doing. He's doing what the FBI brass has been historically famous—or infamous—for since the days of J. Edgar Hoover: He's bigfooting the locals, letting them do the lion's share of the work and then shunting them—us—aside so the FBI can grab all the credit.

I'm a three-star chief in the NYPD, which means I don't take orders from some pushy FBI ASAC. So for a minute I think about pulling IAB out altogether. But that would be letting my professional ego get the better of me. Besides that, I have tremendous respect for the FBI public corruption squad agents who are on the team, their new ASAC notwithstanding. And having gone through a lot of these things, I suspect that before the operation is over, they're going to need us.

So that night the rip crew rolls up in front of the apartment house, six white and Hispanic males in three cars, including a Crown Vic; they kick the door to Apartment 5C and grab the $50,000 that's in the two bags while our surveillance cameras record it. But before the bad guys can get out the FBI SWAT guys move in and, although this wasn't part of the original tac plan, they toss a couple of flash-bang grenades into the apartment— *BOOM! BOOM!*—to give the bad guys a little shock and awe.

Shocked and awed they certainly are. When the FBI SWAT guys swarm into the smoke-filled apartment—FBI! On the floor!—the bad guys quickly drop down and give up. As it turns out, the badges they're wearing are fake, and when we run the plate numbers of their cars, none of them, including the Crown Vic, comes back to the NYPD or any other law enforcement agency. The good news for us is that these guys aren't crooked cops; they're police impersonators, like so many other rip crews we've dealt with. The crew leader turns out to be a bail bondsman from New Jersey, and another member of the crew is a New Jersey bounty hunter.

Still, there are a few little problems with this FBI-led operation.

For one thing, when the flash-bangs go off in Apartment 5C, the 911 switchboard starts lighting up with calls from nearby residents reporting an explosion and fire. We hadn't been expecting the flash-bangs to be used, and by the time we call the emergency dispatch center and tell them this is a police operation, the street is already swarming with sirens-screaming, lights-flashing FDNY fire trucks and buses—that is, ambulances. The entire operation scene is in chaos.

And there's another small problem. When the FBI agents start counting bad guy heads in Apartment 5C, they make a pretty alarming discovery: Six bad guys went into the apartment, but they've only got five bad guys in custody. In the smoke and confusion, one suspect has gotten away, apparently through an open window at the back of the apartment.

Oh, and one other thing. One of the bags that had the cash in it is missing, too.

The deputy chief on the scene is calling me regularly and keeping me apprised about what's going on. (Much as I'd like to be, I'm not at the scene, because my theory of management is to put my best people on a job and then let them do it; too much brass at any operation just gets in the way.) And my instructions to the deputy chief are clear: First, our IAB guys are to grab the remaining bag of cash—which they do—and not give it up for any reason. And second, IAB is to do everything possible to assist the FBI in recovering the missing suspect and the FBI's missing cash.

That's right—the *FBI's* missing cash. Our position, and we're sticking to it, is that $25,000 of the remaining cash is IAB's money, and the money that's in the wind—well, that's the FBI's problem.

Now, given the way the FBI ASAC treated my IAB guys, you may be wondering, Am I deriving any vengeful pleasure from all this? Do I enjoy imagining how the ASAC is going to have to break this bad news to his FBI bosses? Does it make me happy to envision the many, many reams of paperwork the ASAC is going to have to fill out to explain how the operation he masterminded is short one perp and a bagful of FBI money?

No, of course not. That would be wrong. How could you even think such a thing?

In the end, though, it turns out OK for everybody. It seems that when the flash-bangs went off in the apartment, and before the smoke cleared, the missing perp had grabbed one of the money bags and tossed it out the back window, then he crawled out the window and tried to make a Tarzan-style leap to a nearby fire escape—except that unlike Tarzan, he missed and fell five stories to the ground, suffering a nasty compound fracture to his ankle. Unable to walk, this guy crawled on his belly out from behind the apartment and up to one of the ambulances on the scene, where he told the EMTs he was a neighbor who was running over to see what was happening and he tripped and broke his ankle. The EMTs had no idea what was going on, or that a perp was missing—confusion still reigned—so they loaded him into the bus and were about to transport him to the hospital when one of our IAB guys happened to pass by and looked in the back of the ambulance and recognized the "patient" as one of the perps. So the perp went to the hospital, but he went there under arrest.

As for the missing cash—the FBI's missing cash—we finally find it under some weeds and bushes in the backyard of the apartment where the perp threw it. We cheerfully return it to the FBI.

And in fact, the perp falling out of the window in the Bump-in-the-Night case actually plays out in our favor with another FBI unit that IAB often works with—the FBI civil rights unit, which investigates, among other things, allegations of police brutality.

Whenever a suspect is seriously injured during an arrest by NYPD cops, IAB investigates the incident. Sometimes it's a shooting, sometimes a suspect gets a broken arm or leg while fighting the cops—and more often than you might think, it's a suspect who gets hurt jumping or falling from a roof or a window, just like the perp in the Bump-in-the-Night case.

Almost any NYPD cop can tell you stories about doing a vertical and finding a suspect trying to hide by hanging by his fingertips from the roof ledge of a six- or eight-story building. Or about kicking a door on a drug warrant and having a perp jump out of a second- or third- or even fourth-story window, or if it's higher than that, trying to shimmy down a drainpipe or leap to a fire escape or swing like Batman down a TV cable. And sometimes they don't make it.

And sometimes if they don't make it, they—if they survive the fall—or others will claim that they didn't fall at all, that the cops threw them out the window or off the roof. So whenever a suspect is hurt in a fall, we conduct a thorough investigation. We interview witnesses, take statements from other cops at the scene, examine physical evidence like a drainpipe freshly pulled out from a wall or a freshly broken TV cable or the alleged victim's handmarks in the grime on the very edge of a fire escape that was just a little too far away.

And in all my years as chief of IAB, while there were numerous cases of criminals throwing people off roofs, we never had a case where the evidence proved or even strongly suggested that cops had actually tossed a person out of or off a building. Sometimes witnesses changed their stories, in the same way that a witness who claimed to have seen a cop fatally push a twenty-nine-year-old man off a five-story building during the riots after the Kiko Garcia shooting in 1992 later admitted under oath that he had lied. Other times the physical evidence contradicts the allegation. I'm not saying it never happened in the long history of the NYPD, and I remember the aforementioned Sergeant Psycho threatening to throw another cop off a precinct-house roof. But in almost twenty years I never had a documented case of a cop actually doing it.

Still, there are always police brutality lawyers who never let the facts get in the way of a good defenestration-by-cop case. And if the allegation gets a little attention in the press, we'll get a call from the FBI civil rights unit, wanting to see what we've got, to see if some citizen's constitutional rights have been violated by being tossed out a window by police officers. Once we show them the evidence, they'll say, Okay, we guess it didn't happen—this time. But there's always this lingering hint of skepticism, this suspicion that NYPD cops do this kind of thing all the time. It's like they're thinking: C'mon, you're telling us that some guy intentionally jumped out of a fourth-floor window or took a Flying Wallendas–like leap at an eighth-floor fire escape just to avoid getting arrested? Surely the cops must have had something to do with it.

That's exactly what I'm telling them. And after the perp in the FBI-led Bump-in-the-Night case takes a nosedive out the window and breaks his ankle, I'm also telling them: Hey, look, this kind of thing happens all the time, and not just with the NYPD. Do you think your own FBI guys threw that mope out the window?

So like I said, something good came out of our uncharacteristic clash with the FBI in that case. And in fairness, I should say that the FBI ASAC in question eventually came around—or at least he never tried to bigfoot IAB again. IAB's Group 25 and the FBI's Public Corruption Unit agents, especially Supervisory Special Agents Bob Hennigan and Rodney Miller, continued to conduct joint operations just that way—with joint respect, joint cooperation, and joint effort.

But there was still one thing missing from all that joint-ness.

Feds being feds, IAB still never got joint credit at the press conferences . . .

I mentioned earlier that while I was chief of IAB we made it a point to cooperate with New York City district attorneys. But as the Long Island Soprano Cops case shows, there were times when the DAs in the suburban counties also reached out to IAB—and times when we reached out to them.

The case of the NYPD recruit and the hit man is a good example.

In the summer of 2006 we get a call at the IAB Command Center from an NYPD Academy recruit—call him Recruit No. 1—with a strange story to tell. He says he knows this other Academy recruit named Kabeer Din, a twenty-two-year-old Pakistan-born guy who had briefly served as a Baltimore PD cop before applying to the NYPD Academy. They both live in Suffolk County, and sometimes they ride into the city together on the LIRR (Long Island Railroad). It's not like they're close friends or anything—they've only been at the Academy together three weeks—but at some point Din starts telling Recruit No. 1 about the problems he's having with his twenty-four-year-old India-born girl-friend, who also lives in Suffolk County. He wants to get married, Din says, but she doesn't, so now he wants to find somebody who will take care of her—take care of her as in kill her. So does Recruit No. 1 happen to know anybody who's in the hit-man business?

Recruit No. 1 can hardly believe it. He assumes this is some kind of sick joke, that the guy doesn't really mean it. But then he starts to wonder if this might be some kind of Internal Affairs integrity test—IAB is everywhere!—to see if he'll turn Din in. So he calls us—and at first we're dubious. A Police Academy recruit asks another recruit who he barely knows to set him up with a killer for hire? It sounds pretty far-fetched—not to mention unbelievably dumb on Din's part. Also, Din has been through police background investigations and psych screen-ing twice—once in Baltimore, once in New York—and no one detected any problems. He did okay during his brief career with Baltimore PD, and in his even briefer career so far with the NYPD.

Still, we have to check it out. We set up a controlled phone call from Recruit No. 1 to Din, and while we're listening in, Recruit No. 1 says: Hey, you know that thing you were talkin' about? I got a guy who says he can do it for, like, three thousand dollars. He's in the construction busi-ness, he's connected, and he can make sure the "package" will never be found, you know, like buried under a parking lot or something.

So does Din say: What are you talking about? What guy? What pack-age? What three thousand dollars?

No. What Din essentially says is: Great! When can I meet the guy?

Since this conspiracy originated in Suffolk County, and the intended victim lives there, this is going to be a Suffolk County case—if there is a case. We contact Suffolk County PD and the Suffolk County DA and together we work out a plan. Recruit No. 1 will tell Din to meet the "hit man"—actually a Suffolk PD undercover—in the parking lot at a strip mall near the LIRR station in Holtsville. We'll have the hit man's car teched up for audio and video.

So at the appointed time Din shows up, climbs in the car, and makes the deal with the hit man/undercover. He gives him two hundred bucks as a down payment and a credit card to hold as good faith on the balance, and he also gives him his girlfriend's address and photo. No, Din says, he doesn't care how the hit man/undercover kills her, just so long as she's dead and buried and won't ever be found. He also tells the undercover that once he becomes an NYPD cop he can provide the hit man and his Mob pals with guns and access to classified NYPD databases.

We—IAB investigators and Suffolk PD detectives—are monitoring all this from surveillance cars, and at this point we move in and arrest Din. The Suffolk DA charges him with second-degree conspiracy to commit murder—and, it goes without saying, his NYPD career is over.

But here's the really strange part. His girlfriend, the young woman he wanted dead, testifies at his trial—for the defense! Before, she didn't want to marry him, but now that he's locked up for plotting to kill her she can't live without the guy. After Din is convicted, she pleads with the judge to go easy on him so they can get married—a request the judge wisely rejects. He gives the former NYPD recruit seven to twenty years—and he also imposes a thirty-year restraining order barring him from contact with his erstwhile fiancée even after he gets out of prison. The judge says he hopes that by the year 2036 the young woman will have wised up.

Another strange case that had IAB working with suburban detectives and prosecutors happened in Westchester County. It's November 2013, and this real estate developer in Yonkers is asleep in his bed when he wakes up with a searing pain in his head and his pillow covered in blood. Stumbling from the bed, he finds his wife lying apparently unconscious at the foot of the stairs, the victim of an intruder who she says knocked her out, then came up to the bedroom and shot a .22-caliber bullet into the husband's head. It's a miracle he's still alive.

But while he's in the ER, and the Yonkers PD detectives are investigating, they realize that something's not right. There's no sign of forced entry, the wife's injuries are superficial at worst, there's been a history of tension in the marriage, and the wife refuses to cooperate. They're convinced she shot her husband, who for whatever reason is standing behind her on the intruder story—and they call IAB to help with the case. The reason they call us is because the wife is an NYPD employee, a Department psychologist who gives psychiatric screenings to NYPD applicants—which may partly explain why guys like the murder-plotting NYPD recruit mentioned above got into the Academy in the first place.

IAB handles cases involving corruption or misconduct by NYPD civilian employees as well as police officers—and allegedly shooting your husband in the head is pretty serious misconduct. We suspend her and assist the Yonkers detectives in the investigation, but at first there's no indictable case, because the husband is still backing her up on the intruder story. It's only later, after the NYPD psychologist wife files for divorce, that the husband decides that maybe she shot him after all. She's indicted for attempted murder, and as of this writing the case is still pending.

There were a lot of cross-jurisdictional cases like that involving NYPD cops or civilian employees who lived in the suburbs. Most of them didn't involve murder-for-hire plots or bullets in the head, but they were still serious: domestic violence cases with injuries, DWIs with property damage or injuries, NYPD cops getting into fights in bars, you name it. In the NYPD even cops who are off-duty are still on-duty twenty-four/seven, and when they get in trouble anywhere for anything even remotely serious, we have to look into it. So it's important for IAB to maintain good working relationships with cops and prosecutors outside the city—and we did.

IAB worked with nonpolice New York City government agencies as well. For example, at one point we start getting a lot of complaints about money or jewelry being taken from Aided cases in the Bronx, people who were having some medical emergency and had to be taken to the hospital by ambulance. Family members are saying that at some point between the time the cops and the Fire Department's emergency medical technicians (EMTs) arrive at the scene and the time the patient gets to the hospital, Mom's ring or Grandpa's watch or some cash hidden in a bedroom dresser drawer has gone missing. And they're blaming the cops.

But when we cross-check the incident reports, which contain the names of all the cops and rescue workers sent to the scene, we see that while all of the missing property cases involve different cops, they all involve the same team of EMTs from the Fire Department. That's either a hell of a coincidence or one of these EMTs is stealing.

So working with the FDNY Inspector General's Office, we make sure this particular EMT team is in the area and then phone in an Aided call to one of our rented IAB apartments. When the EMTs arrive one of our female undercovers is there, apparently unconscious. It's not easy to pretend to be unconscious, especially in front of trained medical personnel, but this gal is good; I actually saw her practicing for the role, and if I hadn't known better I would have called the morgue to have the body taken away. So anyway, the EMTs put her on a stretcher and load her into the ambulance, along with her purse, and en route to the hospital one of the EMTs fishes some marked bills out of her wallet. Later he's confronted by the IG and IAB investigators and admits to a series of thefts; he's arrested and later fired. We had a number of cases like that.

Okay, sure, there's not a lot of money involved here; you might even think that these are petty crimes, not worth the extensive time and effort we put into them. But civilian city employees take an oath to obey the law just like NYPD cops do, and when they violate that oath there's nothing petty about it. It's corruption, and it undermines public confidence in government agencies. Besides, if it was your mom's ring or your grandpa's meager savings that was being stolen, you'd want the thief caught, too.

I have to emphasize here that in terms of corruption, the FDNY is the same as the NYPD: The vast majority of FDNY firefighters and EMTs are honest, hardworking, and in most cases incredibly brave; it's the one-percenters you have to worry about. And running the integrity tests may have had some deterrent effect even on the one-percenters. Although we only did a half dozen of these integrity tests with the FDNY over a period of several years, the EMT union put the word out to its members over their website that the NYPD was running a slew of these tests—IAB is everywhere!—and reminding its members that they had to act professionally at all times. Which almost all of them would do anyway.

IAB did a number of other integrity tests for city agencies that were having problems. One in particular that stands out is what I call the Bag of Bones case.

Again, we're getting a lot of complaints, this time from Brooklyn, about property missing from DOAs, dead on arrivals, people who are clearly past help when the responding cops and EMTs show up. But when we look at the incident reports, once again it's different cops, and this time it's different EMTs as well. The only common denominator in the missing property incidents is a certain female morgue attendant— officially, a mortuary technician—who helped transport the bodies to the morgue. So working with the ME's office and the city's Department of Investigations, the plan is to take one of our rented IAB apartments, stock it with furniture and clothes to make it look occupied, tech it up with video cameras, plant some marked money, and then phone in a dead body call while the female morgue attendant is on shift.

The problem is, How do we get a dead body in there? We obviously can't use an actual dead body as part of an integrity test, even if it's a John Doe with no next of kin—that would be a violation of the laws concerning the disposition of human remains, not to mention being disrespectful to the dead . . . and more than a little creepy. So instead we get about sixty pounds of cow bones and offal from a slaughterhouse, put it in a duffel bag, and let it sit in the hot apartment for a week or so. Then we call in a "bad smell" report to the local precinct.

For a cop, bad smell calls are the worst. When someone dies alone in an apartment and lies there long enough for the decomposition smell to seep into the hall, you can imagine what it's like inside the apartment. I don't want to ruin your lunch, so just trust me when I say it's not something you ever want to see, or smell. But cops have to do it all the time.

So anyway, the unlucky cops who catch the bad smell call show up and get the building super to let them into the apartment. No one's inside, and the cops don't know whether that bloody, smelly mess in the duffel bag is a cut-up human body or what. So they call the ME's office— remember, the ME is in on the sting—and an assistant ME (AME) shows up with the female morgue tech. He tells the cops the bones are almost certainly not human, but he'll have the morgue tech take them back to the ME's office to make sure. The AME leaves, the cops wait out in the hall—they can't stand the smell—and on the surveillance cameras we see the morgue tech grab $460 in marked cash that's on the dresser. She's arrested as she leaves the building with the bag of bones and the money in her pocket, and later she's fired and prosecuted.

It's actually kind of pathetic. I mean, here's this morgue technician being paid just $37,000 a year to haul around dead bodies, many of them in unspeakable condition, a job that most of us couldn't or wouldn't do for a million bucks, and she ruins her life for a lousy few hundred dollars here and there. You may even be tempted to feel sorry for her—as I am, too. But again, corruption is corruption, no matter the amount of money involved, and the citizens of New York City have a right to expect that city employees will respect their property—even after they're dead.

I could tell you more stories about IAB's work with other agencies, but I think you get the point. Although police officers in trouble get the most attention, public corruption and misconduct isn't just about cops; it's about any public agency that employs human beings, with all the failings and frailties thereof. And as the biggest—and in my opinion by far the best—single anticorruption law enforcement unit in the world, the NYPD Internal Affairs Bureau is in a unique position to help.

The aforementioned Jack Maple may not have thought it would ever be possible. But when it comes to fighting official misconduct and corruption, as far as IAB is concerned, we really are all in this together.

Chapter 11

CANNIBALS IN THE ETHER

It's the late summer of 2012 and a woman named Kathleen has a problem. Her husband, twenty-eight-year-old NYPD Officer Gilberto "Gil" Valle, who works the four-to-twelve shift at the 26th Precinct in upper Manhattan, isn't being as caring and attentive as a new husband and father of a one-year-old daughter should be. When he gets home to the couple's apartment in the Forest Hills section of Queens, he's withdrawn, sullen, uncommunicative; all he wants to do is log on to the Internet and tap away at the keyboard through the wee morning hours.

And there's one other problem: Kathleen has reason to believe that her husband, Officer Valle, may be a cannibal.

The reason she believes this is because when she installs spyware on the couple's shared Mac laptop computer—the spyware records every website visited and every keystroke—she finds that her husband has been perusing some really creepy "fetish" websites, with names like darkfetishnet, fetlife, darkfet, and so on, most of which seem to be concerned with sadomasochism and bondage, and even the torture, murder, and dismembering of women; there are images of women posed naked, hogtied, and covered with blood. She also finds that her husband has been using online screen names like "girlmeathunter" and "girldealer."

At that point, she's out of there. She packs up the baby—and the Mac laptop—and flies home to her parents' house in Reno, Nevada. But then, as she looks deeper into what's on the laptop, it gets worse. She finds that her husband and the father of her baby has been exchanging hundreds, even thousands, of e-mails with other men in which they discuss killing, cooking, and eating women—including her and some of her friends.

This is really sick stuff. The e-mails feature photos of the targeted women, including one of Kathleen in a bikini, along with details such as age, height, weight, bra size. In one e-mail with a guy whose screen name is Moody Blues, Valle talks about murdering a mutual friend of his and Kathleen's, a young woman named Kimberly: *Once she is dead,* Valle writes, *I will take her out and properly butcher her body and cook the meat right away. And that could be out on a rotisserie too.* In another message Valle writes, *I was thinking of tying her body onto some kind of apparatus . . . Cook her over a low heat, keep her alive as long as possible.* In another message he writes, *Her days are numbered. I'm glad you're on board. She does look tasty, doesn't she?* To which his correspondent replies, *You do know if we don't waste any of her there is nearly 75 pounds of food there.*

And on and on, ad nauseam—literally ad nauseam.

To Kathleen, it doesn't sound like these guys are kidding. She's terrified for herself and for her friends and for other women out there. So she contacts the Reno office of the FBI, which contacts the New York Field Office of the FBI, which, since Valle is an NYPD cop, contacts us. That morning Sergeant Joe Clarino of Group 25, the federal liaison group, comes walking into my office with a case file in his hand and a strange look on his face.

Got one for you, Chief, Joe says. This you're not going to believe.

So Joe starts laying it out. And as he's telling me about the case, of course I'm shocked, as almost anybody would be—this is really sick stuff. But I'm really not all that surprised. Ever since the Louima case, I've made it a point not to be surprised by anything.

And it's not like this guy is the first cannibal—alleged cannibal—I've ever heard of. For example, back in the late 1980s, when I had the supervisor duty in Manhattan South, there was a guy named Daniel Paul Rakowitz who I'd often see in Tompkins Square Park—he was hard to miss, since he looked like Charlie Manson and walked around with a pet chicken on a leash—who murdered his dancer girlfriend and then cut her up in the bathtub and allegedly served her body parts in a stew to his fellow transients in the park. (He was later found not guilty by reason of insanity and confined to a mental facility.)

More recently, I'd gotten a call from a friend of mine, Dietrich Reithuber, the chief of the homicide bureau in Munich, Germany—we'd met at the FBI National Academy, an international training program for law enforcement supervisors—who wanted my help in tracking down a potential victim of a cannibal. They had a guy in Germany named Armin Meiwes, aka "Der Metzgermeister," The Master Butcher, who had advertised on a website called the Cannibal Café looking for people who would volunteer to be killed and eaten—and he got about two hundred responses from prospective volunteers, including at least one from the US. Let me repeat that: Two hundred people from around the world contacted this guy and said they *wanted* to be killed and eaten. True, the vast majority of them backed out, but one guy from Berlin actually met with Meiwes and was voluntarily killed and consumed; Meiwes was later convicted of manslaughter. My friend Dietrich was looking for other possible victims, and I helped him determine that the "volunteer" from the US was one of the ones who'd backed out.

So the subject of cannibalism, or at least people fantasizing about cannibalism on the Internet, isn't completely beyond my range of police experience. Still, as far as anyone can remember, we've never had a cannibal or even a cannibal fetishist wearing an NYPD uniform and an NYPD shield and carrying a gun.

But the question is, Is Officer Gilberto Valle a real cannibal? Or is he just playing one on the Internet? Is he really plotting to kidnap and murder and eat women, or is it just some sort of twisted fantasy that he doesn't really intend to follow through on?

Either way, we're pretty concerned about this guy, and although we don't have enough to arrest him—at this point, we can't even prove that he personally sent the messages—until we get it figured out we don't want to let him out of our sight. So we put a twenty-four-hour surveillance on him. We follow him home from the precinct, follow him back to work the next morning, watch where he goes, see whom he talks to. We also run a complete background on him, and discreetly talk to some people who know him.

And the only abnormal thing that stands out about Officer Gilberto Valle is just how outwardly normal he appears. He's medium height, moon-faced, and a little pudgy, kind of a nebbish. He grew up in Forest Hills, parents were divorced, graduated from Archbishop Molloy High School, and then attended the University of Maryland as a psychology major. After graduation he joined the NYPD in 2006, and in the six years since then he's had a thoroughly undistinguished career—no complaints, no significant arrests, no major commendations, average in every way. Currently he's working as a driver for a patrol sergeant.

And the people who know him, cops and civilians alike, eventually tell us that he seems like a regular, normal guy. Of course, cops are hesitant to come right out and say anything bad about another cop, but if they think another cop is strange in some way they'll roll their eyes, or they'll hum the theme song from *The Twilight Zone* or somehow get the message across without directly saying anything. But we're getting none of that with this guy. He's quiet, polite, and has never expressed (except on the Internet) or displayed any hostility or aggression toward women.

And then there are the messages that we've retrieved from the computer that Kathleen took from their apartment. They appear to have been exchanged with people—we assume most of them are men, but who knows?—that Valle met on a website called Dark Fetish Network, or DFN, which has about fifty thousand members—about five thousand of them "active" members—who are interested in rape, necrophilia, erotic asphyxiation, and, yes, cannibalism. Members share photos and tell each other stories about those various activities, but the website's home page has a disclaimer to the effect that it's all just fantasy—"This place is about fantasies only, so play safe!" the disclaimer states.

Another thing about the messages that Valle exchanged: Although the photos of the women he sends with his messages are real, the details he gives about them—where they live, what their jobs are, etc.—are not. Other facts are made up as well. Valle tells his correspondents that he's got a pulley device in his basement to hang women by their heels— but he doesn't have a basement. He says he's got a remote cabin in Pennsylvania where he wants to take women and rape and kill them, but we know from our background check that he has no such place. He says he has an oven that is, quote, *Big enough to fit one of these girls if I folded their legs*, unquote, which he doesn't have. He makes "plans" with his correspondents to kidnap and murder three different women at three different locations on the same day, a physical impossibility. There's no evidence that he ever communicated with his "co-conspirators" by phone, or that he even knows their true names or where they live.

And on and on. In short, there's no hard evidence whatever that Valle physically attacked any women in the past or that he seriously intends to in the future. The more we look at it, the more convinced we are that this is all just fantasizing on Valle's part—sick fantasizing, shocking fantasizing, but fantasizing nonetheless.

Don't get me wrong. I'm not saying that Officer Valle is blameless here. For one thing, when we look at the computer hard drive and check Department computers we find that he has compiled dossiers on almost a hundred women, including his wife, various college and high school female friends, women he met at social occasions, and even the female NYPD sergeant he drives at the 26th Precinct. The dossier files include photos and background information on the women, some of which he got by using Department computers to access the National Crime Information Center, New York Motor Vehicles Department records, and other restricted databases, which is a violation of Department policy and a misdemeanor under federal and state law. (We know Valle did that because he used his Department tax number and personal PIN to log on to the Department computer.)

He also obviously has deep psychological problems that somehow slipped by the Department psychological screening tests when Valle signed on in 2006. Every NYPD recruit has to undergo psych evaluations with a psychiatrist and take the Minnesota Multiphasic Personality Inventory test, but when we check Valle's records there's nothing that stands out—although as far as I know the MMPI and the shrinks don't focus on potential cannibalism issues. Still, not only should this guy not be a cop anymore, he should never have been one in the first place. This is one sick, depraved, deviant individual.

But again, is Valle engaged in an active plot to kidnap and consume women? We honestly don't think so—and more to the point, we don't think there's enough evidence to prove it in a court of law. We want him out of the Department, of course, but we don't think we have enough to put him in prison for the rest of his life.

The FBI and the US Attorney's Office, however, take a different view.

As I explained in the previous chapter, any case involving an NYPD officer that originates with the FBI remains a federal case, with IAB's Group 25, the federal liaison group, working with the feds. That makes perfect sense in a case like this, because while we're primarily working the Valle investigation, the FBI has taken it across state and even international borders. From the messages on Valle's computer they've identified three other guys they believe were engaged in an active conspiracy with Valle to kidnap, rape, and murder women. One of them is a twenty-two-year-old mechanic in New Jersey to whom Valle "promised" to deliver a drugged and bound woman for $5,000; another is a fifty-eight-year-old male nurse in England—the aforementioned "Moody Blues" guy—and the third is a man in Pakistan who goes by the screen name Ali Khan.

Again, we can't see it, as least as far as a criminal conspiracy case against Valle is concerned. But it's the feds' call. So on October 24, after more than a month of investigation, the feds decide it's time to arrest Valle.

As usual in these situations, we want to make sure we can grab him, and his gun, before he can hurt himself or anybody else. So we tail him to his apartment, watch him park his car, give him a chance to settle in, and then stiff in a call to his home phone—This is Officer O'Hara with the 112th Precinct, is this Mr. Valle? It is? Well, sorry to tell you, but your car's been hit, you'd better take a look at it.

Sure, it's an old trick, but it usually works. A moment later Valle walks out in jeans and a University of Maryland sweatshirt, and we and the FBI agents with us grab him. We always try to keep guys like this calm, so after he's in handcuffs one of the guys on the arresting team gently touches him on the shoulder and says, Everything's going to be okay.

But Valle knows better.

I don't think so, he says.

And he's right. We immediately suspend him without pay, and he heads off to the federal Metropolitan Correctional Center in Manhattan, where he is held without bail in solitary confinement. And he's soon to become one of the most infamous and reviled cops in the history of the NYPD— probably second only to Officer Justin Volpe in the Louima case.

The next day, US Attorney Preet Bharara of the Southern District of New York holds a press conference at the federal building in Manhattan to announce Valle's arrest on federal charges of conspiracy to commit a kidnapping—which can get him life in prison—and illegally accessing a federal law enforcement database.

I'm at the press conference, and although as usual I don't take any questions, it's not a pleasant experience. I mean, it's bad enough when as chief of IAB I have to stand up on a press conference dais and tacitly acknowledge that one of our own has been abusing a citizen or robbing drug dealers or running guns or any of the "normal" kinds of cases that IAB handles. But to stand in front of the news media and acknowledge that one of New York's Finest is accused of plotting to cook and eat women? That's something different.

Of course, if Valle wasn't a cop, it wouldn't attract that much attention; it might be a one-day story. But given the opportunity to juxtapose the words "cannibal" and "cop," the news media goes almost berserk with this one. For tabloid headline writers especially, this is a gift.

"CANNIBAL COP!" the headlines scream, not only in New York City but around the world. "MEAT THE WIFE!" is a headline over a story about Valle's wife. "BONE APPETITE!" says another headline. And on and on.

New York Post headline writers had a field day with the case of the so-called Cannibal Cop, an NYPD officer accused of plotting on the Internet to kill, cook, and eat women. Officer Gilberto Valle was found guilty by a jury, but the conviction was later overturned on the grounds that Valle's postings were fantasies he had no intention of carrying out. (*New York Post*)

In the news media, it's almost like the whole thing is just a sick joke—and while it is sick, it isn't a joke. Whether or not Valle is legally guilty of conspiracy to kidnap, he's clearly morally guilty of terrifying innocent women, betraying his family, and violating the oath he took when he joined the NYPD. I'm just glad the guy isn't still a cop; since he's locked up and can't return to work after his thirty-day suspension, under civil service rules we can fire him—and we do.

More than a year later the case comes to trial in US District Court in Manhattan—and the main issue is the same that it has always been. No one disputes the fact that Valle sent the sickening e-mails, or that none of the women he discussed had actually been physically harmed. The question is whether he ever intended to carry out any of his fantasies and committed any overt acts to further the conspiracy. The defense maintains that Valle has been charged with "thought crimes," and that no matter how abhorrent those thoughts may be to normal people, under the US Constitution a "thought crime" isn't a real crime at all.

But the jury disagrees. After a twelve-day trial—Valle's wife testifies for the prosecution, while Valle does not testify—the jury finds him guilty of conspiracy to kidnap and the lesser charge of unlawfully accessing a federal database.

So it looks like we were wrong—there was enough evidence to convict this guy on conspiracy. But then it turns out we were right. In June 2014, while Valle is still awaiting sentencing, the federal judge in the case overturns the conviction on the grounds that there was no evidence presented at trial that Valle was actively conspiring to commit the acts he was fantasizing about. But the judge upholds the conviction for unlawfully accessing the database, and he sentences Valle to time already served—twenty-one months—and orders him to undergo psychiatric treatment and to refrain from visiting any fetish websites. Valle is freed under supervised release, meaning he has to wear an ankle tracking bracelet. In December 2015 a federal appeals court upholds the judge's decision to throw out the conspiracy conviction.

There are several postscripts to the Cannibal Cop case. That guy in New Jersey to whom Valle was supposedly going to "sell" a woman? He was convicted in 2014 in an unrelated case of plotting to kidnap and murder women, including members of his own family, along with a former New York City high school librarian and a former security chief at a Massachusetts veterans hospital. The guy from England, Moody Blues? He, too, was convicted in a separate case in Canterbury, England, of attempting to set up a tryst with a fourteen-year-old girl. All of the men argued, unsuccessfully, that they were just role-playing; none of the men was ever convicted of plotting to cannibalize women with Valle. The guy in Pakistan, screen-name Ali Khan, was never identified.

As for Valle himself, after his release he told reporters he just wanted to get on with his life—which, when you're known worldwide as the infamous Cannibal Cop, is a little hard to do. For example, when Valle posted a profile on the Match.com online dating site—the profile contained no mention of cannibalism—the tabloids were at it again. "CANNIBAL COP COOKS UP ONLINE DATING PROFILE!" one headline read. "CANNIBAL COP HUNGRY FOR LOVE!" said another. After the website yanked his profile, another story said, "He just wanted to meat a nice lady . . ."

Valle also cooperated in making a 2015 HBO documentary called *Thought Crimes: The Case of the Cannibal Cop*—which, as the title suggests, argued that Valle had been prosecuted for his thoughts, not his actions. Valle, for his part, maintained in the documentary that the cannibalism fetish was just a phase and that he no longer has fantasies about cooking and eating women. He also apologized for what he called his "infantile actions."

Well, maybe so. Maybe someday former officer Gil Valle can put it all behind him—although, unfortunately, the NYPD never will. The tale of the Cannibal Cop has become an indelible stain on the NYPD—and it illustrates, in the most extreme way possible, a problem that I saw time and time again during my career as IAB chief.

The problem is that sometimes cops and computers don't mix.

Along with fingerprint collection/identification, radio telecommunications, and DNA technology, the use of computers and information technology has been one of the most revolutionary developments in law enforcement in all of history. And like most revolutionary developments, it has its upsides and downsides.

The upsides are pretty obvious. When I came on the job in 1973 we wrote reports on typewriters and quintuplicate carbon paper—if you're under thirty, ask your grandmother what those were—an archaic process that actually lasted well into the 1990s. Back then it could take hours or even days to get a fingerprint or photo ID, there were no easily accessible national centralized files of known criminals, plotting crime trends involved waiting for paper reports to slowly wend their way through the sclerotic bureaucratic system and then sticking colored pins into paper maps—well, you get the point. The Department was buried in paper, and criminals could often outrun their own paper trails.

But they can't outrun a beam of light in a fiber-optic cable or a wireless data transmission—and cops depend on it. Cops today would be lost if they couldn't get an instant electronic fingerprint ID of a perp, or an instantaneous license plate check, or have access to the Department's criminal database or the FBI's National Crime Information Center or dozens of other databases, or be able to track crime trends on a daily or even hourly basis through the NYPD's CompStat system. In short, computer and information technology have fundamentally altered the way cops operate—not to mention the way the world works in general.

But as every parent knows—and as every cop should know—there are dangers and temptations in computer technology as well.

And that's why we created IAB Group 7—the Computer Crimes Investigations Group.

Group 7 is IAB's own "geek squad," a team of about a dozen combination cop/computer experts, headed when I was chief by Sergeant Yalkin Demirkaya, a big, burly Turkish-born cop and certified computer genius who had been instrumental in setting up the NYPD's vaunted CompStat crime-tracking system in the 1990s. (I was lucky to have been able to draft Yalkin into IAB when he made sergeant, this to the dismay of all the other bureau chiefs who wanted him, and I was luckier still when he decided to stay after his two-year IAB commitment was up. He remains an unparalleled resource and a true friend.) They are our go-to guys and gals on anything involving computers or cyber crimes by cops.

Did we need a program to track corruption and misconduct complaints by every shift in every precinct, or to automatically schedule follow-ups on closed cases, or to instantly flag complaints against any particular cop? Do we need someone who can clone a hard drive without leaving a footprint, or defeat an encrypted data system, or track down an IP address anywhere in the world? Do we need antihacking and unauthorized access prevention and tracking protocols for our files? Or do we just need someone who knows his way around Internet chat rooms and message boards? Whatever we need involving computer technology, the Group 7 guys can do it.

And we keep them busy—because as I said, sometimes cops and computers don't mix.

Most of the time the work-related computer trouble that cops get into is the same kind of trouble that people who work for any business or governmental organization get into. They'll disregard the recommended twelve-hours-from-bottle-to-keyboard rule and send off a drunken rant to a coworker or supervisor, or they'll text a hook-up note to a fellow employee who clearly isn't interested. It's all ill advised, and it can damage a cop's career, but unless there's a crime or a serious violation of NYPD policy involved—a physical threat, sexual harassment, online stalking, that sort of thing—then it's usually not an IAB case.

Internet porn is another computer-related problem that cops sometimes get into. Again, as long as it's not criminal, like child porn, or indicative of some potentially dangerous psychological disorder, like the Cannibal Cop, then it's none of IAB's business—provided, of course, that the cop isn't using a Department computer to access it. We'd occasionally get complaints from other cops about a cop accessing porn on a precinct computer, in which case we would usually just pass it along to the precinct or unit commander or to the borough's investigations unit. The cop involved might just get a "yell" from the commander—a verbal reprimand of the "Knock that shit off!" variety—or maybe a command discipline.

Production or possession of child pornography, of course, is illegal no matter how or where somebody accesses it. And while it wasn't common, we had a few cases of NYPD cops being involved in child porn.

For example, in 2013 we get a tip from an ex-girlfriend about a sergeant in Queens who had persuaded several women to sexually molest their own children, including some infants, while he watched online. We immediately open an investigation, get a search warrant for the sergeant's apartment, and grab his computer. The Group 7 guys find a series of child porn videos so sickening that no one who has to watch them will soon be able to forget.

As for the sergeant, he's immediately arrested and suspended. (As of this writing, the court case is still pending.) Later he's also implicated by federal investigators in another Internet child porn–trading ring involving more than seventy people, including an FDNY paramedic, a New York City rabbi, a Transportation Security Administration (TSA) supervisor, another NYPD cop, an upstate Boy Scout leader, the chief of police in a small upstate New York town—and on and on, most of them outwardly normal and law-abiding people, many of them in positions of trust.

IAB investigators never high-five each other when they complete a case on a bad cop, because every arrest of another cop is an embarrassment to the Department and to ourselves as fellow cops, and therefore nothing to be celebrated. But like virtually all other cops, we despise people who are involved in child molestation or child porn or any abuse of kids—and if another cop is doing it, we take a lot of satisfaction, grim satisfaction, in putting him away. It's not often that IAB gets attaboys from the NYPD rank and file when we arrest a cop, but when we slap the cuffs on guys like that, it's always: Good job, IAB! We're just glad that we don't have to get those kinds of attaboys very often.

Although it's obviously not nearly in the same league as child porn, unauthorized access to restricted law enforcement databases is another problem among cops. From almost their first day in the Academy cops are told that law enforcement databases can only be used for exactly that—law enforcement. You can't use them to get an ID on the attractive woman who lives in your neighborhood, or to run a background check on somebody you met at a party.

Unfortunately, cops sometimes forget that. They also forget that every time they log on to a Department computer it leaves a record of their tax number and personal PIN, and a record of every database inquiry. Just making a restricted database inquiry doesn't raise any flags, because some cops might run a dozen or more license plate or criminal background checks a day. But the record will always be there, and if the cop comes under investigation, like in the case of the Cannibal Cop, we can easily find every database query the cop has ever made.

I said that a single database query doesn't by itself raise any flags, but there is an exception. The names of movie stars and sports figures and politicians and other celebrities are flagged within the system, and if a cop runs a restricted database check on any of them, IAB is alerted—at which point the cop will have to explain exactly why he or she needed to know Bruce Willis's New York address, or the stated height and weight on Kim Kardashian's driver's license. We've had a number of cases of cops running checks on celebrities, and usually they'll say they were just curious, that they didn't really mean any harm.

But while curiosity may not kill the cop, it can certainly damage his or her career. Again, unauthorized access to a restricted law enforcement database is a misdemeanor, even if there's no criminal intent. The cop may not be indicted and fired for running a background check on the attractive woman next door, but it's certainly going to cost him money in the form of docked vacation days and hold up his chances for promotion. The Department takes this stuff seriously.

But as I've said, cops are human beings, and like other human beings they sometimes let passion and jealousy get the best of them. And when you mix passion and jealousy with a cop who also has access to restricted databases, it can cause a lot of trouble.

For example, we had this detective in the 40th Precinct in the Bronx, a twenty-year veteran, a respected guy. His problem is that his girlfriend, also a Department employee, broke up with him, and he's desperate to know if she's seeing any other men, especially other cops. So not only does he start running restricted database checks on some forty people, half of them cops, he also pays an illegal online hacking service $4,000 to hack into their e-mails. He's caught when the FBI investigates the LA-based hacking service and discovers that one of its customers is an NYPD detective—and IAB launches an investigation. The detective later pleads guilty to a misdemeanor and is forced to retire.

In another case, there's an NYPD sergeant in Manhattan who is friends with a Middle Eastern woman living in Canada who is in a child custody dispute with her ex-husband. As a favor, the sergeant runs a federal database check on the ex-husband through a Department computer, which turns up the fact that he's on the classified US terrorist watch list. The sergeant sends a printout to the woman, whose lawyer files it with the court, the argument being: This ex-husband can't have custody of those kids; he's a terrorist! The problem arises when local authorities start to wonder how an NYPD printout of classified information wound up in the court files in a custody dispute in Canada. They call the Royal Canadian Mounted Police, the Mounties call us, and we easily trace it back to the sergeant. His favor for a friend costs him a federal misdemeanor conviction.

Because of the nature of their work, cops have access to a lot of confidential computerized information that the general public has no need or right to see. That includes not only things like background files on individuals, criminal investigation records, crime scene and autopsy photos, but also digital videos from police surveillance cameras like the VIPER program.

VIPER stands for Video Interactive Patrol Enhancement Response—as so often happens in the NYPD, you get the feeling that they came up with the acronym first and then filled in the words to fit. The program uses hundreds of closed-circuit, pan-tilt-zoom cameras to film and monitor activity in and around the public areas of public housing developments throughout the city—halls, stairwells, sidewalks, and so on. The digital images are monitored by cops sitting at TV screens in central locations at each NYPD Housing Bureau Police Service Area, and if they spot a crime being committed they can quickly notify patrol units to respond to the scene.

Although the VIPER program has helped prevent or solve tens of thousands of crimes since its inception in 1997—including murders, robberies, and rapes—it's also been a controversial program. One reason is that most of the cops who are monitoring the closed-circuit TV screens are on modified duty—which is to say, they're cops in some kind of trouble. On any given day there are a couple hundred NYPD cops who are on modified duty, meaning they can't carry a gun or wear the shield or perform full law enforcement duties. Some of them are currently under IAB investigation, some have been found guilty of offenses that aren't serious enough to allow them to be dismissed under civil service rules but are serious enough that the Department doesn't want them on the street. But they're still cops, and they're still being paid, and the Department has to put them somewhere—and where a lot of them are put is the VIPER program. Some City Council members have questioned whether cops in trouble should be posted in a potentially sensitive assignment, but the Department view is that they're closely supervised, and that we really can't afford to take full-duty cops off the street to sit and watch TV screens all day.

Critics like the New York Civil Liberties Union (NYCLU) also complain that the VIPER cameras are an invasion of people's privacy—this despite the fact that they're only a small portion of the estimated forty thousand or more government and private surveillance cameras in New York City. Let's face it, when you're in almost any public area in any city in America, you should assume that you're on camera. And it's worth noting that the NYCLU never complains when a surveillance camera catches a cop doing something wrong.

Still, just because we catch something on camera doesn't mean we're going to release it to the public. If, say, a VIPER camera picks up two people having sex in a public housing development stairwell—and you'd be surprised how often that happens . . . or maybe you wouldn't—we're not going to share it with the world. Unless surveillance camera footage is introduced in a court case, or we release it to get the public's help in identifying some suspects, that video is confidential, available only to investigators on a need-to-know basis, and it's going to stay that way.

Or at least it's supposed to. Unfortunately, sometimes cops forget the rules—with unfortunate results. The case of the guy who killed himself in front of a VIPER camera is an example.

It's 2004, and a VIPER camera in the lobby of the Morris Houses in the Bronx picks up a twenty-two-year-old man kissing his girlfriend good-bye in front of the elevator. Nothing unusual about that, except that after the girlfriend gets into the elevator and the door closes, the guy pulls out a 9mm pistol, puts it in his mouth, and pulls the trigger, killing himself instantly. It turns out the girlfriend had just broken up with him.

The cop monitoring the VIPER camera immediately calls patrol and they respond to the scene. As with any unusual incident captured by the VIPER cameras, the monitors make three copies of the relevant forty-five seconds of video—one goes to the special operations lieutenant, one to the Housing Bureau, and one to the detective squad assigned to the case. Based on the video it's clearly a suicide, not a murder, and the detectives are quickly able to close the case.

And that should have been the end of it. Except that a couple of weeks later, friends start calling the dead man's girlfriend and his foster mother to tell them that the NYPD video of the man's suicide has been posted on a "shock website" called "Consumption Junction," which features gross, violent, and pornographic video clips. To make it even worse, the website is treating the suicide video as entertainment, and racist entertainment, at that—the suicide video is labeled "The Self-Cleansing Housing Projects."

It's true that the dead man had had some problems. He'd been running with street gangs and had a domestic violence arrest. Still, he doesn't deserve to have his last moments turned into an object of fun for a bunch of sophomoric Web surfers hunched over their computers in their parents' basements. And neither do the people who cared about him. They are understandably shocked and upset, and after they contact their City Council representative, the case comes to IAB and Group 7. The question in everyone's minds—the dead man's friends', the politicians', the news media's, and ours—is how did a restricted-access NYPD video wind up on this stupid website?

Actually, for a group of investigators/computer experts like Group 7, this is not a particularly tough case. First they call the operator of the website, who is based in Atlanta, and ask him politely to give them the name or IP address of the person who sent him the video.

Of course, he initially refuses to give it up, citing various First Amendment and privacy issues. And we tell him we certainly understand his concerns, but then we explain, politely, that the video footage is official NYPD property, and that it is in effect stolen property that has been illegally transported across state lines. We also explain that there are these things called subpoenas, and search warrants, and that we have excellent relations with the FBI, which will be happy to send some special agents from its Atlanta field office to his home or place of business to discuss the matter further.

With that the guy quickly caves. He takes down the video footage, and he gives us an IP address that traces back to a former NYPD cop on Long Island who's now with the Suffolk County Police Department. The Suffolk County cop cooperates—he didn't mean any harm by sending it to the website, he says, and he wasn't the one who put the racist label on it. He says he got the video footage from another former NYPD cop who's now an FDNY firefighter. The firefighter tells us he got it from a friend of his, a detective in Brooklyn, who in turn tells us he got it from a sergeant, who tells us he got it from another sergeant in the detective squad in the Bronx.

It seems that the sergeant in the Bronx had been on night duty in the detective squad room and happened to see the video paused on a computer screen at an empty desk as he passed by; it had been viewed by one of the detectives assigned to investigate the suicide. The sergeant was just curious, he tells us, so he took a look, then sent it to his other sergeant friend on the assumption that he might be curious, too. The sergeant never dreamed that it would be spread around, he says, much less wind up on a shock video website. He didn't mean any harm, he says.

Now, things like this traditionally haven't been unusual among cops. They'll often try to shock or gross-out each other with crime- or accident-scene photos, or with bits and pieces of the horrible, disgusting, and disturbing things they encounter on a daily basis; for cops it's a kind of catharsis, a way of dealing with emotional stress. And when it was a case of one cop showing another cop a hard-copy photo from a case file, maybe there wasn't really any harm done.

But to update Ben Franklin's famous saying: Three people with computers may keep a secret if two of them—and their computers—are dead. In the Internet age, once something like this gets out there's no getting it back—and it can cause real harm, not only to the dead man's friends and loved ones, but to the cops who were just curious. In the end, the DA declined to indict any of the cops involved, but the sergeant who first leaked the suicide video got passed over for promotion and all of the cops involved got hit with command disciplines.

Now, so far the kind of computer-related cases I've talked about have been reactive cases for IAB and Group 7—that is, we develop some information about a cop, grab his computer or his smart phone, and backtrack through the electronic record to see what he has already done. But sometimes we have to be proactive, to find out not only where a bad cop has been in cyberspace, but where he's planning on going in the future.

And the case of the cop and a fictional young girl known as "yngbunny90" is a good example.

One morning Sergeant Yalkin Demirkaya gets a call from his computer crimes counterpart at the NYPD Organized Crime Control Bureau's Public Morals Division—basically, the vice squad. Their computer crime guys are a small group of investigators/computer wizards whose job it is to patrol cyberspace in search of criminals—especially child predators. The squad has a potential child predator they think we might be interested in.

I don't have to tell any parent of a young child or teenager just how dangerous, and how common, Internet child predators are. The FBI estimates that every day there are a half million of these creeps online looking for naïve, lonely, and trusting kids to exploit, either by arranging personal meetings or getting kids to send pornographic images of themselves. They're the cyber version of the old-style pervert hanging around a playground—except that the anonymity of cyberspace makes them a lot harder to catch.

To search for these predators, the NYPD's Public Morals Division computer crime investigators, as well as the NYPD Detective Bureau's Computer Crimes Squad and similar units in police departments across the country, put undercover detectives posing as young girls or boys on teen- or preteen-oriented social networking sites, then they wait to see if they get "hit" by a potential predator—that is, an adult, almost always a guy, who wants to reach out and make a personal connection. Usually the predator will pretend to be younger than he really is, somewhere around the targeted kid's own age. It almost never involves an overt sexual suggestion at first; they don't want to scare the kids away, and online predators also know that decoy cops are out there, looking for them. So at first the predators just want to be "friends," to exchange personal information, including photos, and seemingly innocent messages. Investigators call the process "grooming."

Undercover computer cops who work these kinds of cases get a feel for who the predators are when someone reaches out to them online—the words and phrases they use, the things they're interested in, the directions the online conversations take. They can usually tell the difference between a fourteen-year-old boy who really just wants to make friends and a fifty-year-old child molester who thinks he's corresponding with a fourteen-year-old girl. So while making sure they aren't crossing the line into what a defense lawyer can successfully argue is entrapment, they try to draw the guy out, string him along, make him think without explicitly saying so that sex with an underaged girl is waiting for him. And once the predator makes an overt suggestion that they MIRL—meet in real life—and have sex, they can set up a meet and grab him.

Of course, this is a long, complicated, and often drawn-out process; again, the predators know the cyber-cops are out there, and usually they're cautious. But fortunately, some of them are stupider than others.

Which brings us back to the potential predator the NYPD vice squad detective is calling us about.

The predator had hit the vice squad undercover—who was posing as a twelve-year-old girl—in a teen chat room called Mini-Skirt 13. (This is just before the explosion of other social media platforms like Facebook and MySpace, which allow kids to post even more extensive personal information about themselves.) When the undercover online cop draws him out, the predator sends a profile—age, background, likes and dislikes, all of it made up of course—and he tries to set up an innocent-sounding MIRL, as in, Hey, let's go get some pizza!

But the predator's profile also includes a smiling photo of himself, looking every bit of his actual thirty-five years, with a pinched face and a five o'clock shadow—and incredibly, when the vice detectives look closely at it, there, right behind his blue-covered left shoulder, is what is clearly an NYPD holding cell. Since it's not NYPD policy to let perps take selfies in the holding area, they have to wonder: Is this guy a cop?

Which, as it turns out, he is. When they subpoena the records for his IP address and get his subscriber information from his e-mail provider—the subpoena comes with a "do not notify" order so he doesn't know he's being checked out—he comes back as a thirty-five-year-old Transit Bureau cop, assigned to Transit District 2 in Manhattan. He's got thirteen years on the job, a clean record, lives on Long Island, married to another NYPD cop who's a narcotics detective, and they have one young child. And this creep—in deference to his family, not to him, we'll call him Officer Kevin—is cruising the Internet looking for thirteen-year-old girls.

Since he's a cop the vice squad guys hand the case over to IAB. And Yalkin and his crew start putting together a plan to nab this guy.

So far we don't have anything criminal on him. He hasn't overtly proposed any sexual contact with someone he thinks is a minor, at least not that we know about; at this point we don't even have enough to get a search warrant on his personal computer. But we know what he's after, in the same way that cops know that a guy walking down a dark street pulling door handles on parked cars to see if they're locked is looking to boost a car. It's not illegal to pull a car's door handle, but we know if he finds one open, what he's going to do next is a crime.

True, we've already got enough to suspend this guy for thirty days and bring him up on Department charges, because some of his communications with the vice squad online undercovers were made on-duty, with a Department computer, which was another mistake this knucklehead made. But unauthorized use of a Department computer not involving restricted databases is a relatively minor beef, one that under civil service rules probably could only get him dinged for a few vacation days and maybe put on modified duty. And if we pick him up now, what's Officer Kevin—and his lawyer—going to say? He's going to say: Sex? What sex? I never said anything about sex, I just like to talk to young people!

It's creepy, and it's a violation of Department policy, but it's not a crime. So if we're going to get this guy permanently out of the Department, and possibly into jail, we're going to have to sting him.

So Yalkin and his guys create a fictional online thirteen-year-old girl, screen name "yngbunny90," complete with background details: what middle school she goes to; the neighborhood where she lives; parents divorced; lives with her mom, who she says used to be a Playboy bunny and in whose professional footsteps she hopes to follow. Oh, and she also has, like, a super-crush on guys in uniform. We know what teen chat rooms our guy cruises, so when we put her out there he immediately hits, and they start sending private messages back and forth.

Again, our guys have to be careful to avoid anything that looks like entrapment. Our online character can't bring up anything sexual, but she can portray herself as naïve, lonely, vulnerable, a bit rebellious. She says things like, *I hate my mom*, or *School sucks*, or *Boys my age are soooooooo immature!* You might not think that some grizzled, middle-aged, cigar-chomping NYPD detectives could pull off sounding like a young teen, but these guys are good; they can LOL and PIR (parent in room) and KPC (keeping parent clueless) like a bona fide thirteen-year-old.

Officer Kevin, for his part, plays the role of an understanding older man, always ready to listen to yngbunny90's never-ending litany of teen problems, and he's eager to meet her in real life—just for some pizza, of course. He even tells her that he's a cop—after all, she loves guys in uniforms, and who could be more trustworthy than a cop? Which is pretty dumb. I mean, he knows online cops are out there looking for predators, and they're going to be particularly interested in a predator who's wearing a police badge. We know this is on his mind, because he tells her things like, *Hey, you could be a cop. How would I even know?*

But despite the risk, he keeps after her anyway. He's got the same problem all of these guys have. It's not his head he's thinking with.

Or is he? Because suddenly, he drops out of sight. No messages, no communication, for weeks; he's radio silent. So has he changed his ways? Or sought psychiatric help for his problem? Has he realized how dangerous what he's doing is? Or has he somehow made yngbunny90 as a cop?

We can't figure it out. Then at one point we send one of our IAB investigators to take a drive by his house, and there on the front lawn is a big cardboard stork with a sign that says, "It's a Boy!" His wife, the NYPD detective, has just had another baby, and apparently our guy has other responsibilities to take care of.

But soon enough he's back online, grooming yngbunny90—which leaves us pleased and pissed off at the same time. We're pleased the case isn't blown, but we're pissed that this fellow cop, this now father of two, is back to being a low-life, child-stalking predator.

We know that if we're going to make a provable criminal case on this guy, at some point there has to be an actual meet, which is a problem. Our female IAB undercovers are good, but none of them can pass for thirteen.

So we bring in a ringer. There's a young woman, twenty-one years old—we'll call her Megan—who worked for IAB while she was in the Police Cadet Corps and is now about to graduate from the Police Academy. She's tiny, baby-faced, with a teen's voice, but she's got guts and she's eager to do it; for a rookie just out of the Academy to get an investigative undercover assignment is like a dream come true, the first step on the road to getting a detective's gold shield. So we bring her up to speed on the case, have her read through all the Internet messages to study her yngbunny90 character, and put her through a crash course on undercover work, including taking her to a public middle school to study what young girls are wearing these days—which to my admittedly old-fashioned sensibilities is pretty scandalous, lots of spaghetti strap tops and too-short skirts and way too much makeup. But an undercover has to look the part.

All along Officer Kevin has been pressing for a meet, and short of that, a phone number—so we give him one, a disposable burner phone that won't trace back if he runs the number through the Department databases, which, being a cop, we know he probably will. He immediately calls Megan, who's perfect—fast-talking, breathless, with that end-every-sentence-with-a-question-mark "up-talking" teenaged-girl style.

Officer Kevin seems more comfortable, and bolder, on the phone—and we're recording every word. He almost immediately brings up sex, starting with things like, Oooh, you sound hot! and then, over the course of a few days, talking explicitly about having sex, even assuring her that he'll wear a condom. Megan, for her part, is reluctant—I've never done anything like that before, she says—but Officer Kevin is soothing, telling her it'll be okay, that she'll like it, and so on.

Remember, this is a cop who thinks he's talking to a thirteen-year-old girl. Just to have to listen to this is pretty appalling.

Anyway, now that's he talking explicitly about sex acts, we've got him. It's time to set up a meet—and make an arrest. Obviously, we aren't going to send our undercover, Megan, into a motel room or anything like that, certainly not with a cop who's probably carrying his off-duty gun. So Megan says she'll meet him at a McDonald's on Myrtle Avenue in Queens, and then they can go to her house because her mom's at work.

Yalkin and his team will get to make the collar. Yes, they may be computer geeks, but they're also cops—and after listening to Officer Kevin run his ugly little game, they've started to take this guy personally.

Officer Kevin shows up at the McDonald's at the appointed time, a paunchy guy wearing a black "No. 13 Alfonzo" baseball jersey—which under the circumstances is an insult to former Mets slugger Edgardo Alfonzo and the entire Mets organization—but he's still cautious. He stands there for a while, casing the street, but he doesn't make our surveillance van, or our undercover in the waiting cab. When he presses his face against the McDonald's window and looks inside, he sees a big, Middle Eastern-looking guy in a booth talking on a cell phone—he can't hear him through the window, but it's Yalkin, speaking Turkish—and a frumpy, middle-aged woman sipping coffee and reading a newspaper, who's another one of our ghosts. And he also sees Megan sitting at a table in the middle of the room with a cell phone—actually a radio transmitter—on the table.

It's one thing to talk on the phone, but can a twenty-one-year-old woman really pass for a thirteen-year-old girl in person? Maybe not under ordinary circumstances, but this guy desperately wants her to be thirteen. When he sees her, his face lights up. He slides into the chair across from her and, sensing she's nervous, he immediately starts soothing her, telling her it will be okay, he'll take good care of her, it'll be fun, and yes, he brought condoms. He's eager to go to her house and get started.

We're picking all this up in the surveillance van from the transmitter in Megan's cell phone—and now this guy is done. At our signal, Yalkin steps up behind him and grabs Officer Kevin in a bear hug—with a guy as big as Yalkin, it really is a bear hug—and he barks out: Internal Affairs! Don't move! At the same instant our other ghost moves in and pats him down for his gun, although it turns out that for some reason he's not carrying it. We don't want Officer Kevin to know just yet that Megan is an undercover, we don't want him to know just how much we have on him, so acting out her role, she jumps up and says: It's all right! He's a cop! There must be some mistake! He's a cop!

Ignoring her, as planned, Yalkin rear-cuffs him and frog-walks him out of the McDonald's and into the backseat of one of our unmarked cars. And all the while Officer Kevin is pleading: Guys, you gotta believe me, I wasn't going to have sex with her!

But we know better. We take him back to a debrief room at the First Precinct in Manhattan—the initial sex solicitation had occurred there, so he'll be charged in Manhattan instead of Queens—but by that time this guy has wised up and wants his lawyer. He's immediately suspended and charged with felony attempted dissemination of indecent materials, and also with misdemeanor attempted endangerment of the welfare of a minor. The charges are filed as "attempted" because Megan the undercover isn't actually a minor.

Simultaneously with the arrest, IAB detectives show up at Officer Kevin's house in Nassau County on Long Island with a search warrant in hand. It's sad, really. Here's his wife, the NYPD detective, standing there with a new baby in her arms, a toddler tugging at her hand, and we have to tell her what her husband has gotten himself into—and of course she's stunned, devastated. We can tell from the look on her face that this is totally out of the blue; she had no idea. It's what guys like Officer Kevin, or any cop who engages in criminal misconduct, seem to forget—that it's not just their lives they're putting at risk, but their families' lives and welfare as well.

Under Department policy we take all the guns in the house, including the detective wife's gun, which is unfair, because in effect it's unofficially putting her on modified duty. But we figure that her husband probably is going to bail out, and we don't want a gun in the house when he comes home. That's partly because we don't want him to shoot himself, but also because we don't want her to shoot him, which in a situation like this could be a possibility. Sure, we could understand the impulse, but we don't want to compound the tragedy by having to lock up the wife for murder.

With the warrant we also grab all the computers in the house, and when Group 7 looks at Officer Kevin's computer, they find some pornographic photos of what appear to be underaged girls—which earns him another felony child pornography charge from the Nassau County DA.

In the end, Officer Kevin—ex-Officer Kevin—is dismissed from the Department with no pension, no benefits, and in a plea deal he gets a year each on the charges in Manhattan and Nassau County, to be served concurrently. It's a pretty light sentence—but that's not my call.

Because a cop is involved, the arrest and guilty pleas get some press coverage: "COP IN KID SEX STING!" says one tabloid headline. "PERVERT EX-COP ADMITS GUILT IN TEEN SEX SOLICIT!" says another.

Of course, I've been a cop too long to think that the possibility of being arrested and publicly exposed is enough to make these guys stop what they're doing; they're driven by urges beyond the reach of rational thought. But whether it's an ordinary predator, or, far more rarely, a cop who's also a predator, maybe it will give them pause. They at least have to wonder who it is they're reaching out to on the Internet.

They have to wonder, is this really a thirteen-year-old girl?

Or is it us?

Chapter 12

IT'S NOT A COURTESY, IT'S A CRIME

It starts off as a simple case against a dirty cop in the Bronx. But by the time it's over, years later, it has morphed into the biggest police corruption scandal in decades, a web of corruption that involves hundreds of cops.

Funny thing, though. A lot of cops, especially the leadership of the police unions, don't think it's corruption at all.

It's December 2008 when an anonymous call comes into the IAB Command Center. It's a female, young-sounding, and she's angry. We're thinking it's probably an ex-girlfriend looking for some payback on the man who did her wrong, although we never will find out who she is. She won't give the IAB investigator who catches the call her name, but she does give him an earful. There's this cop in the 40th Precinct in the Mott Haven section of the Bronx, she says, his name is Ramos, Jose Ramos, he owns a barbershop on East 149th Street, and this guy who works there, Ramos's best friend, a guy named Marco Mack, is selling marijuana out of the shop. Ramos knows all about it, she says, in fact, he's the boss of the operation, he's a bad cop and somebody ought to do something about it. That's all she's gonna say, good-bye.

Well, I don't want to say this is a routine allegation—no allegation of police corruption is routine. But it's not like Officer Ramos is allegedly moving weight quantities of heroin, or ripping off people for tens of thousands of dollars, or is engaged in a murder-for-hire plot—although eventually all of those will come into play in this case. Still, it's a legitimate allegation, so it gets assigned to IAB Group 21, which covers the South Bronx.

When we pull Officer Ramos's personnel package and start looking around, we find that the anonymous caller's basic information checks out. Ramos is forty, of Dominican heritage, the son of a retired NYPD cop now living in Texas, been on the job since 1993, a former PBA delegate in the Four-Oh precinct, no serious misconduct allegations, lives with his girlfriend, later his wife, a woman named Wanda, in a house in Washington Heights. And yeah, Ramos appears to be the silent owner of a couple of barbershops, although he hasn't registered the shops with the Department as outside businesses, which he's required to do. The two barbershops, both known as Who's First—Who's First I on East 138th Street, and a storefront shop called Who's First II on East 149th Street in The Hub, a commercial section of the South Bronx—aren't exactly upscale hair salons. A handwritten sign on the window at Who's First II advertises men's haircuts for ten bucks, boys' haircuts for eight— which is about as cheap as haircuts go in New York City—and another sign pitches new and used DVDs and CDs for sale.

So we sit on the shops for a while, just watching, and sure enough, Officer Ramos, a slight, thin guy with a pencil mustache, is in and out of the shops all the time. And so is this Marco Mack guy, real name Lee King, an immigrant from Guyana who has a felony burglary conviction on his record, plus some drug arrests; he's a known player in the Mott Haven drug trade. Mack is also driving around in a 2007 Nissan Murano that's registered to Officer Ramos—it's got Ramos's police parking permit on the dash—and he's also living in an apartment that has Officer Ramos's name on the lease.

So right there we've got enough to scoop Ramos up and ding him on Department charges of associating with a known criminal, operating an unauthorized outside business, and unauthorized use of a police parking permit—which may not sound like much, but trust me, in parking-challenged New York City, a police permit is worth a thousand times its weight in gold, and loaning it out to some drug-dealing street mutt is serious business. And in the old IAD it might have happened that way. In the old IAD there was a tendency to grab the lowest hanging fruit, to take down a bad cop on the easiest charges and transfer him to another precinct or boot him out of the Department, because if you looked too deeply, who knew what kind of embarrassing facts—embarrassing to the Department, that is—might come out? But in the new IAB we don't play that way. We want to see where this thing goes—and if any other cops are involved.

So we start building a case on this guy. And one of the first things we do is put an uncle into the barbershop to see what he can see.

Remember when I said that IAB could draft cops with special knowledge or skills? Well, for this case we need a Spanish-speaking cop who used to be a licensed professional barber—and after a quick search of the NYPD personnel files, we find one, a third-grade detective who's actually already an investigator in IAB. We can't order him to work as an undercover—because of the potential danger, being an uncle is strictly volunteer—but the detective is game. We fix him up with a phony background and a back-dated New York State barber's license, along with a "Hello phone" number at IAB if anybody checks him out, and he manages to rent a chair at Who's First II for $125 a week. Of course, a barber is supposed to bring in his own customers, so we start sending in other IAB undercovers to get haircuts from our undercover barber—haircuts paid for by IAB—and listen for any talk around the shop about drug dealing. They pick up some interesting intel, but nothing definitive against Ramos. (Later, citing confidential sources, a newspaper reporter will claim that some of the IAB undercovers were bitching that our "barber" gave lousy haircuts. I don't know about that, but hey, the price was right—free, courtesy of IAB—and our undercover barber later got promoted to detective second grade for his work on the case.)

Meanwhile, working with the Bronx DA's Rackets Bureau, which is then headed by a tough, aggressive prosecutor named Tom Leahy, we get court-ordered wiretaps on Marco Mack's cell phone, and then on two of Ramos's cell phones. And from what we hear over the taps, these guys are into everything—marijuana dealing, car insurance scams, counterfeit DVDs, bogus credit cards, you name it—and they've got a whole network of neighborhood players working with them, guys who've known each other for years. Ramos is stupid enough to be a corrupt cop, but he's cagey enough not to be too specific on the phone, so we don't have enough just from the taps to make a solid criminal case against him.

So we shake the trees a little. At one point, posing as investigators with the NYPD's Trademark Infringement Unit—yes, there is such a thing—we raid the shop on East 149th and confiscate about fifteen hundred bootleg CDs and DVDs. It's no big deal, raids like that happen all the time in New York, against bodegas, barbershops, street peddlers, anybody who deals in knockoffs—which it sometimes seems is everybody in New York City. The idea is to get Ramos and Marco Mack talking about the raid and their counterfeit DVD business on the tapped phones—which they do—without tipping Ramos off that IAB is on his case.

Another time we hear Mack talking on a tap about picking up eight pounds of marijuana from a dealer in Brooklyn. We tail him—he's driving Ramos's car—and after he picks up the dope and heads back into the Bronx, two of our IAB guys posing as borough narcotics detectives pull him over. They grab the dope and then tell Mack that it's his lucky day, he can leave; as far as Mack can tell, it's a drug rip by a couple of corrupt cops. So of course he calls Ramos—we're listening on the tap—and tells him what happened.

We still want to find out if any other corrupt cops are involved with Ramos; remember, he's a former PBA delegate, so he's got a lot of contacts. We figure that when Ramos hears about the drug rip, maybe he'll call somebody he knows in Bronx Narcotics and try to find out which detectives ripped off Mack so he can get the drugs back. But instead, Ramos is pissed off. The nerve of those dirty cops, ripping off his drug-dealing buddy! Apparently he wants to get those two crooked cops jammed up. So he tells Mack to call 911 to report a theft, and the 911 operator transfers the call to the IAB Command Center, which logs the call and takes down Mack's report about two unidentified plainclothes cops in the Bronx who pulled him over for no reason and then stole his wallet—of course, he doesn't say that the only thing the cops actually "stole" was eight pounds of marijuana. So here we've got the target of an IAB corruption investigation, Ramos, helping a drug dealer, Marco Mack, stiff in a false corruption complaint against two other corrupt cops who are actually IAB detectives investigating Ramos for corruption. It's actually kind of funny—and it's actually also an Official Misconduct charge against Ramos, an "A" misdemeanor.

But it's just that—a misdemeanor. Marco Mack is done, we've got him on the eight pounds of marijuana, a serious felony, plus a bunch of other lesser charges, but on Ramos all we've really got are some guarded telephone conversations and some misdemeanors. It's enough to get him out of the Department, but it's not enough for any serious jail time.

Then we catch a break. From the taps on Mack's phone we learn that one of Ramos's crew—a career petty criminal we'll call "Sal"—is planning a score with some phony credit cards. He has a machine in his apartment that can put legitimate credit card numbers on stolen credit card blanks, which he uses to buy electronic equipment that he fences at half price. We tail him and grab him in the parking lot of a Radio Shack loading a van with $20,000 worth of laptop computers that he just bought with the counterfeit credit cards.

Of course we don't tell him we're IAB. We want to turn this guy, make him work for us against Ramos, but if he won't turn, and he knows we're IAB, the first thing he's going to do is tell Ramos that IAB is onto him, and our investigation is blown. So we tell him we're detectives with OCCB—Organized Crime Control Bureau—and as we're processing him on the credit card fraud charge we sit him down in an interview room and give him the standard detective debrief drill, about half of which is actually true. It goes something like this:

Look, Sal, you know you're in some serious shit now, right? This isn't fencing some flat screen that fell off a truck, you know? You read the papers? The DA's hot about credit card fraud this month, it's like a crusade with this guy, and he's going to knock your rocks in the dirt. And look, Sal, let's be honest with each other, you're what, forty-four years old, do you really think you can stand to do a dime with those young-bloods up in Dannemora? You're not built for up north, Sal; they'll tear you up. But we want to help you, and all you have to do is help us. So tell us, do you know anything about guns in the neighborhood that you'll share with us? Armed robberies? Burglaries? How about cops, any rumors about bad cops in the neighborhood? How about drugs, any dealers you can tell us about? Sal, c'mon, we're trying to help you here.

So Sal thinks it over, and finally he says, Well, there's this cop who owns the barbershop . . .

Bingo! Sal gives up his pal Ramos on a plate—marijuana deals, stolen electronics, counterfeit credit cards. And he agrees to work for us as a CI, a confidential informant, in return for the DA giving him a light jolt on the bogus credit card charge—in effect, no jolt at all, assuming he does a good job for us.

So now it's time to put Officer Ramos into some serious crimes.

Earlier I said that the best way to catch a crooked cop isn't necessarily to try to prove his involvement in past crimes, especially when your only direct witness is a low-life criminal like Sal. It's far more persuasive to a jury if you can show the corrupt cop committing fresh crimes on videotape. It's the targeted integrity test thing I talked about earlier—and we decide to run some tests on Ramos.

First, we have Sal the CI tell Ramos about a drug money drop at a sleazy local motel—this while we're listening to the call. There's $20,000 in cash in the room, Sal tells Ramos, put there by a dealer who's waiting for a marijuana delivery, but right now nobody's in the room. Ramos and Sal meet outside the motel, jimmy a window, and crawl in and grab the cash. Of course, it's our room, and we've got the room wired for videotape, and the $20,000 is our money.

Well, actually half of it is IAB money, and the other half belongs to the Bronx DA. From the start we've been working this case with ADA Tom Leahy and his investigators in the Rackets Bureau, so we go half-and-half on all the buy money we use in the Ramos case. Obviously, Sal the CI has to give us back his half of the split, and all the bills have been recorded and marked in the hope that eventually we'll be able to get the rest of the money back after we arrest Ramos. Unfortunately we never get it back—among his many other failings, Ramos has a gambling problem—but that's the cost of doing business.

So anyway, the motel rip is Test One. Here's Test Two. Sal tells Ramos that he's got a guy who wants to buy some stolen electronics, some mope from Jersey or someplace who's looking for a deal. The mope is supposed to meet up with Sal with $30,000 in cash, and then they'll drive over in Sal's car to pick up the stolen stuff. So Sal says to Ramos, why don't they just rip the guy off? Being a cop, Ramos can do a car stop on Sal's car and take the cash. They have to make it look real, though, so the guy won't suspect that Sal is in on it, so it'd be better if another cop helped out. No problem, Ramos says, there's this sergeant in the Four-Oh—Ramos calls him "Dopey Dude"—who'll do anything Ramos tells him to. It's the first time we've got another cop tied in with Ramos's criminal activities.

So at the appointed time, Ramos and Sergeant Dopey Dude, both in uniform, with Ramos at the wheel of a marked police patrol car, pull over Sal's car at the corner of Exterior Street and East 149th in the Bronx. They make a big show of yanking Sal out of the car and putting cuffs on him, yelling that he's under arrest, and they tell the guy in the passenger seat, the would-be stolen electronics buyer, to beat it, this is none of his business. The guy, who looks terrified, takes off running, and as soon as he's out of sight Ramos grabs the $30,000 in cash, which is in a paper bag in the backseat, and tosses it into the patrol car. Ramos and the sergeant un-cuff Sal and they all drive happily away to divide up the money later. Of course, the terrified guy in the passenger seat is one of our undercovers, the $30,000 is our cash, we've got Sal's car wired for videotape, and we've also got surveillance teams filming the whole thing.

Test Three. Sal sets up a meeting at a Bronx restaurant between Ramos and a drug dealer from Miami—Hispanic guy, gold chains, pinkie ring, the whole deal—who's looking for a cop to drive a van with a shipment of heroin in it from the Bronx to Brooklyn. As I said earlier, drug dealers love to have crooked cops transport drugs for them, because if for any reason the vehicle gets stopped by other cops the dirty cop will just flash his shield and be on his way. During the meeting Ramos boasts to the Miami drug dealer—who of course is one of our IAB undercovers, wired—that he can drive around the city with a dead body in his trunk if he wants to, because he's a cop. Ramos drives the van and the "heroin"—it's pancake mix—to Brooklyn and collects $10,000 from our undercover, all on tape.

So now we've run three targeted integrity tests on Ramos, and he has criminally failed every one of them—and it's all right there on video and audiotape. We've got him on charges related to burglary, robbery, and conspiracy to possess and distribute dangerous drugs, and the fact that he was stealing our money and moving our "drugs" doesn't make any difference legally. Three tests may almost sound like overkill, but you have to understand that in each situation we're trying to see if Ramos brings other dirty cops into the scheme. Also, when we finally do arrest him, we want him to know that we've got charges stacked up on him from now until the twenty-second century, and that if he doesn't cooperate, if he doesn't come clean on his own crimes and any other crimes he knows about, especially other crimes involving corrupt cops, the DA is going to come down on him like the proverbial million-pound shit-hammer. It's a leverage thing.

And also, if you're going after a cop like Ramos with just one or two serious criminal charges, you can be pretty certain he'll be bounced out of the Department, but when it comes to a criminal trial, there's always a chance that some smart defense lawyer will get him off. And in fact, in the case of Sergeant Dopey Dude, who helped Ramos with the phony rip on the electronics buyer, eventually he'll be fired from the Department after a hearing, but at his criminal trial his less dopey lawyer will successfully argue that Dopey Dude was only doing a favor for his buddy Ramos, and that he didn't even know the car stop in the Bronx was a rip-off. The point is, you never know what's going to happen in a courtroom, and the more charges you have, the better off you are.

Anyway, we've been working the Ramos case for seven or eight months now, and so far it's not that unusual a case. We've got one dirty cop—one and a half, if you count Sergeant Dopey Dude—that we're going to take off the street, along with dope dealer Mack and several other civilian members of Ramos's crew, including his wife, Wanda, who we've got on tape setting up a phony car insurance claim. It's the sort of good, solid case we do all the time, but not something that's going to garner much public attention. When the DA announces the arrests it'll probably be a one-day story in the papers—"CROOKED COP NABBED IN BRONX CRIME RING!"—and then it will wend its way unnoticed through the court system.

But then, just before we're about to bring the hammer down on Ramos, he gets a call on one of his wiretapped phones.

It's a call that eventually will rock the Department, and the city—and the IAB itself.

At first the call to Ramos doesn't sound like much. It's some civilian friend of Ramos's who just got a ticket for talking on his cell phone while he was driving on Fordham Road in the Bronx, and he wants Ramos to make the $130 ticket go away. No problem, Ramos says, he'll take care of it. Ramos doesn't ask the guy for any money to fix the ticket; it's just a favor. Over the next week or so, while we're listening on the tap, Ramos makes a series of calls to this cop and that cop and another cop, trying to fix the ticket, to make it disappear.

Ticket fixing? Well, okay, compared to Ramos's other crimes, it's not an earthshaker. It's another charge of misdemeanor official misconduct, a charge of misdemeanor obstructing governmental administration, things like that, the sort of stuff that you tack onto the bottom of the multitude of charges in an indictment.

Except that in this case, it's not just one fixed ticket, or a dozen fixed tickets. When we start looking into Ramos fixing the ticket for his pal with the cell phone, the case takes a whole new turn—a turn that leads us to the police officers' union, the Patrolmen's Benevolent Association, the PBA.

A word about the PBA, which represents about twenty-two thousand NYPD police officers. PBA "delegates" are regular working cops who get a little extra money from the union to take care of their members' problems, whether it's a hassle with a boss, a dispute over overtime, even a personal problem at home. Delegates are the fix-it guys for other cops, and each elected PBA delegate represents about a hundred cops. PBA "trustees" are higher up in the union chain, they're also sworn cops, but their only job is to do union business; each NYPD Patrol Borough has its own trustee, as do the various Police Service Areas and Transit Districts. (Detectives, sergeants, lieutenants, and captains also have their own unions, and they're all protected by the civil service laws. Assistant chiefs and above do not have a union, and serve at the pleasure of the police commissioner.)

The PBA and other police union officials do a lot of good things for their members. They're vociferous defenders of cops' rights, they help take care of the families of cops injured or killed in the line of duty, they provide legal assistance for cops in trouble. But too often the PBA leadership and delegates seem to forget that every cop's most basic sworn duty is not only to enforce the law, but also to obey it.

Which brings us back to the Ramos case.

One of the cops that Ramos calls when he's trying to fix the ticket is a PBA delegate in the 40th Precinct. Remember, we're still trying to find out if any other cops in the Four-Oh are in on any of Ramos's criminal schemes, so based on that information we get a court-ordered wiretap on the PBA delegate's cell phone. While we're up on the wire on that PBA delegate's cell phone, we hear him talking about fixing other tickets with another PBA delegate in another precinct, so we get another wire up on that delegate's cell phone, who starts talking about fixing other tickets with another delegate, so we get a wire up on that delegate—and on and on. Eventually we've got court-approved wires up on more than a dozen Bronx cops, almost all of them Bronx PBA delegates or trustees; we've got teams of IAB investigators crowded into the "wire room" at the DA's office, listening in on their conversations. And it seems like these guys are spending half their time fixing tickets!

They're not doing it for money. Nobody's paying them to make tickets disappear. Usually they're not even fixing tickets for members of a cop's immediate family, or even somebody they know personally. Some cop will just call up the delegate and say, Hey, my wife's brother's stepkid got a speeding ticket, can you make it disappear? Or a cop will call and say, Look, there's this friend of mine, he's a good guy, he got a ticket, can you take care of it? And then the PBA guy will start calling around to other cops, trying to track the ticket down and make it go away.

There are several ways to do that. If it's a fresh ticket, a cop can pull it out of the summonses box behind the desk in the precinct and tear it up. Or he can change a digit on the vehicle license plate number, in which case the record won't match and it will be summarily dismissed. Or maybe a PBA delegate will arrange for the guy who got the ticket to plead not guilty, at which point the cop who wrote the ticket either won't show up at the traffic court hearing, or he will show up and then intentionally tank it—Uh, no, Your Honor, I don't actually remember why I stopped this guy. Either way, it's case dismissed.

So maybe by now you're thinking, what's the big deal? All cops do that sort of thing, right? The answer is, No, they don't. Like I said earlier, every cop has discretion when writing a ticket. Most cops I know won't hang a ticket on another cop for parking illegally or a minor moving violation. (Serious violations like DWIs, driving while intoxicated, are another matter.) I've also known cops who wouldn't give a ticket to a woman, any woman, because they couldn't stand to see them cry, and cops who wouldn't write a ticket on any guy with young children in the car, because they didn't want to embarrass Dad in front of his kids. It's officer discretion, and it's completely legal.

But once a cop puts pen to paper in his summons book, that ticket is a legal document. And anyone who tampers with it, or conspires to tamper with it, is not only violating Department policy, he's breaking the law.

I guess you'll want to know, has anyone ever asked me to fix a ticket? Yeah, a couple of times during my career I've gotten a call from a second cousin's wife's brother-in-law, somebody who really doesn't know me very well, and he'll say something like, Charlie, old buddy, I got this ticket, is there any way I can get it taken care of? Sure, I tell him, here's how we're gonna take care of it. If you're not guilty, you go to court and tell it to the judge. If you are guilty, take out your checkbook and write out a check payable to the New York City Department of Finance.

That's how I "fix" a ticket. That's how every honest cop "fixes" a ticket. But the cops who are fixing tickets are not being honest cops—and it's not just a few of them, either. We're talking about hundreds of Bronx cops involved in one way or another with fixing thousands of tickets—most of them moving violations, even a few criminal summonses. And the key players, the facilitators, are the Bronx PBA delegates and trustees who are arranging all this over their cell phones . . . while we're listening in.

Don't get the wrong idea. Not every cop was into this, and not every ticket was "fixable." While we're listening to the wiretaps, we overhear a lot of cops who absolutely refuse to have anything to do with fixing a ticket. And in a lot of the conversations we're listening to, as soon as the PBA delegate finds out the name of the cop who wrote the ticket, he'll say something like, Nah, it won't work, I know that guy, he won't play. And that ticket goes unfixed.

Still, there are enough cops involved in this thing to make it a major scandal. It may not be as bad as the Knapp Commission scandal of the 1970s, when entire precincts were on the pad, or the Buddy Boys scandal of the '80s, or the Dirty Thirty scandal of the early '90s. But this ticket-fixing scheme is still corruption. It's organized, widespread, and systemic; it's costing the city millions of dollars in unpaid fines; and it's not fair to the honest people of New York City. I mean, why should some mope who knows a guy who knows a guy who knows a cop get to skate on a $150 ticket, while some working stiff who doesn't have a cop connection pays the full fare?

So even though we know that going after PBA delegates is going to infuriate the union, and that the ticket-fixing scandal is going to infuriate the public when the news breaks, we can't turn our backs on it.

Of course, for IAB, pursuing the ticket-fixing investigation is not a tough decision. It's what we do. But to be frank about it, it takes some stones for Police Commissioner Ray Kelly and Bronx District Attorney Robert T. Johnson, both of whom have been in on the investigation from the beginning, to let it run its course no matter what. For Kelly it's going to be an embarrassment, a major corruption scandal on his watch, and it's going to have the police unions howling for his head. For DA Johnson, it's probably going to endanger some of his pending criminal cases; as we'll see, it's not going to look good to a jury in a criminal case when the arresting officer has to admit under cross-examination that he's currently under investigation for lying in a Traffic Court hearing to fix a ticket. And for Johnson, who's an elected politician as well as a prosecutor, there are other dangers. What if we hear a cop trying to fix a ticket for a major campaign donor? Or the Bronx borough president's second cousin twice removed? Who knows where this thing is going to lead, and at what political cost?

But despite that, at no time, from beginning to end, do PC Kelly or DA Johnson suggest, hint, or imply—much less order—that IAB or ADA Tom Leahy's Rackets Bureau should ease up, back off, divert resources elsewhere. Of course, if they had, they would have had to find a new IAB chief, and a new Rackets Bureau chief; Tom and I are both committed to this case. But it never happens. We have free rein to see how far this thing goes.

But that's going to take time. Like I said, we've got dozens of wires up, and we're going to be listening in on them for months. Meanwhile, we've still got Officer Ramos out there, ready to be arrested, and we don't want him walking around with his gun and shield for the next however many months the ticket-fixing investigation takes. But if we arrest him now, the wiretaps are going to come out in public and it's going to blow the ongoing ticket-fixing investigation.

So we decide to run one more sting on Ramos. One of our undercovers tails him, close, in one of our IAB undercover cars, and just as Ramos is about to back into a parking space on the street our undercover slides his car into the spot. As expected, Ramos gets out of his car: Hey, buddy, what the hell you doing, that's my spot, I was pulling right in there! There's a brief argument, nothing violent, and eventually our undercover slinks away. Then a couple days later two IAB investigators in suits show up at Ramos's home in Washington Park.

Officer Ramos, they say, did you have an argument with a man over a parking space a couple days ago? Ramos says: Yeah, sure, but it was no big deal, nothing happened. And then the IAB guys explain to him that the man in question had called 911, said he was threatened by a man with a gun, and the car plate number he gave to 911 traced back to Officer Ramos, so it wound up with IAB. While they're telling him this, our IAB guys couldn't be nicer or more understanding. Gosh, Officer, they say, we're pretty sure this is bullshit, the complainant sounds like a nut job, but hey, we gotta investigate it, it's just procedure, standard procedure, and the thing is, while we're investigating we're gonna have to put you on modified duty, so would you mind very much giving us your gun and shield?

Ramos grumbles about it, but he buys it. So now he's on modified duty, working behind a desk in another precinct, and he still doesn't know we're onto him for the barbershop crimes. The funny thing is, while he's on modified we've still got him up on a wire, and he's still planning scams, and he's still fixing tickets. And every month or so Ramos calls IAB, wanting to know when we're going to close the parking space argument investigation, and we have to keep putting him off—Yes, Officer, we're working on it, these things take time, please be patient.

It's weird. But it's that kind of case.

Meanwhile, we're still up on more than a dozen wires at a time in the ticket-fixing investigation. A cop wants a speeding ticket on his daughter's boyfriend to disappear so he won't be disqualified from getting a cabbie license. A cop wants to kill a ticket on a friend of his who remodels kitchens. A cop wants to help his barber by making a ticket disappear. And on and on and on, hundreds and hundreds of them.

Again, there's no overt discussion of payoffs to the cops for fixing the tickets. Why should there be? I mean, sometimes it can take three or four or five cops to fix a ticket, and who's going to pay off five cops to make a $150 ticket disappear? But when you fix a ticket for a guy, it's a favor in the favor bank, and maybe you collect down the road—free haircuts, maybe, or a heavy discount on getting your kitchen remodeled.

In fact, one of the few direct quid pro quos we pick up on the wires is when a Bronx PBA trustee calls a New York Yankees executive to report that he has successfully fixed a ticket for another Yankees front office exec. The PBA trustee doesn't ask for any money, but he does mention that it would be nice if he and his wife got a pass for the exclusive Delta Suite at Yankee Stadium for the game that night. No problem, the Yankees exec tells him.

And it's not just talk about routine traffic or parking tickets that we're hearing on the wiretaps. In several cases, cops tried—unsuccessfully—to quash domestic violence charges or DWIs against other cops. In one case, the owner of a paint store on East 180th Street beats a guy up, badly, for no reason, and when the victim calls 911, the paint store owner calls a cop pal, a PBA delegate, who calls the responding cops on his cell phone and asks them to "make it go the right way" for the paint store owner—after which the cops tank the assault case and file a false report. That's a crime in anybody's book.

Of course, when you're running an investigation involving hundreds of cops, and dozens of IAB and DA investigators and staff members— secretaries, clerks, technicians, and so on—you have to worry about leaks, intentional or inadvertent. You never know if one of the targeted cops just happens to have a cousin whose wife is a clerk in the DA's office or a secretary at One Police Plaza and just might overhear something about cops and wiretaps and fixed tickets.

Leaks can happen. And I'm sorry to say that the first leak about the ticket-fixing investigation came from us, the IAB.

Remember when I talked about the speech I gave to each group of cops we drafted into IAB? How they might not like being in Internal Affairs and investigating other cops, but it was their duty to protect good cops from the bad ones? Well, another part of that speech was about their duty to keep quiet about ongoing IAB investigations, no matter who those investigations involved; in fact, they had to sign a document promising that they wouldn't discuss any ongoing IAB case with anyone who didn't have a need to know—including other members of IAB. (I signed the same form—and I should note that nothing in this book concerns any ongoing confidential IAB investigations.) If they violated that duty it was a form of treason—and treason is a capital offense.

The vast majority of our IAB investigators took that message to heart. But a few didn't.

For example, we had an earlier case we were working with the FBI, looking at a Brooklyn narcotics detective suspected of "shotgunning" major-weight drug shipments for a big-time drug dealer. At one point the narcotics detective thinks he spots us tailing him—he was wrong, we didn't have a tail on him that day—so he calls a friend of his, a sergeant in IAB, and asks if he's being investigated. The sergeant surreptitiously checks the IAB files and calls the detective back and says: Yeah, they got a case on you and it looks like a big one. What they didn't know was that we had a wire up on the detective's phone and we were listening to the entire conversation. The IAB sergeant was indicted and kicked out of the Department.

So yeah, sometimes it happened. Sometimes IAB personnel felt more loyalty to their cop friends, even their crooked cop friends, than they felt to the Department, or the city, or the law.

That's what happened to the lieutenant who blabbed about the ticket-fixing case.

She'd been a sergeant in IAB, a draftee, and she was involved in the Ramos case when it began—not a key player, but enough to know about the initial wiretaps on the PBA cops. Early on in the ticket-fixing investigation she makes lieutenant, and with her two-year commitment in IAB ending, she transfers out to regular duty in the 48th Precinct in the Bronx. Shortly thereafter, she's having a drink at a bar in Rockland County with two other Bronx cops, a lieutenant and a PBA delegate, personal friends, and she tells them: Hey, be careful about talking about fixing summonses on the phone; IAB's got wires up. So of course within hours the word is flying around among the Bronx PBA delegates and trustees. They start telling each other: Look, we gotta be more careful about making summonses go away, IAB's got wires up, we're gonna have to do it face to face from now on.

We know they're saying this because we're listening to them talk about it on their phones.

Let me repeat that: These cops are talking on their phones about not using their phones to fix tickets! I hate to say it, but some of these guys are not the sharpest tools in the shed.

Well, at first we're worried that the ticket-fixing investigation is completely blown, that we'll just have to go with what we have already. And for a couple of months the ticket-fixing chatter slacks off.

But it's strange. A lot of these cops we've got wires up on don't really believe it. We hear some of them say the female lieutenant who leaked the information is a "fucking kook" and "fucking nuts." They know she used to be with "the rat squad"—IAB—and some of them wonder aloud if she's still a rat, if this whole ticket-fixing investigation she talked about is bogus, if it's some kind of unrelated IAB integrity test or something. So pretty soon they're back at it again, on their phones, while we're listening: Hey, I got this buddy of a buddy, he got a speeding ticket, can you take care of it for me?

No investigation can go on forever, and by now we've been on this one for almost a year—almost two years if you count the initial investigation of Ramos and his crew. (That's something that never comes across in TV crime shows, how long investigations can take. On TV, a detective will catch a case, investigate it, make an arrest, and have the perp in court without ever even changing his shirt; in real life, sometimes you can actually watch a cop grow old over the course of a complicated investigation.) We've got more than ten thousand monitored calls and text messages—ten thousand!—made by hundreds of cops talking about fixing tickets. But before we take it to a grand jury, there's one other thing we have to do. We have to stage an IAB raid on every precinct in the Bronx.

So in late 2010, we summon fifty IAB investigators into IAB headquarters on Hudson Street, swear them to secrecy, and lay out the plan. At precisely eleven a.m., you guys hit the Four-Oh, you guys hit the Four-Eight, and so on, every one of the twelve precincts in the Bronx. What we're going to do is scoop up the precincts' copies of summonses, tens of thousands of them, and we have to do it simultaneously at every precinct, because once the word is out that IAB is in the house we don't want to give anybody a chance to start feeding the paper shredder. Unfortunately, one of our IAB investigators, a lieutenant, inadvertently blabs about the raid to a cop buddy, a sergeant in Queens, who quickly alerts a PBA delegate in Queens, who in turn alerts a PBA delegate in the Bronx; fortunately, by the time the Bronx delegate gets the word it's after eleven a.m. and we're already inside the precincts and securing the summonses records. (Both the blabby lieutenant and the blabby sergeant caught suspensions for that one.)

Of course, after the raids on the Bronx precincts, the word is out. The wires on the cops' phones come down, and we and the DA's office start putting together evidence for a grand jury. In early 2011 a special grand jury starts sifting through the evidence in the ticket-fixing case and the case that led up to it, the investigation of Ramos and his crew. Over the next months the grand jury calls more than eighty witnesses, including cops and some of the civilians who got their tickets fixed—including the New York Yankees exec—and under grants of immunity compels them to testify about the ticket-fixing scheme. (Frankly, I wished that some of the civilians who asked to have their tickets fixed would have been charged, but it would have been hard to prove in court—and besides, it wasn't my call.)

At the same time the grand jury is calling in witnesses, we're starting to call cops into a spare, windowless administrative hearing room in IAB headquarters on Hudson Street and GO-15-ing them—that is, ordering them to tell us about the ticket fixing, for which they'll face Department administrative charges, in return for granting them immunity from criminal charges. Eventually, hundreds of cops will walk in and out of that room.

Obviously, any case involving that many people isn't going to stay secret, and this one doesn't. A few weeks after the grand jury probe begins, the word is out—"BIG INQUIRY INTO TICKET-FIXING IN NEW YORK," the *New York Times* headline says—and over the next few months more and more information about the scope of the police ticket-fixing scandal comes out. Pretty soon, the entire city is buzzing about what the papers are calling the "Tix-Fix" scandal.

There's a lot of talk in the press about the NYPD's corrupt "culture," and some writers are suggesting that Tix-Fix is going to be the most far-

ranging NYPD scandal since the Dirty Thirty in the early 1990s. And
the public is paying attention. Instead of saying the usual thing—Don't
you cops have anything better to do?—drivers who are getting tickets
are saying to cops: Hey, who do I have to call to get this fixed? There's
even a scene in the TV police show *Blue Bloods* in which singer Tony
Bennett, playing himself, asks Tom Selleck, who plays the NYPD police
commissioner, if he'll fix a speeding ticket for Bennett's driver—an
obvious reference to the brewing real-life scandal—and Selleck seems
to agree. (I never asked Ray Kelly about it, but if he saw it, I doubt he
thought it was funny. When Kelly was asked if he'd ever fixed a ticket,
his response was "Never"—and no one had ever asked him to.)

As I mentioned before, word about the looming scandal even has
an effect on some of the Bronx DA's unrelated criminal cases. In one
Bronx DWI case, the defendant—a personal injury lawyer, no less—is
acquitted by a jury after two of the cops who arrested him have to admit
on the witness stand that they're under investigation for ticket fixing;
one juror later says of the cops: How can you trust such people? Worse,
in an attempted murder case, another Bronx jury acquits a guy who
was caught on a surveillance camera shooting at a guy in a Mott Haven
apartment building after one of the cops involved in the arrest admits in
court that he fixed two tickets for his sister-in-law—which the defense
attorney says make him a "corrupt cop" who shouldn't be trusted.

Okay, sure, Bronx juries are notoriously anticop. But when a jury, any
jury, trusts a personal injury lawyer and a street player with a gun more
than they trust a cop, you've got a problem.

Within the Department, word of the Tix-Fix investigation has an
immediate impact. No cop is trying to fix tickets anymore, not only
in the Bronx but citywide. Cops who might have legitimately called
in sick on a day they're scheduled to testify in Traffic Court come in
anyway; they'd rather testify with a 101-degree fever than make it seem
like they're tanking a ticket. In the Bronx precincts, even though the
wires have all come down, PBA delegates and trustees have pretty much
stopped taking calls on their cell phones, on any subject—a clear-cut
case of belatedly closing the barn door.

And everybody is wondering: What's the grand jury going to do?
How many cops are going to get indicted behind this ticket thing? Some

of the leaks from the grand jury say twenty cops, some say fifty cops, some say hundreds of cops.

And then in October 2011, after months of work, the grand jury finally makes its decision. And the NYPD finds itself in something close to a state of civil war.

We had known from the start that not every cop who helped fix a ticket would be indicted. Some of the cops we overheard on the wiretaps were only messengers, passing along a ticket-fixing request from a cop buddy in another precinct to a PBA delegate in their precinct. Some of the cops involved clearly felt some pressure from their PBA delegates to not show up on court day or otherwise help fix a ticket. Other cops had only been involved in fixing one ticket, or two. The DA—and through him, the grand jury—isn't going to charge guys like that criminally. The Department will handle them administratively. Eventually three hundred cops will receive command disciplines, docking them up to ten days of vacation pay. Another two hundred more serious offenders are hit with formal departmental charges, with punishments ranging from dismissal to, in most cases, loss of up to forty vacation days—the rough equivalent of a $10,000 fine.

But the organizers of the ticket-fixing scheme, the cops who fixed dozens of tickets, are in serious trouble. So is that former IAB lieutenant who had leaked information on the investigation. And so are Officer Ramos and his crew. In the end, the grand jury returns a sixteen-hundred-count indictment—*sixteen hundred* counts!—charging twenty-one people with various felonies and misdemeanors.

Obviously, Ramos takes the hardest hit. He's been cooling his heels on modified duty for more than year, and when rumors about the ticket-fixing investigation first come out, we pick him up on a wire talking about it. He's not worried, he says, he never took any money for fixing a ticket, he says. This mope has no idea how much we have on him.

And we have a lot. Ramos is charged with attempted robbery (the stolen electronics guy rip-off), attempted grand larceny (the motel rip), transporting what he believed to be a shipment of heroin to Brooklyn, selling counterfeit CDs and DVDs in his barbershops, insurance fraud, and filing of a false report of a robbery (his buddy Marco Mack's phony complaint to IAB). And—icing on the cake—he's also charged with four misdemeanor counts of official misconduct for fixing traffic tickets. His 40th Precinct pal, Sergeant Dopey Dude, is charged in the electronics guy rip-off, and four civilian members of the barbershop crew—Wanda (Mrs. Ramos), Marco Mack (aka Lee King), and two others—are hit with various drug possession, theft, and conspiracy charges. We scoop up Ramos and the rest of them, and put them in handcuffs, even before the indictments are unsealed.

Of course, nobody cares much about the arrest of a dope-dealing, money-stealing crooked cop. But it's the other fourteen defendants named in the indictment that cause a near riot in the NYPD.

One of them is the chatterbox former IAB lieutenant, charged with three misdemeanor counts. Three others are the cops who made it "go the right way" for the friend of the PBA delegate who beat up the guy at the paint store, as well as the paint store owner who did the beating. But ten of the other indicted cops, who are facing hundreds of felony and misdemeanor counts in the ticket-fixing scheme, are all current or former delegates or trustees of the Patrolmen's Benevolent Association.

And when that news breaks, the PBA almost goes berserk.

Even before the indictments were returned, union leaders had been arguing that fixing a ticket for a friend or a family member was "a courtesy, not a crime," that it was a long-standing and common practice in the NYPD, and that no cop should be punished for it. Mayor Michael Bloomberg unintentionally contributed to that argument during a radio interview before the indictments came down, saying that while NYPD officers certainly shouldn't be fixing tickets, that it was an embarrassment for the Department, it was also a widespread practice in many police departments, and he added—quote—*It's been going on since the days of the Egyptians.*

Well, I don't know if cops in the Thebes PD robbed the Pharaoh's coffers by fixing tickets on speeding chariots and illegally parked donkeys. But I bet if they did, Pharaoh wouldn't have given them a command discipline, or even an indictment; he would have had their heads. And so what if fixing tickets was a "common practice"—and I would argue that it really wasn't? Cops splitting up the gambling pad at every level of a precinct was once a common practice. Cops taking bottles of

Scotch on the arm was once a common practice. Cops taking payoffs from tow-truck drivers was once a common practice. Is that the way these guys want the modern NYPD to be?

As for ticket fixing being just a courtesy, not a crime, that's an easy one: Check your Patrol Guide. Or the New York State criminal statutes.

But the union doesn't see it that way. The night before the indicted cops are to be arraigned—along with Ramos and his crew—the PBA sends out a text asking rank-and-file cops to show up in court to support them. When the indicted cops show up, there are a hundred off-duty cops filling the courtroom, hundreds more packed into the halls, and still hundreds more outside on the street, many of them carrying signs that say "It's a Courtesy, Not a Crime" and "Since the Time of the Egyptians"—a reference to the Bloomberg thing. They're shouting encouragement to the indicted cops, jostling reporters and TV crews, screaming curses about the DA, the police commissioner, and of course the "rats" in IAB. When some civilian counter-demonstrators start shouting "Fix our tickets!" the cops heap verbal abuse on them. Like I said, it's a near riot.

Hundreds of rank-and-file officers took to the streets to protest when more than a dozen NYPD cops were arrested after a massive IAB investigation into ticket-fixing. The Patrolmen's Benevolent Association claimed that fixing tickets was just a courtesy—but to IAB it was a crime. (Getty Images)

(To his credit, PBA President Pat Lynch makes it clear the protesting cops aren't there to support Officer Ramos, whom he calls a "drug dealer." The PBA hasn't completely lost sight of its responsibility to oppose lawbreakers.)

At the arraignment everybody pleads not guilty, and the ticket-fixing cops are ROR'ed—released–own recognizance. But Ramos and his crew take a harder hit. The judge slaps Ramos with $500,000 bail—in New York City, an astonishingly high bail for anything less than murder or violent mayhem—and he's off to jail on Riker's Island. His accused crew members are held on lesser bail amounts.

Now it's in the hands of the lawyers.

It's a funny thing about accused cops and their lawyers. A cop can sit on a barstool and rail for hours about the injustice of slick defense attorneys and lily-livered, criminal-pampering judges who allow critical evidence in a case to be tossed out because of an illegal search. But when a cop gets arrested, he'll develop a sudden and profound reverence for the finer points of the Fourth Amendment.

Which is exactly what happens in the ticket-fixing case. One of the first things the cops' lawyers do is challenge the search warrants for the wiretaps—and although the legality of the wiretaps is eventually upheld, it's a process that takes months, and then years. Although the former IAB lieutenant who leaked the investigation was convicted of a misdemeanor and sentenced to probation, as I write this most of the criminal ticket-fixing cases against the cops are still in the courts. (I should point out that nothing I've said about those cases hasn't already been turned over to the defense lawyers or become part of the public record.)

But justice moves more quickly in the case of Jose Ramos, the crooked cop who started it all. In October 2014, after a jury trial, Ramos is convicted on several counts stemming from our initial criminal investigation and later is sentenced to almost fifteen years in prison. But in fact, his trouble is just beginning—and once again, that trouble involves his old pal, and our old confidential informant, Sal.

Go back a couple of years, when Ramos is stuck on Riker's Island on $500,000 bail. Based on the indictments, he knows that Sal is the rat, the guy who put him into those rip-offs and that shotgunning drug deal that IAB set up—and as a result, Ramos would very much like to have Sal murdered. Sal is still out on bail for that bogus credit card scam and is expected to testify against Ramos. Ramos thinks that if he can put Sal out of the way, permanently, the DA won't have a case against him. He's wrong on that—we've got videotapes and undercover IAB cops to testify against Ramos, with or without Sal—but then, Ramos never was the brightest bulb in the chandelier.

So of course Ramos mentions this desire to have Sal murdered to another Riker's Island jailbird, and says he's looking for a hit man to take out Sal. And what does that jailbird do? He does what every jailbird who's looking to get out from under his own charges does. In return for a break on his own crimes, he rats out Ramos to a Corrections Department officer, who contacts his own Department of Investigations, who contacts IAB.

We figure: Ramos wants a hit man? Okay, we'll give him a hit man. We've got an IAB undercover, an African American cop who plays a perfect gangsta killer, and we get the jailbird turned informant to introduce him to Ramos on visiting day at the jail. Ramos explains that he wants this rat taken out, and our undercover hit man, who's wired, tells Ramos, sure, he can get the job done, for five thousand up front, five more after it's over. Life is cheap with these guys.

Meanwhile, Ramos has gotten his wife, Wanda, who was released without bail on the insurance scam charge, in on the deal. All phone calls from Riker's Island are monitored, so he and Wanda talk in kind of a dopey, childish code, but with what Ramos has already said to our undercover, it's easy enough to figure out. He tells Wanda, in code, to take the money for the hit out of his Department pension fund and give it to the hit man.

I mean, does this guy Ramos never learn? He's already gotten jammed up by trusting one low-life criminal, his pal Sal, and now he's put his trust in another low-life criminal, the Riker's Island jailbird. He's already been fooled by two IAB undercovers, the Miami drug dealer and the stolen electronics guy, and now he's being fooled by another, the IAB "hit man." He's already been caught in dozens of incriminating conversations on tapped phones, and now he's talking about a hit for hire, from Riker's Island . . . on the phone!

I guess the answer is no. Guys like Ramos never do learn.

So eventually Wanda takes the cash out of the pension fund, but when our undercover goes to her house to collect the down payment on the hit, she balks, saying she doesn't have the money. I don't think she made our undercover; I think she just decided that, given her husband's less than stellar success record as a criminal, she was afraid to be a part of any murder he had planned.

Still, it's enough. Ramos and Wanda are both indicted on murder-conspiracy charges. After being convicted and sentenced for the earlier barbershop crimes, in January 2015, Ramos pleads guilty to the conspiracy charges and gets another three to nine years tacked onto the earlier sentence.

There's a postscript to the story of Sal the CI. In November 2012, while Sal is still out on bail and waiting to testify in the Ramos case, he reverts to form. He and a couple of pals arrange to steal more than three thousand iPads—fresh off the plane from China, and worth $1.5 million retail—from a cargo storage facility at JFK Airport and drive them in a tractor trailer to a storage facility in Virginia. As we had carefully explained to Sal when we first signed him up as a CI, any further criminal activity on his part would not only greatly diminish his value as a witness, but it would also eliminate any goodwill that we might have for him in return for helping us investigate Officer Jose Ramos. But of course he doesn't listen. So after he's busted on that charge, Sal winds up getting two and a half years in the joint.

Like I said, it's been that kind of case.

So in the end, what did the Ramos/ticket-fixing investigation accomplish? Was it worth the thousands of man-hours, and the years of time, and the hundreds of thousands of dollars that IAB and the Bronx DA put into it?

The answer is, You bet it was worth it.

For one thing, it took a seriously dirty cop—Ramos—off the street and put him in prison. That's worth almost any amount of time and resources.

The ticket-fixing investigation also made the city's traffic summonses system more accurate and more fair. Even while the investigation was going on, as the wide scope of the ticket fixing became apparent, it speeded up the introduction of a new computer tracking system that scanned all summonses as they came in, making it much more difficult to make a summons disappear.

But most important, the ticket-fixing investigation helped change the NYPD culture.

What helped turn New York City around in the early 1990s, what changed it from a crime-ridden, Third World–style hellhole into a safe and vibrant city was the NYPD's decision to not only aggressively pursue serious crimes, but also to start enforcing the laws against low-level and "quality-of-life" crimes—subway fare beating, public urination, aggressive panhandling, and so on. It sent out the message that crime, any crime, wasn't going to be tolerated anymore—and it worked.

Same thing with the ticket-fixing investigation. Although the investigation was concentrated in the Bronx, it sent out a message to every precinct in every borough in the city that corruption, even relatively low-level corruption like ticket fixing, would not be tolerated in the new NYPD. I won't say that since then there's never been a summons or a criminal case that's been tampered with by an NYPD cop. But I can guarantee you that with the memory of the ticket-fixing case still fresh in everyone's mind, no sane cop is going to risk his career and his livelihood by trying to tank a lousy $150 speeding ticket for his cousin's wife's nephew.

The old-style NYPD cops, the cynical hairbags who may look back fondly at the bad old days, may not like it. But everybody understands it.

When a cop willfully and intentionally breaks the law, it's never just a courtesy. It's a crime.

Chapter 13

POLITICS

I had never intended to spend half of my NYPD career investigating other cops. It's not the sort of thing that any young cop dreams about on the day he graduates from the Academy.

But somebody has to do it. Somebody has to be the point man in the never-ending fight against cops who cross the line. And whether I liked it or not, that somebody turned out to be me.

What is amazing to me is that I lasted as long as I did.

You'll remember that back in 1993, when then commissioner Ray Kelly told me he was sending me to the new Internal Affairs Bureau, he had assured me it would only be a two-year gig. And by mid-1996, I had done more than my promised two years in IAB, first as an inspector in charge of the Corruption Prevention and Analysis Unit, then as IAB deputy chief of support services and IAB executive officer, second in command under my friend Chief Pat Kelleher. During those two-plus years we'd done a lot to get the new IAB up and running, and I was proud of that, but I was looking forward to moving on, maybe as—this was being contemplated—the new commander of the Police Academy. I was a one-star chief by then, and the Academy commander job was a one-star chief's position, and I'd always been interested in education. I thought I'd like to help instill in young recruits my love for the NYPD and my faith in the NYPD's core values, and to help teach them how they could contribute to the new NYPD.

And in 1996 it *was* a new NYPD. Beginning with Police Commissioner Ray Kelly and continuing through Commissioners Bill Bratton and Howard Safir, and with the help of visionaries like the aforementioned Jack Maple, the NYPD had begun its transformation into a proactive police department, not just a reactive one, attacking crime at the "quality-of-life" level and carrying through to more serious crimes. The CompStat system pioneered by Maple and others was allowing the Department to track crimes on a daily basis and deploy resources accordingly. And it was working. Murders had been cut in half since 1990, other crimes were plummeting, people were feeling safer on the streets, New York City was becoming not just livable but once again a thriving and vibrant city. As I said earlier, it was already being called the "New York Miracle"—and the NYPD was getting much of the credit.

In short, it was an exciting time to be an NYPD cop—and I was looking forward to sharing that excitement with new recruits. I figured I'd do that for a few years, then move on to something else. I had twenty-two years on the job by then, so maybe in a few years I would drop my retirement papers, finish my PhD dissertation in criminal justice at John Jay, and go into teaching full-time. One thing was certain: I wouldn't be in IAB much longer.

And then one morning in July 1996, Police Commissioner Howard Safir calls me into his office. He's smiling like he's got good news for me. He says he's making me the new chief of the Internal Affairs Bureau, the top guy. (Current IAB chief Pat Kelleher is moving over to the coveted spot of chief of detectives.) It's a three-star chief's position, so Safir says he's bumping me up two grades, from one star to three, virtually overnight; I'm going to be what's known as a "super-chief," one of only seven in the Department. Yeah, it will mean I won't get the Academy commander job, but for a guy who not too many years earlier had thought that passing the lieutenant's exam was going to be the highlight of his career, becoming a three-star chief is pretty heady stuff.

And yet, when I get home that night and tell my wife, Arlene, about this big promotion, this is exactly what she says: That's good news, isn't it? So why aren't you smiling?

She's right. I'm not smiling. For two reasons.

One reason is that I know the average useful professional lifespan of an NYPD super-chief is about three years. That's because New York mayors come and go, and since the mayor appoints the police commissioner, who serves at the mayor's pleasure, that means that police commissioners come and go, which means that super-chiefs come and go. A new PC comes in, he understandably wants his own guys around him in the top slots, and since you're the previous guy's super-chief, suddenly maybe you aren't so super anymore. Sure, if you aren't quite ready to retire they'll usually find some obscure place to park you for a few years until you drop your papers, but who wants that?

Well, as it turned out, my concern that as chief of IAB I would be caught in a rapidly revolving door proved unfounded. As I mentioned earlier, I would wind up spending more than seventeen years as chief of IAB, under four different police commissioners—which was unheard of. I would not only be the longest-serving Internal Affairs chief in NYPD history, but I also would be the longest-serving—or longest-surviving—three-star NYPD chief in modern NYPD history.

That's mostly because the dedication and hard work of the cops under my command in IAB—detectives, sergeants, lieutenants, captains, administrative personnel, all of them—always made me look good. But I was also fortunate to serve almost all of my time as IAB chief under police commissioners who, although their personal styles were completely different, believed in what we were doing in the new IAB—and they wanted us to keep doing it.

I've mentioned them already. The first was Howard Safir, the former DEA and US Marshals Service agent and administrator who Mayor Rudy Giuliani brought in to replace Commissioner Bill Bratton in early 1996 after Bratton and Giuliani butted heads. (More on Bill Bratton later.) Safir, who incidentally was the first Jewish police commissioner in NYPD history, was a lot like the mayor who appointed him: tough, relentless, blunt, and never ready to back down from a fight—of which he had many, particularly with the police unions and the press. A longtime friend of Giuliani's, and an outsider to the NYPD, Safir had zero tolerance for police corruption or misconduct, or for the much-discussed Blue Wall of Silence. He was a consistent and solid supporter of the IAB. His response to any IAB investigation, including the Louima case, was to make sure I had the resources I needed and then trust me wherever it went.

I also served, relatively briefly, as IAB chief under Police Commissioner Bernie Kerik, who was appointed to replace Safir after he decided in 2000 to go into the private sector. Kerik was a former NYPD narcotics undercover detective, a member of Giuliani's protective detail, and the city commissioner of corrections before Giuliani named him police commissioner—a kind of temporary fill-in, since Giuliani was going to be term-limited out of the mayor's office in just sixteen months. As police commissioner, Kerik was . . . well, let's just say that in his heart he was always more of a street cop than an administrator or executive. He liked nothing better than to go out at night with his security detail, all of them tough cops, and actually make arrests. He generally left most of the day-to-day running of the Department to subordinates—including me at IAB. Colorful, affable, and often profane—he could out-cuss a sailor—Kerik also had a complicated personal life and some ill-advised friendships. Although there were never any corruption allegations against Kerik while he was police commissioner, later he was investigated by the Bronx DA and the US Justice Department for tax evasion and for lying during his aborted attempt to become the federal secretary of homeland security. As a result he served three years in federal prison—a reminder, I guess, that it's not just beat cops who sometimes forget the oath they take.

And then there was Police Commissioner Ray Kelly, who was reappointed as commissioner by Giuliani's successor, Mayor Michael Bloomberg, in 2002 and under whom I served for twelve years as IAB chief. Kelly, you'll remember, was the guy who shanghaied me into Internal Affairs when I was a deputy inspector in 1993—for which I have long since forgiven him. Since joining the Department in 1966 after his service as a Marine officer in Vietnam, Kelly had held almost every job there was in the NYPD, from street cop to police commissioner, a position he first assumed in late 1992 under Mayor David Dinkins. Although Kelly was a tough commissioner who initiated many of the concepts that dramatically reduced crime in New York City in the 1990s—including the dispersal of the so-called squeegee men whose shakedowns of drivers symbolized much of what was wrong with New York—he also maintained excellent relationships with the city's many minority communities, an important function in a city as diverse as New York. But Kelly had the misfortune to be linked with a mayor, Dinkins, who was widely perceived as antipolice and soft on crime, so after

Giuliani took over the mayor's office on a tough-on-crime platform in 1994, he unceremoniously moved Kelly out and put tough-on-crime Bill Bratton in—which proved to be kind of ironic. It's ironic because—as we'll see—years later Bratton himself would have the misfortune (in my opinion) to be linked as police commissioner to another antipolice and soft-on-crime mayor in the form of Bill de Blasio.

In any event, after Bloomberg brought Kelly back to the police commissioner's job—Kelly was the first PC in history to hold two nonconsecutive tenures in the job—no one ever mistook Kelly for being soft on crime, or on police corruption or misconduct. He continued many of his predecessors' anticrime policies and even expanded some of them—including the controversial "stop, question, and possibly frisk" program (incorrectly shortened by the news media and politicians to "stop and frisk") that took tens of thousands of guns and other weapons off the streets and saved thousands of lives. As a lifelong NYPD cop who had lived through some of the most troubled chapters in NYPD history, Kelly also understood that another widespread police corruption or misconduct scandal like those that produced the Knapp Commission and Mollen Commission could be fatal to the Department—and consequently he put resources, and his confidence, into IAB. As IAB chief I met with Kelly almost every day to brief him on ongoing investigations and explain new ones, and while he always wanted to know every detail, he never micromanaged. As far as I was concerned, he was the perfect boss, and the perfect commissioner. In fact, with his ramrod-straight posture, close-cropped hair, and Irish pug face, he even *looked* like the perfect NYPD commissioner.

So anyway, although I couldn't know it yet, on that day in July 1996 when I told my wife about my big promotion, I didn't have to worry about being shuffled out of the job after just a year or two. The guys I would be working for were going to back me up.

But as I said, there were two reasons I wasn't smiling on the day I got promoted to IAB chief. The second reason I wasn't smiling was because I hate politics—and by 1996 I'd already been around the upper floors of One Police Plaza enough to know just how savage the politics surrounding the NYPD Internal Affairs Bureau could be.

Don't get the wrong idea. I'm not saying that IAB investigations are political. When we get a complaint or open an investigation, whether it's about a cop on the beat or a senior member of the Department, we go where the investigation leads us—and nobody tells us otherwise. A lot of critics out there won't believe it, but I'll raise my right hand and swear in any court in the land that, with one relatively minor exception—which I'll get to later—no mayor or police commissioner under whom I served ever ordered me or anyone under my IAB command to tank an investigation, or to go after a political rival, or even subtly suggested that I redirect IAB resources away from a given case. If one of them had I would remember, because that would have been my last day as chief of IAB.

I should point out that there are only two people in the NYPD who IAB doesn't investigate if there's an allegation of misconduct or impropriety—that's the police commissioner and the chief of IAB. If something like that comes up, those investigations are handled by the city's Department of Investigations or the city's Conflicts of Interest Board or some other outside agency.

For example, one day in the Bronx there's a traffic accident in which a guy in a white Oldsmobile hits another car, injuring the other driver, and then drives away. A witness gets the plate number, which traces back to my official Department car. That's right, my Department car has been identified as the getaway vehicle in a hit-and-run.

So as soon as I hear about it I notify the Bronx DA's office, the independent mayor's Commission to Combat Police Corruption, and the New York State Police to conduct the investigation—and I think I've got a pretty good defense. My Department car is a brown Buick, not a white Oldsmobile. At my request, the New York State Police tow my car to the lab and forensically determine that it's never been in a collision, much less a recent one. And at the exact time of the incident I was operating the scoreboard in front of a couple hundred people at the Abe Stark Arena in Coney Island where my son's hockey team was competing—which is about as solid an alibi as you can get. It turns out that the witness got one digit wrong on the hit-and-run driver's plate number; later we found the owner of the white Olds, who had conveniently reported the car stolen an hour after the accident.

Anyway, although IAB isn't political, it's constantly involved as the lead investigating unit in politically charged situations—officer-involved shootings, excessive-force allegations, deaths in custody, police corruption. And there are plenty of political people and groups out there who are eager for an IAB investigation to support their preconceived opinions—and if it doesn't, they aren't shy about letting you know. The press, the New York Civil Liberties Union, the police unions, police brutality lawyers, race- and gender-discrimination lawyers, community activists, City Council members—the list goes on and on. There's never any shortage of people on the outside who will tell you how IAB should do its job, or how IAB isn't doing its job, or how IAB shouldn't be doing its job.

For example, to paraphrase Henny Youngman, take the press . . . please.

It's not that I don't like newspapers and TV news. Hey, I enjoy fiction as much as the next guy—and to be fair, sometimes when covering cops in general, and the NYPD in particular, the reporters actually get it right.

But too often I'd see a news story about IAB and have to wonder, Where do they get this stuff?

The press seemed to take it as an article of faith that IAB would, if given the opportunity, cover up anything that was embarrassing to the NYPD. The Louima case is an example. As I mentioned earlier, by the time the story of the assault broke in the press, IAB already had hundreds of investigators working the case, and we were close to positively identifying the officers involved and making arrests. But since we couldn't talk about it publicly until we had indictments, some reporters assumed that we'd been sitting on the investigation, and had only been roused to action by the public outcry.

Sometimes the press simply didn't understand how law enforcement works. For example, remember those cops that robbed the perfume warehouse in New Jersey? The one where they got away with half a million dollars' worth of swag but left behind a truck rented by one of them in his own name? As I explained earlier, after the robbery the local cops alerted the FBI, who alerted us, and we quickly rolled up the cop robbery crew—and since it was an interstate theft case the feds prosecuted the cops involved. But some reporters took that case and other joint IAB-FBI investigations to mean that IAB was being caught flat-footed, that the FBI was the lead agency in rooting out corruption in the NYPD, and that the NYPD wasn't capable of policing itself. And I had to think, Do these guys not understand that that warehouse robbery took place in New Jersey? Do they not realize that New Jersey is another state? Are they unfamiliar with the Hudson River?

Or how about that story on the IAB Command Center logs, the one that said IAB had received fifty thousand "complaints" or "tips" about police misconduct or corruption or brutality in a year, but only opened investigations into about a thousand of them—which therefore proved that IAB wasn't taking corruption and misconduct seriously, that we were ignoring thousands of tips and complaints. I actually sat down with the reporter involved and patiently—or as patiently as I could, given the Sicilian thing—tried to explain the difference between a "log" and a "tip." I tried to get him to understand that, for example, when the aforementioned Barry from Brooklyn calls IAB forty times to report that forty different cops have stabbed him in the eye on forty different occasions, it will generate forty logs in IAB records—but that doesn't quite amount to forty bona fide "tips" or "complaints" about police brutality. But the guy just couldn't seem to get it.

Well, I could go on and on. There were a lot of times when I wanted to publicly correct the press's misinformation about specific IAB cases—not for my sake, but for the good name of the IAB—but I couldn't. For one thing, we didn't talk about ongoing investigations or unadjudicated criminal cases. In that sense we were sort of like the CIA: We can neither confirm nor deny . . . In fact, everyone in IAB, me included, was required to sign a special nondisclosure agreement. So we were seldom able to get the real facts out.

And besides, as Paul Browne, the deputy commissioner for public information under Kelly, often explained to me, if you respond to bad reporting in the press you just turn a one-day story into a two- or three-day story—and in the end you lose anyway. He was right, of course. But it still rankled.

Lawyers were another political headache. Any high-ranking public official can expect to be sued for supposedly permitting improper actions by his or her subordinates, even if he or she wasn't directly involved in the alleged misconduct; it comes with the territory. So as IAB chief I was a named defendant—along with the police commissioner, the New York City Police Department, and the City of New York—in about a dozen lawsuits alleging various acts of misfeasance and demanding millions of dollars in damages. The press picked up on a lot of them, reprinting the lawyers' allegations almost verbatim—and since the city's lawyers wouldn't allow the Department to publicly respond with anything beyond a generic denial of any wrongdoing, some people assumed they were true.

For example, there was a Brooklyn cop we investigated for allegedly trying to set himself up as a pimp, and who was later fired from the Department. He sued us for $30 million, claiming among other things that, one, IAB intentionally targeted minority cops in its investigations (which case statistics indicated wasn't true), and two, at least as I understood the complaint, the IAB female undercover we had posing as a hooker in the case—code name "Candy"—was so good-looking that in effect she constituted a form of entrapment.

In another lawsuit, an IAB investigator claimed that I was among those who had fostered a campaign of harassment and discrimination against him because he was gay—this about a guy who as CO in the Sixth Precinct carried a candle in the AIDS vigil and who often received praise from the NYPD Gay Officers Action League. (Actually, when I first heard about the IAB investigator's lawsuit, my initial reaction was, What? He's gay?) I'm not saying that gay and lesbian officers have never experienced discrimination or offensive comments in the ranks of the NYPD, but I certainly would never have knowingly allowed it to happen.

In yet another discrimination lawsuit, a recently retired female IAB detective claimed that I was among those who not only discriminated against minorities in hiring and promotions—which, again, we demonstrated by the numbers was untrue—but that female IAB employees were routinely coerced to have sex in return for career advancement, which sort of put a whole new spin on the "Affairs" part of "Internal Affairs." In my opinion, even by the low standards of lawsuits that was ridiculous. In fact, while the female complainant criticized my management style, she also later told a reporter, quote: *He [Campisi] is honor-*

able. He still has the old values. He loves his wife and children and he lives for his grandchildren. He is not like a normal chief. He never made a pass at me.

I don't know how that quote played with the "normal chiefs," whoever they were. But it played pretty well in my house.

In the end, we won almost every lawsuit filed against me and IAB (one is still pending)—won in the sense that neither I nor the IAB nor the Department was found to have done anything wrong. Most of the cases were dropped or dismissed outright, but in some cases the City Corporation Counsel, the city's legal arm, paid the complainant—and of course his or her lawyer—a relatively small sum to make the lawsuit go away. For example, in the case of the former Brooklyn cop suspected of being a pimp, he had demanded $30 million in damages but wound up settling for somewhat less than that in "go-away money"—$2,500 to be exact.

"Go-away money" in unfounded or frivolous lawsuits against cops is a sore point with me and with most cops. I can understand the city paying a settlement in cases where the cops committed a crime, like the Louima case, or cases where the cops made a mistake, like the Diallo shooting. I can also understand the arithmetic involved in settling a frivolous lawsuit with a small go-away payment. The way the city's lawyers see it, why spend $100,000 in litigation costs to win a bogus lawsuit when you can make it disappear for five or ten or twenty grand?

The problem is that while the go-away settlements always include a stipulation that the city and the cops involved are not admitting that they did anything wrong, who believes that? Most people figure, why would the city pay if the cops are innocent, so they must be guilty, right? If it were up to me—which it isn't—I'd have the city's lawyers fight every unfounded lawsuit against a cop and not pay out a dime. It might cost some money initially, but in the long run it also might discourage lawsuits that are made up out of thin air.

The police unions were often another source of political headaches. As I said earlier, the unions have a valid role to play, but in cases like Louima and the Bronx ticket-fixing investigation, their leadership sometimes went too far. Protecting your members' rights is one thing, impeding a legitimate IAB investigation is another thing altogether. The case of the "Drunken Hero Cop" is an example—and it's also that one case I mentioned in which political pressure directly affected an IAB investigation.

Here's the scene: It's the wee early hours on a summer night in the St. Albans section of Queens, and an off-duty, fifteen-year veteran NYPD detective from Brooklyn South Narcotics and some civilian friends are having drinks in an unlicensed social club. As they're leaving the club they see four men on the sidewalk doing a major beat-down on another guy. When the off-duty detective identifies himself as a cop and tries to stop the beating, one of the beat-down guys pulls out a handgun and starts firing. The detective pulls out his own off-duty gun and fires four times, hitting the shooter in the left arm and leg—although at the time the detective doesn't know if he hit him or not. After that the shooter and his pals manage to take off in a car. No one else is injured.

What follows is all SOP. An NYPD duty officer arrives at the scene and takes the detective's gun; the ballistics guys will need it for bullet comparisons. Since it's an officer-involved shooting with possible injuries, the duty officer notifies IAB and our call-out team goes to the scene to assist the borough shooting team in figuring out what happened. Meanwhile, an IAB deputy chief goes to Jamaica Hospital, where the detective has been taken for observation—a standard procedure in an officer-involved shooting even if the officer isn't visibly injured. And that's where the problems start.

Remember the Sean Bell case in 2006, when cops shot and killed the unarmed Bell outside a strip club in Queens? In that case there was some suspicion that the undercover cop had had more than just a couple of drinks in the strip club, which could have affected his judgment and led to the shooting. So after that the NYPD implemented a new policy: In any officer-involved shooting within New York City, on-duty or off, that involves a death or possible injury, the officer involved is given a Breathalyzer blood-alcohol test—and if he comes up drunk, he's suspended pending completion of the shooting investigation. All of the police unions complained about the new rule on the grounds that it was demeaning to cops, that it made cops be treated like suspects. But that's the rule: You fire your gun, and if someone is killed or injured or may be injured, you take the Breathalyzer test.

Which is what happens with the detective. At the hospital the IAB deputy chief gives him the test with a portable, handheld Breathalyzer—and the detective blows a .09, just over the .08 blood-alcohol content limit for being legally intoxicated. This isn't good—technically, NYPD cops are never supposed to be drunk and unfit for duty, even when they're off-duty, and they're certainly never supposed to be drunk when they fire their weapon. On the other hand, blowing an oh-nine doesn't necessarily make it a bad shooting, especially if it's in self-defense. So at this point, this detective, who's a good cop with a good record, probably isn't in serious trouble.

Or at least he's not until some reps from the Detectives Endowment Association (DEA) show up at the hospital. Following SOP in a case like this, the IAB deputy chief orders the detective to report to one of the NYPD's Intoxicated Driver Testing Units for a more accurate Intoxilyzer test—which actually is probably going to help the detective, since by that time a couple hours will have passed and maybe his BAC (blood-alcohol content) will have dropped below .08. But the guys from the DEA, which, along with the other police unions, has been looking for a chance to challenge the new Breathalyzer test rule for officer-involved shootings, tell the detective to refuse the order, that it's a violation of their contract. There's a lot of loud discussion and waving of arms, and finally I drive in to the hospital from home, this at about four a.m., to get this straightened out.

Remember, at this point we still don't have all the facts. IAB investigators and the borough shooting team haven't yet interviewed all the witnesses, most of whom scattered when the shooting started. The ballistics guys haven't finished processing the scene to figure out whose shots went where. And we don't even know yet if any of the detective's shots hit anybody; only later is the suspect picked up at a Long Island hospital where he went to be treated for gunshot wounds. All I've got is a detective who's legally drunk, who was in an unlicensed social club—itself a violation of Department rules—and who through his union reps won't follow standard Department procedure for an officer-involved shooting.

So I do the only thing I can do. I take the detective's shield and temporarily suspend him from the Department. All by the book.

Well, judging from the reaction, you would have thought that I had slapped a pair of handcuffs on Mother Teresa. The detective's union takes the story to the press, which takes the position that the detective should be given a medal, not a suspension. "NYPD SUSPENDS HERO COP!" is the general theme, with me specifically as the bad guy. Pretty soon it's a full-blown controversy, with front-page editorials in the tabloids, the rank and file up in arms, and the police union presidents threatening to tell their members not to make any arrests or intervene in life-threatening situations when they're off-duty. Finally Mayor Bloomberg, who hates getting into public beefs with the cops, sends the word down to Commissioner Kelly: Restore the detective to duty—which Kelly does.

This was all very public, nothing underhanded about it; it wasn't like the old days of the IAD, when word would secretly come down from above and an Internal Affairs investigation would be quietly dropped into the "tickler file," never to be seen again. The NYPD press office even issued a press release explaining the decision.

So I guess in the scheme of things it was a relatively minor incident. And as I said, it was also the only time that a mayor or a commissioner directly intervened in an ongoing IAB case while I was IAB chief. But it shows you how much political power the police unions can muster, even when they're wrong.

Another source of political headaches for me and for IAB had nothing to do with police corruption or serious misconduct or any of the other things that Internal Affairs usually is concerned with. No, believe it or not, our most frequent and frustrating political battles were about . . .

Parking.

That's right, parking. I know, I know, in a city and a police department that should be dealing with serious issues—crime, antiterrorism, police corruption, misconduct, and all the rest—we're talking about parking? It does sound foolish, but you have to understand that while parking, or the lack of it, is a major issue in most urban areas, in New York City it's an obsession. I mean, you steal a New Yorker's wallet, or his watch, or maybe even his wife, there's a chance he'll let it slide. But if you mess with a New Yorker's parking privileges, you've got a war on your hands.

And unfortunately, during my watch as chief, IAB got dragged kicking and screaming into the parking wars—with disastrous results.

A little background here: As I said, all of the police commissioners

I worked under had confidence in IAB, but Commissioner Ray Kelly most of all. So whenever something special comes up that Kelly wants taken care of, he calls us in, even if it really doesn't relate to Internal Affairs. Is there a problem with the awarding of tow-truck drivers' contracts? Put IAB on it. Is there a committee charged with drawing up new rules and policies for NYPD undercover cops? Put IAB on it. Does he want to make sure that a Department equipment procurement process goes smoothly? Kelly puts IAB on it. And so on.

This sort of "mission creep" takes up a lot of IAB's time—mine included—and even though we usually get additional resources to do the job, it's still takes away from IAB's primary mission. So whenever we got drawn into one of these sideshows, I'd tell my guys who had to work on it: Hey, I've got good news and bad news. The good news is that the commissioner has faith in us. The bad news is that the commissioner has faith in us.

Which brings us back to the parking debacle.

For years now—this is around 2007—the City Council has been complaining about cars with "Official Police Business" parking placards taking up too many street parking spots, especially around City Hall and the various borough courthouses and government centers. There are thousands and thousands of these parking placards out there, and not just for NYPD vehicles; judges, district attorneys, federal agencies, and other state and city government departments also get the placards for their vehicles, which effectively protects them against getting ticketed or towed. And they're being illegally parked everywhere, not just at expired meters but in bus stops, handicapped spaces, no stopping/standing zones, crosswalks, at fire hydrants, you name it. It's a safety issue—and although the City Council members don't say so, it also makes it harder for City Council members and their staff members to use *their* "Official Police Business" placards to park illegally.

So every time Commissioner Kelly has to appear before some City Council committee, what do they want to talk about? Crime? Police salaries? Department staffing levels? Forget about it. It's parking. What are you going to do about the parking? They're constantly breaking his shoes about it.

And when Kelly looks into it, he finds that the NYPD's system for issuing the placards is a mess. They don't even know for certain how many placards are out there, or who has them, and if they really need them. Kelly wants the whole parking placard system reorganized. So whom does he assign to do it?

Like I said, the good news is that the commissioner has faith in IAB. The bad news is that the commissioner has faith in IAB.

Okay, fine. This isn't a proper IAB function, but we'll do it. So we cut the number of parking placards issued in half—boy, you should have heard the bureaucrats howl about that—and we make it clear to all placard holders that an "Official Business" parking placard is for bona fide official business only, and it certainly doesn't mean you can park your vehicle in a crosswalk or a bus stop. But do they listen? No. They're still hogging every legal and illegal parking spot around City Hall, and the City Council is still breaking Kelly's shoes.

So Kelly decides to get tough. The NYPD is going to start ticketing and towing these illegally parked government vehicles, placards notwithstanding. And when I hear this, I'm thinking: Please, God, no. Not us. Not IAB.

But yes, it's us. As much as I fight it—I knew this was going to be a disaster—Kelly orders IAB to start ticketing and towing illegally parked government vehicles, police vehicles included.

So I assign an IAB lieutenant to oversee it, and he calls in some guys from the various Patrol Borough Investigations Units with some tow trucks, and they start towing illegally parked official vehicles. Now some precinct detective or assistant district attorney or Agriculture Department meat inspector will come walking out of one of the courthouses or City Hall or the federal building, and when he starts looking for his car in front of the fire hydrant where he left it, it's not there anymore—which means that before he can get it out of the impound yard, he, or worse, his boss, is going to have to write a letter explaining what dire official business emergency forced him to park it there in the first place. He won't have to pay the towing and storage fees, but unless he's got a really good excuse, he or his department is going to have to pay the ticket.

It's a huge hassle for everybody—me included. I start getting barraged with calls from other Department bureau chiefs and DAs and federal administrators and even some City Council members, all chewing my leg about their department's official cars being towed: Hey, whaddaya doin', you towed my guy's car! It's like I stole their children or something.

Unfortunately, the towing program worked. The parking situation around City Hall and other government buildings did get better—and not only did the City Council notice it, but the press did as well. In one of the few positive newspaper editorials ever directed my way, one of the tabloids praised Commissioner Kelly for "sending in the Marines"— that is, IAB—to successfully attack the illegal parking problem.

So why do I say it was unfortunate that it worked? Two reasons.

One is that after we got it up and running, I tried repeatedly to pass this towing thing back to where it belonged—the Transportation Bureau—but Kelly wouldn't hear of it; why change it when even the press is saying it's working so well? So because IAB had done a good and effective job, I had this political albatross hanging around my neck for the rest of my IAB career.

And the second reason it was unfortunate is because while towing a few vehicles may sound like a small thing, it damaged the Internal Affairs Bureau. You have to remember that one of the founding principles of the new Internal Affairs Bureau was that IAB was only going to handle serious cases of police misconduct and corruption. The minor stuff, the "white socks" violations—smoking in public view in uniform, not wearing your hat, conducting personal business on duty, and so on—was handled by the individual Patrol Borough Investigations Units or a precinct's integrity control officer. It was the only way that IAB could ever expect to be respected within the Department. But now IAB is towing cops' illegally parked cars? That's about as white socks as you can get—and IAB's hard-fought-for reputation for concentrating on serious corruption and misconduct cases suffered accordingly.

Of course, these are just a few examples of the sort of politicized controversies that IAB so often got saddled with; I could give you a lot more, large and small.

I'm not complaining about it. It comes with the three stars, and I knew that from the day I took the job. Still, sometimes I wondered what it would be like if everybody could somehow put aside their personal agendas and bureaucratic turf wars and petty resentments and work together for some common goal.

Given human nature, you wouldn't think it could ever happen. But one day it did.

And it happened in the worst way imaginable.

It's a Tuesday morning in September, a little before nine o'clock, and I'm in my office on the twelfth floor of One Police Plaza. As usual I've been there since 4:15 a.m., reading through the overnight logs, glancing through the newspapers, trying to move some paperwork before people start coming in and the phone calls and meetings start piling up. It's a beautiful morning, bright, clear, sunny—a Chamber-of-Commerce-brochure kind of day in New York City.

And then at exactly 8:46 I hear it—a kind of low, distant boom.

My first thought isn't a bomb, or terrorism. It's been eight and a half years since radical Islamic terrorists exploded a truck bomb in the World Trade Center in 1993, killing six people and injuring more than a thousand, and terrorist attacks aren't high on most people's radar. I'm thinking maybe it's a gas leak explosion in an apartment building, or an electric transformer blowing up; it happens.

Then I look out my window and there, less than a half mile away, black smoke is rising from the North Tower of the World Trade Center. I call the NYPD Operations Center on the eighth floor of One Police Plaza and the first report is that a plane—a small plane—has hit the tower. Again, I'm not thinking terrorism. This isn't unprecedented. In 1945 a military B-25 bomber got lost in heavy fog and crashed into the Empire State Building, killing fourteen people including the crew. Today is clear, but maybe a private pilot had a heart attack or something and accidentally crashed into the tower.

Then, at 9:03, as I'm watching through my window, telling the Ops Center what I'm seeing, I see another plane, a commercial airliner, swoop in low over the city and punch through the corner of the South Tower in an explosion of bright orange flames and billowing black smoke.

And that's the moment that the city, and the world, changes.

Right now I'm the senior chief in the building. So I tell the Ops

Center: This is not an accident, this is a terrorist attack! Evacuate the building and mobilize on the Triangle!—the Triangle being the mall-like area in back of One Police Plaza. I grab a radio, my cell phone, and an NYPD raid jacket—I usually wear a business suit to work, reserving my uniform for ceremonial occasions—and head out the door. In the Triangle I grab some supervisors and we start organizing the milling crowds of people—civilians on one side, cops on the other, ten cops to a sergeant, a lieutenant to every three sergeants, and so on. I'm not sure yet what we're going to be assigned to do, but I know we're going to be doing something. I call IAB headquarters on Hudson Street to make sure everyone there and at the borough IAB offices is doing the same. I also send teams of cops out to divert traffic the length of Canal Street, blocking off access to lower Manhattan.

Then I started walking, then jogging, then running toward what will soon be known as Ground Zero.

By this time hundreds of NYPD cops, FDNY firefighters and EMTs, Port Authority Police, and other emergency service personnel are at the scene, trying to rescue and evacuate survivors; my police radio is crackling with frantic calls describing the chaos. Thousands of dazed people are streaming out of the buildings as cops and firefighters are rushing in, while people trapped on the burning floors are leaping out of windows, choosing death by falling to death by flames.

And then miraculously, at the corner of Center and Chambers Streets, I see my youngest son, Vincent.

Like virtually everyone else in New York City that day, I'm worried about my family. No one knows if there will be other planes, other attacks, maybe on buildings, maybe on bridges or tunnels or subways. I know that my wife is safe in Queens, and my oldest son, Charlie, is at the Police Academy. But my youngest son, Vincent, is an NYPD Police Cadet who works as a computer tech in One Police Plaza, and he takes the subway to the WTC station every morning. And I haven't heard from him.

So when I see him walking toward me, for a few seconds, with chaos all around us, I'm not a cop, I'm a father. I hug him, and send off a small prayer of thanks. He's a tough kid, but I can tell he's shaken; he saw some of the people leaping out of the burning buildings. Finally I send him back on his way to One Police Plaza and start heading back toward the WTC.

And then, a couple of minutes before ten a.m., a little over an hour after the first plane struck, when I'm still a few blocks away, the South Tower collapses. One moment it's there, some of the upper floors burning but still largely intact, and ten seconds later it's gone, a million tons of steel and concrete collapsing in a roar, sending roiling clouds of acrid, smothering ash and dust and smoke cascading through the surrounding streets. People are running past me, covered in ash, some of them screaming, trying to get away. I can't see, I can't breathe; I can't get any closer. Twenty-nine minutes later the North Tower collapses.

The rest of that day and the days that immediately follow are a blur of work, little or no sleep, and then more work—and trying to come to grips with the enormity of the destruction, and the enormity of the task ahead of us. As a senior chief, I spend most of my time in the Ops Center, coordinating logistics—who needs what, where, and how much of it—grabbing a few minutes of sleep on a cot when possible; it's three days before I get home to see my wife and grab some fresh clothes.

At this point there's no such thing as Patrol Bureau cops, or Detective Bureau cops, or Internal Affairs Bureau cops; we're all just cops. Ordinary Internal Affairs work comes to almost a complete halt, as does ordinary police work in general. Arrests drop by almost two-thirds in the week after the attacks—even the criminals in the city seem stunned into inactivity. And at the same time, there's a huge outpouring of public support for cops and firefighters; civilians are waving flags and cheering and shouting "God bless you!" whenever cops pass by—something I've never seen before, and hope never to see again under these kinds of circumstances. No one is making any complaints to IAB about cops.

So most of our IAB investigators are doing the same jobs that other cops are doing. Some are sent to Ground Zero to prevent looting, of which thankfully there is very little. (A dozen or so civilians, some of them caught wearing stolen FDNY gear, are eventually charged with stealing expensive watches, jewelry, and other items from damaged stores at the site.) Other IAB investigators and supervisors are assigned to security details at bridges and tunnels, or at the morgue, or at the victim and family assistance centers. And some IAB cops are assigned to The Pile and The Landfill.

The Pile is what cops call the mountain of twisted steel and rubble at Ground Zero. At first it's a rescue effort, trying to find survivors buried in the rubble—and although it's a hard, dirty, and dangerous job, cops and firefighters are desperate to be there, because while they're looking for any survivors, they're also looking for their brothers and sisters—the 343 FDNY firefighters and EMTs, the 23 NYPD cops, and the 37 Port Authority Police who never made it out of those buildings alive.

Sometimes cops are working at The Pile even when they shouldn't be. On the day after the attacks, I'm at Ground Zero, talking to some cops who are about to go to work, finding out what they need, when I see that one of them is an old friend of mine, Sergeant George Ferguson, who was an instructor with me at the Academy back in the 1980s. The thing is, I know George is retired from the Department, and therefore has no business being there. The Pile is still burning, rubble is shifting, there are explosions as air pockets open and feed the flames, the air is thick with toxic fumes; it's a dangerous place. But when George sees me looking at him he calls me over and says—Charlie, please don't tell anybody I'm retired, I just want to help, I have to help, please don't send me away.

And I don't. In the days after the attacks, there are a thousand other stories just like that.

Unfortunately, few survivors are found in the rubble, only twenty, with the last one found alive twenty-seven hours after the attack. And there are relatively few people seriously injured, either. The grim fact in almost every case is that if you made it out before the towers collapsed you lived, and if you didn't you died. So while hope remains for days, even weeks, it eventually becomes not a rescue but a recovery effort, with cops, firefighters, and volunteers from across the country painstakingly digging through the rubble, trying to recover the dead and remove almost two million tons of debris.

Some of the debris is being taken by truck to The Landfill, specifically the old Fresh Kills Landfill, a one-hundred-seventy-five-acre plot on Staten Island. ("Kill" is a Dutch word for "stream.") Hundreds of cops—including IAB cops—and others wearing gloves and protective suits are there to sift through the debris in piles or on conveyor belts, looking for evidence (pieces of the planes) or clues to victims' identities (ID cards, documents, articles of clothing) or more important, bodies—or in actual practice, parts of bodies: charred bones, pieces of flesh, anything that might be used for DNA testing. Again, it's hard, dirty, sometimes even revolting work, and it goes on for weeks, then months. And yet cops are eager to do it.

So like I said, in the wake of the 9/11 attacks, IAB cops are out there doing the same jobs that thousands of other NYPD cops are doing. But there is one unique role that IAB plays.

IAB is also tasked to find the living among the dead.

You have to remember that when the towers came down, no one was certain how many people made it out and how many people didn't. Based on NYPD and FDNY records and private company records, along with missing persons reports filed with the Red Cross and other agencies, the initial estimate was that about six thousand people were missing and believed to have perished in the World Trade Center attack.

But to be missing isn't necessarily to be dead. We have to be certain. So we set up the Missing Person Task Force in the IAB headquarters on Hudson Street, staff it with dozens of IAB investigators, and start working our way through the six thousand names on the missing list.

Some of the people on the missing list are quickly confirmed as being among the dead. Cops, firefighters, employees at firms like Cantor Fitzgerald—even if the bodies haven't yet been positively identified, there are records and witnesses to confirm that they were in the buildings and haven't been seen since. But what about the mother from Thailand or Nigeria who calls her embassy and reports that her son, an illegal immigrant who worked under-the-table as a busboy or a janitor in the World Trade Center, is missing? Or the man from California who calls the Red Cross and reports that he thinks his brother was visiting the World Trade Center when the planes hit—and he hasn't heard from him? There are hundreds, even thousands of names of people like that on the missing list. We have to find out who they are.

Sometimes it's just a case of cross-checking the names in various databases to determine that the missing person isn't really missing—at least not under that name. For example, we find one woman who was reported missing under both her married and maiden names; sadly, she died in the attack, but it means one other name is taken off the missing list. In other cases, especially with immigrants whose names don't easily translate into English, it's simply a case of a missing person's name being spelled two or three different ways. And sometimes the database searches and follow-up calls and interviews show that the missing person on the list never existed at all, or has been dead for years. Almost forty people in New York City were arrested for making fraudulent claims about missing relatives in attempts to get survivors' benefits; a few other names on the missing list came from emotionally disturbed people who reported their multiple-personality alter egos or some fictional person as being among the missing.

But with many of the missing, it's a case of someone having called to report a loved one missing and then not notifying anyone when that loved one turned up alive and well; not until our IAB investigators show up at their doorsteps do they or the loved ones even realize that they're on the missing list. In many other cases, we find that a person whose name is on the missing list is, in fact, alive, but for whatever reason he hasn't contacted the person who reported him missing.

In both those kinds of cases, once we or another local, state, federal, or foreign law enforcement agency meet with the person and confirm he or she is alive, their names go off the missing list and onto our "Found In Fact Alive" list. And then we ring the "Found Bell," a small bell that the Missing Person Task Force investigators set up in the hall outside their office to let everyone know that someone once feared dead isn't dead after all.

Over the weeks and months, that bell rings hundreds of times. In a time of fear and funerals and worries about the future, it's one of the few happy sounds I hear.

In the end, through phone calls, checking databases, knocking on doors, contacting foreign embassies, working with the Medical Examiner's Office and other agencies, and weeks and months of dogged, double-shift detective work, our IAB Missing Person Task Force dramatically reduces the estimated number of dead—from 6,000 to 5,000, then 4,000, then 3,000. On the first anniversary of the attacks, through our work and that of others, the official death toll in the World Trade

Center attack stands at 2,801—less than half the initial estimates. Sadly, that number will grow over the years as hundreds of cops and firefighters and other rescue and recovery workers suffer and die as a result of the toxic chemicals they breathed day after day at Ground Zero—including IAB Detectives Sandra Adrian and Thomas Weiner.

Of course, the spirit that drew New York City together in those days couldn't last forever. The waving of American flags, the cheering of cops and firefighters, the shared determination and selflessness—eventually they all faded away, and the city returned to its fractious and divided ways.

Don't get me wrong. I'm not nostalgic for those times. Who could be nostalgic about an act of evil that destroyed so many lives and damaged such a big part of a great city?

Still, I'm proud of the service that the NYPD—including the men and women of the Internal Affairs Bureau—provided in the wake of the 9/11 attacks. In those hard times, they proved to the city and to the world that they really are New York's Finest.

And I'll never forget the ringing of that bell.

It's almost over.

It's February 2014 and Bill de Blasio, the former city public advocate—that's sort of an elected city "watchdog" position—is the new mayor of New York City. Many of the positions he took during his campaign are perceived by the NYPD rank and file as antipolice, especially his suggestion that the Department's stop-and-frisk tactic is inherently racist. So to forge better relations with the Department rank and file he has appointed the well-regarded Bill Bratton as police commissioner.

I said earlier that it was ironic that a guy like Bill Bratton, who had first served as police commissioner under a law-and-order mayor like Rudy Giuliani, would later wind up as PC under a perceived antipolice, soft-on-crime mayor like Bill de Blasio. In fact, this is doubly ironic, since it was Bratton who had greatly expanded the stop-and-frisk policy under Giuliani as a proactive method of getting weapons off the street and reducing crime, which it did.

I should point out that "stop, question, and possibly frisk" has been an NYPD tactic since before I came on the job. A 1968 Supreme Court decision held that cops can briefly detain and question someone if there is "reasonable suspicion"—not "probable cause," just reasonable suspicion—and can search them if there is reasonable suspicion that they have a weapon. What Bratton did was to insist that cops on the street be more proactive in conducting stop-question-frisks—and he held their commanders responsible for making it happen. As a result the number of stop-question-frisks surged—by 2012 the NYPD was making more than 500,000 stop-question-frisks a year—and crime had plummeted.

Yes, it's true that the majority of people in New York City who were stopped-questioned-frisked were young black and Hispanic males—but it's also true that for whatever reason, the majority of crimes committed in the city are committed by members of those same age, gender, and ethnicity groups. I guess the NYPD could have made it a policy to stop-question-frisk more elderly black men or middle-aged white women, but I'm not sure that would have had much impact on crime. In any event, de Blasio shows which side of the argument he's on shortly after he becomes mayor by dropping the city's appeal of a 2013 federal judicial ruling that the NYPD policy is racially discriminatory. Stop-and-frisks plummet 90 percent by the end of 2014, and, unfortunately, what had been predicted by cops in precincts across the city happens: In 2015, amid rising crime rates, the New York City murder rate increases.

Anyway, while it's fair to say that in early 2014 most cops aren't happy about de Blasio being elected, it's also fair to say that most people in the Department are pleased to have Bratton coming in as police commissioner—and I'm one of them. I figure that if we can't have Ray Kelly as PC—Kelly left after Mayor Bloomberg was term-limited out of office—Bill Bratton will still protect the Department against de Blasio's worst antipolice instincts.

But I also know this: With Bill Bratton as police commissioner, the handwriting concerning my personal future in the Department is indelibly on the wall.

I like Bill Bratton, and more important, I respect him. He's the guy who gave me my first star, and he and Jack Maple and others worked miracles in helping to turn around New York City and the NYPD in the 1990s. Throughout his long career as a Boston cop, chief of the New York City Transit Police, chief of the Boston Police Department, and, following his first term as PC of the NYPD, chief of the Los Angeles Police Department, he's proved himself to be a good, brave cop and a brilliant administrator.

True, he's a bit of a showman, a guy who likes the TV cameras. For example, in his first term as PC in the early 1990s, when the 30th Precinct Dirty Thirty scandal was about to break, he made certain he was at the center of attention. Although it was the district attorney and the Mollen Commission and the feds who were actually heading the investigation— the old NYPD Internal Affairs Division had mostly been left out of the loop, with the new IAB under Walter Mack only being brought in at the end—Bratton personally led the well-publicized arrest of two of the officers at the 30th Precinct house. And at a press conference the next day, he held up the two arrested officers' NYPD shields, declared that they had disgraced those shields, and announced that those shield numbers would be permanently stricken from the NYPD rolls. Then he dramatically threw both shields into a strategically preplaced trash can.

(Actually, one of those shield numbers had formerly belonged to a friend of mine, an NYPD lieutenant, who wasn't happy that his old shield number had been designated a symbol of disgrace. Later I helped the lieutenant quietly resurrect the shield number so that his son could have it when he graduated from the Police Academy.)

That sort of headline-grabbing gesture made Bratton a popular PC with the public and the press in his first term—too popular, in fact, for Mayor Rudy Giuliani. Giuliani was a good mayor, the right mayor for New York City at the time, but he never willingly shared a spotlight. After several run-ins with Bratton over his high media profile, in 1996 Giuliani in effect fired him and replaced him with Howard Safir.

But there's another aspect of Bratton's executive style that I know will have an impact on me. In every position Bratton has ever had, he always brings in his own people for the top slots. When he took over as PC in 1994, every senior chief in the Department either retired or was shifted to another slot. And when he takes over again in 2014, I know he's going to do the same.

It's not necessarily a bad management system. In any organization sometimes it's good to have a shake-up at the top. And no one in the NYPD, me included, is irreplaceable.

Besides, I'm going to have to retire in eighteen months anyway, when I hit the mandatory NYPD retirement age of sixty-three, so it's not like I'm going to be here for much longer in any case. Yeah, there's some talk about shifting me to another three-star chief slot, but I'm not interested. I don't want to start a new job and then have to leave in a year and a half.

So when in February 2014, Commissioner Bratton calls me into his office, I know what I'm going to do. We chat for a minute or two, then he says that while he has absolutely no complaints about IAB, and he appreciates the work I've done with IAB over the years, he's decided to make some changes, and there are going to be some moves. And I tell him: Commissioner, I understand that and I think the best thing for me and the Department is for me to retire. We chat a bit more, shake hands, wish each other good luck, and that's it. We're friendly then, and we've remained friendly since.

So I drop my papers, and then I spend the next thirty days filling out paperwork—in terms of paperwork, getting out of the NYPD is almost as hard as getting into the NYPD—and generally getting things in order. We've still got ongoing IAB cases that need attention, including a long-standing IAB–Social Security Administration investigation involving dozens of former NYPD cops who allegedly are fraudulently collecting 9/11-related disability pensions. I won't be around for the conclusion of that case, or other ongoing investigations, but that's the way it is when you're a cop—you're never around for the end of your last case. The case, and crime in general, goes on without you.

Am I sad to be leaving the NYPD? Sure. I'm sad that I'll never wear the uniform again, the uniform that I've worn so proudly for so many years, the uniform that hundreds of thousands of my brother and sister cops have proudly worn before me, and will proudly wear after me. In fact, at this point I've got more years on the job than all but one currently serving cop in the entire NYPD. But like every cop, I've always known the day would come when I'd have to put the uniform away.

And the way I see it, I'm leaving at the top of IAB's game. During my more than twenty years with IAB, we've put the IAB draft system in place, implemented the proactive anticorruption and serious misconduct programs, dramatically increased integrity testing, and—except for that damned towing program—we've shifted the Internal Affairs

Bureau's emphasis away from petty "white socks" violations and toward serious police misconduct. We've reduced corruption cases by two-thirds, even as the number of NYPD cops and civilian employees has grown to fifty thousand. Although we've investigated a lot of corrupt or brutal cops, most of those cases were isolated, involving a few bad cops; we've defied history by passing the aforementioned twenty-year cycle of serious, widespread, systemic police corruption scandals—and with our proactive anticorruption methods and tactics, we don't expect to ever see that kind of historical corruption scandal again. The NYPD Internal Affairs Bureau has gained a national and even international reputation as a model Internal Affairs operation, one that many other police departments copy and emulate. And I'm proud of all that.

So yeah, I'm sad that my NYPD career is inevitably coming to an end. But I'm going out with my head up.

Whenever a cop retires from the NYPD, somebody wants to make a big deal out of it. There's a retirement party, and speeches, and everybody telling stories about you, some of them actually true. For retiring senior chiefs the Department usually stages what's known as a walk-out, with bagpipes and an honor guard and even a vintage patrol car from the year you first came on the job to drive you away.

And that's all fine—but it's not for me. I've made it clear that for me there's going to be no party, no speeches, no walk-out.

So on my last day I shake a few hands, say some good-byes, and then I quietly walk out the door of One Police Plaza. My retirement doesn't officially kick in until midnight, so I'm ending my last shift with the NYPD the same way I ended my first shift with the NYPD more than forty years ago.

I'm just another cop, heading home.

EPILOGUE

Even after a cop leaves the NYPD, the NYPD never really leaves the cop. He or she remains a part of its proud history, traditions, and culture, and the former cop cares about what happens to it.

And since I left the NYPD, I've worried about some of the things that are happening to both the Department I love and respect and to my great city as well.

Yeah, I know, people always look back and say that things were better in the old days. But I'm not saying that at all. When I came on the job in 1973 and for many years thereafter, the situation was almost immeasurably worse than it is today, not only in the NYPD but in New York City as a whole. Crime, drugs, violence, attacks on police officers, racial disorders, corruption, police layoffs, low morale, depopulation as people ran for their lives to the suburbs—they were all almost out of control, and New York City came this close to being unlivable, ungovernable, and un-police-able. It took a quarter century of discipline and hard work by the NYPD, some of the city's best politicians, and the people of New York City to make this city what it is today—one of the safest big cities in the world, and still easily the greatest.

So I'm not shouting gloom and doom here. But I have seen some trends that worry me, not just as a former NYPD cop but as a citizen—trends that, if they continue, could in ten years have us back to where we were twenty-five years ago.

I've already mentioned the drastic reduction in the use of stop-question-and-possibly-frisk tactics by NYPD officers, a trend that I know from my four decades of experience as a cop is going to lead to more illegal weapons being carried by criminals, and thus higher crime rates. The tactic can still be used by NYPD officers, but only under restricted circumstances. At one point the de Blasio administration even proposed that every cop doing a stop-question-frisk be required to give the person a card with the cop's name and shield number on it along with instructions on how to file a complaint against the cop—which is sort of like requiring a doctor to give every patient a business card for a medical malpractice lawyer. Commissioner Bratton headed that one off, but still, if you're a cop on the beat, you know the score. Why risk your career getting involved in a politically charged controversy by stopping, questioning, and maybe frisking that guy who's holding something inside his waistband while he's peering into the window of a frequently robbed convenience store at two a.m.? Sure, if you see a guy actually commit a crime you'll chase him—but that's reactive police work, not proactive police work, and relying solely on reactive police work leads to more crime.

There have also been persistent attempts by the New York City Council and others to decriminalize so-called quality-of-life offenses, or at least to discourage cops from enforcing laws against them—public urination and public drinking, aggressive panhandling, fare beating, plain-view drug activity, all those "small" crimes that as we learned in the 1970s and '80s have a direct correlation with the prevalence of more serious crimes. As commissioner, Bratton has resisted those efforts—but without political support behind them, cops aren't enforcing those laws as aggressively as they should. Almost every New Yorker can tell you stories about the increase in quality-of-life crimes they see every day. The *New York Post* summed up the situation precisely with a photo of an aggressive, emotionally disturbed homeless man openly urinating on a busy Manhattan street, under the headline: "TWENTY YEARS OF CLEANING UP NYC PISSED AWAY!"

Attempts to wrest control of police work away from the people who know how to do it—which is to say, the police—and give it to civilian "watchdog" agencies continue to be a problem. As I was leaving the Department the de Blasio administration and the City Council created a new civilian agency, the NYPD Inspector General, to monitor the Department's handling of things like community relations and stop-question-frisk and to make recommendations to the mayor and the City

Council. Don't get me wrong, there's nothing wrong with monitoring; every police department should be monitored by a civilian agency to make sure it's doing its job and treating the citizens properly. But the NYPD already is monitored by five civilian elected district attorneys and their public corruption bureaus, by two US attorneys and their corruption and civil rights units, by the Civilian Complaint Review Board, by the civilian Commission to Combat Police Corruption, by the civilian police commissioner, by the elected civilian mayor of New York City—and, not least, by the NYPD Internal Affairs Bureau itself. So do we really need to spend millions of dollars every year for another civilian monitoring agency that really doesn't do anything? I think not.

The attitude by some political figures toward cops—and the actual, physical "war on cops" perpetrated by some people—is another disturbing trend, not just in New York City but across the country. During protests over the July 2014 death of Eric Garner, an African American man who died of asphyxiation while NYPD cops on Staten Island were trying to arrest him for selling untaxed "loosie" cigarettes—he had been arrested thirty times before for various offenses—Mayor de Blasio called the death a "terrible tragedy," which it was. But after a grand jury declined to indict any of the officers—which sparked protests across the country—de Blasio infuriated a lot of cops by not backing up the officers and by saying that he had warned his own biracial son about the "danger" he might face during any interaction with what the mayor implied were racist NYPD cops.

It got worse when a career felon shot and killed NYPD officers Rafael Ramos and Wenjian Liu while they sat in their patrol car in Brooklyn's 84th Precinct in December 2014. The killer, a thug with a long criminal record who committed suicide after the murders, had announced on social media that he intended to "put wings on pigs"—in other words, kill cops—in retaliation for the death of Garner and the police shooting death of Michael Brown in Ferguson, Missouri, which also resulted in a grand jury clearing the officer of criminal wrongdoing. Hundreds of NYPD cops famously turned their backs on Mayor de Blasio when he appeared at the hospital where the officers were taken and later at their funerals. Personally I wouldn't have done that—you should show respect for the office, regardless of who's in it—but I know why they did it. The way the cops looked at it, de Blasio was another one of many politicians and community activists across the country who seem to think that the murder of a cop, while regrettable, is an understandable angry reaction by some people to years of brutality and racism by police officers.

Look, I know better than almost anyone that there are some bad cops out there; I spent half my career fighting them. But the idea that all or even a majority of cops are inherently racist, that they come to work each day hoping for a chance to shoot somebody or beat them up, is ridiculous—and so is the suggestion that cops are increasingly brutal or trigger-happy when dealing with suspects. As I pointed out, between the time I came on the job and the year before I left it, the number of people shot and killed or wounded by NYPD cops every year declined by *almost 90 percent*. Any politician who even suggests that cops in general are the primary enemy of any community is doing that community a terrible disservice—and whether he intends to or not, he's putting a target on cops' backs, sometimes figuratively, but too often literally.

After the furor over his performance during the Eric Garner demonstrations, Mayor de Blasio put Bill Bratton out in front on most police-related issues. And he's done some good work. Take police "body cameras," for example. Twenty years ago I was asked by a promotion board what I envisioned would be the single greatest change agent in law enforcement in the future, and my answer was videotape recorders in the hands of cops and citizens that would capture some of the realities of police work; I guess I really would have been prescient if I'd said iPhone 6s Pluses, but it's the same idea. The NYPD under Bratton has begun a pilot program to test the use of police body cameras and expects to soon increase the number of cameras deployed to about five thousand, and maybe many more in the future. I believe they will help protect good cops from false allegations, and help protect citizens from a few overly aggressive cops. But they aren't a cure-all for all police controversies. People have to remember that, as I said earlier, a lot of police work is necessarily brutal, and it always will be, but that doesn't always make it police brutality. Every case of alleged excessive force by the police has to be judged in the context of the entire incident, not just by a few moments' worth of digital images played on the news—and too often politicians and community activists seem to forget that.

Low pay for NYPD officers continues to be an alarming trend, as it has been for years. Currently a rookie NYPD police officer gets a base salary of $42,000 a year, which after six years on the job increases to about $76,000; detectives and supervisors are paid more depending on rank. The pay is far less than it is for cops in suburban departments. Sure, NYPD cops also get overtime, night differential, vacation time, and so on, but remember, this is New York City, where the average rent for a two-bedroom apartment in 2015 is four thousand bucks a month. Remember, too, that we give these cops guns, shields, and the enormous responsibility of enforcing the law—and the responsibility-to-pay ratio for NYPD cops is seriously out of whack. You've heard the expression "You get what you pay for"? With the NYPD, the people of New York City are getting a lot more than they're paying for. But if the city continues to scrimp on police pay, there's inevitably going to be a decline in the quality of recruits and the retention of good cops.

As for the Internal Affairs Bureau itself, since I left there've been some cutbacks in integrity testing and proactive arrests and debriefs of suspects to seek out incidents of police corruption and misconduct. I'm no longer on the scene, and it's not my place to second-guess, but I know a little bit about the subject, so let me offer this observation: Crime and misconduct by cops is the same as any other kind of crime. If you're only reactive, if you don't constantly and proactively seek it out or, better yet, actively try to prevent it, police crime and misconduct is going to increase. Enough said.

And finally, I have one other area of serious concern about the NYPD of the future, and maybe even the NYPD of the present. That is the very real possibility that the NYPD will be infiltrated by sympathizers or even sleeper agents of ISIS or al-Qaeda or some other terrorist organization—cops who are intent on either committing overt terrorist acts themselves or on accessing top-secret NYPD intelligence files and antiterrorism methods and practices to help facilitate another September 11–level mass attack.

Has the Internal Affairs Bureau or any other counterterrorism element of the NYPD ever investigated a case of a suspected terrorist-cop? If they have, I wouldn't tell you—and if they haven't I wouldn't tell you that, either, since that also could have potential intelligence value.

But the prospect of a terrorist infiltration of the NYPD ranks isn't just some vague, half-formed nightmare on my part, a plot from a "Manchurian Cop" movie script. Throughout this book I've described case after case of cops who crossed to the other side, engaging in drug trafficking, gunrunning, money laundering, and every other kind of criminal activity—and in most cases, their motivation was just money. So how hard is it to imagine that there could be an NYPD cop out there who's willing to cross to the other side when motivated by a murderous and misguided but powerful ideology? A cop who would use his shield and his authority to attack otherwise inaccessible high-value targets, such as high-level government officials or critical infrastructure facilities? Or a cop who could use the trust built up over the course of years to penetrate the NYPD's world-class intelligence and counterterrorism apparatus to access classified files or plant false information?

The answer is that it's not at all hard to imagine. Given my experience, it's harder to believe that it *can't* happen than to believe that it can. Currently there are over thirty-six thousand cops in the NYPD, and to believe that not a single one of those thirty-six thousand cops harbors some level of anti-American, pro-terrorist beliefs and connections would be naïve—and trust me, after more than forty years as a cop, and twenty years in Internal Affairs, one thing I'm not is naïve.

Let me make this clear: My worries about a terrorist individual or small cell lurking in the NYPD ranks is not directed at any broad ethnic or religious group. While the current major terrorist threat is posed by radical, anti-American Islamic fanatics, to automatically suspect all of the hundreds of Muslim cops in the NYPD of having jihadist sympathies would not only be stupid and wrong, but also counterproductive. It would be the same mistake the Department made a century ago, when Italian Americans were only grudgingly accepted into the NYPD ranks, and even then were often suspected of having ties to the Mafia— this at a time when it was Italian American cops who were capable of penetrating the criminal elements of the New York City Italian American community, and who were busily putting mobsters in jail. The fact is that to guard against external jihadist threats, the NYPD needs *more* cops who are familiar with the cultures and languages of the Muslim world, not fewer.

So how can the NYPD protect itself, and more important, the people of New York City, against an internal terrorist threat?

There are already certain counterintelligence procedures in place to help guard against infiltration or internal subversion of the NYPD; again, I can't talk about those. But I can offer some general observations.

For one thing, the Department needs better screening and background checks of potential applicants—and a tougher, more pragmatic attitude toward applicants who don't make the grade. Again and again in this book I've described cases of bad cops who never should have been cops in the first place, although nobody seemed to realize that until after they got caught committing crimes. In most of those cases it wasn't a matter of the applicant screening process actively ignoring red flags in the cop's background—obvious things like a prior criminal conviction, family and neighborhood criminal associations, and so on. Instead it was a question of the screening process not doing enough to actively seek out the red flags. In the rush to fill the ranks after layoffs or downsizing, or to increase diversity or acquire special language and cultural skills, the Department too often allowed a lack of negative information in the record to serve as proof that there was no negative information to be found.

Unfortunately, sometimes gaps in a potential cop's background are impossible to fill in, especially when recruiting applicants from immigrant communities. For example, an NYPD applicant who came to the US from Syria as a teenager, a guy who seems perfect in every way, may *say* that he had no criminal record or terrorist connections in the old country, but how does the screening process prove that? Given the chaos in that part of the world, you can't just call the Damascus PD and ask them to run a RAP search (Record of Arrests and Prosecutions) on the guy—and even if you could, how trustworthy would that be? And even if the US national security and intelligence agencies don't have the guy on their radar, that doesn't necessarily prove that he *shouldn't* be on their radar.

So in cases where there are blank spots in an applicant's record, until those blanks can be filled in the Department should assume the worst—and it shouldn't matter whether the applicant is an immigrant from the Middle East or a suburban kid from Long Island. Yes, that might deprive the Department of some applicants with critical cultural and language skills. And it may not be fair to some individuals. But the threat of infiltration by an ISIS-style terror group is too serious for the Department to cut corners.

Of course, all the preemployment background screening in the world can't detect a cop who becomes radicalized after he's on the force. To guard against that threat requires the same sort of vigilance that should be applied to any form of police corruption or misconduct. Part of that vigilance involves constant, proactive Internal Affairs or counterintelligence monitoring of everything from Department computer systems to individual officers' on- and off-duty conduct—a level of scrutiny that might not be acceptable to civilians, but should be applied to police officers because of their special status within society.

And the other part of that vigilance against potential terrorist infiltration comes down to the old admonition: If you see something, or hear something, or even just suspect something, then say something.

Is a cop you know spending time looking at Islamic jihadist websites—or violent right-wing Christian-oriented websites, for that matter? Well, maybe he's just curious. Or maybe he's applying for a job with the Intelligence Bureau and is trying to get some background information for his interview. Or maybe, just maybe, there's a problem there. Has your partner sitting next to you in the patrol car become increasingly bitter or angry about American policies in the Middle East, or perceived injustices toward a religious or ethnic group? Hey, this is America, and everybody's entitled to their opinions—but not everyone is entitled to be a cop. If a cop is acting strangely, we have to find out why.

Sure, probably 99 percent of the time this sort of behavior will not turn out to be anything sinister. But the potential threat posed by that other one percent, or even one-tenth of one percent, could be devastating.

Like I said at the beginning, as chief of Internal Affairs Bureau I was kept awake at night by only a small group of potentially bad cops.

Even now, as a private citizen concerned about terrorists attacking my city and my country, I know that the numbers are small, but that doesn't help me sleep any better.

Since retiring from the NYPD I've kept busy—so busy that sometimes I think I should go back to full-time employment just to get some rest.

I've worked as a consultant on Internal Affairs and security issues for a number of US and international police departments and private companies; I'm also working part-time as the Nassau County Commissioner of Corrections. I've always regretted not completing my PhD in criminal justice, so I'm planning to knuckle down and finish that dissertation. Having never had quite enough time for fishing, I've also traveled to various remote areas of the world to personally investigate reports of game fish that haven't been taken into custody—although once caught I usually ROR them (released–own recognizance). And after so many missed birthdays and hockey games and holidays and family events during my years as a cop, I've made sure I don't miss anything with my four grandchildren. The old joke is true: If I'd known how much fun grandchildren are, I would have had them first.

And I've also taken the time to write this book.

As I said at the beginning, by necessity much of this book has been about bad cops—the small group of criminals who betrayed their oaths and tarnished their NYPD shields. That's because for almost half of my NYPD career, protecting the public and the good cops from those bad cops was my job.

But those bad cops aren't the ones who usually come to mind when I think about the NYPD. The bad cops are easily forgotten. It's the other NYPD cops that I remember.

I remember the cops in the Seven-Three who risked their lives to protect people in the neighborhoods that no one else in the city cared about. I remember the cops walking beats or working details in the cold rain while everybody else was warm and safe inside. I remember cops like Lenny Swindell, cops who never grew cynical, cops who from their first day to their last always followed Lenny's credo: If ya got a job, do the job!

I remember cops like Detective Luis Lopez and so many others who risked and lost their lives in the service of the people of New York City, and the thousands of cops standing at attention at the funerals, eyes filling with tears as a member of the NYPD honor guard knelt down to present a folded American flag to yet another grieving widow or mother or child. I remember cops like the Anti-Crime Unit guys I used to ride around with in the Sixth Precinct, cops driven by the sheer joy of taking dangerous criminals off the streets, and cops in ESU who were never afraid to be first through the door. I remember cops who weren't only great cops but great leaders and innovators, like Ray Kelly and Jack Maple, and the young cop who broke the Blue Wall of Silence in the Louima case not to save his own skin but simply because he saw a wrong that had to be righted.

I remember the cops who didn't fail the integrity tests, the vast majority of cops who did the right thing simply because that's the kind of cops and the kind of people they were. I remember cops rushing into burning buildings, and current and former cops like George Ferguson sneaking onto The Pile to search for their brothers and sisters, and cops in Hazmat suits sifting through rubble in The Landfill, and cops smiling as they rang the Found Bell and took another name off the missing list.

And I remember the cops of the Internal Affairs Bureau, men and women who, however unwillingly at the start, took on the tough, sometimes dangerous and almost always thankless job of making sure that the law applies to everybody, other cops included.

They are the cops I'll always remember when I think of the NYPD.

And that's the kind of cop I always wanted to be.

ACKNOWLEDGMENTS

First and foremost, I want to thank my family, beginning with my father, Charles "Chappy" Campisi, who always preached honesty and integrity and who taught me to work hard for anything I wanted in life; and my mother, Josephine Lamanno Campisi, who told me to face my mistakes, make sure I didn't repeat them, and fight like hell when I thought I was right. My deepest appreciation also to my beautiful wife, Arlene, and my sons, Charles and Vincent, who like every cop's family had to put up with the 2:00 a.m. phone calls, the late suppers, the holidays, birthdays, anniversaries, and hockey games missed. Their unwavering support carried me through the toughest times and gloomiest nights.

I'm also grateful to the overwhelming majority of good, hardworking, honest New York City cops who day in and day out keep our city safe, and especially to the men and women of the Internal Affairs Bureau. They were selected to do one of the toughest and most important jobs in policing, and they responded with true professionalism and dedication. Their courage was exemplified by IAB Detectives Sandra Adrian and Thomas Weiner, whose work during and after the terrorist attack on the World Trade Center led to their untimely deaths because of 9/11-related illnesses.

Writing a book is a team effort, and this book was blessed with a great team. Rick Horgan, executive editor at Scribner, was a guiding light and a firm hand throughout the process; my deepest thanks also to Scribner editor in chief Colin Harrison, art director Jaya Miceli, David Lamb, Sally Howe, and production editor Katie Rizzo. Ruth Pomerance, Mike Harriot, and Molly Jaffa of Folio Literary Management were instrumental in developing this book; their foresight and suggestions proved right at every turn. Jill Menza from Umami Entertainment was the first person to believe in this project, and her encouragement and support never wavered. Eric Lasher and Maureen Lasher of the LA Literary Agency offered wise counsel along the way. Daniel Paisner was a great help in getting the project started. Gordon Dillow helped me focus my thoughts and coordinate my remembrances to tell this story; our friendship developed over the months and I'm sure it will continue into the future. My thanks also to Debbie Weil, Annie Dillon, and Terry and Patty Dillow for their support.

I had the pleasure and honor to serve under some outstanding police commissioners during my time in the New York City Police Department. My thanks to Raymond W. Kelly, the architect of the Internal Affairs Bureau, whose concept of a dynamic, ever-evolving Internal Affairs Bureau was the foundation of our success; William Bratton, whose continued support of IAB was instrumental to the bureau's growth; Howard Safir, who never wavered in difficult times and brought the Internal Affairs Bureau into prominence with clear direction and guidelines; and Bernie Kerik, who gained international recognition in the aftermath of 9/11.

The New York Police Department was blessed with dedicated first deputy commissioners. Among them were Tosano Simonetti, Tough Tony to those who really didn't know him, a man with a heart of gold who always had time to listen, advise, and mentor; Patrick Kelleher, whose hard work, long hours, and attention to detail made him a force multiplier within the Department; Joe Dunne, a commanding presence and very talented man to work with; and George Grasso (now a New York Criminal Court judge) and Rafael Piñeiro, who carried on the traditions of the office. Chief of Department Joe Esposito (now the New York City Commissioner of the Office of Emergency Management) is one of the top operational planners in the entire city, and although we didn't always agree on things, I know he loves the New York City Police Department and always had the Department's best interest at heart.

Deputy commissioners are appointed civilian members of the

Department; they play a variety of roles and bring vast years of experience. Among the best was Jack Maple, a true visionary who ushered in the CompStat system and worked with the Internal Affairs Bureau in numerous ways to enhance our abilities to use statistically informed data to plan and execute proactive measures; Dr. Elsie Scott, one of the toughest, most demanding, and best bosses I ever worked for; Walter Mack, who took the reins of the new Internal Affairs Bureau at a very difficult time and kick-started the bureau; and Michael Farrell, a brilliant man and the go-to guy on any problem. I don't think there was a problem that Mike couldn't solve.

My appreciation also to Chief of Staff Joe Wuensch, an honorable man with a wicked knuckleball, who could see all sides of a problem and develop solutions that were beneficial to all. Also Chief Allan Hoehl, one of the hardest-working chiefs in the New York City Police Department, always willing to shoulder any task and mentor those under his command, a leader who stood out in front of those who proudly followed him. Chiefs James Waters and Tom Galati are leaders with great potential who are just hitting their strides.

During my career at the Internal Affairs Bureau, I had a number of executive officers, and each brought their own special skills to the position. They include Assistant Chiefs John Moakley, who navigated the inner workings of the New York City Police Department like a master seaman, and Gary Strebel, a dedicated man who looked at all sides of an issue and worked tirelessly to ensure that cops were treated fairly. Also Mike Ansbro (who later retired as Chief of the Transit Bureau), Bill Calhoun, Bill Crawley, Ray King, Tom Fahey, and Jack McManus, all of them diligent and dedicated professionals.

There were many other chief executives who deserve to be singled out as well. Assistant Chief Lowell Stahl, a friend and a stalwart of the New York City Police Department, had the ability to resolve problems and maintain his cool under pressure. Also Deputy Chiefs Sal Comodo, Alan Cooper, Tom Mason, and Ed Thompson—nobody could ask for a better team. Inspectors Vito Colamussi, Joe DiBartolomeo, Ariana Donovan, Dave Grossi, Pat Keane, Tim McCarthy, Bill Monteleone, Terry Moore, George O'Brien, Joe Pfister, Phil Romanzi, Tom Scollan, Christine Servedio, and Bob Sharpe, all of whom helped carry the load day in and day out, and Barry Fried, who had many hidden talents that he shared when we needed them most.

My thanks also to Chief of Detectives Phil Pulaski, an invaluable ally whose expansive knowledge of forensics and willingness to share resources was always welcomed, and to Chief Joanne Jaffe, a committed professional who could always be counted on to face any challenge. Thanks also to Chief Ray Spinella, who turns into a whirlwind when given any job or assignment; Chief Carlos Gomez, an extremely efficient leader who has unlimited potential; and Organized Crime Control Bureau Chief Tony Izzo, a strong boss and a good friend. All of New York owes thanks to Chief of Detectives Bill Allee, who helped transform Times Square from a crime-infested war zone into the safe and tourist-friendly place it is today. My gratitude also to Chief Mike Scagnelli, an avid outdoorsman and a great cop, and to Lieutenant Tim Murphy, a trusted confidential aide and someone I could always count on.

The NYPD's Chaplains Unit provides spiritual and emotional support to cops in times of need. Not only do they preside over religious services, they have become an integral part of all official ceremonies. Chief Chaplain Rabbi Dr. Alvin Kass and Deputy Chief Chaplain Monsignor Robert Romano lead an extraordinary group of clergy representing a most diverse religious group to minister to all members of the NYPD.

My heartfelt thanks and friendship go out to Sergeant Yalkin Demirkaya, whose computer wizardry made me look good on more than one occasion, and who urged me to write this book to tell the Internal Affairs Bureau's story. Deep appreciation also to the late Lieutenant John Donnelly and to Sergeant Joe Clarino, who led Group 25; they were instrumental in fostering the trust we built with the federal law enforcement community. FBI Public Corruption Unit Supervisors Bob Hennigan and Rodney Miller developed a true partnership full of cooperation and mutual respect. Thanks also to Lieutenant Fuat Sarayli, a top financial investigator who made sure hidden assets didn't stay that way.

The investigation of police corruption, serious misconduct, and brutality is just the beginning of the process. The development and prosecution of the case must be just as meticulous from start to finish. For that I want to thank the five independently elected district attorneys who during my time as IAB chief served the five boroughs of New York City, and some outstanding members of their staffs, including Brooklyn DA Charles "Joe" Hynes and his Chief of Civil Rights and Police Integrity, Charles Guria; Bronx DA Robert Johnson and his Rackets Bureau Chief, Tom Leahy; Manhattan DA Robert Morgenthau, his Chief Assistant DA Dan Castleman, and his Public Corruption Unit Chief Bill Burmeister; Queens DA Judge Richard Brown, his Chief Assistant DA Jack Ryan, and his Integrity Bureau Chief Jim Liander; Staten Island DA (and now Congressman) Dan Donovan and his Investigations Bureau Chief (and now a Criminal Court judge) Mario Mattei. They were all true professionals and great partners.

On the federal level, I was proud to work closely with the top people in the field, including US Attorney for the Eastern District of New York (and now United States Attorney General) Loretta Lynch; Eastern District of New York US Attorneys Zach Carter and Alan Vinegrad; and US Attorneys for the Southern District of New York Mary Jo White and Preet Bharara, and his Public Corruption Assistant US Attorney Andy Dember.

Corruption and misconduct in the New York City Police Department doesn't stop at the city limits, so our relationship with law enforcement executives outside New York City was very important. For their unflagging cooperation I'd like to thank New York State Police Superintendent Jim McMahon and his Deputy Superintendent Jim Fitzgerald; Nassau County Police Commissioner Don Kane and Suffolk County Police Commissioner John Gallagher; Nassau County District Attorney (and now US Representative) Kathleen Rice; Suffolk County District Attorney Tom Spota; and Westchester County District Attorney (now TV's "Judge Jeanine") Jeanine Pirro.

My appreciation also to IAB Detectives Tom Janow, Dave Woody, and Bill Radford, statisticians and artists who quietly fostered success, and to Detectives Ed Kearney and Harry Schroeder, Community Affairs officers from the 83rd Precinct, who taught me and other kids from the old neighborhood many life lessons that we carried into adulthood. They were extraordinary role models, and we could use more like them today. Also Dr. Douglas Stafford, Long Island University, Brooklyn campus, professor, who taught us to observe, to think, to ask questions, and never to settle for less than what you were capable of achieving.

Thanks also to Mayor's Commission to Combat Police Corruption Chairman Michael Armstrong and his Assistant Commissioners Kathy Chin, Vernon Broderick, Deborah Landis, Edgardo Ramos, and James Zirin. Their commitment to fighting corruption was a welcomed resource.

There are so many others, too numerous to count, who made my years in the New York City Police Department the adventure of a lifetime. I wouldn't change it for anything.

And finally, to the people of the City of New York, my sincere thank-you for giving me the honor and the privilege to serve you for forty-one years.

ABOUT THE AUTHORS

CHARLES CAMPISI was Chief of the NYPD's Internal Affairs Bureau, the world's largest police anticorruption unit, from 1996 to 2014, serving in that capacity longer than any other. In his tenure, Campisi oversaw thousands of internal investigations. At retirement, Campisi was considered a leading authority on police corruption and a key asset to the NYPD, where he supervised 750 investigators. He is known for the development of model strategies for investigating corruption, which have been successfully adopted by law enforcement agencies across the United States and abroad. Campisi holds a BA in psychology from Long Island University and an MA in criminal justice from CUNY's John Jay College of Criminal Justice. Currently a senior VP at the private investigation firm Cyber Diligence, he also works part-time as the Nassau County Commissioner of Corrections. He is a graduate of the FBI National Academy, the Columbia University Police Management Institute, and Harvard's John F. Kennedy School of Government. He grew up in Brooklyn, New York.

GORDON DILLOW is a veteran journalist specializing in law enforcement and crime issues.